Waterton Chronicles

People and their National Park

By

Chris Morrison

For the Bailey Family
your history lives on.

Chris Morrison

Edited by

Ray Djuff

Lethbridge   Waterton Park   Calgary

Waterton Chronicles: People and their National Park (Revised edition)
© 2022   Chris Morrison

All rights reserved. No part of this publication may be reproduced, stored in a retrieval system, or transmitted in any form or by any means, electronic, mechanical, photocopy, recording or otherwise (except for brief passages for the purposes of review) without the prior permission of Goathaunt Publishing.

All inquiries should be addressed to:

Goathaunt Publishing
Box 26
Waterton Park, AB   T0K 2M0
cdmorr@gmail.com

Cataloguing information:

Morrison, Chris
Waterton Chronicles: People and their National Park (Revised edition)
by Chris Morrison; edited by Ray Djuff

ISBN 978-0-9696974-6-6

Subject: Waterton Lakes National Park, Alberta - history; includes index

Front cover photo:

Marjorie Oliver, Vic and Jem Valentine at Cameron Falls, August 1928. Photo by William Oliver.
Ray Djuff Collection

Back cover photo:

Cpl. Andy Ford, Waterton's first Mountie. His posting began in 1919 (summers only). Beginning in 1924 he worked in the park year-round. He was transferred to Banff in 1933.
Quenton Wagstaff Collection

Manufactured by Amazon

Acknowledgements

Waterton Chronicles (Revised edition) is an extended salute to the recent human experience in Waterton Lakes National Park.

It is the story of the connection between the risk-takers, rascals and others in a place of special character and beauty.

My deepest appreciation goes to those professionals who patiently assisted my research and helped in so many ways, especially the "never-say-die" librarians of the Lethbridge Public Library and Andrew Chernevych, archivist at the Galt Museum and Archives.

As well, my thanks for public access to the University of Lethbridge Library, the Parks Canada archive in Waterton Lakes National Park, and Library and Archives Canada.

Not to be discounted is the generous assistance and encouragement of so many Waterton devotees, former and present business people in the park, Waterton residents and, in some cases, their families, friends and even interested bystanders with a long connection to the park.

Ray Djuff, my editor and graphic designer, ever the professional and long-time friend, has added greatly to this effort. He kept me on track and pointed out many things that needed clarification. Even more than that, he went the extra mile to help in other ways by locating materials, doing interviews, providing photos, and maintaining his enthusiasm.

This work is dedicated to Jim Morrison, my husband, whose encouragement made this revision possible. And most of all for his excellent advice and endurance with this project.

Chris Morrison

Preface

Since the first version of *Waterton Chronicles: People and Their National Park* was published in 2008, there have been numerous changes in the park and thanks to determined digging, even more has been uncovered about Waterton's human history than was available earlier.

This is the story of people and how they coped in the park, often despite the best efforts of bureaucrats.

Waterton's past is chock full of accounts of admirable human efforts to eke out a living in a beautiful seasonal but isolated place in the mountains. The reasons why anyone would invest their time, effort and money to build a residence or business from the ground up is as varied as the people involved.

Since 1895 when this tiny part of Alberta's eastern Rockies was set aside by the Government of Canada, the call of the mountains has gone out to all those who have answered it each in their own way. Some did so by investing time and money to build a business or by developing an abiding desire to get to know the place by boat, horseback or on foot. Determination and curiosity can be wonderful attributes.

How did this park come to be? It was obvious from its natural beauty it should be somehow protected and at the same time open to appreciation. The creation of a government reserve was the answer. Waterton was the second national park established in the province of Alberta, the fourth in the nation and there was a lot to learn. As time went by and criticism grew, the government's blanket response—without detailed explanation or definition—was that "the park was being operated in the Canadian public's best interest." The response was dubious.

To understand this story of where we've been is to understand where we might go. From the earliest days of camping to the construction of humble dwellings, hotels and the development of youth camps and the demise of some of them, Waterton has welcomed everyone. Services that appeal to tourists have been the goal of business people. Those that didn't appeal met their end. Allowing lot leases and construction of private residences, while strictly regulated, has been a dream come true for a variety, if limited number of people in both Canada and United States.

It takes all kinds of people to enrich a place and in Waterton they've come and stayed, and some have come and gone. Some are memorable, humorous, even distinctive, for good or bad. This is the story of how the park came to be, how the residents, both seasonal and year-round, contributed to a sense of place, stand on guard for its preservation and serve as informal ambassadors. It bodes well for a positive future.

Waterton's human history is both varied and rich but is ever changing, sometimes not because of the circumstances but despite them. Change has meant both improvement and deterioration, building a sense of place and planning. We've come full circle since 1895.

This revised and updated edition of *Waterton Chronicles: People and Their National Park* is the culmination of ever-evolving events and circumstances. And renewed archival digging has assisted in both discovery and understanding.

When you learn the long history of this park, its visitors and residential and commercial lessees—it can only enrich an appreciation for this place, the fourth national park in the country.

Chris Morrison

Table of Contents

Chapter 1   **With Posterity's Blessing**   6

Chapter 2   **Accommodations: A Roof Overhead**   46

Chapter 3   **Entrepreneurs: Like Nobody's Business**   84

Chapter 4   **Golf Course: Breaking 100**   120

Chapter 5   **Summer Camps: The Memory Makers**   136

Chapter 6   **Gone But Not Forgotten**   162

Chapter 7   **Buildings: With Sticks and Stones**   180

    Photo Credits   300

    Index   302

The north-south Waterton Valley is as impressive in person as it is in print, capturing the international setting with Waterton Lakes National Park in the foreground and Glacier National Park in the distance. The deepest natural lake in the Canadian Rockies, Upper Waterton Lake begins in Glacier and runs north to Waterton before turning east for its long journey to the Hudson Bay.

Chapter 1

With Posterity's Blessing

John George "Kootenai" Brown had it right when he said of Waterton: "This is what I have seen in my dreams, this is the country for me." Countless people have felt the same way. There's no place like it.

Brown first caught sight of the three Waterton lakes in 1865 as he was passing through, but he never forgot this special spot on the eastern front of the Canadian Rocky Mountains. It was more than a decade before he would return, bringing with him his young Métis wife Olivia Lyonnais and their children, putting an end to his wanderings. Brown and his family not only made Waterton their permanent home, they also set the stage for all those who felt as he did about its glacier-carved mountains, valleys and lakes, welcoming all who followed.

If there is a single defining characteristic of Waterton Lakes National Park, and a key to understanding its modern human history and development, it is the park's accessible isolation. Waterton's western boundary in the southwestern corner of Alberta abuts British Columbia and the Continental Divide to the west, and Montana, at the Canada-U.S. border, to the south. The park is a destination that is at the end of the road. Its seclusion has been that way since 1895, when some of what we now know as Waterton was first set aside by the federal government and called Kootenay Lakes Forest Park.

With Banff and Jasper national parks to the north and closer to Alberta's largest population centres of Calgary and Edmonton, Waterton became the playground of southern Albertans and often northern Montanans, those groups historically making up the bulk of regular visitors.

For many years Waterton was described as a place "where the prairies meet the mountains." It's a fitting description. Unlike other areas along the Rocky Mountain front, there are no foothills.

This abrupt meeting of the prairies and mountains was a surprise to William A. Buchanan, the new publisher of *The Lethbridge Daily Herald*, on his first visit in 1909: "I had never driven into the mountains before and the distance was most deceptive. . . . What we thought would be a few minutes turned out to be several hours. The mountains keep leading you on, making you believe they are close to you when they are quite a distance away."

Visitors—who often hail from the bald, flat prairie—revel in Waterton's unusual and spectacular mountain landscapes. And once they begin to investigate the park, they soon swap stories of adventures about exploring the peaks and valleys, laugh about the ever-present wind, compare photos of one-of-a-kind flora, and brag about the diverse wildlife they've seen.

This is a place that takes hold of both the heart and psyche of visitors—as much today as it did for Kootenai Brown, whose name was synonymous with the pioneer days of the park. He earned his moniker through his association with the region, then called Kootenay Lakes, and the Kutenai Natives who came to trade with him.

Born in Ireland in 1839, Brown led a rogue's life until finally settling in Waterton. He was variously a soldier in the British army who served in India, a gold miner, a policeman in British Columbia during the gold rush, a bison hunter with the Métis on the plains, a pony mail rider, a U.S. army scout who was reportedly a captive of Sitting Bull, and a wolfer. When he moved to the Waterton lakes in the late 1870s, he had just been acquitted of murder in Montana Territory and was looking for a new life in Canada.

Upon arrival, Brown capitalized on his experience with Natives and went into business with H.A. "Fred" Kanouse, operating a store on the eastern shore of

"Kootenai" Brown

Lower Waterton Lake where Indigenous people traded furs for supplies.

When Brown's trading business began to change as European settlers started to arrive and Natives roamed less, tending to remain on their reserves or reservations, he sold out to Kanouse for $250 and built successive cabins at various locations at various times. One confirmed site was where Blakiston Creek flows into Middle Waterton Lake. The location had the benefit of being closer to travelled routes and offered greater opportunity to interact with those passing by.

Even so, it was a lonely life for Kootenai, with Olivia tending the household and their children. The nearest settlement was Fort Macleod, 105 kilometres (65 miles) to the north.

The couple had three babies, two of whom survived past childhood and their births may have compounded Olivia's frail health; she died in 1884 at the age of 35. Kootenai buried her on the western shore of Lower Waterton Lake at a place which would become the Brown family grave site. Devastated by his loss but aware of the complexities of raising children alone in such a wilderness locale, Brown sent his children north to be properly cared for and educated.

Isolation with a beloved partner was one thing; isolation with no one was quite another. Brown threw himself into a variety of occupations, including fishing, hunting, ranching and guiding. Four or five years after Olivia's death, Isabella, an Edmonton-born Cree, came into Brown's life. He called her "Nichemoos," a Cree endearment meaning "sweetheart."

With Isabella's arrival, hospitality returned to Brown's home, becoming the code of the lakes for the rest of his life.

Isabella Brown, Kootenai's second wife, outlived him by 19 years. Friends took her in and helped her communicate with park officials and others, since she spoke Cree but no English.

Joe Cosley

"Boys, come right in. You are welcome as the flowers in May," Brown told Joe Cosley the first time he and a companion visited. Cosley, then a U.S. forest ranger in Montana, became a good friend of the Browns and recalled some of Kootenai's finer points: "He opened his doors to all comers and treated them with hospitable care. I learned later that he had a host of friends who held him in the highest esteem."

It was little wonder. Isabella was reportedly a good cook who didn't mind sharing meals with unexpected guests. The company was welcomed, especially after a winter made longer by Waterton's incessant, howling wind and an absence of visitors.

Well educated, Kootenai Brown was a good conversationalist with uncommon intelligence, and a man who was not averse to liquid refreshments. A visit to the Browns had all the makings of relaxation. Nothing combines so well at the lakes as good food, good times and good friends. It has been ever thus.

For all the credit Brown would later receive as Waterton's first citizen and park manager, he was not the first European to visit the area and record the event. That distinction goes to Thomas Wright Blakiston, a 26-year-old lieutenant in the Royal Artillery who showed up at the lakes in 1858 as part of the Palliser Expedition.

Financed by the British government, the Palliser Expedition was given the three-fold task of mapping portions of Western Canada, searching for possible railway routes through the mountains to the Pacific, and appraising the land for settlement.

Blakiston's own role was to locate the North Kootenay Pass, taking magnetic measurements along the way to confirm that it was wholly in British territory.

The Canada-United States border was first marked with stone cairns like this one near Cameron Lake. It was partic-ularly important as it indicated where the southwestern tip of Alberta, the eastern boundary of British Columbia and the northern boundary of Montana come together. It stood for many years until replaced with an iron survey marker.

He arrived at the Waterton lakes, which he described as "a very windy spot," on Sept. 8, 1858.

"After two hours' travelling on level ground along Red Stone Creek, we emerged on the Saskatchewan Plains, just six geographical miles north of the 49th Parallel and camped at Waterton lakes, two miles east of the mouth of the pass," he wrote, slipping in the name "Waterton," without explanation.

It is assumed that he named the lakes for Charles Waterton, a fellow Englishman and well-known ornithologist of the day. Although Charles Waterton never visited the area, the name stuck and the government of Canada eventually replaced the name Kootenay Lakes, which had served for decades.

Blakiston left the lakes after two days when a sudden snowstorm—typical weather for that time of year in the mountainous terrain—sent the party packing. But his brief time in Waterton became a claim to immortality. The park's tallest mountain (2,910 metres; 9,597 feet) was named in his honour, as were the valley he descended and the creek that cuts through it, although for many years it was known as Pass Creek.

Two years after Blakiston's group, a joint U.S.-British survey party came to Waterton from the west, surveying the 49th Parallel to establish the international border through what is now British Columbia. They determined that the boundary neatly bisected 11-kilometre (6.9-mile) long Upper Waterton Lake. Among the Northwest Boundary Commission members was artist James M. Alden, whose sketches provided some of the first views of Waterton, the final stop of the surveyors, who had started at the Pacific coast.

Following in their footsteps was another joint survey party in August 1874, this time coming from the east to mark the border across the prairies as far as Waterton, where the previous surveyors had ended their work.

While the American and British-Canadian boundary surveyors were eager to finish the work to avoid another season in the field, their stay in Waterton was marked both by business—astronomical observations and building stone monuments to mark the position of the 49th Parallel—and pleasure.

Like so many visitors to Waterton who have since

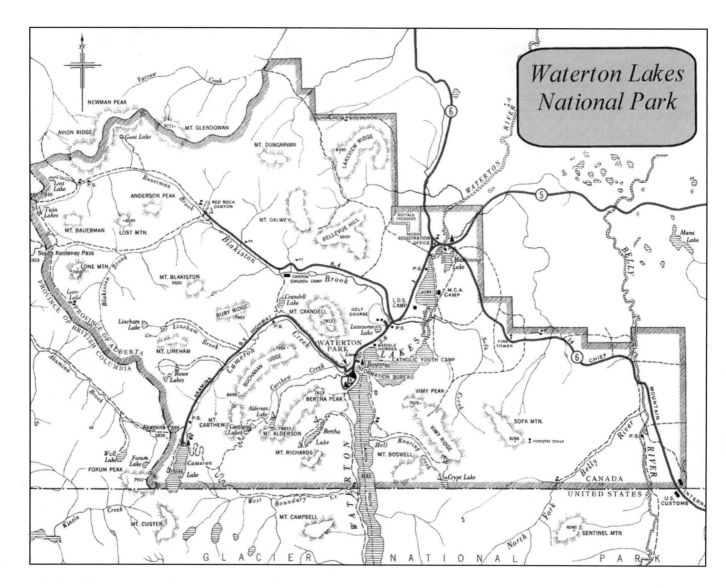

Waterton Lakes National Park

followed, the men tried their hands at fishing, hoping for some respite from a monotonous diet. Thomas Millman, an assistant surgeon with the British-Canadian group, wrote: "Cap't [Albany Featherstonhaugh] and I went fishing for the day. Got quite a haul. The heaviest weighed 3 lbs. Found them very delicious."

As a parting gesture, members of the British-Canadian group chose to name some of the geographical features for themselves, something they had not done elsewhere. The names included: Cameronian Mountain for Donald Roderick Cameron, the chief commissioner; Anderson Peak for Samuel Anderson, chief astronomer; Mount Galwey for William James Galwey, assistant astronomer; Mount Boswell for William G. Boswell, the party's veterinary surgeon; Mount Richards for Capt. George Henry Richards, commission member; and Mount Rowe for Lieut. Valentine Rowe, also a commission member.

It was in the wake of the 1874 boundary surveyors

that the Browns arrived and stayed, becoming the first year-round, long-term residents in what is now the park.

As European settlement expanded in southern Alberta and new communities were created, more people came to the lakes. Pioneer residents began to wonder how long this place would remain unspoiled. Brown, who had earlier promoted the region's bounty, was also beginning to note the toll on natural resources.

It was just such observations that prompted Frederick W. Godsal, an Englishman-turned-Alberta rancher and an acquaintance of Brown's, to take pen in hand. Godsal wrote to old friend William Pearce, the federal superintendent of mines, to remind him of a recommendation Pearce himself had made some years before to set aside the Waterton lakes as a park.

"I think [the lakes] should be reserved forever for the use of the public otherwise a comparatively small number of settlers can control and spoil these public resorts," Godsal wrote in September 1893. Pearce forwarded the letter to his Ottawa superiors, where it made the rounds of cautious civil servants and elected officials. It took nearly two years for T.M. Daly, the minister of the Department of the Interior, to act and turn the idea into reality.

"Upon the strength of Mr. Pearce's approval of Mr. Godsal's suggestion," Daly wrote to A.M. Burgess, his deputy minister, "You have my authority for making the proposed reservation for park purposes. Posterity will bless us."

Kootenay Lakes Forest Park was established on May 30, 1895, with several changes in both name and size over the years.

Hunting was forbidden in the new reserve, but other resource protection was lacking. Timber could be harvested under permit, and petroleum prospecting and the staking of mining prospects, although regulated, were allowed. That fact was jolted home when Mormon pioneer William Aldridge and his 12-year-old son Oliver stumbled across an oil seepage on Cameron Creek in the Akamina Valley, west of the present Waterton townsite.

Aldridge, his wife Anna Rolph and six children (later to total 13) had arrived in the park about 1892 and tried to raise cattle. When the herd died because of the harsh winter, Aldridge began a commercial fishing operation from a squatter's camp he built on the northwestern shore of Middle Waterton Lake then informally known as Aldridge Bay, near Linnet Lake.

When Aldridge found oil, the family abandoned the lakes and moved to the Akamina Valley, about eight kilometres (five miles) to the west. There Aldridge and his family collected oil by pooling it in pits they dug and scooping it or soaking it up with sacks, wringing them out into 19-litre (five-gallon) cans. They sold the oil for $1 a gallon for use as medicine and as a lubricant. In 1904 Aldridge sold out to the Vancouver Western Oil and Coal Co and moved to Cardston.

When they left the valley, it was with a measure of sadness for they had buried an infant close to their cabin. Alexander Aldridge was born July 1, 1902, and died just weeks later. According to his brother Frank, the pregnant Anna was taking the children on a picnic to a site across Cameron Creek when four-year-old John slipped and fell in the icy stream. In rescuing the child, Anna was badly bruised and soaked by the bitterly cold water. As a result of the trauma, she gave birth to Alexander two months prematurely.

"The baby died from malnutrition as mother was unable to nurse him and we had not milk or any baby foods," Frank said. The baby was buried in a crude wooden coffin and the grave was marked with stones. In 1966, Frank Aldridge requested and received permission to install a metal plaque at the grave site.

The Aldridge discovery and subsequent exploitation of oil encouraged others to search for petroleum in the region. Wildcatters were quick to move in, drilling off and on at various locations, including the Akamina Valley, near Cameron Falls, and along the shore of Upper Waterton Lake on property now occupied by the Bayshore Inn.

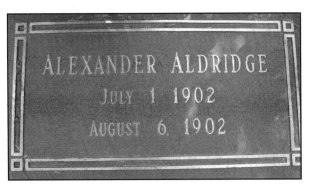

Alexander Aldridge was buried in thick forest near Oil City along Cameron Creek at a time when this area was not part of Waterton. This grave marker was placed at the request of family members.

John Lineham of the Rocky Mountain Development Co. purchased about 648 hectares (1,600 acres), which was then freehold land, in the Akamina Valley and had 437 lots surveyed for a residential development he called Oil City, selling a few lots to the public in an initial offering.

Lineham drilled for oil and found it in 1902. The well flowed at 300 barrels a day but proved to be a "nine-day wonder" and was commercially unsuccessful. Its demise ended hopes for further development of Oil City.

The Pincher Creek Oil and Refining Co. was equally unsuccessful in its attempts to make a discovery in the same general area as Lineham's company. Another outfit, Western Oil and Coal Co., selected a drilling site in 1904 several hundred metres north of Cameron Falls, where it erected an office, blacksmith shop, stable, engine house and two buildings to house and feed the crew. For all their efforts, they finally hit oil in 1905, but it came to the surface at only one barrel a day before a wall caved in and the well was plugged. The camp was abandoned in 1907 and stood for half a dozen years until it was dismantled.

To Kootenai Brown and others who knew the lakes intimately, "Alberta's first oil boom drove home the danger of people flooding into the mountains and foothills and the resulting impact upon the wildlife and natural resources of the area," according to William Rodney, Brown's biographer.

It wasn't just unsightly, abandoned drilling sites that were a concern. The drilling companies were using timber at a dizzying pace: 1,100 cords of wood just to generate steam to run the drilling rigs and hundreds of board feet of timber for construction purposes. It could only get worse: more than half the forest park had been staked for petroleum exploration.

Federal bureaucrats hadn't been totally oblivious to the situation. In 1901 they appointed 60-year-old Kootenai Brown the fisheries officer, largely a public relations position created to provide an official presence.

Lula Nielson recalled encountering Brown in 1906 after a day of fishing with friends. A bit leery when he hailed them from horseback, they quickly identified him by his red shirt and long greying hair.

"We knew it was Kootenai Brown," Nielson said. "His first remark was, 'How many fish have you got?' We were plenty scared for we knew that he was

Frederick W. Godsal

the big boss in that area." After looking at the fish and commenting that it was a fine catch, Brown said, "I'm having a dance over at my house tonight and you tell everyone you see that they are invited."

As an official, he'd done his duty cleverly and made friends in the bargain. But Brown could do nothing about forces larger than the growing number of tourists. Developments such as the oil drilling continued to trouble him.

It was all too much for Godsal. In September 1905 he again wrote a letter, this time to the minister of the Interior in Ottawa, seeking an enlargement of the park and the safeguarding of this scenic location. The following March, the government sent W.T. Margach, chief forest ranger with the Department of Interior, to inspect the park. Margach disagreed about the need to enlarge the park and suggested in his report that recreation must come second to commercial resource

development, although he conceded that drilling should not be allowed along the shore of Upper Waterton Lake.

The protection would come in stages, starting in 1906 when the forest park became a forest reserve. To reinforce those efforts, Kootenai Brown was appointed "forest ranger in charge" effective April 1, 1910. The appointment was an acknowledgement that the government had to establish more control if the park was to be properly maintained.

The appointment was suggested by John Herron, member of Parliament for Alberta and a friend of Brown's. Despite the fact Brown was 70 years old, Herron was sure the spry Kootenai was up to the task.

Finally, on June 8, 1911, Waterton was designated a dominion park, the country's fourth. It was also the smallest at 35 square kilometres (13.5 square miles), not even reaching the international boundary on Upper Waterton Lake.

As tiny as it was, park administrators were moving to develop the new park into a tourist destination. Howard Douglas, the commissioner of dominion parks, declared that "the finest summer resort in Alberta will be established on the Waterton lakes." He predicted that "as soon as the townsite is laid out, a branch of the Canadian Pacific [Railway] will no doubt be built to Waterton, and this will ensure the success of the scheme." He was incorrect on that note. No rail line was built to serve the park.

Behind the scenes, dominion land surveyor W.F. O'Hara had nearly completed his work in Waterton, which was finalized and approved in 1911. O'Hara's survey consisted of plans for 172 lots at two locations, one along the west side of Upper Waterton Lake (today's townsite) and a grouping along the entrance road near the Middle Lake.

There was also a survey of lots near the Lower Lake which was withdrawn from the plan early in 1918 because the location was deemed "too distant from the business section to attract prospective lessees."

Applications for lot leases were not accepted until October 1911, as officials in Ottawa scrutinized and approved O'Hara's work, and had maps and paperwork prepared. Forty-two-year renewable leases would be issued if the applicant paid one year's rent

This early oil drilling rig was located on today's Evergreen Avenue in Waterton townsite, north of Cameron Falls. The effort resulted in a dry hole and eventually the buildings were torn down and the lumber reused.

in advance and erected a building with a minimum value of $300 within 12 months. The most desirable residential lots were those on the lakeshore, which rented for $15 a year; rent for other lots was $10.

Squatters such as Jack Hazzard and Christian Jensen, both of whom had built hostelries in 1911 in anticipation of a lease rush, filed formal applications for the land they already occupied. In general, by 1913 some lots were reserved exclusively for businesses and others were designated for residential use. Development of Waterton as a resort had begun.

The lease applications with the associated paperwork added substantially to Brown's duties as he became a go-between for applicants and Ottawa bureaucrats, even though only a few lots were offered at a time. Suddenly his job became far more than guarding the park. This added administrative workload was to set the tone for future park administrators.

During Brown's last days as the park manager, the government conceded it had made a mistake in

Sue Laszynski at a naturally fed oil pool near the national historic site commemorating the first oil well drilled in Western Canada. The pool, a combination of water and oil, has long been an attractant to bears.

1911 when it set the size of the park at just 35 square kilometres. It had provided too little area for wildlife protection. So, in 1914 the park was increased more than thirtyfold in size to l,096 square kilometres (423 square miles), its border extended north to the Carbondale River, west of Pincher Creek and just shy of the Crowsnest Pass. (The current park is half that size.) While it was a major concession to the role of the national park, there was little visitor accommodation and just a small increase in park staff.

The added workload, the greater area to guard and Brown's failing health came to a head just days after Canada entered the First World War in August 1914. Brown, then nearly 75 years old, was forced to retire. Robert Cooper, a forest ranger who had worked for Brown since 1911, was put in charge. He became Waterton's first superintendent, by official title, and was responsible for a staff of four men.

"I was appointed to my present position on 17 August 1914 and took over the superintendence of the park about a week after. The conditions in the park when I took over control were primitive," Cooper later wrote.

The conditions would stay primitive for the duration of the war, as federal money for improvements was diverted to the war effort and Cooper was instructed to authorize work that was "only absolutely necessary." Ignoring instructions from his superiors, he got into serious hot water and was dismissed in 1919 for incompetence.

With one exception, little by way of park improvements was accomplished during the Great War. The exception was the completion in 1915 of a wooden bridge over the Waterton River for travellers coming from Cardston and Lethbridge. No longer did automobiles or horse drawn wagons have to ford the river either at a site near today's park entrance road or at Waterton Mills.

Annual visitation to Waterton more than quadrupled between 1914 and 1918 despite the war, increasing to 9,000 from 2,000 people over the period. A population explosion in the West through immigration and the popularity of the automobile contributed to the increase. Licensed drivers in Alberta, who numbered 3,700 in 1913, totalled 20,000 by 1917.

Kootenai Brown did not live out the war. He died in 1916 and was buried beside his first wife, Olivia. His second wife, Isabella, would join them in the family plot in 1935.

Even before the First World War ended on Nov. 11, 1918, interest in leasing land in the Waterton townsite was picking up and a handful of cabins were completed. Southern Alberta had transitioned from frontier to settled, and residents now had the resources and time for leisure pursuits.

By September 1919, George Ace Bevan, the new park superintendent and a war veteran, had the names of 43 people who wanted to apply for lots while he awaited a new survey to expand the townsite by an additional 86 lots between Evergreen and Fountain Avenues.

Business people were beginning to sniff out possibilities, as well, but before development could proceed there was an unexpected delay.

After several consecutive years of drought on the prairies, the Reclamation Service, a branch of the Department of the Interior, proposed construction of a dam in the park, a 12.2- to 18.3-metre (40- to 60-

Boundary Revisions and Name Changes

The protected area known as Waterton Lakes National Park has seen numerous changes since 1895, both in size and in name, due in part to differing ideas and the various federal government departments that were responsible for its administration over the years.

Designated	Name	Size
1895	Kootenay Lakes Forest Park	54 sq. miles (140 sq. km)
1906	Kootenay Lakes Forest Reserve	54 sq. miles (140 sq. km)
1911	Waterton Lakes Dominion Park	13.5 sq. miles (35 sq. km)
1914	Waterton Lakes Dominion Park	423 sq. miles (1,096 sq. km)
1921	Waterton Lakes Dominion Park	294 sq. miles (762 sq. km)
1930	Waterton Lakes National Park	220 sq. miles (570 sq. km)
1947	Waterton Lakes National Park	204 sq. miles (528 sq. km)
1955	Waterton Lakes National Park	203 sq. miles (526 sq. km)
2000	Waterton Lakes National Park	195 sq. miles (505 sq. km)

Early roads into the park were only marginally better than wildlife trails until the 1920s, when they were graded and gravelled. Construction of bridges at Waterton River and Blakiston Creek made automobile crossings safer and more reliable. Otherwise, rivers and creeks were only safe to cross at times of low water.

foot) high barricade at the Narrows between the Upper and Middle lakes. Waterton seemed the logical place for an irrigation dam to serve southern Alberta farms because the existing lake would simply be topped up by spring runoff to create a storage reservoir, and the Narrows seemed a natural place to put a dam.

Parks Branch staff abhorred the idea. A dam would turn Waterton into a game reserve with a few hiking trails, they said, submerging the townsite and, in general, spoiling the park. To allay concerns about destruction of the townsite, newspaper stories, based on nothing but speculation, suggested a new town could be located on high ground northwest of Linnet Lake. That idea was discounted by park officials because the land was too "precipitous and impossible for building sites."

So important was agriculture to the province, the idea of enhancing productivity was equated with a bright economic future and deemed far more important than budding seasonal tourism in Waterton.

Truman W. Crofts was willing to sacrifice his new cabin, built in 1918 on Mount View Road, in favour of a dam. As a Lethbridge area farmer, he was among those to argue for irrigation and eventually became the first chairman of the Lethbridge Northern Irrigation District.

While discussions continued about the feasibility of a dam at the Narrows, in May 1920 parks commissioner J.B. Harkin put a moratorium on new land leases and building permits in Waterton. As for those who had applied, complied with their building commitments and were awaiting a lease, Harkin had no choice.

"I would recommend that leases be issued in these cases," he wrote in a memo. If the dam was built and compensation required, it would be dealt with later.

Clara Thompson, a prominent Spring Coulee, Alberta, business woman who had applied for a lot on Fountain Avenue, withdrew her application specifically because of the uncertainty. A few others did likewise.

Surprisingly Godsal, a one-time friend of the park who had moved to Victoria, British Columbia, wrote

The business section of Waterton townsite, seen above in 1919, was developed slowly by entrepreneurs, as was the number of residences. Following the First World War more backcountry trails were built, allowing the use of saddlehorses to take riders to the park's high country lakes.

to support the dam. In a rambling 1,000-word letter to *The Lethbridge Herald* in April 1922, Godsal noted the importance of irrigation to agriculture:

"Rocky mountain scenery will not fill empty stomachs however satisfying to our own enjoyment. Our sport and enjoyment must not be at the cost of others' suffering. . . . After all that has been said, is any great, real harm going to be done by deepening Waterton Lake?"

By contrast, local resident Henri "Frenchy" Riviere, a provincial game warden and honorary Waterton warden, suggested drought-stricken farmers move to the northern part of the province, thus eliminating the need for a dam.

Since a dam at the Narrows would back up Upper Waterton Lake into adjoining Glacier National Park in Montana, it was essential for Canada to get U.S. permission to do an irrigation survey across the boundary. It was two years before it could be arranged through the co-operation of the International Joint Commission, responsible for matters related to the cross-border flow of water.

In the end, it was the objections of Americans that brought the matter to a conclusion. Raising the level of the lake into Montana was adamantly opposed by the United States government, as well as private citizens. George Bird Grinnell, Glacier park's "godfather" and greatest supporter, told Harkin in 1922: "The project is to the last degree shortsighted."

While this was not the last proposal to build an irrigation dam in the park, the long and loud opposition set a precedent for efforts that followed, in 1941, 1951 and 1962.

The one plan for park improvement that was unaffected by the dam proposal was development of a golf course. Located on higher ground than the townsite, at the base of Mount Crandell, the golf course was an instant hit with visitors when it opened in 1922.

The end of the dam debacle meant the public was again allowed to apply for townsite leases and the park experienced a tourism boom that extended over the remainder of the decade. Poor roads—some no better than wide trails—were eventually graded as automobile use continued to increase throughout the 1920s. Plans were being made, work was underway, and development was taking off.

Many residential lease applicants, like Eleanor Delong of Lethbridge, hired a contractor to erect their cabins. It was just the boost needed for two Cardston builders, Doug G. Oland and James C. Scott. They were willing, able and ready to take on the work.

Carl Carlson, a local carpenter, decided he would build one cabin at a time—on his own rather than by contract—applying for a lease in his own name, erecting the cabin and living in it until a buyer was found. Then he used the money to start again.

Carl Danielson, another local tradesman, built several cabins as fast as the rules and his finances allowed, retaining ownership and renting the cabins to others. Some lease applicants did their own building. There were options enough to suit everyone if the park superintendent approved the construction plans.

Entrepreneurs lost no time providing tourists with what they needed, expanding the variety of services offered in the park. The new and improved businesses made the park attractive to visitors, but one large new establishment in particular drew people like a magnet: the Waterton Dance Pavilion.

"Dancing made this park," said Nahor Dilatush, whose café, hotel and store across the street from the pavilion benefitted from the influx of dancers. In fact, the building of the dance pavilion was a tide that

The townsite's first official campsite was near Cameron Falls. The number of visitors soon outgrew the site and other areas were opened for camping. Today the townsite campground has few tall trees, but continues to attract campers and RVers.

Following construction of the dance pavilion, at right, Waterton started to come into its own as a tourist attraction, a reputation further secured by the 1927 opening of the Prince of Wales Hotel on the knoll. Doug G. Oland and his partner Jim Scott built both structures, as well as many residences in the townsite.

raised all ships. Hotels, rooming houses, campgrounds filled quickly because of the people who came for the dances, made all the more popular by the excellent music. Every business in Waterton flourished because of the dances.

The biggest investments of all in Waterton during the 1920s were the $1-million Prince of Wales Hotel (1927) and the $25,000 excursion boat *Motor Vessel International* (1928), both built for the Great Northern Railway of St. Paul, Minnesota. The hotel and the boat were not important simply because they were new and expensive. They represented first-class service, unsurpassed by any operations of their kind inside the park or nearby, and that fact was advertised across North America.

The Great Northern Railway had been drawn to Waterton as a means to expand its tourism developments in Glacier park, which was on its Chicago to Seattle main line. While not serving Waterton directly—bus and saddle horse connections did that—the Great Northern used its promotional capability in ways that

Doug G. Oland

Jim Scott

locals couldn't match. North America-wide advertisements for the railway's chain of hotels and chalets in Glacier included its new Waterton hotel and boat—unprecedented international exposure at no cost to the Canadians.

There were two other spinoffs from the Prince of Wales Hotel which made a huge impact on life in the park.

First, the Great Northern was able to persuade Alberta government officials to give it a licence to open Waterton's first beer parlour. Despite numerous previous individual efforts to get a beer licence, it was the railway's influence and reputation that succeeded in ending Waterton's dry spell, albeit three years after Prohibition had ended in the province.

The railway was also able to persuade provincial authorities, after buying interest-free government bonds, to upgrade the road between Cardston and the park. This was the main route used by many southern Albertans, especially those from Lethbridge, to get to Waterton.

But more importantly for the railway, it was the

route its passengers took by bus to travel between Glacier and Waterton via Cardston, in the days prior to construction of Chief Mountain International Highway.

The contractors who built the Prince of Wales Hotel had faced enormous problems hauling supplies from Cardston to Waterton for its construction and Great Northern officials now demanded an all-weather road to bring its guests into the park. The highway improvements greatly enhanced access and soon there was scheduled bus service linking Waterton and Banff parks, via Calgary.

With the boost in tourism in the 1920s came the establishment of a larger, year-round population in the Waterton townsite. Although the permanent population was relatively small, this community had needs just like any other and at the top of the list was a school. This became acute during the construction of the Prince of Wales Hotel, when an influx of 200 workers, many of whom had arrived with their wives and children, swelled the student population.

Waterton's educational system had begun in September 1925 when Florence Keith was hired to teach 19 students in eight grades. Since there was no school building, classes were held in a private home, 105 Mount View Rd., for the first school year. With the influx of the hotel builders the following year, classes

were held in the lobby of the Waterton Lakes Hotel and Chalets and various private homes.

A wood frame and stucco school on Fountain Avenue was completed in the fall of 1927. The contract went to George Baker, who in turn subcontracted it to carpenter Harry Cummings. It was a 7.3- by 10-metre (24- by 33-foot) standard one-room school. It was enlarged to two rooms by Oland & Scott Construction in 1929.

The tax base, increased substantially with the addition of the Prince of Wales Hotel, and was now broad enough to support the cost of a larger school. In its

The first school house, above, was a small building erected by Harry Cummings and later greatly enlarged by Oland & Scott Construction of Cardston.

The park's second registration office was on the entry road across from Linnet Lake. It was replaced when officials noticed that golfers entering the park never reached this location and thus avoided paying the entry fee. A new office was built at the junction of Highways 5 and 6 in the 1930s that ensured everyone entering the park paid up.

Tourists on their way to Cameron Lake on the newly opened Akamina Highway (later renamed a parkway) pause to take in an elevated view of Waterton townsite and Vimy Peak. Drivers entering Waterton could buy an annual park pass, which got them a metal badge (below) they could attach to their vehicle radiator, or a daily paper permit.

first year operating a business in Waterton, the Great Northern paid $2,400 in school taxes, almost half of the school's $5,077 expenses in 1927.

Besides offering education, the school was a hub for what cultural and social life there was in the winters in Waterton, and for many years it was used in the summer for church services by congregations without their own buildings.

The growth of the town, measured by its developments between 1919 and 1929, was remarkable and by the end of the decade only one commercial lot on Waterton Avenue remained vacant.

The great economic boom that made the 1920s roar and Waterton suddenly so vigorous began to

slow with the onset of the Great Depression of the 1930s, but tourism continued and so did building, although both were at a less intense pace.

The federal government's establishment of unemployment relief camps during the Depression went a long way to provide facilities in Waterton that might not have otherwise come about when they did. The men who worked in these camps through the end of 1935 built the Chief Mountain International Highway, improved the Akamina Highway to Cameron Lake, cleared brush, cut trails, built camp shelters and other buildings, and added another nine holes to the golf course.

Another bright spot during the economic gloom of the 1930s were the summer dances, which took on a novel variation with the aid of the excursion boat *M.V. International.* Called the Midnight Frolics, the once-a-week event was designed to skirt Alberta laws prohibiting dancing and drinking on Sundays by moving the dance to Goat Haunt, Montana, at the head of the upper lake.

With no objection from the boat's owner, the nighttime cruise became a regular feature. By law dancers at the pavilion could only cut a rug until 11:59 p.m. on Saturdays. Then the orchestra would lead the way to the boat and Capt. Peter Primrose and his crew would cruise to Goat Haunt, where a rustic log chalet provided space for dancing and beer was sold. Montana had no Sunday prohibitions. The conviviality of the Midnight Frolics was long and fondly remembered.

Not so fondly recounted was the forest fire of 1935, a truly harrowing experience. The fire began on Aug. 8, started by lightning on the west side of Upper Waterton Lake in Glacier park. Members of the U.S. Civilian Conservation Corps attempted to fight the fire in the Boundary Creek Valley, but it was flared by the wind, forcing the men to evacuate the site. Within two days, the blaze spread rapidly northward from the Canada-U.S. boundary toward the townsite, billowing black smoke that hung in the valley, making breathing difficult and heightening fears about personal safety and property protection.

Hundreds of Canadian and American firefighters joined forces to attack the fire while the Waterton park office staff handled the logistical problems. C.K. "Cap" LeCapelain, engineer in charge of the Canadian section of Chief Mountain Highway construction, rushed his men from the road camp to the fire, bringing tools and equipment.

About 100 men from the Blood Tribe reserve also volunteered to join the crews. Capt. Primrose of the *International* placed himself and the vessel at the disposal of the park superintendent to move men and supplies, while local resident Les Morrow piloted his freight boat *Linnea* at all hours, delivering food, fuel and equipment to the staging areas and a lakeshore mess camp.

Waterton residents did what they could to protect their property. They ran hoses through the town, fed by dozens of pumps that drew hundreds of gallons of water from Cameron Creek and Upper Waterton Lake, to soak anything that could burn. As the fire neared, embers and ash rained down and the smoke got thicker, stinging eyes.

The Motor Vessel International, *built for the Great Northern Railway, was launched in 1928 and carried passengers to Goat Haunt at the head of the lake with commentary by the captain's wife, Winona Primrose. It was also used to carry men and equipment during the 1935 forest fire, below, that threatened the town.*

Chief Mountain International Highway, the long-awaited road link with Glacier National Park, was a Depression relief project on the Alberta side and a contract project on the Montana side. It was opened to traffic on June 13, 1936. A new Waterton registration office, bottom photo, was also completed at the junction of Highways 5 and 6 and was used until 1990.

Despite all the efforts, officials feared the worst. A message relayed from the fire line: "Get word to the people at Waterton if they don't want to take their own chances, to move out of town as the fire is out of control . . . it is hard telling where it will go."

Just as police initiated the evacuation order, the wind shifted to the north and the fire stalled 2.4 kilometres (1.5 miles) from the townsite, then moved southward. The evacuation order was rescinded shortly after. The town was saved by the very forces of Mother Nature that had put it in danger.

It was the worst scare in the 20th century history of the park and one of Waterton's brightest moments—a practical show of co-operation among Canadians, Americans and Indigenous people in a time of crisis.

After their firefighting diversion, the relief camp workers returned to finish the job on Chief Mountain Highway. It was opened in the spring of 1936 and for the first time Waterton and Glacier were directly linked by a road, and one with scenic views.

The opening of Chief Mountain Highway followed the 1933 completion of the transmountain Going-to-the-Sun Highway in Glacier, the first road through the interior of that park and over the Continental Divide. The eastern terminus of Sun Highway was St. Mary, Montana, and many travellers who reached there decided to head north to see Waterton. It was just the boost Waterton businesses needed during the Depression, and the amount of American traffic that headed north picked up when the route was made shorter by the completion of Chief Mountain Highway.

Waterton's fortunes were turning around, and it was the perfect time to celebrate.

The first weekend in July 1936, less than a month after the opening of Chief Mountain Highway, and with the reopening of the Prince of Wales Hotel, the park was packed with celebratory events, drawing more than 6,000 visitors in 2,000 cars.

Topping the list was a ceremony by members of the Rotary clubs of Alberta, Saskatchewan and Montana to mark the Waterton portion of Waterton-Glacier International Peace Park, the world's first such designation.

The U.S. celebration had been held at Glacier Park Hotel in 1932, the year both Parliament and Congress granted the special peace park designation by legislation. Since the peace park idea had originated at a Rotary gathering held at the Prince of Wales Hotel, it was only fitting the Canadian celebration be held there, but the hotel was closed from 1933 through 1935.

With the hotel reopened, the delayed dedication was led by Rev. Samuel H. Middleton, the Rotarian who had proposed the peace park idea. He was, principal of St. Paul's Residential School on the Blood Tribe reserve east of the park, and a longtime Waterton supporter active in community events.

In a separate ceremony in the townsite that weekend, a stone cairn was dedicated to the memory of Kootenai Brown, who had died 20 years earlier. The cairn was also Rev. Middleton's idea, but he was assisted by others who had also known Brown, not the least of whom was Arthur H. Harwood, Waterton's postmaster, who had been a friend of Brown's. Located at the east end of Cameron Falls Drive near the lakeshore, the cairn was unveiled before a crowd of 300 people by Senator William A. Buchanan of Lethbridge, a park cabin owner, and Alberta Lt.-Gov. W.L. Walsh.

The third large spectacle was a gathering of First World War veterans from Alberta and Montana who met to form an international legion and elect officers and committee members. Three Waterton men were among them: Peter Gairns, vice-president; Fred Udell, secretary-treasurer; and Walter "Waddy" B. Foster, a committee member.

The weekend was pivotal: it marked the beginning of an upsurge in visitation that did not slow until the Second World War and reinvigorated a community spirit in Waterton that lasted for decades.

Sense of community had been prevalent in Waterton ever since the opening of the Prince of Wales Hotel and the resulting influx of new residents.

Ensuring the wholesome development of resident youths, a Boy Scout troop was formed in 1933 as a winter activity. The troop, sponsored by the newly formed Waterton branch of the Canadian Legion, was led by Cpl. Andy Ford, an award-winning marksman, First World War veteran and the park's Royal Canadian Mounted Police officer.

The new scout master began by teaching the boys how to shoot and used the indoor swimming pool, adjacent to the RCMP buildings, as a rifle range. Pool owner Dell Ellison, himself the father of three boys, readily agreed to its use.

Teenager Frank Goble was among the first Scout participants. Years later, in 1955, when he was the father of three boys, Goble revived the scouting tradition in the park, helping ensure Waterton boys handily won the Senator Buchanan sports trophy for winter camping skills several years running.

Not to be left out, the girls in the park were organized into a Girl Guide troop in 1934 by Sibyl Kemmis, with the assistance of Marjorie Harwood. Other adults in the community pitched in to help both girls and boys earn proficiency badges, offering knowledge in their various areas of expertise. When the Girl Guides were revived in the 1950s, so was the participation of parents and resident adults. Restaurateur Linnea Goble, for example, taught groups of young people how to cook.

The lettering on the arches on both Highways 5 and 6 into Waterton were changed to acknowledge the international peace park designation following the passage of legislation in 1932.

Children and adults alike found that winter presented the biggest challenge to living year-round in the park. Making the best of things, however, was seldom viewed as a hardship.

Skiing and skating parties were often formed on an impromptu basis, and shinny hockey enlivened windless days and evenings. In some years, a Waterton hockey team challenged others in the district. But however inventive residents were at having a good time, the amenities so taken for granted by people outside the park were not available, and created an awareness that Waterton was well behind the times.

"As kids, we couldn't wait to grow up and leave," said June Rackette Miles, who attended school in the park beginning in 1937.

One of the greatest inconveniences was the lack of running water in the winter. The water lines were buried just below the surface or lay on top of the ground. The water supply had to be turned off and the pipes drained before freeze-up, leaving residents to their own devices.

"In the wintertime we used to haul our water from the creek," said Delance Strate, whose house on Evergreen Avenue was several hundred yards from Cameron Creek.

"We caught rainwater, icicles and everything else to wash with," said his wife Theressa, the mother of eight who did a lot of washing.

Even more than an inconvenience was the reality of compromised fire protection. In a town where wood or coal was used to heat homes, the risk of fire was always present. If park wardens, who were responsible for firefighting, were even able in winter to get to where the equipment was stored and then get it over snowy roads to the scene of a fire, there was no guarantee that they could find available open water at the lakeshore to pump and put out the blaze.

It was a string of winter fires during the 1930s that brought home the town's vulnerability: the Kilmorey Lodge in 1933; the Lee cabins and a horse stable in 1937; the dance pavilion and three private residences in 1938; and another residence in 1939.

Rev. S.H. Middleton

"The presence of a 'fire bug' in the park is feared," *The Lethbridge Herald* reported. "Local people are so alarmed about fires this winter in unoccupied buildings, some of them are hiring night watchmen."

As suddenly as the structural fires had started, they stopped. Park residents gave a collective sigh of relief and the rebuilding, both physical and spiritual, began.

Another sore point in the community was the absence of a facility available to residents of nearly every other town in southern Alberta: a cemetery. For many years, the only exceptions that had been officially made were the burials of Kootenai Brown and his two wives, but there were at least three other burials which were unofficial and not revealed until decades later.

When the idea for a park cemetery was first raised in 1922, park superintendent George Ace Bevan dismissed it. "I hardly think that the day has arrived yet for such action," he said. "Our permanent residents are very few yet and it seems to me that such action at present might be premature."

Superintendent Herbert Knight requested in 1931 that Ottawa officials reconsider a park cemetery and together with Rev. Middleton scouted several potential sites, finally settling on one near the Middle Lake. But the selection was academic. By 1933, all new leases in the townsite were issued for summer-only occupation to discourage a permanent settlement. If people didn't live in the park year-round, the thinking went, they didn't need a cemetery.

Senator Buchanan brought up the idea again in 1938 and received a curmudgeonly reply from officials: "It should be noted that the persons who use the park cemeteries [in other parks] do not pay for the care and upkeep of same. The whole area has to be suitably fenced and kept in attractive condition as all such places are open to the public. This means regular yearly expenditure of park funds and the understanding here is that conditions in Waterton Lakes Park do not necessitate a cemetery inside the park boundary. This is the stand which the Department has taken for years."

Like year-round water supply, the matter of a cemetery would have to be taken up later, after the Second World War which sidelined all new government expenditures in parks.

Waterton business people pressed on as usual during the early years of the war, welcoming travelling Americans who continued to pour across the border.

According to E.R.J. Forster of the Alberta Motor Association, Americans were on the move because they had more disposable income for vacations due to war work, although they were not yet involved in the fighting. And with European travel out of the question and a monetary exchange rate in their favour, they eagerly headed for Canada. They could get good value, as well, since price controls set by the Canadian Wartime Prices and Trade Board helped prevent profiteering on accommodations and meals.

Waterton residents became models of determination during the world conflict, rallying around the war effort in many ways. They went far beyond waving goodbye to their young men and women and

When RCMP Cpl. Andy Ford, left, wasn't enforcing the law in the park, he was a willing supporter of community and youth programs. Drawing water in the winter months was a tiring but necessary task since there was no year-round water system until 1953. Park resident Chuck Underwood used a yoke to supply water for his family of five.

Linnet Lake is usually first to freeze and is sheltered from the winter winds so local hockey players in the 1920s and 1930s would practise there in comparative comfort.

Park residents showed their support for the military during the Second World War by building this temporary "war hut" where funds were raised for Canada's overseas effort. Park visitors were eager to buy raffle tickets and home-made craft items in support of soldiers, as well as for victims of bombings and for refugee relief programs.

writing them letters. In short, they used ingenuity to fuel patriotic home fires.

Lillian Haug and Adelle Rackette wanted to raise enough money through the sale of war stamps to buy a naval depth charge. They canvassed the town and in less than a week had sold more than $75 in war stamps.

Others formed a local Red Cross group to make bedding and clothing for European refugees, and they held fundraising garden parties at the fish hatchery grounds just north of the park registration office.

Park employee George R. "Joe" Annand proposed that all park workers donate one day's wage to the war effort. The 30-day drive in the spring of 1941 resulted in a very high per capita purchase of war bonds: $280.

"This, in consideration that park workmen, with the exception of wardens and administration office employees, were for the five months previous on part-time winter work, was a remarkable rating," said Leishman McNeill of the national war savings committee in Calgary.

When Annand's group suggested they join the Banff and Jasper Spitfire Fund, to raise enough money to build a fighter plane, the idea was rejected by residents in the northern parks simply because they felt the addition of "Waterton" to their name would make it too long. So Annand's group carried on alone.

Defying criticism of a long name, they adopted the tag "The Waterton Lakes War Drive for Bombed Out Areas of Great Britain" and raised nearly $1,500. Their enthusiasm never wavered, even when they were advised by the federal government that tourists, mostly Americans, were not to be "molested" for war relief. Tourists from the United States turned out to be fascinated and very generous in their support.

A gun-metal, grey coloured "War Hut" in the shape of a huge army tank was set up on Waterton Avenue, south of the dance hall, and it became the most photographed building in the park as Americans snapped a visual reminder that Canada was at war prior to their own entry in December 1941.

At the hut, visitors could purchase home cooking, patriotic emblems, flags and donated items. Volunteers staffed the hut and collected items to be raffled for the Queen Elizabeth Fund in support of the "afflicted people of England."

Among the prizes to be won: a set of fishing tackle donated by Ben Higgs, the druggist; a quilt made by Elenora Hunter, a park resident; a large pastel Native portrait by Jim Rackette, a First World War veteran, talented artist and park employee; a handmade rug donated by Hanna Presley, a rooming house owner; a silver fox fur donated by the Parkview District, north of the park; a used light delivery truck, donated by park employee Art Dayman; and a pinto pony donated by horse concessioner Ed Schrempp and Peter Gairns, a First World War veteran and park employee.

"No place in southern Alberta—perhaps in the whole of Alberta—has a finer record than Waterton in its support of the Queen's Canadian Fund for Air Raid Victims," claimed a national news release originating from Montreal.

After the attack on Pearl Harbor by Japan, tourism in Waterton went into a tailspin. Visitation dropped 70 per cent in 1942 from the year before. Gasoline rationing and rubber tire shortages on both sides of the Canada-U.S. border curtailed many a trip to the park. Bus line routes were reduced and service to the park was cut to one day from seven days a week.

Suddenly, this national park paradise at the end of a road was a very long way from home when distances were measured in miles per gallon of rationed fuel and wear and tear on rationed rubber tires. But inventive ways around the gas and rubber restrictions were found.

Those who could not find new tires could have their existing ones retreaded. Employees of some companies had access to gasoline, sometimes collected literally by the cupful from "empty" barrels. With care, determination and often a smile and a wink, gasoline could be found to run a car to Waterton or power a motor boat for fishing.

When the diesel power plant at the Prince of Wales Hotel, which also provided electricity to the town, was shut down by fuel restrictions in 1943, cabin and business owners had to revert to kerosene lamps and limited use of gasoline-driven light plants. Like most rural areas in Alberta, Waterton had not yet received electrical service.

Everyone made substantial use of ice for their refrigeration. It was one commodity in ample supply, thanks to entrepreneurs like local carpenter Carl Carlson who cut and stored ice by the ton each February.

It was this attention to detail—ice for cold beer, chilled meat and dairy products—that was essential in serving the tourists who kept arriv-

ing during the war years, especially men and women from around the Commonwealth who were training at airfields across southern Alberta.

Robert Miles, an English flight lieutenant training with the Royal Air Force at the Pearce aerodrome east of Fort Macleod, was one such tourist, hitchhiking to the park in late July 1942 with five buddies for a seven-day visit. They rented Dell Ellison's apartments, just across from the marina, and immediately began enjoying the park by boating, fishing and then trail riding.

"Cowboys in the village hire out horses at moderate rate," Miles told his parents in a letter. "It was a perfect day and so we went down and secured a horse each, telling the owners that we would pay them upon our return, not knowing how long the ride would take." Their destination was Bertha Lake.

"Great snakes! What a view," Miles wrote. "Imagine a colossal bowl in the mountain with precipitous cliffs around you hemming the lake in on three sides, and that is the general setting of Bertha Lake.... One could imagine such a lake to be an anglers' or a poets' paradise."

Rainy weather finally sent Miles and his buddies back to their base, but it was, he said later, a visit of a lifetime.

Encouraging members of the military to enjoy

Ice cutting was an important task for summer use as a refrigerant at the fish hatchery, restaurants, stores and homes. Special ice houses were built for both commercial and domestic storage. Park employees cut ice for park needs while Carl Carlson cut and stored ice for commercial sale.

their time off, Col. D.E. Macintyre of the Canadian Legion War Services believed affordable park accommodation was in short supply and sought permission to build a dormitory in Waterton for 80 servicemen. Ottawa had no objections and in the spring of 1943 park superintendent Herbert A. DeVeber selected two lots on Waterton Avenue (now part of the campground) where no trees would have to be removed. The project, however, fell through.

The reality of war was taken seriously on the home front. Waterton men organized an "air raid precaution" in which a siren at George Baker's Park Transport Garage was to alert the town in the event of "an enemy action." Park accountant George Swedish gave first aid lessons while a fire protection committee was set up that included George Baker, Silas Dickson, Nahor Dilatush, Eddie Bell and Delance Strate.

The Second World War saw Waterton's year-round population sharply reduced, as at least 47 able bodied men and two women enlisted in the military, without a single loss.

Ethel and Jean Carnell, the daughters of Hannah Carnell Presley, both saw service overseas. Pte. Ethel Carnell enlisted in 1942 with the Royal Canadian Corps of Signals and was stationed in Edmonton and Calgary before being assigned to England. Lieut. Jean Carnell, who was a registered nurse, enlisted in 1943 in the U.S. Nurses Corps and served in Milan Bay, the Dutch East Indies, Manila and the Philippines. Both women were discharged in 1946.

During the war park superintendent "Cap" LeCapelain accepted a related assignment, becoming the Canadian liaison officer for construction of the 2,200-kilometre (1,367-mile) Alaska Highway. A civil engineer with much road building experience, LeCapelain was highly suited to his new job and in 1946 he was presented with a civilian award, becoming a Member of the Order of the British Empire.

Stanley Dilatush, son of business owners Nahor and the late Mabel Dilatush, chose not to enlist but instead became a civil servant. The University of Washington graduate went to work as an air traffic controller for the Civil Aeronautics Administration at an army base in Pendleton, Oregon. It became his life-long career.

Still others headed off to work in war industries. Gerald "Slim" Udal, a Waterton boat operator, was one such war worker. Since he was a skilled carpenter, Udal was needed to help build airport buildings at various locations.

Brothers Rae Baker, left, and Alf pose with their uncle George Annand prior to his 1939 departure for training in the air force. Annand became a prisoner of war when his plane was shot down on a mission over Germany.

Those who stayed behind were also active in supporting the war. Mechanic Art Dayman headed a committee in 1942 which launched a four-month campaign to collect recyclable materials, netting over $200.

Even three energetic boys, Calvin Goble, Alf Baker and Robert Ayris, scoured the town pulling a wagon and pushing a wheelbarrow to collect hundreds of pounds of metal and rubber that netted $25. They also helped the committee members load more than three tons of metal from the Belly River district and abandoned oil well drilling sites in the Akamina Valley.

In preparation for Christmas at the Jim and Adelle Rackette home on Evergreen Avenue, baking was begun and despite rationing of butter and sugar, some was set aside for baking to be sent to troops overseas.

First World War veteran John Pittaway with his sons, from left, John Jr., Bert and Denis, who all served in the military reserve prior to the outbreak of the Second World War. John Jr. joined the RCMP, while Bert and Denis joined the army.

Bo Holroyd, left, a First World War veteran and chief park warden, strongly approved of the enlistment of his eldest son Art, who joined the Royal Canadian Air Force.

"Mother baked Christmas cake in tobacco tins for the boys overseas and I helped make the candies," said June Rackette Miles. The candies were crafted from almond-flavoured mashed potatoes rolled in bittersweet chocolate. "I guess the community helped with ration coupons to buy the ingredients as we couldn't possibly have saved enough to undertake the job."

It was Christmas parcels like these, supplemented with knitted items, that helped George Annand Jr., Waterton's only prisoner of war, stay alive. His parents Joe and Betsy and his sister Betty Baker got the devastating news in September 1943 that George, 28, a sergeant flight engineer, was listed as missing during an air operation over Germany.

His bomber was caught in searchlights and had taken a direct hit. It took two months for his family to learn George had survived and been captured. The entire community shared the worry. A year and a half later, on Victory in Europe (VE)-Day, May 7, 1945, George's family received word he had been seen by a military chaplain when his prisoner of war camp was moved north. A few weeks later, he was sent to England. He had spent time in seven prison camps.

Annand returned to Waterton in June 1945, where a welcome home party was hosted at the school by the newly formed Lions Club. He was presented with the gift of a wallet from the community, and he expressed his appreciation for the life-saving food parcels sent via the Canadian Red Cross.

When the war in Europe ended, Waterton residents celebrated with services at All-Saints Anglican Church conducted by Rev. Middleton. There was also an impromptu dance at the school and a bonfire at the ball diamond along Windflower Avenue, complete with the burning of a Hitler effigy.

The sense of community in Waterton swelled when the Lions Club, established in 1945, launched two major postwar projects: a community hall and a ski run in the townsite. With an initial membership of just 30 men, the Lions was the only service club formed in the park and over the years it flourished. The first executive officers were a cross section of the town's most active citizens: Ernie Haug, Sr., president; Nahor Dilatush, vice-president; James Rackette, secretary-treasurer; A.H. "Pop" Harwood, "lion tamer;" Harry Reeves, tail twister; and directors Hugh Leavitt, George Stewart, Albert Roper and George H. Delany.

The Bertha Peak ski slope south of Cameron Falls, boldly named "Suicide Ski Run," involved the labour-intensive job of clearing brush by Lion's members aided by Boy Scouts. The 366-metre (1,200-foot) long slope was a cherished winter site enjoyed by both skiers and spectators.

The Lions Hall gave members, as well as all Waterton residents, a place of their own to hold dinners, dances and social events. One of the most popular winter gatherings was weekly square dances, which led to competitions throughout the region in the 1950s. Cleaning bees, hall maintenance and fundraising for improvements were done by volunteers as a matter of community pride.

The 1950s were a golden age for tourism in Waterton, which became a microcosm of trends seen elsewhere. The townsite population boomed as travel became easier with better roads and bigger cars, and more facilities were added to cater to tourists.

Hopes in southern Alberta were raised for improved travel when, in April 1947, the provincial government optimistically announced a five-year plan for a new Lethbridge-Waterton highway that would be hard surfaced and shorten the trip by 32 kilometres (20 miles). It took 11 years to follow through.

In the postwar prosperity, general interest in cottage leases picked up as did outdoor recreation, which took a new direction with the popularity of power boats and the introduction of water-skiing. The sport was taken up with marathon-like intensity.

Oblivious to the icy temperature of water melted from mountain snowpacks, Kent Cahoon and Michael Carnell water-skied to the head of the Upper Lake in early September, wearing only bathing trunks and lifejackets. They were towed by Stan Kretz's *Deeidra*. Not to be outdone, Barney Reeves of Waterton and Art Baalim Jr. of Lethbridge skied non-stop for more than 37 kilometres (23 miles) behind a boat driven by Dick Allison of Waterton while Lynn Cahoon of Cardston served as spotter. Their record was beaten the following summer when Julie Dowsing of Toronto and Kent Cahoon of Waterton made a 45-kilometre (28-mile) ski run behind Barney Reeves' boat.

Owning a cabin in the park presented one small drawback. Spur-of-the-moment weekend trips to the park over improved roads were so easy that cabin owners could find themselves overwhelmed by unexpected

Members of the Waterton Lions Club raised funds to buy a surplus military building and have it relocated to Fountain Avenue as their hall. The project had more than its share of difficulties, but the volunteers were up to the challenge. Although the Waterton club eventually folded, the building is still in use and is owned by the community association.

friends "dropping in" to stay a while. Many a Waterton cabin owner, fed up with being expected to provide unending hospitality, threw up his hands and sold out.

As one female cabin owner said: "Guests would arrive and stay, for sure. The decision to sell came one day when I tended my three little ones plus some more while preparing dinner for the returning fishermen. Enough was enough."

Even so, summer cabin life had rustic charms. Amenities were few and routines different from the places people called home the rest of the year. Many cabin owners were dependent upon wood for cooking, heating and hot water so young people learned early that filling the wood box was a chore with their name on it if they wanted to please adults and make the most of vacation privileges.

Electricity was primarily for cabin lighting and radios. Most people had an ice box rather than an electric refrigerator. Block ice was delivered to the door, but when it melted, emptying the water pan was another job for careful children. Although many cabin owners had bathtubs, the "Saturday night bath" might be waived if the kids had spent the day swimming. In any event, grey water went into cesspool tanks because there was no sewer system. And everyone had an outhouse until a sewer system was installed in the mid-1950s.

While telephones were readily available in the postwar period, they were expensive as all but local calls were long-distance, so few cabin owners bothered with them. To have one meant extra expense and the likelihood that people without a phone would be constantly using theirs.

By the 1950s the streets in the park were paved and every kid whose parents would pack their bike from home was in seventh heaven pedalling to his or her heart's delight. And because it was a tourist town, there were movies every night, except Sunday, a luxury unknown in other small towns. Board and card games filled the evenings, time for kids and adults alike to socialize and visit neighbours.

Television reception was finally available in 1962 when Alf Baker and other members of the local TV association got permission to erect the equipment to rebroadcast Lethbridge station CJLH. It was described as "a dream come true," especially in the winter for the 60 families then living in the townsite year-round.

With visitation to Waterton more than doubling

Farmers Bay, located on the north side of Mount View Road on Emerald Bay, provided boaters limited mooring sites for a few years. It is not known why Famers Bay was so named nor when the moorings were eliminated.

to 349,500 in 1960 from 172,000 in 1950, there was immense need for upgrades and expansion to tourist facilities. They were made slowly, as government funds allowed, but the improvements came at a price: increased involvement by politicians who began asserting stricter control on many aspects of national park operations.

Arthur Baalim, an outspoken and influential Lethbridge business leader and long-time Waterton cabin owner, called for a 10-year program to improve the town's appearance and provide proper camping grounds and docks, which he described as "a mess."

Caught flat-footed by the influx of postwar tourists, the federal government rushed to improve existing campgrounds and then develop new camping facilities. In 1958, one of the largest summer crews to date, 110 people, was hired to supplement the regular park staff. Gradually, the combination of additional staff and money began to show results, both in the backcountry, where trails and shelters were improved, and in the front country, with the realignment of

When television reception was finally available in the townsite, it was only because of the efforts of residents who sought permission to erect an antenna just off the Bear's Hump trail on the side of Mount Crandell.

For many years a children's playground was located on Cameron Falls Drive, where it meets Windflower Avenue. It has since been relocated to a field immediately east of the Community Hall.

Chief Mountain Highway, among other projects.

One of those other projects was something residents had wanted for decades: a cemetery. The matter came to a head in September 1952 when long-time, well-known resident George "Joe" Annand died. The family's request that he be buried adjacent to the Kootenai Brown family plot was flatly turned down by J.A. Hutchison, acting parks director in Ottawa: "The sentimental attachment the family has for the park and the desire to have interment made there is understandable, but I am sure that you will agree that were we to depart from established policy and permit Mr. Annand to be buried in the park, a precedent would be established for further requests of a like nature which it would be very difficult to refuse and we would end up with a cemetery to manage and maintain."

Annand was buried in Lethbridge, but it was the last straw for park residents. Within weeks they submitted a 53-name petition to superintendent Jim Atkinson requesting a local cemetery. Atkinson's support of the request, plus the death of another park resident, Ernie Haug, Sr., just after the petition was submitted, convinced Ottawa officials that a cemetery was necessary.

The cemetery site was chosen in May 1954, just west of the entry road at the base of Mount Crandell, with space allotted for 252 graves. By the end of summer 1955 cemetery regulations were finalized, fees established, and perpetual care of plots outlined. Burials were limited to permanent park residents and owners or lessees of real property in the park unless formal exceptions were authorized by officials in Ottawa.

The cemetery was to be ready for use as soon as it was consecrated. Before that could be done, however, Cecile Ada Carlson, another long-time park resident and wife of Carl Carlson, passed away Oct. 31, 1955. Her plot had to be specially hallowed for burial.

On June 17, 1956, Rev. G.R. Calvert, the Anglican bishop of Calgary, consecrated the balance of the cemetery with assistance from Rev. Middleton, who would be buried there himself in 1964. Two religious sections were initially allocated, one for Protestants and one for Roman

Use and possession of firearms in Waterton have long been banned to protect wildlife. Roadside "sealing stations" were located near the park entrance, the sign leading some visitors to wonder if there were seals in the park.

Catholics. That summer, Annand was reinterred in the Waterton cemetery.

Today, rules governing who can or cannot be buried in the cemetery are at the discretion of the park superintendent after years of extremely tight regulation; fewer than one-quarter of the burial sites have been filled.

With the cemetery matter initially settled, attention returned to tourism, as private enterprise was busy trying to meet the needs of the ever-growing number of visitors.

Officials gave the go-ahead for two new motels. The first was owned by builder Wilfred Forry of Lethbridge, who opened the El Cortez in June 1955. The second, the Frank-Lin Motel, was started by restaurant owners Frank and Linnea Goble in September 1956.

When Bessie Hacking, owner-operator of the Northland Lodge, sought permission to build a

motel on a site across from Linnet Lake, her proposal was vetoed. Bureaucrats in Ottawa said the new El Cortez and Frank-Lin motels provided adequate new accommodation.

Yet two years later, news was leaked that the Great Northern Railway, owner of the Prince of Wales Hotel, was planning to build a motel in Waterton, presumably with park approval. The project never got off the ground, though, and the railway sold the Prince of Wales Hotel a few years later to Tucson, Arizona's Don Hummel and his company Glacier Park, Inc. The railway got completely out of the accommodations business.

The proposed new tourist facilities gave rise to the prospect of making Waterton a winter resort, made possible by Calgary Power's installation of year-round electricity in 1947 and the park's establishment of year-round water and sewer service in 1953.

Convinced that Waterton had the makings of a ski

Both cross-country and downhill skiing were popular in the park. Cross-country skiers took to the trails while downhill skiers preferred the route dubbed "Suicide Ski Run" on Bertha Peak, which served until the mid-1960s.

resort, Ernie Haug, Jr. and Frank Goble, on behalf of the Lion's Club, enlisted ski school operator Bruno Engler of Banff to assess the potential of the park.

After just one visit in April, Engler gave it an excellent review, suggesting the need for only modest cutting and clearing. Suddenly, with skiing Alberta's fastest growing sport, Waterton had all the makings of a pot of gold.

But park officials withdrew their support of skiing development in Waterton when heavy snowfall resulted in avalanches which boomed down Bertha Peak in 1954 on the very slope Engler had recommended. It was the worst recorded avalanche in the 20th century.

The Waterton Ski Club continued to operate for local members only, eventually finding a niche when it held a truly novel, late-spring event in May 1952: the Akamina Ski Championships at Cameron Lake. Without the benefit of a ski lift, participants did not have an easy time of getting to the starting area. Rowboats and eventually the *Lady Cameron* tour boat provided by George Baker took the skiers to the south end of the lake, where the competitors trudged up the mountain

to start their races. Despite the effort, the event ran for 10 seasons, ending in 1961, attracting skiers from Alberta, British Columbia, and Montana.

As the dream of creating a ski resort in Waterton faded, another hope for the park was revived. There had been talk ever since 1917 of building a road from Cameron Lake, west across the Continental Divide into British Columbia, then south to Montana's Glacier National Park where it would link to Going-to-the-Sun Highway. The 1950s push for what was optimistically dubbed the Akamina-Kishinena Highway was spearheaded by the Rotary Club's international peace park committee, looking to create a circle route to connect Waterton and Glacier parks.

Renewed support for the route grew slowly, aided in 1955 by civic leaders and park officials from the two countries who traversed it by horseback to prove it was feasible. While the idea did not languish, neither did it flourish. It would take several more decades before it was resolved.

Meanwhile in the townsite, a $500,000 Olympic-sized, heated outdoor swimming pool was opened in 1960 on Cameron Falls Drive. The facility included dressing rooms, laundry facilities and mechanical room, office space and a four-room residence for the supervisor, plus parking for 180 cars.

The new pool demonstrated that government-funded facilities were finite, an either/or proposition, and something would have to go. In this case, the new pool rang the death knell for life guard-supervised swimming at Linnet Lake.

The men's dressing room there was razed in 1960 and the ladies' facility was moved across the road to the park compound for use as storage space. The lake itself, no longer chemically treated, returned to its naturally weedy state and fell from favour, but swimming was never prohibited. Signs warning of swimmer's itch, however, deterred most people from going into Linnet Lake.

The high level of optimism created by the opening of the new swimming pool sank with the government's oppressive handling of a 1960 land rent review which affected park lessees, a group that existed only in the western national parks.

Following the recommendations of a Queen's University study, the government announced it would change the leasing terms and phase in greatly increased land rents based on assessments. The scheme replaced the original, affordable flat rate formula with perpetual renewals.

Created with only minimal public input, the proposal gave way to rumours, fear, suspicion and finally anger. When leaseholders protested, a royal commission was appointed which sided with lessees, who felt they had no voice in policy formulation. It was only a temporary reprieve, but the process, along with the government's heavy-handedness, created a legacy of animosity.

In preparation for the new regime it planned to impose, the government had requested in 1959 that residents elect a five-person advisory council to provide a forum with the government. The first advi-

Carl and Cecile Carlson were among the first permanent residents in the townsite. They operated "Happy Landing," a boarding house across from the RCMP office. Carl was a builder and an ice cutter.

J. J. "Jim" Morrison of Lethbridge was a angler who often vied for fishing honours with Art Baalim. This Mackinaw lake trout weighed in at 18 kg (39 lb.), a trophy fish devoured with gusto by family and friends.

The heated, Olympic-size pool opened in the townsite in 1960 featured many conveniences: swimming lessons, diving boards, a wading pool, swim suit and towel rentals, all watched over by three life guards. The new pool brought an end to supervised swimming at Linnet Lake, below, which began in 1923 and eventually had two changing buildings.

sory members were Frank Goble, chairman; George Baker, vice-chairman; George Delany, secretary-treasurer; and members-at-large Hugh Craig and Sibyl Reeves.

Frustrated, in part, over lease matters, petty complaints and the government's repeated unwillingness to compromise, the council was disbanded in 1970 when the members resigned as a body.

Parks Canada historian William F. Lothian wasn't far off in describing the lessees' mood as "a rising hostility." Businessman George Baker summed up public opinion when he stated the administration of the townsite had "been sort of a dictatorship."

While the federal government charged fees to local

businesses and cabin owners, the money went into its general coffers with no guarantee an equal amount would be reinvested in the park. As well, lease-holders had no formal say in how their funds were spent, a system Baker said was entirely wrong.

"Any businessman with an ounce of brains wouldn't consider investing in a national park under the new policy," snapped Waterton restaurant owner Frank Goble, after the government proposed to eliminate lease renewals.

There were other negative factors, as well, which came to the notice of the public when a master plan for the park was proposed in 1967. It was a trial balloon for some startling ideas that stunned the public, one of the most radical being the suggestion that visitors not be allowed to drive their own cars into the park; instead, transportation by bus would begin from the park gate. Another was removal of "unnecessary" services, without spelling out what was meant but hinting that any activity that could be done outside a national park would be eliminated from Waterton. The proposed master plan also called for the purchase and removal of cabins for unspecified government redevelopment.

The master plan was modified and approved by Ottawa bureaucrats in June 1977, with revisions being made every 10 years or so since. Its effect was most evident to frequent Waterton visitors in the frenzy of changes in services in the park from the 1960s onward.

Facilities began to disappear completely, government services were sometimes abandoned and the park's character, so loved for generations of visitors, fell away bit by bit.

Closed were a number of facilities that were more economical to remove than to replace or administer: the fish hatchery (1961), Bridgeview Cabins (1966), George Baker's Cameron Lake Auto Bungalows (1967), the YMCA's Camp Inuspi (1969), the public horse pasture (1973), Snowshoe Cabin Road and the lower horse corral at Crypt landing (both 1975); and Cameron Lake campground (1975), to name but a few.

Marion Virtue, an outspoken Waterton cabin owner, didn't see the changes at Cameron Lake as progress. "Where once the road wound up to the lake through stately pines and graceful spruce, and where chipmunks and squirrels darted about, we were now confronted with two separate, long stretches of citified cement with glaring white painted dividers, a supermarket style parking lot. . . . Picnickers are no longer welcome here as the quaint roomy, log shelter that had weathered many a storm and wintry blast

There were many changes in the park in the 1960s and 1970s, all of which were justified by operations. Among those falling victim to removal were the fish hatchery on Highway 6, above, the associated fish rearing ponds near Cameron Falls, below, and an outdoor amphitheatre. The latter was replaced with an all-weather theatre on the fish ponds site.

and housed many family gatherings got the hatchet last year, as did the fine one at the far end. Perhaps Parks Canada's last word for Cameron Lake will be a supermarket-type hamburger and Coke stand," she wrote in a newspaper opinion piece.

As if bureaucratic tinkering wasn't enough of a problem, the park's reputation as an out-of-the-way family recreation spot was tainted when Waterton and Victoria Day became synonymous with "wild weekends" which kept the police busy enforcing liquor and traffic laws. The timing in May was partially tied to high school graduation celebrations and the Victoria Day long weekend, which traditionally marks the beginning of the tourist season.

A new camping section for those with trailers was opened in 1960 to separate tenters from recreational vehicles, which were just coming into their own with vacationers. The two parts of the campground were linked by a bridge over Cameron Creek.

The police came down hard on troublemakers in 1962, but their efforts were sharply criticized by Waterton business people. Chamber of commerce president Doug Allison, said, "I don't know what got into the police or on whose authority they are acting, but I definitely think they are giving Waterton a bad name."

The beginning of the so-called hippie era didn't improve the situation. In response, youth hostels sprang up across the country, but Waterton had no such facility. A transient camp was set up away from public view in 1971 near Lonesome Lake, below the golf course. The camp, which had one building and two kitchen shelters, helped eliminate problems in the crowded townsite campground and was supervised by a second-year university student.

After the first summer's trial with no reports of problems, the camp was set up again the following summer, but not quite as successfully. A tip led to an early morning drug raid by the RCMP resulting in charges against six young people, one of whom was from Waterton, and another a camp counsellor. The camp was permanently closed the next year.

Whenever a female was arrested and jailed in Waterton, the RCMP called on Donna Cohen, co-owner of the Emerald Bay Motel, to serve as matron and execute the strip search. The transient camp kept Donna quite busy making sure none of the detainees had a stash of marijuana "and just about all of them had a stash," said Donna's husband, Manny Cohen. It was many decades later, in the autumn of 2018, that marijuana possession was legalized in Canada.

The discontinuation of weekend dances at the pavilion, along with some wet, snowy Victoria Day weekends in the 1970s, put a damper on the partying and it eventually petered out.

Waterton's business people are, by nature, optimists and during these unsettled times they once again resurrected the Akamina-Kishinena loop-road proposal.

In August 1969 a group of 80 retraced the horseback route through the Akamina-Kishinena valley, this time using 28 four-wheel-drive vehicles. The participants proved that it was a passable route and just to reinforce the point, repeated the trip in 1970.

Art Bell, whose parents owned a park cabin and who was a member of the Lethbridge Coulee Cruisers, a four-wheel drive vehicle club, was an eager participant on both treks. He later recalled that it was very slow going: "There were 23 creek crossings in a one-mile stretch, and it was the same creek."

Also among the drivers were Waterton hotelier Manny Cohen and service station operator Butch Sloan. Cohen was enthusiastic about the route, saying "British Columbia must realize it would also benefit from the road," which would have provided access to Fernie and the East Kootenay.

It was the British Columbia government's final re-

In both 1969 and 1970, off-road vehicle enthusiasts from southern Alberta and Montana participated in a trek between Waterton and Glacier through the Kishinena Valley to demonstrate the feasibility of building a loop road there to link the two parks.

fusal in 1977 to allow the road through the province that ended the dream, dashing the hopes of Cohen and other businessmen that the road would be "the making of Waterton" and finally end its status as a no-through-road destination.

Providing Mother Nature's markers to this era

were three major floods, in 1964, 1975 and 1995. As calamitous events, they stand out in local memory, none more so than the inundation of June 1964, unequivocally the "flood of the century." It was a catastrophe the likes of which had not been experienced since the Waterton townsite was established in 1911.

The stage was set by a combination of factors: a heavy snow pack was suddenly melted by two days of heavy, warm rain driven by strong northerly winds which prevented the runoff from flowing out of the Upper Lake fast enough. It created a witch's brew of swollen lakes and streams.

Cameron Creek became a torrent crashing over the falls and scattering natural debris over both the foot and vehicle bridges in the townsite. Boulders and heavy gravel rumbled along the creek, which tore a new course and overflowed its banks on its way to the lake. At the same time Upper Waterton Lake, fed by many other rapidly flowing tributaries, rose at the rate of 30 centimetres (12 inches) an hour until it crested nearly three metres (nine feet) above its normal level.

Nola Madge and her two children, Marty, 5, and Jo Ellen, 2, had just settled in for the summer at the family cabin on Vimy Avenue, north of the townsite campground. Assuming all was well, Nola's husband Paul headed home to Milk River in the family car.

As the lake level continued to rise, superintendent Fred Browning ordered the campground evacuated, but the nearby Madge cabin was ignored by staff sent to raise the alarm. Since there was no car to indicate anyone was home, staff never stopped to check. Madge, whose mobility was impaired, had no idea of the impending danger, despite the heavy, steady rain, nor was she aware that telephone service had been cut.

"All night I heard noises and thought it's just a shutter banging, and I won't bother to get out of bed to fix it," she said. The next morning when she turned on the radio, she heard a report of flooding in Cardston. "When I looked out the west door, the water was hitting the house and creating a whirlpool around it."

The night noises were logs and propane tanks drifting around the cabin in the ever-rising water. She spotted neighbours and called to them, but the rushing water and high winds muffled her cries for help. No one knew she and the children were in the house. Struggling to the second storey of the cabin,

The worst flood in the history of Waterton inundated townsite buildings in 1964. Waterton Avenue, above, was awash and took weeks to dry out and be cleaned up. Below, owners of cabins to the northeast of Cameron Falls discovered the creek had overflowed its banks and cut a new course around their buildings.

she threw open a window and waved a dish towel at a park vehicle driven by Kay Kenley, the park maintenance supervisor.

"She was just screaming and waving. That's how we noticed them," said Kenley, who had just rescued her neighbours across Windflower Avenue, Henry Matkin, 89, and his brother Joe, 74. Kenley, driving a road grader for its stability in the fast-flowing water, made his way to Madge's house.

"When I opened the door, the chesterfield met me," he said.

Kenley got the trio into the grader, but they were far from safe. The children were standing on the seat of the cab and were still in water, and Nola was standing in water up to her knees in the cab. When he backed up and hit a low spot, the grader tipped

precariously and became stuck as waist-deep water flooded into the cab.

"I wasn't sacred for myself, but for those two little kids standing on the seat," Kenley said.

It was businessman Frank Goble who came to the rescue with his Land Rover. With the aid of a 91-metre (300 foot) climbing rope, Goble and others secured one end to his vehicle and set off to retrieve the Madges and Kenley through a terrific current. He quickly got the two children to safety and went back for Nola.

"I was barely able to hold her," Goble said. "We couldn't pick up our feet because of the current and had to slide along. It was up to our knees."

And then Nola went down, dropping into armpit-deep water, losing her balance and her purse. She

Flooding in Waterton reoccurred in 1975, much to the horror of those who owned residences and businesses. The park was closed until the water receded and repairs could be made.

The floods of 1975 and 1995, although not as horrific as 1964, were reminders of the power of nature. Each was slightly different in intensity, but the result was the same: the park was temporarily closed, and residents were evacuated to the Prince of Wales Hotel, which became a refuge both for its high ground and for its independent sewer, water and electrical systems.

Town and park cleanup began as soon as the water subsided and for most people operations returned to near normal within days. Each flood was both terrifying and memorable.

It was a blessing that only buildings, not lives, were lost in any of these floods, but nature isn't always so kind, as was demonstrated by the park's only fatal bear encounter.

Allison Muser, 5, was killed July 1, 1977, while playing near Cameron Creek in the Little Prairie picnic site off the Akamina Highway. The Musers, a family of four that had moved from South Africa to Regina, Saskatchewan, just four years before, sued Parks Canada for failure to inform them of the presence of bears, to control the bear population, to provide a means for escaping a bear attack, and for not supervising the picnic site.

"We had no more thought of a bear being there than of there being a lion," said Anne Muser, Allison's mother. Parks Canada settled out

said, "Oh there goes my purse!" to which Goble shouted, "To hell with your purse."

"If Frank Goble hadn't grabbed me, I would have been washed away. . . . There was no way I could have made it by myself," Madge said.

Thanks to the efforts of Kenley and Goble, everyone got to safety but the memory remained vivid long afterward.

The property damage to commercial and residential buildings, plus lost revenue and public facilities, was never accurately totalled.

of court with the family and introduced a concerted program of distributing bear warning pamphlets, erecting signs and carrying out a determined bear management program, which remains in place.

There were other changes made in the park, as well. The government opened a new, 25-unit Belly River campground along the Chief Mountain Highway, and a 128-unit Crandell Mountain campground. New picnic areas were located along the park's roads, and an improved boat launch was installed at the townsite marina.

Trail riding continues to be a traditional and memorable activity for park visitors, especially for those not accustomed to horses. As one visitor quipped: "Horseback riding is great exercise ... for the horse."

The removal of the fish ponds on lower Evergreen Avenue, and elimination of an amphitheatre closer to the lake on the same street, gave rise to a new indoor interpretive theatre in 1974. That theatre was closed several summers prior to a new one established within the new Visitor Reception Centre on Cameron Falls Drive.

Rather than remove the marina or the golf course under the new master plan, these facilities were leased on long-term agreements to operators as the park began to withdraw from the expensive business of conducting business. In 1993, Waterton Inter-Nation Shoreline Cruise Co. was given a 25-year lease in exchange for $1 million in marina improvements. Upon expiry of that lease, another was granted to the same lessee.

A 25-year lease of the golf course was awarded in 1994 to the Waterton Park Community Association, which received a temporary two-year extension. A new course lessee was selected in early 2021 based on a request for proposals. Again, the term was for a 25-year period. Lakeland Golf Management, based in Winnipeg, Manitoba, was the successful proponent chosen to manage, operate, maintain, and make capital improvements to the golf course as the facility began its 99th year of operation.

Drumming up visitors at the end of summer, before the start of school, was often left to the Waterton Chamber of Commerce, which provided entertainment to attract people at a time when visitation often falls off. To that end the chamber created Beargrass Days, in late August 1986.

A festival-like atmosphere, reminiscent of Waterton Days in the 1950s, was reintroduced with Beargrass Days. Among 20 events were scuba diving and windsurfing contests, bed races, a chili cook-off, Native dancing, a parade, talent contests, a swim meet, golf tournament, and a dance. Beargrass Days ran its course for the next 11 years, ending in 1997.

About the same time, a new generation of cabin owners with a different outlook came onto the scene. These were adults who had grown up in the park and now had a strong urge to see community building begin anew through volunteerism.

They helped several groups get off the ground and operate: the Waterton Natural History Association (1983), the Waterton Lakes Leaseholders' Association (1986), the Waterton Park Community Association (1993), and the Green Team (1994).

Although operation of the townsite and its services are the responsibility of Parks Canada, lessees were given limited municipal authority at the end of the

1990s with the election of a council for Improvement District No. 4, established under Alberta's Municipal Government Act. The council continues, with a mandate to work with park officials in an advisory capacity and to oversee provincial property assessments, bill for and collect school taxes, and decide other limited matters. It was as close to taxation with representation as Waterton would see in the 20th century.

It was with the council's unanimous endorsement that Carol Watt became the first Waterton resident to receive the Governor General's Caring Canadians Award in 1996 for her many contributions. Nominated by residents, Watt, the wife of a park warden and a registered nurse, provided winter emergency nursing assistance to one and all in the tradition of earlier Waterton nurses. She also helped organized the first major recycling initiative and for many years was a mainstay in the United Church.

Emblematic of the new spirit of co-operation that is possible between bureaucrats and volunteers, if only briefly, was the cemetery wall project. Built to honour long-time visitors and cabin owners who can't be buried in the cemetery due to regulations, this memorial was proposed and implemented by the Waterton Natural History Association.

Award-winning Medicine Hat artist James Marshall was commissioned to design and sculpt the wall in 1996 and it was erected at the back of the cemetery. The association paid for the wall by selling plaques to honour the deceased with a connection to the park. The wall was dedicated at a public ceremony June 29, 1997.

A second cemetery wall was announced in July 2015. Commissioned by the Waterton Park Community Association, the new wall was again designed and built Marshall and his staff. It was completed in the summer of 2016.

Today, fewer than a dozen families winter in the park. One of the chief reasons is that government employees, no longer required to live in the park, are paid mileage to live elsewhere. As a result of the declining population, the school was closed in 1995, a blow to the community and an emotional loss to the parents who had attended the school themselves or whose children were enrolled there.

Just eight children in four grades attended the school in its last year: Jodi Shouting-Wynder, Brian Van Tighem, Kelly Baker, Ryan Dolan, Joey Shouting-Wynder, Katie Van Tighem, Ryan Hammell and Corey Van Tighem. Lisa Lenz-Hofer taught all of them.

Residents with school-age children have the option of sending them to Pincher Creek by bus or driving them to schools in Mountain View or Cardston. The closure of the Waterton school persuaded some parents to live in nearby towns rather than subject their children to a long daily commute.

Nothing plants human memories deeper than terror, which in turn can lead to long-lived memories. Such was the case when the Kenow forest fire advanced toward Waterton in early September of 2017.

The fire got its name from Kenow Mountain in British Columbia, 10 kilometres (six miles) from Water-

Jim Marshall of Medicine Hat, the award-winning designer and builder of the first memorial wall at the park cemetery, was contracted to build a second wall. The park's memorial walls provide a place for the commemoration of people with park ties but who can't be buried in the cemetery due to restrictive regulations.

ton's western boundary, where an Aug. 30 lightning storm ignited a blaze. By Sept. 1 the fast-moving fire, fanned by a ferocious wind which changed direction hourly, was out of control. Too big to fight from the air and too remote to reach by ground, the fire went without suppression. As well, British Columbia's emergency crews had their hands full with other much larger and more dangerous fires elsewhere in the province.

Day after day for a week smoke from the Kenow fire filled the Waterton valley, obscuring the mountains and turning the sky into a wall of grey. During that time, the wind pushed the fire eastward over the Continental Divide and just into Waterton, raising the anxiety levels of park residents.

In an attempt to quell the apprehension of both town residents and outside neighbours, park officials issued an evacuation alert Sept. 5 and called a meeting the next day at the Community Centre to explain the situation. Those present were advised of the possibility of a mandatory evacuation order.

Calling in experts, Parks Canada worked closely with partner agencies and neighbouring jurisdictions as the fire progressed eastward. Crews created fire breaks and helicopters dropped water on hotspots to stop the spread of fire. Fire retardant had also been sprayed on picnic shelters, washrooms, and other park facilities.

In the townsite, high-volume water pumps and sprinkler systems were installed around the edge of the community, drawing water from at least two locations at the lake.

Then on Sept. 8 at 1:15 p.m. a mandatory evacuation was issued both personally by park employees and also by electronic means. Residents had two hours to leave the park.

Three days later on Sept. 11, the fire grew, fanned by a strong wind, as it roared through terrain that had dried out during the hot summer. At about 10 p.m. the fire "blew up" sweeping through the park, then moving outside the park boundary, to the north and east.

The damage done by the Kenow wildfire was significant. It burned approximately 193 square kilometres (74.5 square miles) of land in Waterton, 38 per cent of the total park area of 505 square kilometres (194 square miles). Some 156 square kilometres (60 square miles) of land outside the park's boundaries was also burned.

There was a significant impact on built infrastructure in the park. Along the 16-kilometre length of Akamina Parkway and Red Rock Parkway's 15 kilometres, guardrails, signs, picnic areas and parking areas were affected despite the efforts of facility protection crews. Over 80 per cent of the hiking trail network in Waterton was affected by the fire.

In addition, the visitor centre, Crandell Mountain Campground, about half of the buildings at Canyon Youth Camp, all of Alpine Stables, some staff housing, and electrical systems were destroyed.

That the townsite was saved—not one building in the townsite was destroyed—was truly a herculean accomplishment on the part of the firefighters from

The Kenow forest fire of 2017 threatened Waterton townsite, but was contained to Mount Crandell and Bertha Peak. A Coaldale and District fire department member paused to take this image at the height of the blaze, showing the water tower at the Prince of Wales Hotel highlighted by blazing bush and trees.

18 towns and cities across southern Alberta who had volunteered to come to Waterton to fight the Kenow wildfire.

Just how close the blaze came, once residents could see it for themselves, was evident in a kind of "post-traumatic fire disorder" that affected some in the community. Not one life was lost during the fire, a blessing in its own right.

After residents were allowed to return on Sept. 20, public appreciation for the efforts of the firefighters was seen everywhere in the townsite in the form of handmade signs. The following summer, a special public thank you event was hosted by park residents to which all the firefighters were invited. Every lessee in Waterton was given a lawn placard to personally acknowledge the efforts of the firefighters.

* * *

Regardless of the many changes experienced in the park over the years, what Kootenai Brown said in 1865 upon first arriving in Waterton—that "this is what I have seen in my dreams"—still rings true today.

That this is a truly unique place in the world has been recognized by four different official designations.

The first came in 1932 when Rotarians on both sides of the Canada-U.S. border successfully lobbied their elected federal representatives to pass legislation establishing Waterton and Glacier as an international peace park, the first in the world. There are now more than 100 peace parks around the globe, dedicated to the notion that mankind can live in harmony.

In 1979 Waterton was recognized as a biosphere reserve by the United Nations Educational, Scientific and Cultural Organization (UNESCO). It was acknowledgment of the relationship between people and the natural environment with its Man and the Biosphere program. Waterton was the first national park in Canada and the second site in the country to be so honoured. Glacier park had received the designation in 1976.

Waterton and Glacier combined were designated a World Heritage Site in 1995, recognizing the distinctive climate and landforms, their "triple divide" waters which flow to three oceans (Arctic, Pacific and Atlantic), and their exceptional natural beauty.

The most recent designation was given in 2021, when Waterton and Glacier became the first international transboundary Dark Sky park, which required

Evening scenes like this are gone forever after Waterton installed new dark sky-friendly lighting in the townsite to meet the certification requirements of the International Dark Sky Association.

them to meet specific standards for outdoor lighting, which allows visitors to experience the night sky at its best.

It is with posterity's blessing that Waterton continues to be a place where moments make memories that last a lifetime, and a location that is not just geographic, but a place in the heart.

The Hazzard Hotel, the first in the townsite, was opened July 1, 1914, in time for the joint celebration of Dominion Day in Canada and Independence Day, July 4, in the United States. The number of vehicles and visitors who showed up for the festivities is a testament to the determination of tourists to get to Waterton at a time when roads were poor and bridges over rivers and creeks were few.

Chapter 2

Accommodations
A Roof Overhead

Waterton's tourism pioneers started offering accommodations years before the government sent out a survey crew to lay out a townsite in the fall of 1910. They set the standard for others who followed, sending customers home who were eager to return and spread word about what was available.

William O. Lee established his camp business in 1908 with "tented villages" at two sites in Waterton: the Maskinonge and Linnet Lake, then called Mirror Lake. His was a complete operation providing transportation to and within Waterton, and meals and tents for customers. He also widely publicized his operation in newspapers and through handout materials complete with photographs and written descriptions.

Lee was a go-getter who had moved to Cardston from Utah in 1902 with his second wife Armenia and five children from his late first wife. Motivated to provide for his family, which would grow to 10 children, he was an energetic businessman involved in several Cardston businesses at once. Two of those, tent-making and a livery operation, gave him an instant advantage in establishing his Waterton operation.

To get to Lee's camps, Lethbridge citizens could board the Alberta Railway and Irrigation train to Cardston, arriving in time for lunch, then travel by Lee's horse-drawn carriage or wagon, arriving in Waterton in time for dinner. In all, it was a 12-hour trip over crude roads. Today the journey can be made in 90 minutes.

Lee's Tented Village included tents that were rented either unfurnished or "equipped" with spring cots, mattresses and bedding. "All you need bring with you is your fishing tackle and your appetite," visitors were advised. They could choose from the American plan (meals included) or European plan (no meals). Those who chose the latter, and brought their own

provisions, could rent a tent with a cook stove, table, benches, utensils and dishes for 75 cents a day for one person and 50 cents a day per person for parties of two to four.

There was a choice of two sites. One was at the Maskinonge not far from Henry Hanson's sawmill, which was on the east side of the Waterton River near the present-day picnic area. Lee had come to know the Swedish-born Henry Hanson and his wife Julia when he hauled mail to the post office at the sawmill, which was no longer used after a major flood in the spring of 1908 that ruined Hanson's business.

Lee's Maskinonge operation featured picnicking, boating, fishing, mountain climbing and an evening dance at Hanson's, where a dance floor had been constructed on floating logs for impromptu gatherings. Lee's customers mingled freely with area residents at the dances. Although phonograph music was a standby, guests who brought fiddles, harmonicas, banjos and other instruments were encouraged to play. After the dances, Julia Hanson served refreshments for a small fee. It was the start of a friendly relationship between the Lee and Hanson families that would span decades.

William O. Lee

W.O. Lee & Sons' other tent village site, on Aldridge'Bay near Linnet Lake, was called the Upper Camp. It offered a sheltered location, excellent fishing and berry-picking.

The two camps were open from June 15 and Sept. 15 with Lee offering both stage and boat transportation between the camps for 50 cents a person. The return stage fare from Cardston to the park was $3, with children under 12 half price.

Lee encouraged his customers to make Waterton a three-day outing, leaving Cardston on Saturday with the return to Cardston on Monday in time to catch the train for Lethbridge. It was, he noted, "an outing for the busy man that cannot be equalled anywhere."

One of the first groups Lee hosted was nine female school teachers who intended only to spend a couple of weeks. They were so taken with Waterton and the tent accommodations they stayed the entire summer. Word of mouth advertising began immediately.

Lee was an exceptional promoter in his own right, and he strongly believed his tented villages would be successful. He convinced David H. Elton, former publisher of Cardston's *Alberta Star* newspaper, to visit and write an article about the operation. Elton's half-page piece, an exceptionally glowing tribute to both Lee's operation and the mountain region, appeared as a special feature in *The Lethbridge Daily Herald* in February 1909. Scenic photographs and shots of splendid catches of fish accompanied the story.

Lee had the photographs made into postcards, which he distributed widely, and he turned Elton's text into a 16-page, nine- by 14-centimetre (3½- by 5½-inch) pamphlet. He handed out both to anyone he felt would find them of interest and even supplied Kootenai Brown, then Waterton's forest ranger-in-charge, with copies for his use. Lee was the first to widely use printed materials to promote Waterton, five years ahead of the government's efforts.

After only one season in the tenting business, Lee had competition.

Bert Riggall and Jack F. Hazzard, both from nearby Twin Butte, formed a partnership and in 1909 offered fishermen tent camping with meals at a site on the shore of Upper Waterton Lake, near today's Bayshore Inn Resort. Riggall built two boats and the pair set up three sleeping tents and a cook tent, but the camp lasted only one summer and the two men went their separate ways.

With Lee's "experiment" working out nicely, he began considering expanding the market for it. In the spring of 1910 he wrote to resort operators at Lake McDonald, Montana, which was about to become part of Glacier National Park, hoping to spread the word about his facilities "so we can interchange mountain climbers this summer."

Competition returned in the summer of 1910, this time from Riggall and a new partner, Cyril J. Watmough, who set up a camp at Cameron Bay. This partnership, like the last, was short-lived. According to Riggall's daughter, Doris Burton, "a terrible wind blew his boats out of the lake" and onto the shore

Lee's Tented Village was widely advertised through the use of photo postcards in a manner that was worth a thousand words: contemporary tent facilities in a mountain setting with ample fishing available.

among the trees, collapsed tents and smashed dishes. Riggall and Watmough called it quits, going on to other joint ventures outside the park.

Lee's operation, however, flourished, thanks not only to his advertising efforts, but also to his growing reputation for providing good service. His Upper Camp at Aldridge Bay was an ideal location, well

Jack Hazzard's first accommodation was on the lakeshore, now the site of the Peace Park Plaza. It consisted of a few small buildings and several tents. A small motor boat, operated by Carl Danielson, took visitors cruising on the lakes.

protected from Waterton's notorious winds, yet close to the water and towering mountains, with a horse pasture nearby. The bay had been named for William Aldridge, a squatter who had arrived about 1896 but moved to the Akamina Valley in 1898.

When surveying for lots in Waterton began in 1910, Lee pressed authorities for official permission to use the Upper Camp site, making it clear he was willing to fulfill all the requirements and pay the necessary fees. Since details like lot sizes, land rent fees and application procedures were yet to be worked out by the federal government, as an interim measure Lee was given commercial camping privileges, paying $1 per tent per month and $5 for the season to rent four row boats.

Dominion land surveyor W.F. O'Hara had barely finished his work when Lee wrote to Kootenai Brown to formally apply for the four lots encompassing his Upper Camp. Lee was very likely the first person to apply for a lease in Waterton, months ahead of the October 1911 date officials announced they'd begin accepting offers.

There was a note of urgency in Lee's request, as he said he was seeking early lease approvals because he wanted to erect a building at the Upper Camp in time for the coming tourism season. Unfortunately, William Lee died unexpectedly from a stroke two weeks later. His tent camp business closed, at least for the time being, and Lee's wife Armenia and their 10 children returned to Cardston.

Christian F. Jensen

The site of Lee's tent village didn't remain vacant for long. In the summer of 1911 Christian F. Jensen, a 41-year-old dairy farmer from Aetna, Alberta, south of Cardston, spent $650 to build a five-room frame house and an accessory building on the spot, becoming the first person to open a hotel in the park, even though at the time he had no legal right to use the land.

Besides offering beds, meals and rowboat rentals, Jensen provided auto transportation to and from Cardston. When applications for leases were officially invited in the fall of 1911, Jensen put in for the two lots he already occupied. He was granted two 42-year leases.

Believing forgiveness was easier than permission, Jack F. Hazzard followed Jensen's example and built on a waterfront property, at the site of today's Peace Park Plaza, before he had the legal right to do so. He put up an 8.4- by 9.8-metre (28- by 32-foot) rough log building, built a dance floor and an icehouse.

When park officials began accepting lease applications late in 1911, Hazzard formally applied for three lots, two of which he had already built on. His applications received approval in January 1912. With that, Hazzard became the biggest lessee in the new townsite of Waterton. Now a lawful businessman, he expanded his rental accommodations by erecting 20 tents and three log cabins for tourists.

Following Hazzard's lead, Jensen also erected tents. He purchased Armenia Lee's stock to expand his facility in 1912, but it was his last season in the park. Jensen relinquished his leases in February 1913, sold his buildings to Kootenai Brown for $200 and returned to his Aetna farm. Brown acquired a lease across the road, had the hotel moved and renovated, and lived there with his wife Isabella until his death in 1916.

With Jensen's departure, Hazzard became Waterton's principal hotelier. To secure his position, he acquired a fourth adjacent lease and began construction of a proper hotel in September 1913, one an area newspaper described as "quite an imposing structure."

The $12,000, two-storey, 15.2- by 6.7-metre (50- by 22-foot) building had "a commodious dining and sitting room," a kitchen, an office and a store-room on the main floor. Upstairs were 10 bedrooms, with a veranda on the south and west sides of the building.

The Hazzard Hotel opened on Saturday, July 4, 1914, three days after Dominion Day. Jack Hazzard arranged a full day of sports including horse races, foot races, boxing matches and promised "a general good time."

Jack Hazzard

Little is known about Jack Hazzard, who came to Alberta from Ontario. A life-long bachelor, he filed for a homestead north of the park, in the Spread-Eagle district, and supplemented his income by hauling logs and cooking for logging camps.

Hazzard knew little about running a hotel, but he was willing to try. He was dubbed "Haphazard Jack" for his lackadaisical approach to managing the hotel, which was said to sometimes run itself.

Appointed Waterton's postmaster in July 1915, he hauled the mail from Twin Butte to Waterton. Finding his horses to haul the mail was occasionally time-consuming and when he was thus occupied, visitors were left to check themselves in and out of the hotel on the honour system.

In a burst of patriotism, 43-year-old Hazzard, two years under the upper age limit, enlisted in the Canadian Expeditionary Force in March 1916 and was sent to Calgary to train with the 192nd Battalion. He was sent home three months later. His enlistment documents record that he was "unlikely to become an efficient soldier."

Limited construction took place in the townsite

Hazzard's hotel was sold in 1921 to Isaac Loren Allred, who put an addition onto the north end of the building to increase its room capacity. The name was also changed to the Lakeshore Hotel.

The steamboat Gertrude *was out of service and abandoned by owner Henry Hanson on the shore of Emerald Bay until converted in 1917 by Harry Lee into a floating tea room that operated for two years, until it was sunk.*

during the First World War, but Harry Calder Lee had an idea. The son of William O. Lee, Harry returned to the park in 1916 and joined Cal Hunter of Lethbridge, who had been operating a tent camp for the last two years. Together they erected a new tent village, near the townsite entrance on the mountain side of the entry road. Their operation accommodated 75 overnight guests and featured a wood-floor dining tent for 150.

According to Theresa Davis Strate, who worked for Lee, the washstands in the tents were made of two wooden crates tipped on end, and cold water was delivered to the campers by employees. "It was kind of rough," Strate recalled, although she said the food was good and the prices were reasonable.

Lee and Hunter worked together until the end of the summer of 1916, selling supplies from a small store and renting fishing equipment and a few boats to supplement the camp income.

Looking for additional opportunities, Lee made a deal that summer with old family friend Henry Hanson to rent his out-of-service steamboat *Gertrude*, which had been abandoned on the shore of Emerald Bay for several years. Lee obtained a permit from the government to refloat the *Gertrude* and moor the boat just across from his tent camp. He substantially renovated the nine-year-old wooden vessel, installed a kitchen, created a dining area and called it a tea room.

The floating tea room was described as serving "tastily prepared" meals with a view that was nothing short of magnificent, as described in an article in *The Lethbridge Daily News*.

Guests looked out across the water to "Mount Sophia [now Vimy Peak] over whose summit the sun rises, casting a delightful reflection on the water below, causing the very walls and ceiling of the dining room to sparkle as though it were set with a million diamonds."

With this novel new business underway, Lee applied to lease two townsite lots on Mount View Road, now occupied by the Crandell Mountain Lodge. By the summer of 1917, he had erected two three-roomed log cabins, one on each lot, and the following spring his lease documents were finalized.

The new boat-based tea room-restaurant lasted only two seasons, suffering the abuse of harsh winter winds and the crush of lake ice since the *Gertrude* was left in the water. Park officials condemned the steamboat and it was later scuttled in Emerald Bay, where its remnants lie today. For many years it was known as Steamboat Bay.

The loss of the *Gertrude* did not sink Harry Lee's ambition. Since his father's death, he had worked diligently in Cardston, continuing the mail delivery business from Cardston west to Hillspring, Glenwood and Mountain View. He had also established an automobile tire business, as well as providing an undertaking service, both outside the park. The two new rental cabins he had built in Waterton were a logical business progression from his father's tenting operation.

Harry Lee's ideas for new business opportunities were brought up short, however. The influenza epidemic of 1918 claimed the 30-year-old in November, only months after he had fortuitously transferred the leases on his Waterton properties to his wife Emily.

With three small children to raise, Emily was largely dependent on the money earned from the seasonal cabin rentals. She seized the opportunity, starting in 1919, and added a few supplementary tents. The completely furnished cabins went for $4 a day or $25 a week, which included "everything but grub," as the promotional material put it. The tents were available furnished or unfurnished, starting at 75 cents a day.

Down the street to the east from Lee's cabins, Jack Hazzard was by 1919 tiring of being a hotelier, even if he did have a monopoly. It was an enviable position following the First World War, when visitation to the park revived, thanks in part to government funding of developments like the golf course and better roads, including a wooden bridge over the Waterton River into the park.

Hazzard took on a partner-manager, Isaac Loren

Allred, 33, who ran the hotel. In December 1920 Allred bought out Hazzard and changed the name to the Lakeshore Hotel. Hazzard returned to the logging business and later joined Carl Carlson, a Waterton carpenter, in an Akamina Valley sawmill operation for a short time before moving on to opportunities outside the park.

Within a week of buying the hotel, Allred approached parks officials with a proposal to build more rental cabins, increasing the number that Hazzard had erected from three to nine. Park superintendent George Ace Bevan recommended approval of the proposal.

Bevan advised his Ottawa boss that "the three cabins . . . have been very popular with the public in the park ensuring as they do strict privacy. [The additional cabins] will, I am sure, be even more so and help to fill a long-felt want in the matter of accommodation in Waterton Lakes Park."

Completed in time for the 1921 season, the furnished cabins were rented for $3 and $4 per day, depending on size, and Allred's management of the hotel was favourably mentioned in the Lethbridge newspaper. Under Allred's vigilance, the hotel had an experienced, dependable staff and featured a good and all-important dining room.

Although his operation was intended for summer use only, Allred was in for an unexpected extended

Lee's Cabins were located on the site of today's Crandell Mountain Lodge. W. O. Lee and his wife Emily built and operated the facility until the 1918 flu claimed his life. His wife took over management of the cabins.

winter operation in 1921 and 1922, when he was asked to accommodate the park crew doing preliminary work on the new Akamina road to Cameron Lake.

By 1923 Waterton was definitely southern Alberta's fun spot. One Saturday night that summer, it was reported that two well-known Lethbridge lawyers were forced to sleep on the Lakeshore Hotel's billiard table because the number of visitors exceeded accommodations.

"Both the learned gentlemen are glad that Proprietor Allred did not charge them by the hour [as was done for playing billiards]," *The Lethbridge Herald* reported.

Allred was not to one to become stale in the same business, although he preferred to operate only one business at a time. He sold the hotel building in 1924, but not the leases on the four lots associated with it, to Mark C. Rogers of Lethbridge. Allred moved on to build and operate the town's first swimming pool, west across the alley from the RCMP detachment.

Mark Rogers was a high-profile businessman who headed Rogers and Co., which was involved in successful oil and gas prospecting in southern Alberta. Always on the lookout for investment opportunities, Rogers hoped to be the first to get a licence to sell beer in his hotel now that Prohibition had ended in Alberta—but it was not to be.

Despite flamboyant announcements about what he would do were he successful in getting a beer licence, Rogers had no idea of the red tape he was up against. The province of Alberta refused to grant Rogers a licence. Although he had a $100,000 building plan, which included a new hotel and 25 furnished chalets, what he did not know was that park approval was required for nearly every aspect of the project.

In the meantime, he hired Lethbridge contractor Thomas Stubbs to build the new hotel and chalets and brought in a crew to begin the work of tearing down the small cabins Hazzard and Allred had erected. The 1914 hotel was left standing to provide interim visitor accommodations.

Hoping to create the semblance of an attractive townsite, government officials insisted on architectural standards and drawings, at least those which pleased the eye, even if they proved to be a bit weak on building quality or standards.

When Rogers' drawings were amended by officials, he angrily stopped construction. There were several differences of opinion between Rogers and officials. Acting park superintendent Herbert Knight told parks commissioner J.B. Harkin in Ottawa that Rogers was "obdurate on this matter and has withdrawn his men from the park and states he will either remove or sell the material on the ground."

Senator William A. Buchanan of Lethbridge was drawn into the hubbub and wrote a confidential memo to Charles Stewart, minister of the Department of the Interior who was in overall charge of national parks, expressing his fear of "disaster" if the department rejected Rogers' much-needed development.

"On account of the location of Waterton Lakes away from the railroads, very few men are tempted to invest in a hotel or chalets," Buchanan wrote. "Rogers happens to have made [a] considerable amount of money and when he wants to spend it in providing facilities for the people, I am one of those who believe in encouraging him."

After Rogers' lawyer got involved, Harkin finally allowed completion of the work planned for the summer of 1924. It took most of the summer to work things out to everyone's satisfaction, but by that time the prime construction season had ended. By Labour Day, 17 of 25 chalets were completed and occupied. They were built in a quasi-Spanish style, each with two rooms and a veranda. Rates were $5 a day or $30 a week.

All appeared on course until the end of September 1924, when Mark Rogers was found dead of a gunshot wound at his Lethbridge home. A coroners' jury was unable to determine how the gun was discharged and could not decide if the death was accidental. Although a note was found following his death, the contents were not disclosed to the public.

Rogers' sudden death left Waterton business people shocked and wondering what might happen to the hotel development. Isaac Allred, who still held the land leases but did not own the buildings, stepped back in. He spent the winter looking for someone who would buy the property.

Rumours and speculation—a staple of Waterton life to this day—took on new vigour when in April 1925 a group of men came for a visit. Among the group were J.T. Beckett, a passenger agent for the St. Paul, Minnesota-based Great Northern Railway; George W. Noffsinger, owner of the Park Saddle Horse Co. in Glacier National Park; J.W. McNicol, a

The chalets constructed at the Waterton Lakes Hotel added substantially to the rooms available in the park. Completed in 1925, they were designed by a government architect, renovated several times and served the public for almost 40 years. The mound of rocks at left served in lieu of signs to direct street traffic at several intersections in the townsite.

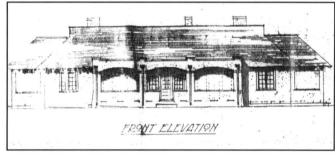

FRONT ELEVATION

local good roads enthusiast; and H.H. Granger, secretary of Rogers and Co.

Since several officials of the railway were said to have been "making quiet investigations" in Lethbridge, Waterton's unfinished development was immediately linked to their presence. The rumours, many of which were printed in the local newspaper, expressed the hope that the Great Northern, which had built hotels and chalets in Glacier in Montana, would buy the Rogers hotel and encourage extension of north-south transportation between the parks. While the 1925 entourage was indeed looking at prospects in Waterton, the Rogers hotel was not one of them.

Three weeks later, Louis "Eddie" Poulin, a well-known Calgary sportsman and businessman, purchased the Lakeshore Hotel and Chalets and immediately began making improvements inside and out. Poulin, who seldom spoke to the press, made an exception this time and expressed the view that people

in Calgary were beginning to take notice of Waterton and he expected a record season. The hotel name was changed for the third time, becoming Waterton Lakes Hotel and Chalets.

As an alternative accommodation, just south of the hotel a tent camp was set up by Cal and Elenora Hunter, moving from their previous site on Emerald Bay. Hunter was granted permission to sublet the lot, on Waterton Avenue at the end of Cameron Falls Drive (now a parking lot), for the camp.

A rough cabin immediately to the north, erected by lessees Thomas Hodgins and Benjamin Metcalfe of Lethbridge, provided a place to cook meals. The lot was planted with hedges and walks were laid out. A light plant provided electricity for both the tents and the grounds. Hunters' Camp offered meals, furnished tents complete with firewood, and fishing rowboats were available for hire.

Fishermen were drawn to the Hunter Camp to share stories and discuss strategy. Both Hunters were keen and superb anglers, known for their ability to haul in the big ones, specimens of seven to 14 kilograms (15 to 30 pounds), and lots of them. Elenora's July 8, 1920, record for the largest fish caught in the park, a 23-kilogram (51-pound) Mackinaw lake trout, has never been broken.

Since accommodations were at a premium, a few cabin owners began to rent their premises to the public. Among the first was Elsie Baker, wife of William Baker, who owned several cabins. She found herself competing against rooming houses, a less expensive but popular option for vacationers in the 1920s.

Waterton's first rooming house, opened in June 1924, targeted a select clientele: businesswomen and members of women's clubs wishing to spend a week or two in the park.

The facility was located near the marina on Mount View Road, facing Emerald Bay. Built by Dell H. Ellison of Aetna, Alberta, it was the first of several businesses in which he and his wife Tay would be involved over the next 40 years. The 12-bedroom Ladies' Lodge had a big lounge with a fireplace, a kitchen, dining room and showers with hot and cold running water.

The second rooming house was built in 1926 for Ada Kemmis at the corner of today's Evergreen Avenue and Mount View Road. Named the Kilmorey

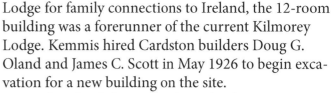

Cal Hunter

Lodge for family connections to Ireland, the 12-room building was a forerunner of the current Kilmorey Lodge. Kemmis hired Cardston builders Doug G. Oland and James C. Scott in May 1926 to begin excavation for a new building on the site.

Pincher Creek lawyer Arthur Charles Kemmis, husband of Ada, had applied for the lease in 1911 and had a three-room cabin built in August 1914 from materials salvaged from an abandoned oil drilling camp near Cameron Falls. The 4.9- by 4.9-metre (16- by 16-foot) log house was only the second privately owned building, after the Hazzard Hotel, to be erected in the townsite.

The lease was transferred to Ada in October 1916 while Charles was serving in the First World War as a lieutenant-colonel. Following the war, the couple became permanently estranged and Ada took in boarders at her Pincher Creek home to help support herself and her two daughters.

The opening of the Kilmorey in 1926 benefitted from her boarding house experience and became her year-round home. It also established Ada, 44, as the second businesswoman in the park after Emily Lee, who had been running two rental cabins across the street since 1917.

Ada Kemmis, who was born in Putney, England,

Dell and Tay Ellison's Ladies' Lodge was the first rooming house in the park. The couple owned and operated both rental cabins and other businesses in Waterton.

and had lived in Pincher Creek since the age of five, never remarried. Her daughters Helen Aileen and Sibyl Olphert would have long connections with the park.

The completion of the Kilmorey came within months of the start of work on the future Waterton showpiece, the Prince of Wales Hotel, built for the Great Northern Railway. Plans to build the $1-million hotel had been announced in March 1926 in New York City. Waterton's business people were ecstatic, saying this was just the kind of investment and high-profile backing that would bring the park to the fore.

With no apparent hard feelings, Eddie Poulin welcomed the competition, noting not only the physical distance between the two hotels, but also the fact they would cater to different clientele: his mostly to southern Albertans; the Prince of Wales to Americans on railway tours. And in the meantime, Poulin briefly profited from the building of the Great Northern hotel. During the winter of 1926-27 his chalets were rented to family men working on the hotel and his hotel's dining room provided classroom space for their children's education.

Oland & Scott Construction was selected to build the Prince of Wales Hotel on the knoll above the Narrows and overlooking the townsite. Oland & Scott had already demonstrated their abilities in the park with the completion of the large, new dance pavilion on the lakeshore, as well as many cabins.

Oland & Scott's abilities were tested again and again as the contractors faced repeated and unexpected challenges in building the Prince of Wales Hotel. Blueprints were drawn and drawn again as changes became the norm, with Great Northern boss Louis W. Hill frequently changing his mind about the hotel's design. During the winter of 1926-27, the hotel was transformed from a four-storey structure with low-sloping roof to one that was seven storeys with a high, peaked roofline.

Then there was the weather. A December 1926 storm brought winds so strong the hotel was blown 20 centimetres (eight inches) out of plumb and building materials were scattered all over the hill. The snow was so heavy at times the men who should have been building the hotel had to stop to shovel snow to get access to materials and the site.

As winter turned to spring, the road from Cardston, where all the building supplies were stockpiled, was churned into "a sea of mud" by laden transport trucks.

The first Kilmorey Lodge was built in 1926 for Ada Kemmis at the corner of Evergreen Avenue and Mount View Road.

The Prince of Wales Hotel construction crew gathers on the roof of the unfinished building on a rare windless day in February 1927. Below, the first incarnation of the hotel's kitchen wing, which was extended in 1928.

Incredibly, 11 months after ground was broken, the 90-room Prince of Wales Hotel was opened on July 25, 1927 (now referred to as "Christmas in July" by hotel staff).

The hotel reeked of class, from its design to its services. A guest had only to make a request and it was attended to by the uniformed staff, whether it was a desire to rent a horse or play golf, have shoes shined, have a meal delivered to a room, or be driven to the dance downtown. No other hotel in the park—or southern Alberta—provided service like the Prince of Wales. Room rates started at $8.50 per person and included three meals.

The hotel influenced life in the park in numerous ways. It provided seasonal jobs and training for area residents who might otherwise not have been employed in tourism. It was responsible for increased park visitation, not only by bringing guests to Waterton from Glacier, but also itself becoming a tourist attraction.

Combined with advertising by the railway across the continent, Waterton's profile rose from being a lo-

GREAT NORTHERN LAND IS ADVENTURE LAND

visit the new

PRINCE of WALES
HOTEL

in the Canadian Rockies adjoining Glacier National Park

This summer will mark the opening of the beautiful new Prince of Wales Hotel in Waterton Lakes National Park—adjoining Glacier National Park on the north across the international boundary in the Canadian Rockies.

The completion of this commodious new hotel now enables tourists to achieve the thing long wished for—to enjoy in one memorable visit, the fascinating outdoor sport of lake-bejeweled Glacier National Park and the awe-inspiring panoramas of the Canadian Rockies.

After enjoying the thrills of an international vacation in Glacier and Waterton Lakes National Parks you can see *all* the Pacific Northwest at slight extra cost via Great Northern. Low round trip summer fares now in effect. Mail coupon today for full information about an Adventure Land Vacation.

GREAT NORTHERN
a dependable railway

The Great Northern Railway widely advertised the new Prince of Wales Hotel to ensure tourists were made aware of its presence so close to Glacier National Park, which was served by its line. The hotel was the first in the park to be licensed to serve beer.

cal destination to an "international playground."

Waterton Avenue also got a shot in the arm from the presence of the Prince of Wales Hotel as park officials released previously restricted lots to lessees with ideas for attractive commercial buildings.

Mabel Dilatush, of the Tourist Café, applied for a lot immediately to the south of her restaurant. Like other local business folks, Nahor and Mabel Dilatush had profited from the hotel, catering meals to the construction crew. Oland & Scott had originally hired tent camp operators Cal and Elenora Hunter to feed the workers but when the crew complained about the portions, Oland was forced to replace them and chose the Dilatushes. Mabel took over cooking for the building crew.

In 1927, the Dilatushes hired Oland & Scott to begin a two-and-a-half storey building, the Stanley Hotel, on the new lot. It was named for their only child. The building was the town's first and only "commercial block," with the ground floor designed for two businesses—a pharmacy and a mercantile—and a hotel above which had nine small but modern, furnished rooms and two additional rooms in the garret "for rush business." Each room had hot and cold running water at permanent washstands and one shared bathroom down the hall. Meals were available next door, at the Dilatushes' Tourist Café.

When Eddie Poulin decided in April 1928 it was time to sell the Waterton Lakes Hotel and Chalets, he had no trouble finding a buyer. It was Associated Breweries of Canada Ltd., which in turn created a holding company to own and operate the business, appropriately named Waterton Lakes Hotel and Chalets Co.

Associated Breweries, headed by German-born Lethbridge businessman Fritz Sick, not only bought out Poulin, but also purchased Allred's four lot leases, bringing the entire property under one management.

The new company's officers were all men from the region. One of the most colourful directors was 40-year-old Lethbridge lawyer James Stanley Kirkham, who often wrote a humorous civic affairs newspaper column under the pen name Mrs. Irma Peach. He established Lethbridge's Garden Hotel in 1925 and was an outspoken member of the Alberta Hotelmen's Association.

Another director was Minnesota-born Paul Kuschel, also 40, who was operating the Arlington and King Edward hotels in Pincher Creek when the Waterton opportunity arose.

Funding for the Stanley Hotel, centre, came from the profits made by Mabel and Nahor Dilatush, the owners of the popular Tourist Cafe, who had the contract to feed the Prince of Wales Hotel's construction crew.

E. Al Neils, Kuschel's nephew, also a native of Minnesota, was appointed hotel manager. He had experience as a clerk and bartender at a Pincher Creek hotel.

With the promise of a $15,000 injection toward improvements, the new owners were eager to make their mark and Neils was charged with overseeing completion of the 1928 renovations. This time, plans were approved by park officials well in advance and contractor Thomas Stubbs, who had done the work for the late hotel owner Mark C. Rogers, was hired to make the alterations, which were quickly completed.

The hotel's exterior was substantially improved with an arched veranda and stucco to match the chalets. The hotel lobby was relocated and a ladies' sitting lounge and six guest rooms were added, bringing to 20 the number of rooms in the hotel proper. Running water and lavatory fixtures, including showers, were installed in both the hotel and chalets, greatly modernizing the facilities. Rates were $2 per day in the hotel and $6 per day or $30 per week in the chalets.

The one addition to the hotel most anticipated by the public—one which had eluded Rogers and then Poulin—was the licensed beer parlour. The new owners, possibly aided by the fact the parent company ran

Lethbridge's Sick brewery, received the licence June 22, 1928, and promptly opened the park's second beer parlour.

The Prince of Wales Hotel's tiny Tap Room, opened the summer before, was supposed to be limited to hotel guests, but the public was welcome at the Waterton Lakes Hotel and Chalets. The new parlour was a 7.6- by 18.3-metre (25- by 60-foot) addition on the south side of the hotel. As per provincial government liquor regulations, the beer parlour was divided into two sections: "gentlemen" and "ladies and escorts."

The Waterton Lakes Hotel and Chalets continued to operate under the same ownership for many years, seemingly unaffected by the Great Depression. Some of its success was its location, close to the very popular dance hall and other downtown businesses. Its variety of accommodations also helped. It was the only operation to offer both hotel and chalet accommodations, separately priced, under one management and at a single location.

With the improvements to the Waterton Lakes Hotel, Hunters' tent camp just to the south of it seemed out of place in the up-to-date and developing business district. In fact, the summer of 1928 was Cal

Tent camp operators Elenora and Cal Hunter moved their operation from Waterton townsite to Cameron Lake in 1929 where, besides tents, they also rented rowboats to anglers and served delicious chicken dinners to the public.

and Elenora's last on Waterton Avenue. Their sublet was cancelled by the lessees, who intended to renovate their building now that the street was showing marked improvements from an upswing in tourism to the park brought on, in part, by the opening of the Prince of Wales Hotel. But the resilient Hunters weren't finished with the tent camp business for quite some time.

In 1929, a year after the 16-kilometre (10 mile) Akamina Highway was opened to Cameron Lake, the Hunters moved their tent camp and rowboat rentals there, becoming the first to provide both accommodation and boat services at that location. According to Frank Goble, who worked at the Cameron Lake tent camp as a boy, the Hunters made a name for themselves at the new location by specializing in chicken and trout dinners, which they served in a big dining tent.

Others were making changes, as well.

In the townsite, Ada Kemmis, who had purchased the cabin next door to her Kilmorey Lodge from Cardston physician Clarence Watson Pickup, began renovations in the fall of 1929. A second storey was put on the Pickup residence for additional guest bedrooms, but it was only a temporary improvement. She later razed the building.

The Depression gave rise to more rooming houses. The first was opened in May 1931 by Lenore Costello and was advertised in the newspaper, something new for this type of less-expensive accommodation, which usually depended on word-of-mouth promotion.

It was named The Tavern, in the Quebec tradition of the operator, but never served alcohol. It consisted of two adjacent but unconnected cottages immediately south of Cameron Falls (402 and 404 Evergreen Ave.).

The one at 402 Evergreen, owned by Robert and Estella Oldroyd of Carmangay, Alberta, was sublet to Lenore Costello, the proprietor of The Tavern and the estranged wife of a health officer of the British Colonial Service stationed in the British West Indies. Next door, at 404, the cottage built and owned by Doug G. Oland of Oland & Scott, was sublet to Charles F. Reilly, a First World War veteran and one-time Waterton magistrate. Reilly, in turn, sublet it to Lenore Costello, who was his sister.

The cottages had a wonderful, east-facing view of the lake and Vimy Peak, and were a quiet, semi-secluded, "restful vacation" spot.

Costello made several improvements to The Tavern, including installation of showers, and a comfortable lounge and card room. The dining room was open to the public (generally, rooming houses served meals only to overnight guests) and offered breakfast, lunch, afternoon tea and dinner, as well as catering to parties. Room and board were available from $3 to $5 per night; rooms without meals were $2.50 and up. The Tavern closed in 1935.

Bellevue Lodge was an 11-room house, also opened in 1931, on one lot now part of the area occupied by the current Visitor Reception Centre. It was owned and operated by Erik and Olga Hagglund, who later opened the three-suite Green Timber Apartments next door to the south. Both leases were purchased by the government and the buildings demolished in the 1970s.

Still another rooming house started out as the personal lodge built for the Great Northern's Louis Hill in 1928. The Carthew Lodge (now Northland Lodge) was built at Hill's whim by Oland & Scott. It was designed with a living room, dining room, kitchen and six bedrooms to accommodate 18 people. It had two bathrooms, a fireplace and oak floors throughout. A "fair sized basement" provided storage space. On the outside were two balconies and a stone terrace at the front of the house with a flight of stairs leading to the road below.

Although Hill visited the park many times after the lodge was completed, there is no evidence he ever stayed there. Instead, Hill and his entourage stayed at the Prince of Wales Hotel, perhaps because everything and everyone there was at the ready.

Fred and Grace Udell became caretakers of the property for Hill, it serving as home for them and their five children. In the summer of 1931, Grace Udell began renting rooms to visitors.

Ada Kemmis's Kilmorey rooming house operation, meanwhile, was about to undergo major changes. She contracted local carpenter Edward Johnson to demolish the Pickup cottage next door and replace it with a new building with eight bedrooms and two light housekeeping suites upstairs, and a large sitting room and dining room downstairs. Harry Northover Reeves, who would become Kemmis's son-in-law, was responsible for finishing the interior.

The new structure, known as the White House, was often referred to as the Kilmorey Lodge annex and became Kemmis's private, year-round residence, but the upstairs bedrooms were rented during the summer months and the large dining room was open

Advertised as "The Tavern," this residence was primarily a short-term boarding house which never did serve alcohol. It opened in 1931.

The 11-room Bellevue Lodge, on the west side of Windflower Avenue at what is now the site of the new visitor centre, was run by owners Erik and Olga Hagglund. They also operated another rooming house next door, to the south, called Green Timber Apartments.

The second Kilmorey Lodge, at right, was destroyed in a 1933 fire. Owner Ada Kemmis had the lodge rebuilt and later, it was attached to the "White House," her personal residence behind the trees at left.

to both Kilmorey Lodge guests and the public. Meals were served in the first years by two local women, Anna and Katinka Anderson.

Disaster struck Mrs. Kemmis' Kilmorey Lodge two years later, on Feb. 22, 1933. That evening the lodge was destroyed by fire during a blizzard. Kemmis and her daughter Sibyl were safely next door in the White House when the fire broke out and able to save only a few furnishings from the lodge. The cause of the fire was presumed to have been a faulty chimney, but no cause was officially determined.

The destruction of the Kilmorey came at the most inopportune time. That spring, Waterton was taken by surprise when it was announced the Prince of Wales Hotel would not be opened. The hotel's owner publicly blamed a declining numbers of rail passengers to Glacier, but privately discussed the need for a new road to directly link the two parks and shorten the bus trip between them. The hotel did not reopen until 1936, only after such a road—Chief Mountain Highway—was completed.

Kemmis vowed to rebuild her fire-ravaged lodge and two weeks later announced plans for a modern, two-storey building that would be connected to the White House next door by sun porches.

Delays plagued the rebuilding. Kemmis became ill and underwent two major operations at the Cardston hospital. When she was finally well enough to examine the plans prepared by the government's archi-

tectural branch, she was not pleased and sent them back with revisions, asking for a one-year extension to start work. When park superintendent Herbert Knight saw the plans, he noted that a two-storey building would dwarf others in the area and recommended a height limit of one and a half storeys.

During the summer of 1933, Kemmis and daughter Sibyl continued to provide rooms and meals at the White House while details for the new lodge were being worked out. It was not until the end of September 1934 that construction began on the new Kilmorey Lodge.

Doug G. Oland, who by then had parted company with James Scott, was hired to do the work and by the end of October he had the western portion of the building closed in. It was ready for guests in 1935, but the plan to join the adjacent White House to the new Kilmorey Lodge, now in its third iteration, was delayed.

Park officials responded by encouraging development of new accommodations for the increasing number of tourists arriving in Waterton by car. Auto bungalows, the precursor to today's motels, were seen as the answer to tourists' needs. Between 1933 and 1948, four auto bungalow operations were opened in the park.

Park officials first floated the idea of auto bungalows in 1931, putting out a public tender. In exchange for building a minimum number of sleeping cabins and agreeing to operate them according to an established standard on a percentage-of-profit basis, the successful applicant would be granted a lease on a large portion of land.

No one responded. They tried again in October 1932, offering two locations: one in town along the west side of Cameron Creek and the other 16 kilometres (10 miles) away at Cameron Lake. No one submitted a tender for Cameron Lake, but the town location was taken up by the partnership of Erik Hagglund and James Fisher, the only applicants.

Swedish-born Erik and Olga Hagglund had moved to Waterton in 1931 from Bellevue, Alberta, with their three children, Hilding, Esther and Linnea. Erik distinguished himself in Waterton as a builder, including constructing their home at 418 Evergreen Ave. It was the first of many properties he and Olga would own.

At the time of the government tender, Erik and Olga were running a rooming house, so the auto bungalow opportunity would benefit from both their skills. Their entrepreneurial spirit set an example for their children, who later with their spouses all went into their own accommodation businesses in the park.

Erik's partner in the Waterton Auto Bungalows

Erik and Olga Hagglund

was James Fisher, whom he knew from Bellevue where Fisher ran a garage with his brother and had access to the necessary furnishings and fixtures at wholesale prices.

The Hagglund-Fisher partnership was granted the concession and the architectural division of the Parks Branch drew up the plans for the one-room bungalows, all of which were identical. Each was furnished with a bed, table and chairs, cooking stove, a sink, shelves, kitchen utensils and a small cupboard. All had private toilets, running water and electric lights, but the shower facilities were central to the site.

Rates, set by the government, were reasonable: single cabins, $2 per day, $12 per week; double cabins $2.50 per day, $15 per week. Bedding, if supplied, was 25 cents extra.

The first 10 Waterton Auto Bungalows were opened for business on June 27, 1933 and proved an immediate success.

By the time the Chief Mountain Highway was completed in 1936, accommodation providers were prepared. Waterton now had more rooms than ever, and it was ready for the surge in visitation that followed.

Ada Kemmis certainly heard opportunity knocking. She bought a lease on Waterton Avenue in the fall of 1937, had the existing building razed and be-

Waterton Auto Bungalows were the first of their kind built in the park, a precursor of today's motels.

gan construction of the Ballinacor Hotel, which was opened in 1938. The name was another nod to her estranged husband's Irish heritage.

The two-storey Ballinacor was built under the supervision of local carpenter Harry Cummings. The hotel had a dining room, living room, curio shop and ice cream parlour on the main floor, with 18 bedrooms upstairs and bathrooms at both ends of the hall.

Still intent on establishing auto bungalows at Cameron Lake, in August 1937 park officials again put it out to tender, this time with new information. If the Akamina road were to be extended west over the Continental Divide into British Columbia and then south to Glacier park in Montana, Cameron Lake would be on a thoroughfare and would have incredible potential.

Four contenders submitted bids: J.P. Gregory, a labour foreman who had worked in the park for the past 12 years; Fred Udell of Carthew Lodge, who had been house officer, doorman and caretaker at the Prince of Wales Hotel and was a First World War veteran; Harley H. Boswell, a career hotelman who was manager of the Prince of Wales Hotel; and George Baker, who owned and operated several businesses in Waterton townsite.

Each man made the government an offer. They ranged from a percentage of gross receipts to a five-year flat fee which thereafter would lead to a percentage of gross.

From the point of view of the four bidders, there were several things to consider: the shortness of the Cameron Lake season due to its higher elevation, the investment required to build the cabins at a period when money was tight, the operating expenses, and the lowest possible fees each thought the government would accept.

From the government's standpoint, the successful bidder needed experience in the accommodations business, the ability to make good on the investment, run the operation to its standards, and offer competitive concession fees.

Boswell, who had been managing the Prince of Wales Hotel for five years, was the man who met all the criteria except one. He was only willing to offer three per cent of gross and declined to increase the amount, even on second consideration.

In the end, park officials decided on George Baker who, although he had no accommodations experience, was able to finance the building of the Cameron camp and offered the government 10 per cent of gross. In 1938 Baker was given a 21-year lease on less than half a hectare (just over one acre) at Cameron Lake.

Waterton hotelier Ada Kemmis had an existing building on the lakeshore side of Waterton Avenue razed so Harry Cummings and his crew could construct a new facility, the Ballinacor Hotel, which opened in 1938.

George Baker had come to Waterton from the Twin Butte area in 1922 when his parents William and Elsie built the first of several rental cabins in the park. Since then, George had become involved in a variety of park businesses.

The Cameron Lake cabins were designed by the government's architectural division, whose goal was "artistic and comfortable buildings." Cautious that the cabins not be anything like summer cottages, officials rejected Baker's own design, which entailed a sleeping porch and veranda in each cabin. The development was located by park officials so it was far enough from the public campground, which had been enlarged in 1936, to ensure a distinct division between the two areas.

As a new concept for Cameron Lake, the auto bungalows' success was imperative to the Parks Branch. It lay in the class of accommodation that was provided: park officials wanted to ensure the auto camp was "an asset and credit to Waterton Lakes National Park and a profitable venture for yourself," superintendent C.K. "Cap" LeCapelain wrote Baker.

At 1,660 metres (5,446 feet) above sea level—370 metres or 1,200 feet higher than the townsite—Cameron Lake is late to recover from winter's ice and snow and early to see its return, which allows only eight to 12 weeks for construction. Doug G. Oland was hired to build the cabins, but his work was delayed until park officials built a bridge over Cameron Creek so materials could be trucked to the site. It took all summer of 1938 to complete the bridge, the auxiliary buildings and the first six 4.3- by 5.5-metre (14- by 18-foot) cabins. Two more cabins would be added later.

George Baker outbid several others to develop an auto bungalow camp at Cameron Lake. Opened east of the creek in 1939, see map below, it featured six small cabins. Baker slowly added two more cabins, a restaurant, store and gasoline service. The camp was built on the hope of a through road, dubbed Kishinena Highway, to Glacier park, but it was a dream that never happened.

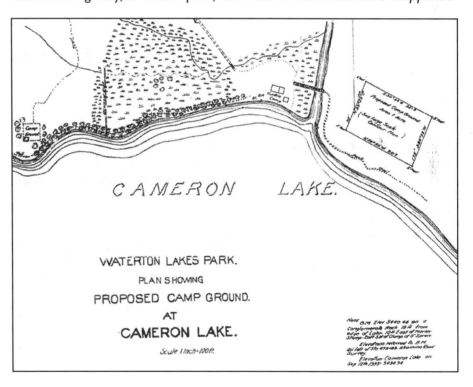

CAMERON LAKE.

WATERTON LAKES PARK.
PLAN SHOWING
PROPOSED CAMP GROUND.
AT
CAMERON LAKE.
Scale 1 inch = 100 ft.

Baker's new, electrically lit, one-room auto cabins were full when they opened July 1, 1939. They were in a group on the east side of the lake, at the Summit Lake trailhead. Hidden from the road and facing the lakeshore, they were tucked among the trees and linked by red shale paths. There was no running water, and toilets were outdoor privies. Rates, approved by the government, were $2.50 a night for a single cabin, $3 for a double and 50 cents a night for sheets and towels.

It had been Cal and Elenora Hunter's tent camp, set up in 1929 at the lake, that proved the tourist potential of Cameron, but the summer of 1939 was the Hunters last season and they retired to the townsite. Cal died in 1940, at the age of 72. Elenora remained active in community affairs and died four years later, at age 77.

Canada's entry into the Second World War in 1939 slowed development in Waterton but did not stop it.

That fall, a call for tenders was made for a small development outside the townsite on a 10-year renewable lease. Long-time businessman Ernie Haug, Sr. was the successful bidder for the site, across the Waterton River and east from the park entrance kiosk.

Built as the International Coffee Shop and Service Station under the Imperial Oil banner, it was intended to be a brief refreshment stop for motorists travelling on Highway 5 from Lethbridge and Cardston, and for those northbound on Chief Mountain Highway from Montana. It opened in May 1940.

The main restaurant-store building included a kitchen, coffee shop and office, as well as a staff residence with a living room featuring a massive, 1.8-metre (six-foot) stone fireplace, and laundry facility. While the war was still underway, Haug began thinking of the future development at the site, but it was one that had to be held in abeyance until the war ended.

Meanwhile, within the boundaries of the townsite, other developments went forward during the war which included construction of the Crandell Lodge at the corner of Evergreen Avenue and Mount View Road, the joining of the Kilmorey to the White House next door on Mount View Road; renovation of the Ladies' Lodge near the marina; and Erik Hagglund's Waterton Auto Bungalows expansion along what is now lower Evergreen Avenue. And at Cameron Lake, George Baker expanded his auto bungalows operation.

Crandell Lodge, across Mount View Road from the Kilmorey Lodge, was built to provide furnished housekeeping apartments. Hilding Hagglund, son of auto bungalow and rooming house operators Erik and Olga, purchased the leases for the two lots from Emily Lee. Lee's two log rental cabins had mysteriously burned to the ground in the winter of 1937.

Although Lee wanted to rebuild, she had limited resources and was, like many lessees during the Depression, in arrears on her land rent. When she sold the leases, it ended a 30-year history of the Lees in the park.

Hilding Hagglund's idea of building an apartment house was precedent setting in two ways: no apartment houses had been built before, nor had park officials ever allowed construction of one large building on two residential lots. The prominent location, however, gave officials pause and the original plan Hagglund submitted was revised to meet a new architectural style. Since the site was on the main road coming into town, everyone who entered the townsite would see it.

Immediately, Hagglund's neighbour, Ada Kemmis, registered an objection. Although she said she was opposed to an apartment house because of zoning, in

The International Coffee Shop and Gas Station, just beyond the registration building at the junction of Highways 5 and 6, opened at the start of the 1940 season. Developed and operated by Ernie Haug, Sr., it offered travellers a convenient place to stop, refuel and have a snack.

fact, when she had requested permission to expand the Kilmorey Lodge over two lots in 1933 she had been denied. Park officials would later relax that prohibition, based on the decision made for Hagglund's building.

The two Hagglunds, father and son, began erecting Crandell Lodge in 1939, calling in help when it was needed. Joe Shaw of Cardston did both the interior plastering and the exterior stucco. The Hagglund family selected the original furnishings from Eaton's department store in Lethbridge, where the store manager accommodated them by extending the hours so they could complete their selection.

With money in short supply and banks unwilling to approve a loan for a building on leased land, financing came from friends and family. Hilding's mother, Olga, hemmed sheeting and made draperies as well as supplying table cloths that were hand-woven by her sister in Sweden.

By late June 1940 the Crandell Lodge, named for the mountain that rises above it, opened for business. It had four three-room apartments, four one-room apartments and four single bedrooms. Each apartment had modern amenities such as a private bath, deluxe furnishings, kitchen, and fireplace, plus decorative touches like framed Canadian art prints, candles on the fireplace mantle and live houseplants. The apartments and rooms were available by the day or the week, ranging from $2 to $5 per night.

In 1944 Hilding Hagglund married Florence Moss, the school teacher who had come to Waterton the

Crandell Lodge was built on the site where a pair of rental cabins owned by Emily Lee had once been, until they were destroyed by fire. Built over two lots and originally as an apartment building, the Crandell set a precedent that would allow expansion of the Kilmorey Lodge, across Mount View Road, also over two lots.

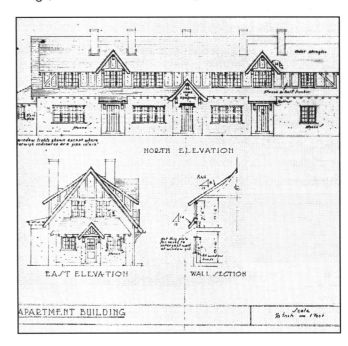

previous year. After Hilding's death in 1946, Florence married Peter Hominuke. But she was a determined owner-operator and ran Crandell Lodge for the next 40 years, until 1986.

The early years of the lodge were characterized by several challenges, according to Florence Hominuke's account. Lack of year-round electricity was one of them. In fact, the entire townsite did not receive year-round electricity until Calgary Power built a line into the park in 1947.

Only a few Waterton businesses, such as restaurants, had their own light plants—noisy machines at best. For many years the town depended on the Prince of Wales Hotel to supply electricity, but during the off-season, as well as three Depression years and during the Second World War when the hotel was closed, no electricity was provided. Coal oil lamps were standard issue.

Coal oil was also used in the Crandell Lodge cook stoves, sometimes producing smoke that discoloured the walls and ceiling if the stove was not operated correctly. Both coal and wood were needed for the furnace, hot water heater and the units' fireplaces. Lodge linens were washed in a wringer washer, line dried at the back of the property and ironed.

"But how the New York and other tourists from far away loved the [smell] of laundry dried in Waterton's fresh air," Hominuke said.

The change in park policy on a building spanning two lots in a residential area allowed Ada Kemmis to fulfill her dream of linking the Kilmorey to her White House next door. Doug G. Oland skillfully joined the two buildings, facing the exterior of the White House with the same half-log siding used on the Kilmorey. From the lakeshore it was nearly impossible to tell those two buildings were joined. The newly enlarged Kilmorey Lodge opened in June 1940.

Also in 1940, Dell Ellison renovated his 12-bedroom Ladies' Lodge, creating six suites, which proved to be a popular improvement. The name was changed to Lakeview Apartments and was no longer restricted to ladies only.

That same summer, an 11- by 14.6-metre (36- by 48-foot) store and tea room-dining room was completed at Cameron Lake Auto Bungalows. It was arranged in the shape of a cross, with a stone fireplace in the middle. Mr. and Mrs. Bert Matkin were hired to manage the cabins and tea room in 1941. A rustic lunch counter was added to the tea room, with the restaurant featuring chicken and fish dinners.

At each cabin, George Baker installed running water and a central comfort station with showers and flush toilets; the privies were removed. Baker also built a dock and rented 14 row boats and five canoes to the public. He later added excursions aboard the

The Lady Cameron, *introduced in 1952, was the only motorized boat ever regularly used on Cameron Lake, thanks to the need for crew transportation in the case of a forest fire. Brian Baker, grandson of boat owner George Baker, would serve on it as a "bilge boy."*

Lady Cameron, a 22-passenger cabin cruiser which was the only motorized boat allowed on the lake.

When James Fisher sold his share of the Waterton Auto Bungalows to Erik Hagglund and the paperwork was finalized in the summer of 1940, Hagglund continued to expand. By 1947 he had added 15 cabins and accessory buildings, and then sold the operation to his daughter and son-in-law, Esther and George Allred.

Esther had been a school teacher and assisted George in running their Twin Butte store before they bought the bungalows. Hagglunds' sale of the auto cabins was one of several management changes that occurred in the immediate postwar years.

At the Waterton Lakes Hotel and Chalets, there had been a shakeup in management during the war. In 1943 two key directors of the hotel company died of natural causes: James S. Kirkham in May and Paul Kuschel in September. Kuschel's widow, Flora, became responsible for maintaining the operation and after 1944 she hired Albert Roper to manage it.

That same year, the Canadian Legion War Services, which was looking for a hostel, expressed interest in buying Kemmis's Ballinacor Hotel. With building materials and manpower in short supply, the organization wanted to take over an existing structure, suggesting it could turn the coffee shop into a canteen. The purchase was recommended to the federal Budget Board but while park officials had no objections and were even willing to forgo land rent, the sale did not go through.

Instead, Flora Kuschel, who was overseeing the Waterton Lakes Hotel and Chalets next door, bought the Ballinacor from Kemmis in May 1945 and personally managed it with her daughter-in-law Justine.

The purchase of the Ballinacor led to its consolidation into the hotel next door. Eventually, the Ballinacor name would disappear, rebranded as Kootenai Lodge in 1956, as would much of its visual identity. The building still stands today but has been architecturally blended into the Bayshore Inn Resort.

Also after the war, Ernie Haug, Sr. requested permission to expand his International Coffee Shop and Service Station near the park entrance road by building a few simple overnight cabins for travellers. They would have a minimum of amenities to avoid competition with townsite facilities.

Superintendent Herbert A. DeVeber supported Haug's idea and told his superiors: "During the past four years there has been an acute shortage of accommodation in the townsite, and it was not uncommon at the height of the season for visitors to have to leave the park and seek accommodation in the towns of Cardston and Pincher Creek. Provision should be

James S. Kirkham

made for the establishment of another auto bungalow camp as soon as sufficient building materials are available."

Business people in the townsite would have none of it, sure they were being cut out of the tourist flow. Several of them wrote letters of protest to the park superintendent, so authorities denied Haug's request for the time being. They later reversed their decision.

Haug never got to see additional development at the site; he died in December 1952. His son Ernie, 27, was in charge of the operation for a time but his mother Lillian eventually sold the lease in 1960 to Jack Ensign of Pincher Creek and Peter Morrison of Red Deer.

They implemented Haug's suggestion and erected five simple Tudor-style cabins north of the service station, which was about six metres (20 feet) above the Waterton River, offering an impressive view of the mountains.

Leonard and Victoria Hutchinson of Taber bought the lease in 1961 and operated the facility until 1966.

In the course of the ownership changes, the business was renamed at least twice: Entrance Cabins and Service Station, and Bridgeview Cabins and Service Station.

Back in the townsite on Mount View Road, Rosedale Apartments increased by three units in the July 1947 under the ownership of Frank and Linnea Goble. Each apartment could accommodate four people. By the spring of 1950 Rosedale included five modern suites with coal, gas or electric ranges, and tubs or showers. They were rented by the day, week or month.

Ernie Haug, Sr. never got to see his proposal to add cabins at the International Coffee Shop and Gas Station fulfilled, but new owners took up the idea and got permission for five units, built just to the north.

Reeves Lakeshore Bungalows were completed in 1947 and immediately proved popular. The 20 units were located on a windblown lakeshore site near the south end of Waterton Avenue, across from today's campground.

The Northland Lodge, on Evergreen Avenue, was a joint venture between Earl and Bessie Hacking and Hugh Black of St. Mary, Montana. Black had motels and a restaurant just outside Glacier National Park.

Down the street, new long-term managers were also found for Kilmorey Lodge. Kirk and Jean Bell of Montreal stepped into the job with enthusiasm. Kirk Bell, a Second World War veteran who had served in the Royal Canadian Air Force, was 35 when he took over the operation. He had just left his job in the Moore Corp., then the world's largest maker of business forms. Bell became very active in Waterton business circles, serving as president of the Waterton Chamber of Commerce and a vice-president of the Canadian Rockies Tourist Association.

At Carthew Lodge, Grace Udell, estranged from her husband, found she was unable to support herself and left Waterton in 1947, moving to Fort Macleod where she hoped to earn enough money to make repairs on the building. She did not return for the 1948 season and following the death of owner Louis W. Hill that April, the lodge was put on the market.

Hugh Black bought the lodge for $6,000 in 1949. Black was a successful restaurateur and motel operator in St. Mary, Montana, just east of Glacier National Park. Earl Hacking of Cardston became his Canadian partner and by July 4, 1949, Hacking and his wife Bessie were running the lodge.

Meanwhile, the auto bungalow concept had proven so successful, park officials offered another tender to the public in 1945. Preference was given to war veterans not holding other concessions in a national park. Eight applications were received, but only one applicant was a war veteran: Harry Reeves, who had served in the First World War with the 31st Battalion of the Canadian Expeditionary Force in France.

Reeves won the bid also because he had experience in the hospitality business, having operated the Kilmorey since 1938 with his wife Sibyl, Ada Kemmis's daughter. Reeves was a skilled carpenter who had worked on a Banff Springs Hotel addition before coming to Waterton. He was said to have also done much of the interior woodwork at the Prince of Wales Hotel.

The site for the new auto bungalows camp was the mostly treeless shore of Upper Waterton Lake, selected by the government. Reeves asked if the location could be changed, hoping to get permission to build on the north side of Emerald Bay below the Prince of Wales Hotel, but the request was denied. He was told if any cabins were to be built at that location, they should be built by the hotel's owner or its associates. So, Reeves went ahead at the original site.

He was required to have three categories of cabins: deluxe, modern and economy. By the end of 1947, seven 4.9- by 6.7-metre (16- by 22-foot) cabins and 13 4.9- by 6.1-metre (16- by 20-foot) cabins were built, as well as an office with a heating plant. The improvements were valued at $30,000, a substantial investment at the time. Like other auto camp operators, Reeves paid the government a percentage of his gross revenue in lieu of land rent.

The doors to Reeves Lakeshore Bungalows were

opened in 1948. Rates began at $6 per day for two people. Despite the windy location, the cabins were very popular. Adjacent to the cabins on the north was a large government community building where evening interpretative programs were presented and outdoor movies were shown. And it was a short walk to Cameron Falls and town's amenities, such as the movie theatre, dance pavilion, beer parlour, grocery and other stores.

The postwar rush to meet visitor needs eased and it was not until 1955 that another accommodation was built in the townsite.

The El Cortez Motel (now Bear Mountain Motel) was named at a time when all things Spanish had wide appeal in both Canada and the United States. The location and design were the brainchild of Waterton's most established builder, Doug G. Oland. He intended to build the motel and have it operated by his daughter Mary and son-in-law, Tim O'Brien.

Oland got approval for his plans, but when family circumstances changed, he contacted Wilfred Forry of Forry Construction in Lethbridge who eagerly took over the development. Forry purchased the lease and used Oland's plans.

The first phase of the concrete block and natural stone motel opened in June 1955. There were 12 units large enough for four people each and two units to accommodate six people each. Every unit was heated with its own panel furnace. There was one hot water

The design of the El Cortez Motel was startling in comparison to other park buildings. The flat-roofed accommodation done in a Mexican style was the first concrete block motel in Waterton townsite.

heater between every two units. Government approved rates were two persons $8; four persons $11; six persons $14.

The motel was laid out in an L-shape and was painted in terra cotta with lime green trim. The flat tar and gravel roof was constructed to hold 10 centimetres (four inches) of water for cooling purposes in the summer and to help fireproof the building. Over the next few years, Forry added additional units, bringing the total to 35.

Close on the heels of the El Cortez was the Frank-Lin Motel. It was started in September 1956 following a government call for tenders on the site the year before. The name of the motel was a combination of Frank and Linnea (Goble). The facility was built as a 19-unit development on three lots (now the eastern portion of the Aspen Village Inn on Windflower Avenue).

The $63,000 deluxe motel was designed by architect E.R. Saran of Calgary who announced that it would be one of the best in Alberta. Since the motel then consisted of separate, flat-roofed buildings, it could be completed incrementally. The complex accommodated 63 guests, a sizable addition to the number of available rooms in the townsite.

Over the next several years, a succession of new owner-managers came to the park.

In 1959 Harry and Sibyl Reeves, wishing to retire, decided to begin looking for buyers for their two accommodations: the Kilmorey Lodge and their auto bungalows, the Reeves Lakeshore Motel.

The Kilmorey was sold in August to Kirk and Jean Bell, who had managed the property since 1949. The Bells' interest in tourism was soon parlayed into a second role for the Kilmorey. The lodge became an official representative-outlet of the Alberta Motor Association, handling reservations and providing road and weather reports, services that were in heavy demand.

Always responsive to tourism, the Bells took note of a government suggestion made in the 1950s to emphasize Canada. "Being able to present something different to a tourist is the greatest attraction a tourist-conscious nation can offer," they were told. Bell chose to display the Union Jack, then Canada's national flag, on a short pole on the lodge's front lawn and it soon became a tourist attraction.

"You'd be surprised how many American tourist take pictures of their wives and children standing beside our Canadian flag. It's something that's definitely Canadian and they really go for it," Bell said.

The Bells kept the lodge until in August 1960, when it was sold to Ray and Olive Graham of Calgary who extensively renovated the aging building, increasing the number of rooms to 28. They owned the lodge for the next 10 years.

Early in January 1960 the sale of the Reeves' other accommodation, the Lakeshore Motel, was made public. The business was purchased by Reidar Lundstad and Clarence Bowie, both of Lethbridge, for an undisclosed sum. The fact that the exchange made the front page of *The Lethbridge Herald* was an indication of the lodging's popularity.

Another motel announcement hit the newspaper in July 1960. Fred Ganske and Oscar Lundgard were going to build a new motel in Waterton. The three lots immediately to the south of the marina were cleared for the construction of the 22-unit, two-storey Emerald Bay Motel, at the corner of Mount View Road and Waterton Avenue. Construction of

The Frank-Lin Motel was a variation of the individual auto bungalow cabins. It was designed to be duplex buildings. Much later the flat roofs were altered, becoming metal and peaked, to give the complex an up-to-date appearance.

The Emerald Bay Motel was a concrete block structure that faced the marina. Construction, below, began in 1960 and it opened the next summer. It was purchased by the government and razed in 1991 to increase parking.

the $100,000 motel began in September 1960 and opened the next summer. Flat roofed and sided with redwood, the building faced the water and the Prince of Wales Hotel.

At the Waterton Auto Bungalows, George and Esther Allred were negotiating a sale to Ingwall Sundal and Andy Briosi of Picture Butte, Alberta. As the dealings went on, Andy Briosi and his wife ran the business for the Allreds. The Briosis had no experience in tourist accommodations, but they learned quickly and had a lot of chuckles doing so, especially dealing with American guests.

While one family from the southern United States completed their registration card, Briosi said, "We couldn't help but notice how the children were looking us over and when they had no sooner got out of the office door, we heard one of them say: 'Mother, they're not like you said at all. They even dress like we do.' No doubt their parents had told them they were going up north into Canada where Eskimos live, and the kids expected to see them the minute they crossed the border."

A man of the prairies, Briosi got a quick education

in the ways of mountain wildlife. On one occasion, a farmer from Taber, Alberta, took a cabin for a week for his distraught, overworked wife and daughter, then headed home. The first morning, the daughter tore into Briosi, claiming they hadn't slept a wink for the racket going on in the attic.

"This seemed strange for we had rented this cabin all summer and no one had complained, but knowing [the mother's] condition, thought it best to move her to a different cabin," Briosi said. "My thinking was that she was in worse condition than the husband thought."

The next night new guests moved into the offending cabin and Briosi warned them they might hear animals in the night such as birds or squirrels, "knowing damned well that these slept at night." That was no problem, the guests said, they were quite used to night sounds in the park, and nothing could keep them awake.

The next morning, Briosi said the "old man came in furious."

"What in hell have you got in that cabin? That is certainly no park sounds," the man said.

Determined to solve this mystery, Briosi spent the next night in the cabin.

"All night long [there was] running, jumping, squealing, sliding, scratching. Now I just couldn't help thinking of that poor woman that came up here for a rest and relaxation and she went through this all night."

Briosi finally called a park warden for help. In short order the warden determined the noise was caused by a family of packrats, known to be nocturnal, and explained how to trap them. In all, seven of the noisy critters were removed. None of their kind returned. Nor did Briosi after the deal to purchase the operation fell through.

In 1961, new owners Gunnar Holte and Hans Nordlund, who ran a construction company in Lethbridge, bought the Waterton Auto Bungalows from the Allreds.

With their company getting the contract to build the new United Church in Waterton that summer, Holte and Nordlund were able to use the bungalows to house their crew while renting the balance of the 25 cabins to the public. During their tenure they remodelled the interior of some of the cabins and put stucco on the exteriors for a fresh look.

Also in 1960, the Waterton Lakes Hotel and Chalets and the Ballinacor, by then renamed Kootenai Lodge, were sold by Leigh and Flora Kuschel to brothers-in-law Ab Swinarton and Hugh Craig of Fort Macleod.

The Swinarton-Craig partnership represented two of the most knowledgeable hospitality operators in southern Alberta.

Swinarton was a second-generation hotelman who was born in Fort Macleod. His name was synonymous with his hometown's accommodations: the

American Hotel, the Empire and the Queens. He became a silent partner in the Waterton operation while Hugh Craig and his wife, Ann, were front and centre.

Long-time restaurant operators in Fort Macleod, the Craigs had a wealth of experience in the business. Later in life, when Hugh became known as "Mr. Hospitality" and "Mr. Tourism," he always credited his success to his wife Ann.

Very soon after the purchase of the Waterton Lakes Hotel and Kootenai Lodge, plans were unveiled for changes and improvements in the accommodations. The first change was in the name. Except for the Kootenai Lodge portion of the property, the operation became known as the Lakeshore Village.

There was some measure of irony that the Balli-

Hugh and Ann Craig

nacor Hotel was renamed Kootenai Lodge in 1956 just before the purchase since Hugh Craig had been born in Ireland. Had Craig known the origin of the name Ballinacor, he might have been tempted to change it back.

For the first several years, the gift shop at the newly named Lakeshore Village was run by Ann Craig, who was also in charge of the waitresses and chamber maids as well as handling the money. Credit card use was not widespread in those days, and handling cash was a major task.

Hugh commuted to Waterton on weekends from Fort Macleod, where he ran the Java Shop. He took the money to the bank in Fort Macleod on Monday mornings. Meanwhile, Ann kept the cash under her bed in a sweater box since there was then no bank in Waterton.

Both Craigs' daughters, Linda and Svea, worked at the motel during the summers and learned first-hand the ins and outs of its operation. Some of the work involved was pure logistics. An essential was laundry, which was contracted to a commercial facility in Lethbridge 144 kilometres (90 miles) away.

"We had to have four times the number of linens we needed since it would be several days before they would be returned," Linda Craig Mackenzie said. While driver Ralph Nelson was in the city on the laundry run, he also picked up beer for the bar and food for the restaurant.

"Twice a week we brought in goodies from the

Kootenai Lodge, which began life in 1938 as the Ballinacor Hotel, was later incorporated into the Bayshore Inn to provide staff housing upstairs, and a giftshop, dining and cocktails for the public on the main floor.

Marquis Hotel bakery and sold them in the coffee shop counter. Lots of cottage owners and campers used to come in for this," Mackenzie recalled. Cookies were also a particularly popular item for hikers' lunches.

Hiring staff for the Lakeshore Village and Kootenai Lodge also took planning. Most of the staff came from the local area. The going rate for wages was 65 cents an hour and staff paid $10 a week for room and board. Waitresses and chambermaids wore uniforms that were provided but had to have their own white shoes.

Ann Craig was very strict about appearances, Mackenzie said. "The girls got several white aprons, but they had to keep them clean and ironed and the collars on the uniforms were detachable so they could be washed regularly. And their hair had to be done properly."

Mackenzie was herself a member of the uniformed staff for several seasons. At first her duties included simple tasks like filling the pop and cigarette machines. Each season a new job was added to her duties. Her goal was to become a cashier. Eventually she enrolled in hotel and restaurant management courses

and worked in the hospitality industry in Calgary.

In time, management of the gift shop was handed over to Mary West. While gift shop employees didn't have uniforms like other staff, they were expected to "dress up" and be very neat. Appearances were important to a well-run facility.

In the fall of 1963, Craig and Swinarton brought in the wrecker's ball to remove the last of what Jack Hazzard had built in 1914 and the many subsequent owners had cobbled together and renovated time and again. The new construction was to be like a phoenix rising from its ashes. Only the beer parlour wing on the south side of the building was untouched.

According to Mackenzie, the old Waterton Lakes Hotel was replaced with a partially stone-faced building with room for a gift shop, and the much-needed services of the Canadian Imperial Bank of Commerce. Also included was space for sleeping quarters for bank staff, male hotel workers and Greyhound bus staff. The new building, 7.3- by 23.7-metres (24- by 78-feet) joined the old beer parlour and the L-shaped chalet grouping. It was supposed to be ready by June 8, 1964.

"There were about 17 chalets, numbers 34 to 50.

The floods of June 1964 and June 1975 damaged the ground floor of the Lakeshore Motel and Lodge, now the Bay-shore, as well as the town's only beer parlour. It took weeks to remove the debris, and clean and restore the buildings.

I remember Number 43 was a corner suite that had two bedrooms and was really deluxe," Mackenzie said. These ever-popular chalets featured private bathrooms and some had cooking facilities with dishes. They were left standing for the time being while plans were drawn up for a modern replacement.

The delay in making the replacement proved fortuitous as Mother Nature had a major surprise in store. Heavy rains and subsequent flooding—the worst of the century—closed the park June 8, 1964, as Upper Waterton Lake inundated much of the business section of the townsite and disabled the sewage lift station. Had new accommodations been erected, the flood waters would have ruined them.

As it was, the existing facility suffered its share of damage, Mackenzie said. Once the water receded, affected buildings had to be dried, carpet lifted, furnishings repaired or replaced, and walls repainted. The flood was a major setback for all those affected.

"There was a lot of silt associated with the water," Mackenzie said.

It would be another 10 days before business could resume. That summer the park saw 70,000 fewer visitors, due in part to the negative and widespread publicity about the flooding. It was a test of character and determination for Waterton business owners.

For Albert Dray and Leonard Ully of Lethbridge, the start of the 1964 season could hardly have been worse. The partners were the new owners of Reeves Lakeshore Motel, which they renamed Allen's Lakeshore Motel. Their cabins were out of service for weeks as they scrambled to recover from the flood.

By May 1965 Craig and Swinarton were ready to get on with their plans to expand the Lakeshore Village. Construction began on a 7.9- by 53.6-metre (26- by 176-foot) two-storey motel that would add 22 units to the operation, bringing the total number of rooms to 51. The rooms all had private balconies and a feature cedar wall. Five of the old chalets had been removed to open the view and provide space for parking.

The $100,000 facility was rechristened the Bayshore Motel at its grand opening, on June 26, 1965. Owners Craig and Swinarton had selected the word "motel" in deference to the travelling public, which tended to shy away from "hotels," which were considered swanky, stuffy or overpriced. The Bayshore's rooms were $16 a night, Mackenzie said, which "seemed very expensive to me."

Soon, plans were also announced for additional rooms. The remaining 12 chalets were torn down in the fall to make way for a second building on the site. With the expanded facility, Hugh Craig stopped commuting and took on full-time management of the Bayshore Motel.

Food service was of major importance. Home cooking was a feature of the coffee shop in the Kootenai Lodge.

"Dad was always there for breakfast and a girl would help him cook," Mackenzie said. Her mother, Ann Craig, started every day . . . baking powder biscuits. In the dining room, a featured dinner menu item was prime rib, served with Yorkshire pudding. On Sundays, a very popular smorgasbord was available, an innovation the Craigs introduced to Waterton.

Almost overnight government officials had a change of heart about how some things were being done in Waterton. In an unexpected move, commercial activity was almost exclusively confined to the townsite. The two exceptions were the horse concession and the golf course.

The auto bungalows that park officials had encouraged in the 1930s and 1940s quietly became the target of buyouts and removal in the 1960s and '70s. The first to go was Baker's Cameron Lake cabins.

Park staff had begun secretly discussing removal of Baker's Cameron Lake facility in 1960 on the premise that sewage from the camp could potentially affect the townsite's water supply downstream. The following year, an internal report made it clear a decision had been made to halt all overnight use at Cameron Lake and plans were being made to replace those facilities with ones for day-use only.

Officials had been hesitant to talk to Baker about his expiring lease and put him off by agreeing to grant only a short-term lease. But without a long-term lease, Baker's plan to make further improvements was uneconomical.

Park officials were finally forced to show their hand in 1964, when heavy rains washed out portions of the Akamina Highway leading to Cameron Lake. Fearing that Baker might submit a claim for loss of business due to the closure of the road for most of the summer, Ottawa ordered the park superintendent to take steps to acquire the property.

Although the Crown was within its legal rights to take possession, it wanted Baker to go willingly. The superintendent was advised to offer Baker $13,000, or Section 9 of the leasing agreement would be invoked. Under Section 9, Baker would get nothing.

Although Baker originally wanted $25,000, faced with Hobson's choice, he took the $13,000 with the proviso he be allowed to complete the 1965 season. He vacated the site on Oct. 31, 1965. The tea room building and one of the cabins remained in place for several years to accommodate seasonal wardens and the campground caretaker. Ten years later the

George Baker's cabins at Cameron Lake were bought out by the government, which later removed not only the cabins but also the public campground.

campground was closed and in 1976 Cameron Lake was designated a day-use only site, which it remains today.

Park officials felt the time had also come for removal of other outlying developments, including Bridgeview Cabins at the Waterton River site. The Hutchinsons sold the property to the government for $15,000. The contents of buildings were disposed of by Hurlburt Auction of Fort Macleod and the buildings by the Crown Assets Disposal Corp.

While the Waterton Auto Bungalows lasted longer, all of that type of accommodation was earmarked as outmoded and was gradually removed.

The Waterton Auto Bungalows and the Emerald Bay Motel had both been purchased by Emanuel and Sam Cohen of Calgary. They bought the bungalows in 1967 and the motel in 1968, lured by the prospect of being able to make a living by working only five months a year.

"We knew nothing!" Manny Cohen said of their new businesses. "We were green." But Manny soon learned the ropes and joined the Alberta Motel Association. While he and his wife Donna ran the bungalows, Sam and his wife Gea tried their hand at the Emerald Bay Motel. After two years, Ivy and Bay Penhove were hired to manage the motel.

Manny and his wife took over the motel in 1974 when the Waterton Auto Bungalows were purchased by the government. The Cohens took the contents of the 26 cabins to the dance hall, where a "going out of business" sale was held.

"People were fighting for one of those little washstands," he said. The cabins were sold individually and removed from the park. They were used as farm outbuildings in many cases. "You'd be driving around southern Alberta and see them in farmers' yards all over the place," Cohen said. In 1976 the bungalows site was redeveloped into a walk-in campground.

Allen's Lakeshore Motel was also purchased by the government after a major flood in 1975 damaged the buildings. Remaining units were demolished in April 1978 and the site returned to a natural state.

Rooming houses and cabins with rentable rooms or suites were also phased out. By the mid-1960s many were beginning to show their age and were falling below standard. "They are the last to be occupied,

Fred Weatherup

with the primary demand being motels and housekeeping units," noted a park report. The last rooming houses ceased to operate at the end of the 1970s.

One new accommodation was erected. The Windflower Motel, named for the street of the same name, was built in 1970 by Arlen and Flora Leavitt on the site once occupied by the Central Auto Court, which had been destroyed by fire in 1966. The Leavitts saw potential in Waterton and acquired the Ponderosa Motel next door (formerly the Frank-Lin) from Wayne and Arminta Anderson.

The 1970s were turbulent times for accommodation lessees in the park, with government policy threatening to pull the rug out from under commercial operators.

Some, like the Florrys, decided to leave. The El Cortez Motel was sold in the early 1970s to Joe Roberts of Lethbridge, who operated it only for a short time and then sold it April 1973 to Alf and Rae Baker, who owned the motel until 2003.

Others, like Hugh Craig, chose to stay and fight. In 1972-73 the Craig-Swinarton team put up one more addition to their Bayshore complex: the units that now face the Peace Park Plaza.

But in June 1975, Mother Nature did it again, delivering another major flood. Before the summer was over, Craig and Swinarton, both 68 years old, had had enough and began discussing the sale of the business to Fred Weatherup, a Lethbridge auto dealer and businessman. The negotiations, which began eight months before, were completed on March 1, 1976, for "in excess of $800,000," according to Weatherup's public statement.

Fred Weatherup had first expressed interest in the accommodation business in Waterton in 1974 when he attempted to purchase the Prince of Wales Hotel for a reported $1 million. He created a stir by demanding that the hotel be owned by Canadians, but Don Hummel, head of Tucson, Arizona-based Glacier Park, Inc., which had bought the hotel from the Great Northern Railway, was not interested in selling—at least not to Weatherup.

Weatherup dropped the idea and shifted his focus to the Bayshore. He formed a company called Canadian Rockies Hotel Co., a name surrendered by the Great Northern in 1960. Weatherup then renamed

Today's Bayshore Inn was built on the site of the Hazzard Hotel, on the east side of Waterton Avenue with easy access to services and shops.

his new property the Bayshore Motor Hotel and Kootenai Lodge.

Weatherup had been a park visitor for many years. His wife's family had owned a cabin since 1951 and it was from this vantage point that Weatherup observed how business was done in Waterton.

Of the many owners at this Waterton Avenue site, 47-year-old Weatherup was the most memorable for his aggressive ideas and in-your-face confrontations with authority. Throughout his brief tenure as a park hotelier, Weatherup's minimal regard for authority became legendary and he demonstrated it in daring ways.

Once on a trip to Waterton by helicopter, he directed the pilot to set down in the town's swimming pool parking lot, a violation of several park regulations. It was an error he did not make again.

Weatherup had no end of ideas for his newly

purchased establishments and in the tradition of all those who had gone before him, said he would renovate, redecorate and make building additions. It was a bit of irony that Fort Macleod-born Weatherup had, as a teenager, once worked for Hugh Craig at the Java Shop. It proved once again that southern Alberta was a small place with intricate connections.

As company president, Weatherup was eager to share his grandiose plans with the news media and in the process inadvertently tipped his hand to park authorities. Within 10 days of acquiring the Bayshore, Weatherup said he would replace the 100-seat dining room in the Kootenai Lodge with a Hy's Steak House, an upscale chain operation with outlets across Western Canada. In addition to refurbishing all the rooms, he said he would also build a heated swimming pool and within two years he planned to stay open year-round.

Weatherup had no idea what the park regulations were or that he was legally obliged to comply with them. Among those regulations was a prohibition against private swimming pools. And to keep the motel open year-round, he would be required to have written permission from park officials.

As a precursor to his year-round plans, Weatherup began discussions with park officials to have snow cleared from Linnet Lake in the winter to improve skating there and to have more park roads plowed, in particular the Akamina Parkway to Cameron Lake. "We expect to pressure the park into opening the Cameron Lake road," he told the news media. He dismissed the danger of avalanches.

Within a few weeks all of Weatherup's ideas, including a helicopter ski service, were squashed. Park superintendent Jean Pilon refused permission for winter operation because the park budget couldn't provide for winter visitor services, warden service or road clearing. Pilon did, however, offer to reconsider the ideas the following year in light of a park master plan and commercial study, which was being completed. The Bayshore and Kootenai Lodge were closed for the season on November 1, 1976.

Dave Cruickshank, who was a silent partner with Weatherup, had been appointed manager of the Bayshore. He was a distant relation by marriage who would later have several Waterton businesses of his own. Cruickshank, thoroughly disillusioned with how things were going with Weatherup and the hotel operation, withdrew from the partnership.

The winter of 1977-78 was a test of year-round operation in Waterton for Weatherup, whose motel, lounge and dining room were open on weekends until early January.

Gerry Muza, then manager of the Bayshore, said the motel had received many inquiries about a weekend retreat in Waterton, with people looking

Rick and Mary Kratz and their children Luke and Miriam.

for an alternative to Banff. But the winter business "was hardly a rousing success," *The Lethbridge Herald* reported. Travellers' road warnings were issued for three of the four weekends the motel was open.

Still, Weatherup soldiered on, planning to close for a few weeks' maintenance and reopen in February 1978. Guests could rent double rooms with cooking facilities for $24.50 a night and find meals ranging from $2 for hamburgers to $15 steak and lobster. The lounge, complete with live entertainment, would be open. In the end, the winter operation experiment was a flop.

After four summers Weatherup announced late in 1979 his intention to sell the Bayshore and concentrate his business interests on industrial opportunities in northeastern Alberta. Mary and Rick Kratz, Lethbridge motel owner-operators, took possession on Dec. 1, reopening it the following spring. The reported price was "in the neighbourhood of $1.5 million."

The Kratzes, both 36, had been in the accommodations business since 1972, learning the ropes the hard way elsewhere. "We did everything—lived on the premises, cleaned rooms, checked people in," Mary said of their learning experiences. What was very new to them was the seasonal aspect of the Waterton operation: opening, hiring staff, closing. It was like starting a new hotel every spring.

Full of enthusiasm, however, Rick Kratz noted that "there's a lot of potential for Waterton," calling it the only remaining quiet national park in Canada. "There are a lot of people who want to have a rest when they holiday," he said.

For once, the new owners initially said nothing publicly about renovating, although Mary Kratz admitted later that she had visions of many improvements.

Across the bay on the knoll above the lake, the Prince of Wales Hotel was sold in 1980 to Greyhound

Food Services, a U.S. company now renamed and under a parent operation known as Viad Corp., based in Phoenix, Arizona.

At the Emerald Bay Motel, Manny Cohen said he knew the writing was on the wall for his operation when he applied in 1977 for permission to add a restaurant. According to Cohen, park officials refused, saying they planned to build a museum nearby and wanted the motel site for a green space. The museum was a "story" other businessmen would also hear, but one that never came to fruition.

Cohen sold the Emerald Bay to Parks Canada for $365,000 in 1977 and park officials announced their intention to remove the motel, but "only after additional rooms were developed in the community." Until those replacement rooms were built, the motel would be operated under an agreement with Dee Ruperell of Calgary, whose company shared maintenance responsibilities for the motel with the government. Even after rooms were added to existing facilities, it was not until 1991 that funding was found to tear down the motel and it was eventually turned into a paved parking lot for the marina.

The replacement rooms park officials had spoken

of came after Mary and Rick Kratz finalized plans to renovate the Bayshore Motor Hotel in 1983. That September, at the end of the regular season, Lear Construction began work on a $1.5-million expansion of accommodations and the renovation of the Waterton Avenue dance hall. It was the largest investment to date in Waterton hospitality operations and gave the property a new face.

Gone was the beer parlour, first opened in 1928. And completely renovated was the 1938 dance hall, which was changed into a two-part structure, with convention facilities for 200 people and the Thirsty Bear saloon with a mezzanine. First planned for demolition, the old dance hall was saved on the recommendation of the architect because "it had too much character to tear down." The convention centre proved to be an important addition to facilities in the townsite and helped maintain business during the spring and fall "shoulder" seasons.

The name was changed to the Bayshore Inn and was advertised as "Waterton's luxury lakefront inn."

It now took more than 75 people to run the new 70-room facility, including both Mary and Rick Kratz and their two adult children, Miriam and Luke, who

Waterton Lakes Lodge Resort is out of the way of most local traffic, with ample parking on site.

Waterton-Glacier Suites has many popular amenities and is one of a few Waterton facilities open year-round.

initially managed major portions of the operations.

The future of Crandell Lodge took on new possibilities after it was sold to Gordon and Lil Casey in 1986. The Caseys hoped to divide the building into nine condominium units. Half of the units, priced between $22,000 and $42,000, went quickly but when the balance of the units did not sell, the plan folded. The Crandell resumed life as a lodge.

The Caseys sold the lodge just four years later, in 1990, to Doris and Alan Hochstein, who substantially redecorated the 17-unit facility and built a residence behind it. Alan, raised in Pincher Creek, was the son of Toots and Cyril Hochstein, who had built a cabin in the park four decades before. The lodge changed hands again when it was purchased by Jamie Creason in 1997, who became fourth owner. Today, Crandell Lodge is owned by Waymarker Hospitality.

The dream of operating a year-round accommodation in Waterton remained long after Fred Weatherup departed. It was achieved when Leslie and Gerry

Muza bought the Kilmorey Lodge in 1987. The sale was followed by many renovations.

The Muzas moved the dining room from the lake to the Mount View Road side of the building, created handicap accessible rooms in its place, and redecorated and renovated part of the lobby to create a licensed lounge. They also built a gazebo in 1989 for summer outdoor dining.

The Muzas added the Windflower Motel and the Ponderosa Motel, both on Windflower Avenue, to their operations in the 1990s. The two motels were homogenized into the Aspen Village Inn and the buildings were given a new look, with faux-stone entrance posts and steeply pitched, red metal roofs replacing the once flat roofs.

The Muzas sold the 23-room Kilmorey Lodge and the 51-unit Aspen Village Inn in 2007 to Waymarker Hospitality, a partnership of four southern Alberta businessmen who already owned the Crandell Lodge and the Waterton Lakes Lodge Resort.

The lodge resort had started life as The Lodge at

Waterton Lakes and was built by a company headed by Ed Romanowski on the site of the park's swimming pool. Unusual at the time, a Peigan blessing and the planting of a tree marked the official start of construction on the $8.1 million lodge.

The 80-unit facility comprised nine buildings and was opened in 1998. It included a recreation centre and health spa, small indoor pool, whirlpool with hot tub and a 20-bed hostel. Due to financial difficulties the accommodation changed hands at least twice, then in 2004 Waymarker Hospitality purchased the operation and renamed it Waterton Lakes Lodge Resort.

Meanwhile in 1991, the Kratzs were approached with "the right deal at the right time" and they sold the Bayshore Inn to Razia Nathani Suleman, Andy Nathani and Karim Karim of Vancouver. Like the Craigs and Kratzs, the new owners immediately involved family members to supply much of the critical management for the business.

"I don't think you could run a huge project like this if not for family," Suleman said after her company branched out to build and operate the 26-unit Waterton-Glacier Suites in 1998, later adding a restaurant, known as Red Rock Trattoria, to its year-round operation. Located on Windflower Avenue, the facility replaced two cabins, both of which were built in the 1930s.

Although the Kratzs had been spared during their ownership of the Bayshore, the new owner, Mani Krupa Investments Inc., was dealt several nasty hands by Mother Nature. It experienced more weather crises in the first decade of business than all previous owners of the hotel combined.

In 1992 an unseasonable storm known as an August Singularity struck Waterton, dropping more than 30 centimetres (one foot) of snow on the townsite, bringing all traffic—coming and going—to a full stop. In June 1995, another flood inundated the ground floor of the Bayshore, ruining carpeting and

Rebuilding of the Kilmorey Lodge, destroyed by fire in 2009, has taken a record-breaking period of time due to construction difficulties and requirements.

furniture, and closed the park to all visitors. And on June 8, 2002, a storm blanketed the park with 90 centimetres (three feet) of snow that knocked out electricity for days, closed the road into the park as well as the all-important inter-park link, the Chief Mountain Highway and customs operation at the border.

As the new century began, ownership and management of Waterton lodgings continued to see new faces.

The El Cortez Motel, closed in 2003, was reopened under the name Bear Mountain Motel when it was purchased in 2004 by Andy and Beth Towe. The new name has historic roots. It was a variation of Black Bear Mountain, the first name given to what is now Mount Crandell.

The Towes sold the motel to Jim and Ashley (Uibel) Riddle in the winter of 2015. Ashley's parents, Ross and Lorna Uibel, are owners of Caribou Clothes, Big Scoop Ice Cream Parlour and Big Chunk Fudge Shop on Waterton Avenue and have been in business in Waterton for many years.

By 2007, Waymarker Hospitality purchased the Kilmorey Lodge, which brought to four the number of accommodations in Waterton under its ownership. The Kilmorey was destroyed by fire on Jan. 20, 2009, and was still under construction in early 2022.

It's been more than a century since William O. Lee set up the first accommodations in Waterton. He was correct in believing there was opportunity to be had in hospitality business in the park.

*As many as 150 parked cars would clog the business section of Waterton Avenue in the 1920s and 1930s when-
ever there was a dance scheduled at the pavilion, above right. People came from across southern Alberta and even
Montana for the dances, drawn by live music performed by top entertainers. Local entrepreneurs credited the
dances for making the park, with the economic spinoffs benefitting every business in Waterton.*

Chapter 3

Entrepreneurs
Like Nobody's Business

Small, independent businesses are the norm in Waterton. The park's off-the-beaten-path location and the seasonal nature of tourism have meant that corporations operating chain outlets have generally skipped Waterton for more lucrative and year-round tourist destinations.

Instead, there's a tradition of family ownership and many of today's business people have ties to the park's pioneers. It seems once tourism gets into the blood of the determined, it can stay there for generations.

The Baker name is the oldest continuously associated with the park. It spans five generations and represents a diversity of business operations, from cottage rentals to a mountain equipment outlet. It began with William and Elsie Baker in the early 1920s.

William J. Baker came to Canada from Sussex County, England, in 1907. He was in search of a homestead and when he found what he wanted, in the Gladstone Valley north of the park, he summoned his wife Elsie and their three small children to join him. William raised cattle and work horses. The latter were hired out for railroad work, dam building and logging. The Bakers moved in 1918 to the Twin Butte district, immediately north of Waterton, primarily to increase the land available for their livestock. The move tied their future not to livestock, but tourism.

By the summer of 1919 their oldest son George went to work in Oil City, but his job turned out to be as short-lived as the flow of oil and he moved north to work in the Turner Valley oilfield. By 1922 George had had enough and returned for good to Waterton, where his mother had a cabin on the lakeshore (site of the present-day Park Transport building near the marina).

George Baker at the Motor Vessel International's *boat house at the head of the lake.*

Over the next three decades as opportunities arose, William and Elsie amassed eight park leases, and built structures on each of them, in turn renting them to tourists. Some leases were in William's name, others in Elsie's.

Renting cabins served as a business example to George, but he had other things in mind. His interest in motor mechanics, picked up in the oilfields, spurred him in a new direction. He built his own log cabin on a lot in the vicinity of park headquarters, then across from Middle Waterton Lake. At the back of the lot he had a small garage.

He began a hauling business with a second-hand Ford Model T truck he bought from Dewitt Johnson, another young Waterton businessman. George put $100 down on the truck and hoped he'd be able to earn enough to pay off the $400 balance. He sold gasoline out of a barrel to supplement his summer hauling income and worked winters for the government.

"I was a business manager, front-end man, mechanic and truck driver combined," George Baker recalled on the 30th anniversary of his venture.

Ever since Jack Hazzard had opened his hotel in 1914, the difficulty of and need for transportation to and from Waterton to provide provisions for the hotel and visitors was evident. Getting building materials to the townsite was inconvenient at best due to poor roads and few bridges, and the need for a hauling company was urgent. Baker helped fill that need.

Moving people to the park was another matter. With no public transportation available, each visitor was on his own. Hotel guests who came by their own horse-drawn conveyance, as most did, needed a livery stable for their animals, a service which Isaac

George Baker spent $4,000 to build the Central Garage in 1927 at the corner of Mount View Road and Waterton Avenue. Baker, below third from left, had a full-service operation, with mechanics ready to serve the public.

L. Allred quickly provided the year the Hazzard Hotel opened.

Allred was a 27-year-old, Utah-born resident of Caldwell, Alberta, who had moved to the small farming community east of the park as a child with his parents. Now married to Mattie Ellison of Cardston, Allred's entry into the livery stable business was timely as a companion operation to the new hotel.

The stable was on the northwest corner of Waterton Avenue and Cameron Falls Drive, suitably distant from the hotel to separate guests from the associated noise and odor. With room for 22 horses and a 10-tonne capacity hay loft, the stable was just the right size for the customers it served. The next year, Allred added a large pole corral, and he expanded his business by providing guides and renting horses for those wishing to take saddle horse day trips.

By 1917 Allred had built a log residence across the street, on the lakeshore (now a parking lot), so he was always available. But the stable was doomed, due to the growing popularity of the automobile, which in turn spawned gasoline and garage businesses.

Dewitt Talmadge Johnson, a 27-year-old from Fort Macleod, opened Waterton's first garage and gas pump in 1919, locating it across from Hazzard's hotel on the lot now home to Akamina Gifts. He also hauled freight between his hometown and Waterton. He shut down his garage-gasoline business in 1923, converting the building to another purpose, while he continued his hauling service.

The timing of Johnson's garage business closure was perfect for George Baker, but he wasn't fast enough. Two men beat him to the punch by getting approval to build a service station on the corner of Waterton Avenue and Mount View Road (now a parking lot), east of Elsie Baker's cabin.

Leonard J. Rexford of Granum, Alberta, and his partner Claude A. Ferguson of Cardston sold gas, oil, tires and auto parts, plus provided the services of a mechanic. They also offered a much-needed passenger service, as well as a hauling service, focusing on the Waterton-Cardston route to connect with the daily train from Lethbridge. The pair provided the service though the summer of 1925. Before the next spring, both men had died.

This time George Baker was quicker off the mark, buying the garage-gas station, Ferguson's trucking equipment and Rexford's cabin, which was adjacent to the station. Baker made the site headquarters for his own Park Transport Co. and in case anyone failed to notice the new ownership, he painted the small building red.

Construction of the Prince of Wales Hotel began in the late summer of 1926, bringing many new people to town, and Baker's business did so well he soon saw the merit in building a fully equipped garage. By September, now in partnership with his father, George announced construction of a "fully modern 50 feet by 75 feet garage costing over $4,000" which was to be opened in the spring of 1927. At nearly the same time, he began building a new residence at 136 Evergreen Ave. which was considerably closer to the new business. This brought his residential holdings to two and he sublet his original log house.

Baker's new Central Garage was a fully equipped, electrically lit facility with gas and oil pumps, free air for tires, a battery charging station and a mechanic available to do repairs. Baker hired help during the busiest part of the summer. It was also the office of the now growing Park Transport Co. In 1928 Baker bought two new trucks and to serve tourists, a large White Motor Co. bus to meet the Cardston train and provide sightseeing tours around the park.

Baker also had begun capitalizing on other opportunities. He introduced himself to Louis W. Hill, head of the Great Northern Railway, and in September 1929 was hired to install launching improvements at the company's boathouse, the winter storage site of the *Motor Vessel International*, near the head of Upper Waterton Lake. It was an entry into working with the Great Northern that boosted his boat freighting business. Baker also took on a variety of other jobs for the Great Northern when the Prince of Wales Hotel closed in the fall, becoming a local agent to represent the company and assisting the caretaker as required.

In 1929, George Baker purchased Charles "Dippy" Carnell's small excursion boat *Alleas* and rowboat rental business, then hired Boer War veteran George David "Cap" Thomas to manage the business. Two

An attendant pumps gasoline at Ernie Haug's International Service Station on Windflower Avenue, one of three gas stations in Waterton in 1931.

years later, Baker sold the *Alleas*, which was put into service on Crowsnest Lake northwest of the park. He replaced it with the 50-passenger *Altyn*, which he brought from Glacier park in Montana.

By 1931 the commercial garage business in Waterton had grown to the saturation point. There were three in town: Baker's Central Garage, with gas pumps, a workshop and storage for 14 cars; Delbert H. and Tay Ellison's Waterton Service Station (now Pat's Waterton) at 224 Mount View Rd., built in May 1928, which they owned for the next 26 years; and George Frederickson and Ernie Haug's International Service Station (303 Windflower Ave.), with two gas pumps and storage for 10 cars.

When Baker wanted to build yet another station, parks officials refused permission, for the time being. "It is better that a few businesses should prosper and maintain their premises up to the required standard than a lot of businesses with competition so keen that none pay and the places fall into disrepair, giving the park and townsite an uncareful appearance," park superintendent Herbert Knight reasoned.

With only $26 in cash to his name but plenty of assets, Baker decided in 1932 to build a larger garage on Mount View Road (now Tamarack Outdoor Outfitters). Using spare lumber already on hand, Carl Carlson and Erik Hagglund began construction of the new building, which had been designed by the government's architectural division. The garage provided plenty of space for auto repairs and the sale of hardware, eventually adding gasoline pumps.

Shortly after he had the new garage built, Baker began buying and selling boats. In 1935 he bought the *Montalta*, which was used as a work boat. He sold his row boats to another local man, Gordon Morrison, in 1937 and purchased the freight concession from Les Morrow to serve the head of the lake.

Baker's Park Transport Co. became one of only two commercial operators to land at Goat Haunt. The other was the excursion boat *International*. To accommodate his freight boat and facilitate loading and unloading, Baker was allowed to build his own dock at

George Baker built another garage on Mount View Road. It was the last to sell Imperial Oil products in the park.

the Emerald Bay marina, aptly named "Baker's Dock."

On Aug. 1, 1935, George Baker married Betty Annand Nixon, becoming stepfather to six-year-old son Alf. The following year Rae Baker was born. Both later worked to help develop George's various businesses. The marriage brought together two families with much in common.

George "Joe" and Betsy Annand and five-year-old Betty had emigrated in 1913 from Scotland to Caldwell, Alberta, where Joe operated a dairy farm for several years. Two years later, son George was born.

Each summer the family took up residence in Waterton close to their cows, which were moved there for summer pasture. The Annand Dairy became the town's supplier of milk year-round, by truck in the summer and by horse in the winter. Joe quit the dairy business in 1928 and began a 23-year career working for the park.

Daughter Betty, then 20 years old, went to work at the Prince of Wales Hotel, where she was a chambermaid. The experience served her well when she married George Baker and became an integral part of his businesses, putting in long hours at the same time raising their two sons.

Betty's brother, George, went to work for her husband in 1937 after he completed two years of mechanics training at the Provincial Institute of Technology and Art in Calgary (today's Southern Alberta Institute of Technology). He later followed in

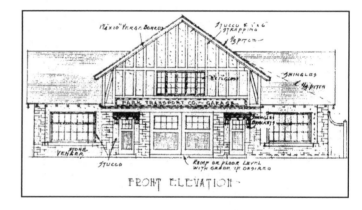

his father's footsteps, taking a permanent job with the park, becoming a mechanic and shop foreman.

William and Elsie Baker continued renting cabins to tourists, which became their sole occupation and allowed them to winter in Victoria, British Columbia. Betty's mother, Betsy Annand, also rented a duplex cottage, known as "Vimyvue," near the park headquarters. Each half had four rooms.

George Baker just never seemed to stop looking for opportunity or say "no" to a worthwhile business idea. In 1938 he was the successful applicant for the Cameron Lake Auto Bungalows, which featured a restaurant, boat rentals and tour boat. Back in the townsite, he took over operation of the telephone switchboard system in 1938 from Arthur H. "Pop" Harwood, who was also postmaster. The telephone switchboard, located in Baker's Mount View garage, was a vital link with the outside world at a time when only a few permanent residents had their own phones.

Telephone use grew rapidly, though, and Baker was required to hire four women to staff the switchboard. Baker provided staff for the telephone service for the next 26 years and was honoured by Alberta Government Telephones (now Telus) for his continuous efforts in 1964, when automatic switching equipment was installed and his service no longer needed.

Baker was also responsible for Canadian Pacific Railway's telegraph communications. A summer-only service, it sometimes required both of his sons to run messages around town trying to find total strangers in the campground so telegrams could be delivered.

Elsie Baker died in 1952 at the age of 73, leaving her first cabin lease on Mount View Road to George and a lease at 206 Fountain Ave. to her daughter Ella Baker Broomfield. William J. Baker died in Victoria in 1965, but by that time had divested himself of his Waterton leases.

George Baker parlayed his inheritance into a new building, intended strictly for storage and not a public garage. Located two doors east of the park administration office, the two-storey Park Transport facility had the same Tudor styling as the Baker garage to the west and across the street. Oland Construction was responsible for erecting the 16.8- by 19.2-metre (56- by 64-foot) structure. The building was used for overnight summer storage of Glacier Park Transport Co.'s red buses, and winter storage of Baker's boats and equipment. More than 70 years later, it continues to serve as a storage building.

One of the dairy wagons that served summer residents and campers in the townsite.

In 1955, Cliff Ott purchased the site of Baker's first gas station, the Central Garage, and operated it until the end of the 1959 season. It was demolished and replaced by the Emerald Bay Motel.

George Baker, Waterton's best-known businessman, died in December 1968 after a brief illness. He was 66. His wife Betty continued to live in their home on Evergreen Avenue until 1982, the same year she was voted Waterton's Citizen of the Year. She died in 2006 at the age of 97.

Alf and Rae Baker carried on the family businesses following George's death, adding to and changing them to suit the times and economic conditions. Today, Rae and Shirley's son Brian Baker and his family continue to operate their business, Tamarack Outdoor Outfitters, at the site of George's garage on Mount View Road. The Park Transport building remains in family ownership, as well.

* * *

Throughout the 20th century, Waterton's favourite nighttime activity was dancing. The earliest dances in Waterton were held at various rustic venues.

Lula Nielson was said to have hosted the first dances in the townsite, but few details have survived. Nielson, a Utah-born Cardston businesswoman, installed what may have been the first rough dance floor in 1915 on Evergreen Avenue, opposite what would become the Kilmorey Lodge. The summer proved to be too wet for much dancing on the small, semi-open floor, so that fall Nielson had it moved down the road to the present site of the Bear Mountain Motel. Dances were held there throughout the summer of 1916, but during the following winter Nielson had a cabin built on the site, ending the dances on her property.

The first all-weather dance hall was built in the summer of 1917 on Waterton Avenue, south of Hazzard's hotel. Charles A. Fairweather, a mechanic from Fort Macleod, invested $1,200 in the 7.2- by 18-metre (24- by 60-foot) Lakeshore Dancing Pavilion. He sold the building in 1920 to two other men from Fort Macleod, Ernie Haug, Sr. and Eudor Brosseau. Although Brosseau dropped out of the business sometime later, for Haug it was the beginning of his self-employment in Waterton.

Ernie Haug was born in 1891 in Regina, Saskatchewan, where his German immigrant father, also named Ernie, was a member of the North-West Mounted Police working as a wheelwright and carpenter. When the elder Ernie was transferred to Fort Macleod, his whole family took up residence in the southern Alberta town. In 1913 he resigned from the police force to open his own business, specializing in making and repairing wheels for grain wagons.

Ernie Eugene Haug was by then 22 years old and

had distinguished himself by winning a speed contest in typing and shorthand, skills much sought after in offices of the day. Haug was strongly attracted to the outdoor life of the Rockies and became well acquainted with Waterton and Kootenai Brown.

In 1914, Haug became the office assistant to Waterton superintendent Robert Cooper, who succeeded Brown. As a park employee, Haug had accommodations as well as workspace at headquarters, across from Middle Waterton Lake in what is now the park compound. While it is unclear how long Haug held the job, it is known that he was a witness to the signing of Brown's will in May 1916, attended Brown's funeral that July and was still living in Waterton in September when he joined the Canadian Expeditionary Force to fight in the First World War. Cooper signed his enlistment papers.

Ernie Haug, Sr.

It was with a certain amount of pride that Haug enlisted since, by all accounts, back in Fort Macleod residents were treating his German-born parents with considerable disdain. He began training in Calgary in September 1916 but for undisclosed reasons resigned from the military and was "struck off service as a special case" in January 1917. He returned to Waterton.

By 1920, Haug was overseeing his newly acquired Lakeshore Dance Hall. He did more than just manage it and hire the musicians. The popular bachelor fussed over his customers at the nightly dances to make sure they were properly served. Many of the dancers were his friends and clients.

Haug was also an avid outdoorsman, hunter and guide with a vast knowledge of the mountains. "He has no equal regarding knowledge of the mountains, passes and trails of Waterton Lakes Rockies," an area newspaper reported.

Haug fit in well with men and women alike, honing his people skills in the winter of 1922 in Cardston, where he managed the skating rink. He gradually built a far-reaching reputation.

Haug changed the name of the Lakeshore Dancing Hall to the Waterton Pavilion Dance Hall and looked for ways it might be improved. A general store, operated in connection with the dance hall, ensured that this valuable Waterton Avenue property was wisely utilized both day and night. The store sold "everything for the camper."

But Haug had a bigger vision, one that was for a better type of dance hall.

He submitted rough drawings to the park superintendent. In February 1923 he received approval for a "fine new dance pavilion," but it was another three years before Haug had the necessary backing to erect the new building.

Meanwhile in early 1923, garage owner Dewitt Johnson decided to get into the dance hall business, too. He took on a partner, Julius T. Lockead, also from Fort Macleod, and renovated the garage (now Akamina Gifts) into the town's second dance pavilion with a costly new hardwood floor. They called it The Palace.

A third Waterton dancing spot was also touted by the local newspaper. Goathaunt Chalet, at the head of Upper Waterton Lake, opened in 1924.

The rustic Goathaunt

Dance Hall
Waterton Lakes Park

The Lakeshore Dance Hall opened in 1917 but was supplanted in 1926 by a much bigger dance pavilion next door, so it was repurposed and became a store.

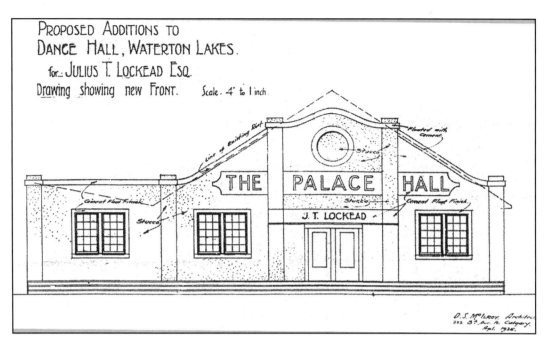

PROPOSED ADDITIONS TO
DANCE HALL, WATERTON LAKES.
for: JULIUS T. LOCKEAD ESQ.
Drawing showing new Front. Scale. 4' to 1 inch.

THE PALACE HALL

J. T. LOCKEAD

O. S. McILROY, Architect.
Apl. 1926.

The Palace dance hall, on the west side of Waterton Avenue, was created in 1923 by converting it from a garage. That was the first of numerous renovations to the building that is today Akamina Gifts and Book Nook.

Chalet, a 15-metre (50-foot) long log building with a large fireplace and a kitchen, was financed by Les Morrow and Henry Hanson with major log work done by Walter Foster. Morrow and Foster lived in Waterton and Hanson lived just east of the park. Hanson was no stranger to hosting dances, having done so at Waterton Mills nearly two decades before. Morrow, primarily a boat man, joined forces with Hanson in 1923 to help complete the chalet.

For the first time, visitors could choose where to dance and the competition, although brief, was lively. While Alberta in those days prohibited dancing on Sundays, Montana had no such restriction, giving the Goathaunt Chalet an edge on Sabbath activities.

Haug joined forces in 1924 with Dave "Slim" Mac-Lean from Pincher Creek and the two were able to sublet The Palace from Lockead after only one season, thus creating a monopoly in townsite dancing.

That summer was a prosperous one and in October Haug married the very popular Lillian Webb, the Fort Macleod Jubilee Queen, and brought her to live in Waterton. Lillian's father, like Ernie's, had been a Mountie in Fort Macleod, where she was educated. The quiet Pincher Creek wedding was followed by a surprise Waterton reception attended by more than 100 people, such was Haug's popularity.

Lillian, then 23, had been working in the Fort Macleod post office for several years, which gave her considerable business experience, a boon to Ernie's operations, until four-year-old Neil Ernie Haug was adopted in 1929.

In addition to his regular job, Ernie Haug, Sr. was a kind of one-man Waterton publicity department. He wrote hundreds of inches of articles for the *Calgary Herald*, *Albertan* and *The Lethbridge Herald* daily newspapers, keeping readers informed of park news, recounting area history and praising the wonders of Waterton's outdoor pursuits. Although his newspaper articles frequently mentioned his dances, he maintained a balance in his articles to keep readers up to date on all aspects of Waterton news, both private enterprise and government work.

A much-watched-for item was the annual announcement of the season's opening dance, to which hundreds of people flocked. For cabin owners and regular park visitors, it was an opportunity to renew acquaintances after a winter apart.

Known as jitney dances, they featured a live orchestra, often with four or five pieces. The customers were admitted free of charge, but to dance the men bought tickets for 10 cents a dance or 12 for a dollar. The price remained the same for many years. Just how big a business 10-cent dances were was evident by the fact that Haug and MacLean could make a living from them.

Finally, three years after getting approval, Haug's new, bigger dance hall became a reality. The opening of the Waterton Dance Pavilion in 1926 was not without a lot of help from others. Haug held the leases on Waterton Avenue where it was built; William Cromarty, a government architect, created the plans; Archie MacLean, a Pincher Creek farmer and the father of Slim, would hold the mortgage on the building; and Cardston contractor Oland & Scott Construction erected the dance hall.

The $20,000 dance hall was large enough to accommodate a thousand people and was not only the largest building in the park at the time and the largest dance hall in Western Canada, it was also Waterton's largest single private investment. Completion of this impressive building helped to establish the reputation of contractors Doug G. Oland and James C. Scott, who later that year were awarded the contract for the million-dollar Prince of Wales Hotel.

The dance hall was stunning. "It is so much beyond the average idea of a dance pavilion that one can hardly conceive of its proportions," *The Lethbridge Herald* reported.

The building was 34.1 metres square (112 feet square) to accommodate 1,100 dancers with coat check rooms, gentlemen's smoking room, an ice cream parlour and refreshment bar on the main floor. Upstairs was a three-metre-wide (10-foot) balcony for spectators. The attractive exterior was finished with pebble dash stucco. Two thousand panes of glass in hinged windows provided plenty of fresh air on warm evenings and the electric lights within sparkled through to the street.

Bessie Jensen, centre, and two friends are ready to cut a rug at the dance pavilion, where tickets like the one below were needed to access the dance floor.

Its most important feature was the white maple floor. "This floor shall not be laid until all other construction work is completed and all dirt and grit cleaned out of the building. After the floor has been laid it shall be scraped down to a perfectly level, smooth, flat surface, sand papered and filled with Johnson's Prepared Paste Wood filler and then finished with two coats of approved floor varnish," the building specifications demanded.

Senator William A. Buchanan of Lethbridge told the press the new hall was "the finest building in the park and the biggest boost so far." Ben Metcalfe, who had a cabin two doors to the south and who was also the manager of the Lethbridge Hotel, said: "It is a beautiful building . . . you have one of the finest pavilions in America." And Eddie Poulin, owner of the Waterton Lakes Hotel and Chalets, said: "It is certainly a wonderful building. I have never seen any better dance hall than this anywhere, not barring Montreal."

The first dance was held May 15, 1926, and for the next 12 years the Waterton Dance Pavilion was the focal point of evening entertainment in the park. More than 165 cars were parked on the street opening night, a good sign for all the businesses in town.

The jitney dance format was continued in the new hall. No admission was charged but for the first time there was plenty of room for spectators, who showed up to listen to the music and watch the dancing from the perimeter of the floor or from the balcony. Tickets were sold inside throughout the evening and ticket-takers were stationed at gates to the dance floor. No liquor was ever served at the dance hall, although it was available from bootleggers.

The opening of the Waterton Dance Pavilion caused some business changes in the town. The Pavilion Dance Hall immediately to the north was converted into a general store and operated by Slim MacLean, who bought out Haug's interest in the property in 1929. The Palace dance hall across the street was remodelled in 1926 for the third time and became the Beach Café. Both businesses benefitted from the new dance hall by staying open late to serve those attending dances.

Haug's connection with the new dance hall was brief. In 1929 he sold half of his interest in the lease to Slim MacLean and sold out completely in 1932. Haug then moved on to other opportunities.

Even while the new dance pavilion was the focal point of park entertainment, Haug was having a new, $2,100 residence built at 103 Fountain Ave. To help pay for the new house, in the winter of 1926-27

The Waterton Dance Pavilion, opened in 1926, was a magnificent addition to Waterton Avenue, drawing dancers from all over southern Alberta. The centre pillar was a structural device but also added interest to the 34.1-metre-square building. The balcony was popular with spectators, who could watch dancers and listen to the music for free.

The business district on Waterton Avenue underwent a transformation of pride with the opening of the dance pavillion in 1926 and Prince of Wales Hotel in 1927. Business owners co-operated to get the street, seen here in 1923, graded and wooden sidewalks installed on either side, vastly improving the streetscape. The board of trade printed a tin fish radiator badge, sold for 25 cents, to show support for Waterton. The badges now sell for thousands of dollars.

he took a job as clerk with Oland & Scott Construction, which was building the Prince of Wales Hotel.

For the next several years Haug was involved in a variety of other business ventures, including cabin sales and rentals for others, and as an insurance agent. He became a key participant in the board of trade and active in community affairs, serving as secretary-treasurer of the Waterton school board.

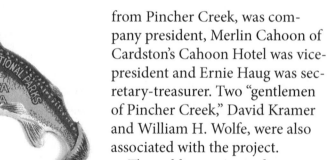

In April 1930 Ernie Haug's focus turned to two new possibilities when he purchased a lease on the last prime lot on Waterton Avenue, at the northwest corner at Cameron Falls Drive (now Zum's Eatery & Mercantile).

Just two years before superintendent William Cromarty had noted the lot was "likely to become a most important corner of the main street."

In the summer of 1930, it was announced that $100,000 would be spent to build a 60-room hotel on four lots, including the one Haug owned. Waterton Investments Ltd. of Pincher Creek was sponsoring another company, Waterton Lakes Building Corp., and all it needed was the money.

H. Bossenberry, member of the Alberta legislature from Pincher Creek, was company president, Merlin Cahoon of Cardston's Cahoon Hotel was vice-president and Ernie Haug was secretary-treasurer. Two "gentlemen of Pincher Creek," David Kramer and William H. Wolfe, were also associated with the project.

The public was invited to purchase stock in the company to finance the three-storey hotel, which was to offer medium-priced rooms and provide ground floor retail space. The name selected was Kootenai Lodge, for pioneer Kootenai Brown.

Although Oland & Scott Construction began work on the basement, the hotel was never built. The timing couldn't have been worse: the Depression was well underway and investment funds were either tight or non-existent.

In May 1932, when the Kootenai Lodge Hotel Co. formally advised park officials it didn't have the necessary funds to proceed, the lease applications for three lots were cancelled. Haug, however, held on to his lot. The name Kootenai Lodge was held in abeyance until 1956, when Flora Kuschel adopted it to rename the Ballinacor Hotel.

In 1931 George Frederickson, who had previously owned a rowboat and trucking business, joined Haug in the International Service Station on Windflower Avenue. It was owned by Imperial Oil Ltd. Haug was the manager and Frederickson did the mechanical work.

The partnership did not last. Frederickson contracted a fatal illness which required expensive medical treatment and he soon became dependent on the government for medical assistance. He was forced to relinquish his lease and residence at 405 Windflower Ave., and sell an unfinished cabin at 403 Windflower, next door.

When Frederickson died in December 1936, Haug pursued the business alone, concentrating on making extensive additions to the garage, installing new equipment for oil changes and adding car washing to his services. In 1938 he purchased the station from Imperial Oil.

Two years later, Haug expanded his park business 9.6 kilometres (six miles) beyond the town, to a site near the park registration office, north and east of the Waterton River bridge.

The International Coffee Shop and Service Station sold Imperial Oil products and was "an attractive asset to the park." The coffee shop was decorated in the style of the day, with black and white checkered flooring, a native stone fireplace and leather upholstered chairs at the food counter. Large windows commanded a view of Lower Waterton Lake. An information desk provided free road maps.

Haug, meanwhile, still had hopes for the vacant lot at the corner of Waterton Avenue and Cameron Falls Drive. It was an anomaly that officials allowed him to retain the lot without building on it.

In 1946, despite personal illness, Haug told officials he and unnamed Lethbridge associates intended to build apartments and a coffee counter on the site. He submitted a rough plan in February 1947, promising to provide drawings by January 1948 if officials gave him the go-ahead.

Among themselves, park officials doubted Haug had the money to complete the project, but he was good to his word on the plans, which included retail space for two stores. However, he was told the plans were "too plain" and needed to be drawn by an architect. Finding one in the postwar building boom was nearly impossible. When he failed to also find partners to fund the project, it was shelved permanently.

Ernie Haug, Sr. died in December 1952 at age 60.

Over the course of the next few years, his business and residential properties operated but were eventually sold by his widow Lillian and son Ernie. Lillian died in 1987.

After his father's estate was settled, Ernie Jr., went to work for the park, a career he concluded as maintenance supervisor 31 years later, in 1989. He married Maxine Higbee in 1949 in Waterton's All-Saints Anglican Church, where she was walked down the aisle by her boss, Nahor Dilatush from the Tourist Café.

Together Ernie and Maxine raised their four children in the park and were among the most active community supporters until they moved to Pincher Creek in 1990.

* * *

The year 1932 proved to be an important one for the dance hall business in Waterton. Ernie Haug, Sr. had sold his remaining half of the dance hall lease to Neil "Pat" MacLean, whose brother Slim MacLean owned the other half. The brothers formed a partnership, and the dance hall business would change significantly under their ownership.

Slim, noting that the dance hall was only used during the evening, decided to bring in some daytime business by introducing indoor badminton. Four courts were laid out and a supply of racquets and shuttlecocks was ordered then rented to participants. It was an ideal place to play badminton since Waterton's notorious winds wreaked havoc on outdoor games. The new business proved so popular that by July, MacLean had hired an instructor.

It was an innovative use of the building, but the MacLeans' biggest coup was in the choice of the 1932 dance orchestra. Whether it was talent or luck is not known, but that spring Slim MacLean auditioned Mart Kenney via radio from Vancouver and hired his orchestra for the prime period of July 1 through Labour Day.

Mart Kenney and his Western Gentlemen were a sensation. Not only did they play every night, but they also found a way to skirt the Alberta government's prohibition against Sunday dances. They simply moved the dance to Montana, beyond the reach of provincial law enforcement.

On Sunday evening July 17, 1932, about 200 people, including the orchestra, boarded the *Motor Vessel International* for a special excursion up the lake. At the Goathaunt Chalet, an impromptu dance was begun, and beer was sold to those who imbibed. After the cruise, the entire crowd returned to the

Mart Kenney and his Western Gentlemen were a sensation when they played at the dance pavilion from 1932 to 1934, with occasional return engagements over the years. Their music was broadcast over the radio from Waterton.

Waterton dance hall, where the Kenney orchestra entertained with skits and musical novelties until 1 a.m. Monday.

Known as the Midnight Frolics, the weekly event provided Kenney and his musicians with extra wages and dancers with one-of-a-kind entertainment on an otherwise dull Sunday when the Lord's Day Act forbade many commercial activities.

These moonlight cruises and late-night entertainment became a tradition lasting long after Kenney moved on to other venues. In later years, the rules were fudged slightly, and a dance began during the early morning hours of Monday.

Kenney and his group were part of "an epoch in radio history of Alberta" when their music was broadcast live to the nation. *Rocky Mountain Melody Time* debuted on Tuesday, July 24, 1934, as a half-hour program aired by the Canadian Radio Broadcasting Commission, forerunner of the Canadian Broadcasting Corp.

"The orchestra started with tom toms and brass,

the announcer punched out 'Rugged Rhythm from the Land of Rugged Peaks,' the orchestra drifted into *The West, A Nest and You, Dear* while the announcer crooned, 'From beautiful Waterton Park, nestled in the heart of the Canadian Rockies, it's the music of Mart Kenney and his Western Gentlemen.' And so, we began to broadcast," Kenney said in his memoir.

The weekly Waterton radio program made the band one of the most popular in Canada, with a large American audience, as well.

"We started getting fan mail from all parts of Canada and the American border states," Kenney recalled. When fan letters began arriving in Waterton, the business people knew they had accomplished their goal. The broadcasts had been organized and financed by Waterton's business people as an innovative way to advertise the park.

Minnie Harwood, wife of the postmaster and telegraph agent in the park, handed Kenney his first fan telegram, all the way from New York. It read: "Where have you boys been all this time?"

Goathaunt Chalet, at the head of Upper Waterton Lake, became the destination for Midnight Frolics, where Waterton visitors could skirt Alberta's prohibitions against dancing and drinking alcohol on Sunday. The chalet was rustic inside, but that mattered little to revellers.

The band's theme song, *The West, A Nest and You, Dear*, became a top recording for RCA Victor and jitney dances at the pavilion in Waterton were never more popular. Unfortunately for the MacLeans and Waterton, the broadcasts were so successful they launched Kenney's career and the orchestra moved on to bigger and more lucrative venues.

The MacLeans, meanwhile, continued to pursue daytime entertainment, which sometimes included wrestling matches. Western Canadian champion Jack Ellison, brother of local businessman Dell Ellison, was a well-known contender, as was Frank Pilling, brother of Peter Pilling of the Park Meat Market. More than 100 people, including a few ladies, attended the matches.

In 1935, Pat came up with yet another idea: vaudeville entertainment. A trick roper and a slack rope walker from the Calgary Stampede performed every Saturday night, and once a special entertainer, "Little Miss Mary Higgins" of Helena, Montana, gave a tap-dancing exhibition.

Brothers Pat, left, and Slim MacLean.

And then in January 1938, southern Albertans received the most shocking front page news to emanate from Waterton: the shuttered, unheated and unoccupied dance pavilion, pride of the town for the past 12 seasons, had burned to the ground and was "a pile of smoldering ashes," according to *The Lethbridge Herald*.

The fire occurred Jan. 3 about 1:30 a.m. By the time the general alarm was sounded, the interior of the building was "a blazing inferno." The cause of the fire was never determined despite an investigation by RCMP and the provincial fire inspector that went on for months. While arson was suspected, it could not be proved.

The loss to the community was felt by business people and residents alike, but none more so than Archie Mac-Lean, father of Slim and Pat, who held a $10,000 mortgage on the uninsured building.

Archie MacLean, who was born in Ontario, had moved to Pincher Creek in 1902 from North Dakota with his wife Elizabeth "Bonnie" and their two sons. Archie made a successful living as a farmer and became renowned for his threshing operation before going into the hauling business. When the Prince of Wales Hotel was built and sloppy roads prevented trucks from getting through, Archie was one of the teamsters hired to haul materials by horse from Cardston to Waterton.

The dance hall was Archie's only commercial investment in the park and while he and "Bonnie" assisted in selling and taking jitney tickets, it was his sons who were in the limelight of the operation.

So important was the dance hall to Waterton and so central was its location in the townsite that three months following the fire, with the investigation still underway, Pat MacLean was told by the park superin-

tendent that if he didn't intend to rebuild and submit plans soon, someone else would be allowed to build it.

MacLean quickly made an announcement that the hall would be rebuilt. A collective sigh of relief came from Waterton's business people, who feared a great drop in visitation without a dance hall.

Although Jean Rankin of Twin Butte, Alberta, who had a saddle horse concession, was reported to be the person to back the new hall financially, it was Ed Schrempp's name that was added to the lease documents in 1938.

A partner in Rankin's horse business, Schrempp had just spent the summer of 1936 helping organize and build the new Twin Butte Hall, north of the park. With contacts in the building supply business and a sideline in hauling, Schrempp's involvement in the new dance hall made a certain amount of sense. Once the Twin Butte Hall was completed, Schrempp also served on an entertainment committee that hired orchestras for dances there.

In addition to finding someone with money to invest, the MacLeans had to find someone to build the new hall. Next door to the north, the new Ballinacor Hotel was going up, utilizing the local tradesmen. Who was chosen to build the new dance hall has been lost to history, but it is known that it was not Oland & Scott Construction, the company that had built the original structure.

Southern Albertans were promised in May 1938 that the new dance hall would be ready by July 1. To meet the deadline, Cecilie "Squish" Parke, daughter of a cabin owner, and band leader Merv Huston got

Merv "Hupp" Huston, fifth from left, and His Merry Gentlemen were hired for the July 1938 opening of the new dance pavilion (below, under construction). The first dance was packed. The new pavilion replaced the previous dance hall, which was destroyed in a January fire.

together to paint the roof, a relatively arduous task for two young people.

The replacement building was quite different from the original. It was slightly smaller, had no interior balconies and a minimum of glass. The orchestra stand was opposite the entrance rather than to one side, as in the old building.

The architectural plans were drawn by E. Ouellette of Pincher Creek and approved in concept by the government in May. Until the government engineers approved the structural details, only the foundation could be built. One delay followed another.

Gordon Brewerton, who owned the movie theatre on Windflower Avenue, was given permission by the park superintendent to host dances, after the movie was shown, until the new hall was ready. Brewerton had a hardwood floor installed and to recoup the cost and the orchestra's salary, he and MacLean suspended the jitney format, replacing it with an admission charge of 50 cent per person.

The opening of the new dance hall—still unfinished—was finally set for Saturday, July 23, 1938, and was "packed to the doors when it opened." Merv "Hupp" Huston and His Merry Gentlemen from Edmonton provided the music. Huston went on to become the dean of the University of Alberta School of Pharmacy and an award-winning published humorist who even years later never lost touch with the park, introducing his wife and children to its wonders.

The decision to rebuild the dance hall was well justified. That summer, for the first time in its history, Waterton's visitor numbers exceeded those of Banff, and it looked like nothing could stop Waterton's popularity. Waterton business people were ecstatic.

Acting park superintendent C.K. "Cap" LeCapelain, however, was not so optimistic about what was going on. He closely monitored the dance hall for the six weeks it operated in the summer of 1938.

The next summer, he laid down the law. Schrempp and MacLean were given two extensions to finish the flooring, stuccoing and painting, but when they failed to meet the deadline, LeCapelain shut down the hall. Seeing the superintendent meant business and losing about $400 while the hall was closed, Schrempp and MacLean snapped into action.

"Workmen swarmed all over the dance hall," LeCapelain wrote to Ottawa officials. "Four plasterers were engaged on the stucco work, several men were busy wielding paint brushes and a further gang [was] laying the floor."

Within four days the hall was reopened "with the clear understanding that this activity would continue until the exterior paint work had been finished." The

The Anderson Sisters of Lethbridge were wildly popular, drawing large crowds whenever they played in the park.

hall still lacked—of all things—minimal fire protection, but extinguishers were on order. The public didn't seem to mind the disruption, especially since during the shutdown the superintendent let the dances again be moved to the theatre.

The enforced completion of the dance hall proved effective and crowds of over 1,000 people were reported attending dances when the hall reopened. With increased American visitation, international traffic at Chief Mountain customs was second only to the Coutts-Sweetgrass border crossing.

In the fall off 1940, MacLean was able to buy out Schrempp. The terms of the deal were not made public, but Schrempp took possession of the cabin Archie MacLean owned at 102 Fern St., selling it later that year to James Fisher of Raymond, Alberta. Meanwhile, Pat's son Laurie lent a hand at the dance hall.

With the entry of Canada into the Second World War on Sept. 10, 1939, subsequent gasoline and rubber rationing reduced some travel to the park, but the dances continued unabated as airmen and soldiers from area military bases made the park a regular destination for rest, recreation and an overall good time—when they could get leave.

Throughout the war, the very popular Anderson Sisters of Lethbridge drew in crowds. Waterton was a career highlight for the four-woman orchestra, which played across southern Alberta and British Columbia.

Kicking off the first postwar summer, Mart Kenney returned for a one-night performance on June 8, 1946. Even though it had been 12 years since Kenney's last Waterton appearance, the dance sold 1,100 tickets and was a runaway success.

"Pat came up to my room after the dance, just ecstatic and dumped all the money on the bed with one grand gesture," Kenney recalled. They had a cold drink while a member of the orchestra counted the take. Over the next 20 years, Kenney returned many times for one-night stands, drawing some of the largest crowds of the season.

The winter of 1950, with record snow levels and driving winds, proved the 1938 dance hall had not been built to the same standard as its predecessor. Local carpenter and dance hall neighbour Carl Carlson was featured in a newspaper photo shovelling snow out the window of the dance pavilion in January. The snow had blown in through cracks in the roof.

It seemed new dance attendance records were being set every year and the July 1, 1950, weekend was no exception, when 1,800 paying customers crammed in to dance for a return of the Anderson Sisters, the most successful band since Mart Kenney.

Pat MacLean might have been a little nervous when the newly formed Lions Club decided to erect

Bonnie and Archie MacLean were the first of a family line that operated busnesses in Waterton. It now extends to a fifth generation.

When a horrific spell of winter weather occurred in 1950, Carl Carlson was hired to remove snow that had blown inside the dance pavillion.

a hall on Fountain Avenue, but the fear of competition was soon dismissed. MacLean's hall was used for public summer events; the Lions Hall became a community facility used primarily for private events and local gatherings during the winter. And MacLean helped the local Lions Club each year by hosting its annual summer fundraising carnival.

When square dancing became popular in the early 1950s, Waterton residents were enthusiastic participants and arranged an event for MacLean's facility. The Mountain Square Dance Jamboree, which included both a workshop and dancing, was regularly attended by 300 dancers for several years in the 1950s.

The jitney dances ended in 1956. "The admission dances are much more satisfactory for young people who really want to dance," Pat MacLean said.

Always on the outlook for new entertainment, in 1958 MacLean booked television entertainers and recording artists Gene Diougy and his band, and Tommy Common and his all-star Country Revue. In 1959, MacLean began hiring as many as three different orchestras to play in a week.

By the early 1960s, with young people increasingly driving their own cars, the Waterton Dance Pavilion became the place to be on a long-weekend. Dances, sometimes attended by a thousand people, were on the rise once again. During July and August dances were held to live music three nights a week and in mid-week a record hop was the featured entertainment. But trouble was associated with these gatherings when secretive and off-premises alcohol consumption got out of hand.

The end was in sight in 1974 when park authorities questioned the need for certain businesses in the park, including dance halls, beer parlours, lounges and even curio shops.

In the spring of 1977, the dance hall was purchased by Fred Weatherup, who announced plans to convert it to a family recreation centre, including a cafeteria, with electronic games and nightly disco dancing.

Pat MacLean retired to Pincher Creek with his wife Annie after 41 years of operating the dance hall. To those for whom the dances held fond memories, it

Nahor Dilatush and Florence, his second wife, seen below with an unidentified woman at right, ran the Tourist Café on Waterton Avenue for many years. The cafe's "all white help" sign would not be tolerated today.

was the end of an era. Pat MacLean died in 1988 at the age of 86. Annie died in 1996. She was 94.

By 1980, the scheduled dances had come to an end. The Waterton Dance Pavilion was converted to a roller-skating rink. The change in use was, more than anything, a reflection of popular pastimes.

When new owners Mary and Rick Kratz decided to renovate their adjacent Bayshore Motel, they originally planned to tear down the 1938 dance hall but were convinced that a small convention centre and bar could be incorporated into the building.

In all, five generations of MacLeans have worked in the park. The first was Archie and "Bonnie"; then Pat and Annie; their son Laurie, who had a variety of jobs. The family of Carol and Dave Cruickshank own Zum's Eatery and Mercantile, BeaverTails, a ladies clothing store, the Stanley Hotel (now staff housing), as well as Akamina Gifts and Book Nook.

* * *

Husband and wife Nahor and Mabel Dilatush distinguished themselves by conducting several types of business at once. "The Dills," as they were known, had moved to Alberta from New Jersey shortly after the First World War. They farmed on the Piikani Nation reserve at Brocket for a time, then settled in Fort Macleod where Mabel was known as an excellent cook and Nahor sold farm machinery and automobiles.

The Dills' lives changed dramatically when fellow Macleod resident Dewitt Johnson had an offer they couldn't refuse. They bought his two-year-old Tourist Café in 1924, the first free-standing restaurant in Waterton. Its only competitors were the Nixon Café and the dining room at the Lakeshore Hotel.

Both Dills worked in the restaurant business, but the couple was ambitious and kept an eye out for available property and opportunity.

Their first year in the park, the lots immediately to the south of the Tourist Café (now Waterton Park Café) had been reserved by park officials for "parking," but the wisdom of releasing the lots for development was realized and in 1926 they were opened for lease application. Mabel Dilatush snapped up two lots to the south. The Stanley Hotel was built on the first lot in 1928 and a butcher shop was built immediately to the south.

The west side of Waterton Avenue as it looked about 1928. The two-storey Stanley Hotel, centre left, was built for Nahor and Mabel Dilatush.

The two-storey Stanley Hotel had ground floor retail space for two businesses. The space on the north side was rented by T.E.H. Patterson, a Cardston pharmacist who ran a combination drug and souvenir store. It was a much-needed service as, the newspaper noted, "for years you have been coming down to spend a holiday and have packed your car with everything possible in case of emergencies and sudden sickness. That day is gone and past."

H.L. Higgs bought out Patterson's Cardston drugstore the next year and with it came the sublet for the Waterton business. For the next 39 years, until 1968, a Higgs was associated with the pharmacy in the Stanley Hotel. H.L. Higgs's son, Ben, took over in 1945 after serving in the Second World War, establishing yet another family business tradition in Waterton.

On the south side of the hotel, space was leased to Waterton Lakes Supply Store, operated by William A. Fraser, a well-known Pincher Creek merchant.

William Fraser and his wife Katherine, both former teachers, had moved to Pincher Creek in 1906 where they ran a dry goods store. Fraser prospered in that town, where he dabbled in a variety of partnerships and ventures.

Leo Schmidt

The Frasers' supply store offered just about everything a visitor could want: tents for rent, groceries including fresh meat, hardware and cooking utensils, sporting goods, clothes, shoes, linens, china, Hudson Bay and English point blankets as well as coats, moccasins, gauntlets and slippers with Native beadwork.

In the spring of 1930, the Dills built the Park Meat Market, which was designed so that its mirror image could be added to the south side of the building. The Dills chose to "go small" on this building for two reasons: they had competition in the butcher business and the Depression had just begun.

Alvin Caldwell's butcher shop on Windflower Avenue (now the site of a commercial-residential building) was the first one in Waterton. Caldwell had sold it to the Strate Brothers in 1927 and whether there was enough business for two butchers was not known.

Nahor Dilatush sublet his butcher shop to J. Tinney of Calgary. Tinney left in 1932 and Quality Meat Market of Cardston took his place. It was soon evident there was plenty of meat and grocery business to go around.

The Dills continued to operate the Tourist Café, the Stanley Hotel and rent commercial space, and by 1934, in the midst of the Depression, they also had seven cottages for rent. It was a good business mix, but it took its toll on Mabel's health.

Mabel Dilatush, 40, died in a Ponoka hospital in August 1935. There were five leases in her name alone and it would take years before Nahor had either the time or inclination to transfer them to his own name.

When William Fraser, who was renting one of the two commercial spots in the Stanley Hotel, moved his business back to Pincher Creek in 1936, the vacancy was filled by Nahor, who opened Dill's General Store.

Dill married for a second time in 1936. Florence Schmidt of Pincher Creek, who had been a waitress at his café the previous year, became the new Mrs. Dill and eventually the town's longest active businesswoman. She ran the general store until 1994.

Florence took a keen interest in the Waterton businesses as well as the many people who visited the park. In 1939, purely as civic pride, she created a flower garden between the Tourist Café and the Stanley Hotel, an addition which drew praise from visitors for generations. Included were a small, neat lawn and a selection of three dozen types of colourful flowers planted amid gravel paths.

Nahor Dilatush was a consummate manager who believed in personally attending to his café. He catered to the late arriving crowd that attended the dances across the street.

The café regularly advertised in the Lethbridge newspaper as having "all white help." It was a frequent claim made proudly in those days when anti-Chinese sentiment was popular. Such wording today would be considered racist and not allowed.

The Dills' ability to find and keep long-serving employees at their general store was legendary. Hilda Hewlett, for example, went to work for the Dills in the late 1930s and remained throughout the 1940s as manager. She and her husband were well acquainted with the Dills, having sublet their butcher shop for a few years. Later, Eva Maclean of Lethbridge became manager of the store and worked there for many years.

In 1957, Nahor sold the Tourist Café to his brother-in-law Leo Schmidt. Schmidt had begun working in the café in 1936 and was well acquainted with its operation. Schmidt stayed open around the clock in July and August with the help of a staff of 22.

The café became something of an institution for its homemade pies and Schmidt was widely known for cooking with an ever-present cigarette dangling from his lips. He operated the café until his death in 1988 at the age of 70.

Throughout his summers in the park, Nahor Dilatush was active in community affairs and became chairman of the board of trade and eagerly participated in the Lions Club. He was a strong supporter of those eager to open businesses in Waterton and, depending on the individual, offered his personal financial

help. He worked in the park until his death in 1967. He was 73.

Florence Dilatush gradually sold off their residential properties, but managed the store, which became known for its woollens and linens. She retired in 1994 and died in 2003 at the age of 91.

* * *

After accommodations, the most essential tourism businesses in Wateton were restaurants.

Close on the heels of Dewitt Johnson's Tourist Café came Nixon's Waterton Lakes Café, owned and operated by Florence "Ma" Nixon and located to the north of today's Akamina Gifts.

Ma Nixon, who described herself as a Twin Butte housewife, worked in the park beginning in 1919 and signed her lease in 1921. The following summer her husband William began hauling lumber for the building, which was opposite the Hazzard Hotel.

Nixon did so well that by 1928 she was able to enlarge the restaurant building and added booths. Nixon's ads also used of the words "all white help." She offered home-cooked meals and homemade bread, pies and cakes, which she sold to campers and cottagers. Picnic lunches were always available by request.

In 1939 after 20 years in Waterton she retired and

Florence "Ma" Nixon opened her café in 1922 across from the Lakeshore Hotel on Waterton Avenue. She operated the restaurant for many years, finally selling her property to Frank and Linnea Goble in 1941.

Delany's Grocery and Meat Market, now Rocky Mountain Food Mart, was built by Carlson & Hagglund and opened in 1936 on Windflower Avenue. For many years it was open year-round.

in 1941, Nixon sold the café to Linnea and Frank Goble for $4,500. It was promptly renamed Frank's.

Both Linnea and Frank were long-time residents of the park. She was the daughter of Erik and Olga Hagglund and had moved to Waterton in 1931. He was the son of Oliver and Arletta Goble and had been there since 1927. When each finished school in Waterton, Linnea went on to become a teacher while Frank stayed in Waterton, working as a trapper and eventually getting a job as a cook. First working in a relief camp and later a Parks Department work camp, he acquired considerable experience in cooking for large numbers of men, but by 1939 the crew cooking job was finished.

The following spring, the couple rented space in George Delany's grocery store on Windflower Avenue (now Rocky Mountain Food Mart) where Frank established a photo finishing business and sold souvenirs. At the same time, they rented out units in the Rosedale Apartments (216 Mount View Rd.) gaining not only additional income, but more importantly needed experience and an understanding of rental accommodations.

Linnea and Frank Goble

When the opportunity to buy the Nixon restaurant presented itself, the Gobles, although pressed for money, couldn't pass it by and borrowed from family to make the purchase and stock the kitchen.

Frank went into the military in the spring of 1944 and Linnea, by then the mother of small children, was thrown into the restaurant's operation and management under less-than-ideal conditions. Rationing of butter, sugar, coffee and other staples made running a restaurant a challenge during wartime.

In October 1951, the Gobles began building a bigger, more modern restaurant which incorporated an attached retail shop on the south side. The new restaurant was typical of its time, with both booths and a counter with stools. Frank's Café became known as "the café with the grizzly." Both Gobles were expert hunters and many of their trophy specimens, taken from outside the park, were mounted and displayed in the café.

As their restaurant business thrived, the couple decided to get into the motel business, building the Frank-Lin Motel in 1957.

The Gobles went on to become vital members of the community and raise their children in Waterton. They sold the restaurant in the 1970s to Lucy Lee and Co. It was renamed New Frank's.

The Goble's business neighbours next door on Waterton Avenue were the Ellisons, a couple who got into business in Waterton at the urging of relatives.

Dell and Tay Ellison were influenced by Dell's brother-in-law, Isaac L. Allred, who had owned several leases in the park. In 1921 the Ellisons built the first grocery store, on the west side of Waterton Avenue (now a parking lot). A pioneer merchant, Ellison was described by Lethbridge Mayor Dave Elton as being "a man of sterling integrity, well-known and well-liked by all who know him."

The Ellisons built Waterton Motors (now Pat's Wa-

Frank's Restaurant, promoted as "the café with the grizzly bear," replaced Nixon's Café in 1952. Frank Goble learned to cook when he worked on the Chief Mountain Highway crew. Both Frank and his wife Linnea were avid hunters and downed many trophy specimens, which were displayed at their business.

terton) in 1928 and soon added a number of rental cabins to their enterprises. When Isaac Allred moved to Calgary, Dell Ellison took over his swimming pool in 1931, making improvements and renaming it the Crystal Pool. The pool continued to operate until the late-1940s.

The Ellisons, who wintered in California, began selling their Waterton holdings in 1953, starting with the service station, which was purchased by Pat Carnell Jr., a long-time park resident. It was then sold to Butch Sloan of Cardston in 1959, who sold it in 1985 to Pat Seerey, brother of former Bayshore Inn co-owner Mary Kratz. Seerey, in turn, sold the business in 2013 to the Wammes family whose sons Jordon and Tyler operate it.

One of the last of the Ellisons' leases to be sold was

their original grocery store on Waterton Avenue. The store, which also sold china and souvenirs, had been rented by brothers Don and Orzie Steed for two years before they purchased it and Ellison's cabin on Mount View Road in 1958 for $23,000.

Waterton had been a part of the Steeds' summers for more than 10 years. Don Steed, a druggist who worked at Ben Higgs' pharmacy, soon saw the potential in the tourist trade.

"Don needed just two things to get started: some extra capital and someone to run the business for him," Eula Steed wrote in her memoir. Her husband Orzie, Don's brother, was just the man. A school teacher with summers off, Orzie was also an experienced accountant.

Orzie and Eula painted the store white with red trim and gave it one of Waterton's catchiest names, Steed's Holiday Needs. Over the course of its existence, it specialized in penny candies as well as some groceries and souvenirs. "The store had a very humble first year," Eula recalled.

They were encouraged by an Irwin Specialty (Toy) Co. salesman to bolster their inventory. "It was a good thing he came along because it set Don and Orzie to thinking seriously about tourist merchandising," Eula said. "And if they hadn't done that, we would have gone under."

Dell and Tay Ellison and two of their sons.

One summer, the hottest item in town was the floppy rubber sandal known as "thongs" or "flip-flops." Eula Steed, who ran the store, said the salesman told them: "Order big, you'll never regret it."

"We did order several huge boxes of them at the glorious sale price of 59 cents a pair. We sold all of them before we could get our breath, then ordered more, but every time we ordered them the prices went up. Everyone still wanted them, so the Irwin salesman said, double your price, and we did. . . . We sold them for three seasons by the gross."

With their lease expiring in 1966, the Steeds proposed to replace the building with a small store and 22-unit motel. Park officials, who had their eyes on the site for a green space with parking at the rear,

turned them down. After several years of discussion, officials gave them the choice of selling back the lease or building a $100,000 "store complex" development. The Steeds choose the former and the park tore down the building and constructed a parking lot.

Another Waterton business that had its beginning in family ties was the Good Hunting China Shop (now Akamina Gifts).

When Ada Kemmis sold the Ballinacor Hotel in 1945, she bought the Beach Café across the street and had it renovated to become the Good Hunting China Shop, running it with the help of her daughter, Aileen Rhodes. Aileen and her husband Dusty Rhodes, a Lethbridge banker, lived in a small apartment at the rear of the store.

The shop became well known for its quality merchandise, which included bone china, earthenware, glass and silver. The public was cautioned with a polite notice: "Lovely to look at, delightful to hold, but if you should drop it, consider it sold."

According to Rhodes' nephew, Brian "Barney" Reeves, who worked at the store, two complete patterns of dinnerware china were always in stock, and a shipping service was available, on request. Reeves, a "china boy" in 1956 and 1957, was responsible for unpacking the stock in the spring and repacking it in the fall. He said he sometimes demonstrated the strength of the bone china to customers by standing on a turned-down cup.

Good quality china was in high demand by tourists. Druggist Ben Higgs, down the street in the Stanley, had "the largest display in Canada of world-famous Irish Belleek china" with an exclusive on that product.

At the south end of the block, Barney Reeves' parents, Harry and Sibyl Reeves, went back into business after a brief retirement from their auto bungalow operation. Harry Reeves had opened Lakeshore Bungalows in 1948. He and Sibyl sold the business in 1960.

The Good Hunting China Shop became a "must visit" for tourists who favoured imported tableware. A heavy snowstorm in the winter of 1950 caused major damage to the structure, but most of the merchandise had been packed away the previous fall. However, any tourists who broke a piece china were told to consider it sold.

They built Reeves Corner House, at Waterton Avenue and Cameron Falls Drive, in 1962. It housed a china and gift shop, a beauty parlour, and McGuire's Woolen Shop, a second location for McGuire's of Lethbridge. The building's extensive exterior rock work was said to have been done by Harry Reeves.

Aileen Rhodes retired in 1965 and the Reeves retired again in 1972. The nature of the business had begun to change, according to Barney Reeves, who noted "there were more lookers and touchers and less desire for quality merchandise."

When the Reeves sold the building and the business, it was renamed Red Rock Gifts and was operated by Doris and Bill Huculak.

McGuire's continued to operate through the summer of 1987 and was then supplanted by R&W Wool Co. owned by Rod and Wendy West, who bought the building and converted the south side into a restaurant, Zum's Eatery and Mercantile. When the Wests retired in 2005, the building was purchased by Dave and Carol Cruikshank of Lethbridge.

* * *

A proposal to build a "moving picture theatre" popped up very early in Waterton's history, April 1918. Lula Nielson, a Cardston theatre operator, hoped to build a cinema at the north end of Waterton Avenue (now a parking lot). Although she made an application for a lease and submitted a rough building plan, she did not follow through.

Eight years later another theatre hopeful, William Peacock of Carmangay, Alberta, made an application to build at the other end of the street (114 Waterton Ave.).

"Movies are to be the next addition to Waterton's already long list of amusements and recreations," an August 1926 newspaper reported. "Mr. Peacock has not yet decided whether to build this year or next spring."

But Peacock waited too long. The lot was leased by the Dilatushes, who later built a butcher shop on the site.

That fall Dell Ellison was given permission to

The movie theatre in Wateton, built in 1935, showed films six days a week with matinees on Saturdays. It also sometimes provided space to roller-skate.

use his store to show movies, but only in the winter months. In 1928 at Ellison's request, the architectural division drew up plans for a major theatre building that would have been a credit to any town in the province. It was to have included a 154-seat theatre with an orchestra pit and stage, dressing rooms, hotel rooms, restaurant, market and a beauty parlour. Although Ellison had hoped to tear down his existing store and replace it with this theatre, he was not able to find the money and the plan was shelved.

Peacock, however, had not given up on the idea of showing movies in Waterton. While he couldn't erect his own building, he was a licensed projectionist and obtained permission from park officials in July 1930 to show movies in the school. At the time, all aspects of theatre operations were regulated by provincial legislation. With only 85 motion picture theatres in the entire province, this was quite a coup for a summer resort.

On July 25, 1930, *The Green Goddess* starring Oscar-winning actor George Arliss had two showings in Waterton—both were "packed to the doors."

The following year Gordon Brewerton and his brothers, who owned theatres in both Cardston and Raymond, Alberta, became interested in Waterton.

Brewerton applied for a lease on the northeast corner of Cameron Falls Drive and Windflower Avenue in 1932, but with economic conditions still

tenuous due to the Depression, it took longer to build a theatre than anticipated. Brewerton proposed using a temporary structure called an "airdome," but park officials turned down the idea. Finally in December 1934, the building's foundation was ready for the 13-by 21-metre (44- by 70-foot) structure, which was constructed by local contractors Carl Carlson and Erik Hagglund at a cost of $6,500.

The theatre opened June 13, 1935, with seating for 300. Movies were shown daily at 7 and 9 p.m., except Sundays, with a 3 p.m. matinee on Mondays. Since the Prince of Wales Hotel, which had provided the town with electricity, was closed during the Depression years, Brewerton was forced to provide his own light plant, but it was not an insurmountable obstacle and authorities felt the movie theatre was an asset to the park. The theatre proved to be a popular addition to evening entertainment.

Brewerton decided to try something different in 1940 and the theatre was used for afternoon roller-skating. Although he had hoped to include this as a Sunday activity as well, park officials denied him the privilege.

Movies, it seemed, were not financially successful. The following year no movies were shown, much to the disappointment of park residents and visitors. But in 1945 roller-skating was available in the daytime, with movies shown at night.

Wayne Sommerfeldt, who grew up in the park, remembered the skating: "We roller-skated on the old type of skates that you screwed onto the soles of your shoes, and we skated to music, and then at night they would set up the chairs and have a show."

The Brewerton family continued to operate the theatre until 1975, with Gordon's wife Lottie taking over following his death in 1959.

Larry and Edith Becker, Pincher Creek theatre owner-operators, purchased the theatre in 1976 and changed the name to Alpine Cinema and later to Waterton Lakes Opera House. The couple later parted just before celluloid movies were eliminated in favour of digital technology, which required a substantial investment in new equipment. After 35 years and the best popcorn in town, 2011 was the last season for movies on film.

The next year the theatre was renovated by a Twin Butte restaurateur to accommodate a Mexican restaurant, bar and place of stage entertainment on a rent-to-own basis. In the summer of 2014, a patio was added for outside seating on the south side. Finally in 2019 the theatre was sold by Larry and Andrea Becker and movies returned to Waterton, albeit on a schedule and with conditions that conformed to COVID-19 health restrictions.

* * *

Boat excursions on the Waterton lakes may have begun as early as 1915, when Jack Hazzard introduced a small steam launch to ferry visitors around. The following year, Carl Danielson, a blacksmith and carpenter, operated a boat for Hazzard which was the subject of some safety concerns.

Silas Carpenter, commissioner of police, expressed his alarm about Danielson and the boat in an April 1916 letter to parks commissioner J.B. Harkin: "He is said to be a drinking character and very often under the influence of liquor while running this boat which is a pleasure craft, said to be often taxed beyond its capacity. If this state of things

Henry Hanson poses in his boat Linnea *at Goat Haunt. Walter Foster and his dog are in the smaller, unnamed row boat. Foster was helping build the Goathaunt Chalet for Hanson and Les Morrow.*

continues there is likely to be a serious accident. I would, therefore, respectfully recommend that the person employed by Mr. Hazzard to operate this boat be required to pass an examination before being allowed to act as engineer on it and the number of passengers carried on this boat be limited in its capacity."

Carpenter's worries about Danielson were eased somewhat by the passage of Prohibition that summer, and the number of days the weather permitted boat tours. Danielson ran trips according to demand.

It was true that Danielson routinely piled in the passengers. One newspaper report said the craft, about the size of a small lifeboat, was loaded with 16 people on many of these trips. But since no one drowned and he had no accidents, visitors didn't seem to mind. Danielson continued to operate the boat until at least 1919.

The early years of the excursion boat business were marked by plenty of competition. One of the pioneers was Henry Hanson, who had begun running boat excursions as early as 1916 and found a niche by personally providing narration on his tours. A knowledgeable individual, he pointed out places of interest as the boat cruised over the international border on Upper Waterton Lake and into the northern-most part of Glacier National Park.

Hanson, former owner of the sawmill near the Maskinonge, got into the tour boat business for two reasons: he had eight children and a wife to support and because he already owned a boat large enough to take people out on the lake. The 12-metre (40-foot) boat *Gertrude* had been built for use at the sawmill.

Linnea, named for Hanson's second daughter, had been built specifically for use in Waterton. The craft was an uncovered launch with a powerful 60-horsepower gasoline engine.

Hanson, however, was an individual who was thick on ideas but thin on cash. After a number of short-lived ventures, he turned his attention to the head of Upper Waterton Lake, obtaining a permit from Glacier to land at Goat Haunt.

He transported passengers between Waterton townsite and Goat Haunt at the rate of $1 per person return or 75 cents one way. The traffic, which depended on trail riders originating in the south, failed to generate much income for Hanson because of the limited days the trails were free of snow and open to horses.

Still running tourist excursions in 1923, Hanson

Walter Foster takes a rest from his log building at Goathaunt Chalet, which opened in 1923 as a dancing venue and restaurant. The chalet eventually became the Glacier park terminus of Motor Vessel International cruises.

got permission to build a chalet at the head of the lake but wasn't in a financial position to make much progress until he took on a partner, Les Morrow.

Morrow had come to Waterton from Spring Coulee, Alberta, to work on oil wells in the Akamina Valley. An enterprising bachelor, Morrow escorted fishing parties out on the lake, hauled freight and took on whatever physical labour he could find. The opportunity to become the part-owner of a business at the head of the lake seemed to be well timed and he threw in with Hanson, providing a cash infusion for Hanson's newest scheme.

The Alleas *and sister tour boat* Fairy *were among the first used on Upper Waterton Lake. Passengers sat under a roof, which protected them from the sun.*

After an array of delays, the Goathaunt Chalet was finally opened to the public in 1924. Hanson and Morrow rented row boats by the hour at the chalet, which was, at best, only a rustic building where groceries and other items were sold. They also ferried passengers and freight to and from the Waterton townsite.

In the summer of 1925 and in need of more money, Hanson and Morrow sold their boats and equipment to the Park Saddle Horse Co., which established a tent camp at the site. The deal consisted of the *Linnea*, an unnamed 5.1-metre (17-foot) motor boat and four row boats.

Morrow bought back the lot in October 1925, but it was too late for Hanson. He died that fall and Morrow was left to run the business on his own. He took over where Hanson left off and had a permit issued in his name for the exclusive right to land boats at Goat Haunt and continued to operate the chalet. It was a tidy arrangement which conveniently served the Park Saddle Horse Co.

Charles "Dippy" Carnell went into competition with Morrow in 1926. He had two small excursion boats, *Alleas* and *Fairy*, and some innovative ideas for his business. He and an associate, Val Pelletier, built two attractive floating boat docks which featured a

Les Morrow

covered loading area, ticket office, repair room and accessory shop.

Carnell spruced up the *Alleas*, repainting the hull and refitting the engine, arranging the seats to ensure comfort, and installed folding glass windows in the event of inclement weather. As a touch of uniformity, he outfitted his employees with hats labelled "boatman."

Carnell's idea for his floating docks was not well thought out. In early December 1926 a windstorm with 145 km/h (90 m.p.h.) gusts that wreaked havoc on the unfinished Prince of Wales Hotel also did major damage to his docks. They were torn loose of their moorings and blown out on the lake, where they were, the newspaper reported, "smashed to atoms by the high waves."

So intense was the wind "the entire surface of the lake was like a huge blizzard, the spray being whipped along at a terrible rate of speed for hundreds of yards inshore. Trees were blown down everywhere and outhouses are scattered all over the townsite." The next spring, Carnell rebuilt a similar single dock which he could pull ashore in the fall.

Meanwhile, Les Morrow's business was doing well. His brother Tom, who had just moved his family to

Waterton from Spring Coulee, joined him to expand the excursion business and develop the freight work.

There was a surprising amount of work for the two boatmen. They hauled hay and supplies to the park ranger and saddle horse company at Goat Haunt, they ferried horse riders to Waterton to see a bit of Canada and take in the dances, then took them back to their tent camp after midnight. And they had regular day customers who they toured around the lake.

Tom Morrow operated his own boat, the *Miss Waterton*. It was the first of three successive boats with that name. The 6.7-metre (22-foot), two-tonne boat had been purchased from Tom Scott, a Waterton cabin owner and Pincher Creek resident.

In the summer of 1927, construction of a new 250-passenger *Motor Vessel International* added to Morrow's freight business. The major pieces of the *International*, which had been constructed in Kalispell, Montana, were knocked down and hauled to Waterton, then shipped to Goat Haunt, where they were reassembled. It meant a substantial amount of freighting for the Morrows, who built a scow which they could pull behind the *Linnea* for large loads.

Charles "Dippy" Carnell's floating boat dock was the first marina building, but was wrecked when a December 1926 windstorm smashed it "to atoms."

When the *International* went into service in June 1928, it was unmatched in Waterton for size and luxury. Passengers could move about, finding sun, shade or protection from inclement weather. Built specifically to carry passengers on this sometimes rough lake, it provided a safe, comfortable ride under the capable hands of a professional captain who was Coast Guard certified for both Canada and the United States.

"It was posh to ride the big boat," recalled Isabell Morrow Holladay, whose father Tom and uncle Les were among the first to suffer business losses once the *International* began operating. The *Linnea* was declared too old to be safe for excursions and became strictly a freight boat. But it was only with Morrow's permission that the *International* was initially al-

lowed to land at the head of the lake. He still held the sole landing concession.

The competition from the *International* drove Carnell from the boat business and soon after he ran into financial difficulties. By 1930 he sold his boats to George Baker, whose water-based business depended on rentals rather than excursions.

Carnell tried to establish another business in 1932, but his venture in retailing out of the MacLean building north of the dance pavilion failed. Newly married and in financial difficulty, he left the park the next year and eventually moved to Fort St. James, British Columbia.

The decline of the Park Saddle Horse Co.'s camp at Goat Haunt hurt Les Morrow's operation. In 1937, after more than a decade in the boat business, Morrow sold out to Baker and left Waterton for good. He moved to British Columbia, where he worked as a builder until his death in 1956.

The *International* curtailed cruises during the Second World War due to gasoline rationing, the U.S. restriction against passengers unloading at Goat Haunt, and a lack of qualified boat captains as they were needed for naval service. The big boat was dry-docked for the war years.

Small, more fuel-efficient excursion boats, however, operated during the war. The *Donna Kay*, introduced in 1944, was skippered by Gerald "Slim" Udal. It was one of several small sightseeing boats used to fill the gap created by the absence the *International*.

Cliff Ott's seven-passenger mahogany Chris-Craft *Deeidra*, the first of two boats with that name honouring his daughter, was another popular excursion boat used during the war. In June 1945, Udal acquired a boat once owned by Doug G. Oland. It was a beautiful, white 25-passenger launch Udal called *Miss Waterton*.

With the end of the war, visitors had three tour boats to choose from and competition for excursions

The Motor Vessel International *was built at the head of Upper Waterton Lake, where it continues to be stored each winter. It went into service in June 1928 and over the years has carried many Canadian and U.S. dignitaries.*

began in earnest. The *International* was the largest and only one to have landing rights in the United States; the *Deeidra* was by far the smallest but fastest, capable of making the 22.5-kilometre (14-mile) return trip to Goat Haunt in just 40 minutes; and the *Miss Waterton* was the newest, boasting a skipper, Slim Udal, with personality plus.

Udal was one of those rare individuals who was universally liked and who had more than the average number of good friends. The fact that he'd saved the life of Nahor Dilatush during a bear hunt stood him in good stead as an outdoorsman, as well.

When he came to Waterton in the late 1920s, Udal was hired by George Baker to drive a truck and do the mechanical work at Baker's garage. But Udal was a man of many talents who tried his hand at several jobs. In 1932, he became a licensed government guide and worked for a saddle horse company.

In 1937 Udal married June Perrett of Mountain View, Alberta, whom he had met when she worked in the park. The couple moved into the "Victoria Cottage" (202 Evergreen Ave.), which became their summer home. They spent their winters in Victoria, British Columbia.

Slim and June were away from Waterton for a few years doing war work, but when they returned the introduction of *Miss Waterton* re-established Udal as a major player in the boat business. His fleet also included the *Eileen*, named after his mother, plus 12 inboard motor rental fishing boats, a very up-to-date improvement in rentals.

Udal's round-trip tour boat fare was $1 per person, 50 cents per person less than the *International*, but without U.S. landing rights. His business benefitted both by being a good operation and from his personable manner.

"Slim was very well liked," his widow June said, noting that he was a man who had always loved the water and this lake. Raised in Maple Creek, Saskatchewan, Udal found no pleasure in living on the bald prairie. By comparison, Waterton was paradise to him.

He hired boat boys to help with the rental boats and they vied for his approval. "They all wanted to say they were the Number 1 Boat Boy because they all wanted his admiration. The kids just loved him," June said.

In 1949, Cliff Ott built a new *Deeidra*, a 9.7-me-

Cliff Ott, who owned and operated the Deeidra, *ran a tour boat business in Waterton for many years.*

tre (32-foot) semi-enclosed boat with two Chrysler Crown motors capable of making 56 km/h (35 mph). The boat, with room for 36 passengers, made hourly trips to the head of Upper Waterton Lake. When Ott decided to get out of the excursion boat business in 1955, he found a willing buyer in Stan Kretz.

A tragic boating accident in June 1958 set Waterton residents on their ears. Slim Udal was killed while fine tuning his self-built speed boat, which he was preparing for upcoming events in conjunction with Waterton Days, an annual festival. After his death, the haunting presence of his boats on the lake did nothing to lessen the sense of loss among those who knew him.

A year or two before he was killed, Udal had sold *Miss Waterton* to Bill Boyce of Lethbridge, who in turn sold it to Stan Kretz in 1959. Kretz also purchased *Eileen* following Udal's fatal accident.

Miss Waterton continued to be used as a tour boat until 1965, when it was sold to Art McMartin and

taken to Shuswap Lake in British Columbia. The fate of the *Eileen*, however, was somewhat more heart-warming. After many years of occasional use, the boat was purchased by Locke Marshall of Mountain View, Alberta, nephew of the Udals, who restored it to its original glory for his personal use.

The purchase of Ott's *Deeidra* became a genuine starting point for Stan Kretz's excursion boat business, which more than 50 years later is still going strong.

Kretz, a school principal, first came to Waterton in 1949 and got a job with the government as a summer fish warden at Cameron Lake. He returned every year through 1953. His wife Vivian joined him, and both became enamoured with the area after having spent most of their lives on the prairies.

The Kretzes became interested in having their own business in the townsite and in 1954 rented five motor boats and one canoe to visitors. Although the boat rental business was not singularly lucrative, it was a part of several other businesses they tried. They also owned and rented out the "Cozy Cabins" on Mount View Road starting in 1956. For a brief time, while still renting the boats, they owned and operated a grocery called Stan's Store (114 Waterton Ave.) featuring "broasted" chicken.

Beginning in 1961, Stan Kretz, by now the father of three, devoted his summer energies entirely to the boat business. He had both rentals and the excursion boats *Deeidra*, *Miss Waterton* and, on a smaller scale, the *Eileen*.

As a novel way to attract customers to the marina, Kretz came up with the idea of setting up speakers and a record player to broadcast music while the *Deeidra* was at dock. A favourite record was *Goodnight Irene*, which he played over and over.

Kretz's boating business, Waterton Inter-Nation Shoreline Cruises, soon expanded with the purchase of the 40-passenger, 12-metre (39-foot) *Wanda Mae* in 1965. Boat-builder Art Burch constructed the vessel for Kretz at his Flathead Lake, Montana, facility. The boat was sold in the mid-1990s to Doug Averill of Flathead Lake Lodge in Montana.

The *Roddy Paul* was added in 1970. This 50-passenger, 12.5-metre (41-foot) long boat has twin Perkins diesel engines. It was partially built by Canoe Cove boat works on Vancouver Island and shipped to Art Burch for completion, then trucked to Waterton.

The most popular name for a tour boat was Miss Waterton. *The first was owned by the Morrow brothers, top photo; the second was owned by Slim Udal, middle photo; and the current boat, below, is owned by Waterton Inter-Nation Shoreline Cruises.*

Kretz retired as principal of Calgary's North Haven Elementary School in 1971 and concentrated on the boat business.

He sold the *Deeidra* in 1972 to Ken Hurlburt, a Waterton regular who, after about a decade, sold it to Cliff Ott's son.

Kretz got a 10-year lake touring and boat rental concession in 1972. He continued to rent his five motor boats and single canoe but was now building the excursion business. The *Connie Marlene* was put into service in 1973, having been constructed as a duplicate of the *Roddy Paul* by Canoe Cove boat works from the same boat mould.

The third *Miss Waterton*, a 125-passenger 17.3-metre (57-foot) long vessel was introduced in 1984. It was also built by Canoe Cove, but this time with the assistance of the Kretz's son Rod, who worked on all aspects of the boat's construction.

Stan and Vivian Kretz

Kretz's chief competition was the *International*, which was still the only tour boat allowed to land at Goat Haunt. But in 1986 he bought the *International* from Glacier Park Boat Co., which had operated it for a decade. With it, Kretz also acquired the concession to land his boats at Goat Haunt.

Parks Canada privatized the Waterton marina in 1993 when it granted Waterton Inter-Nation Shoreline Cruise Co. an exclusive 25-year lease in exchange for $1 million worth of improvements to the facility.

When the lease was renewed, the second generation of Kretzes—Rod and Nancy Kretz and Wanda (nee Kretz) and Ed Robinson—had surrendered the business to the third generation of boat operators, their children. Stan Kretz died in 1989 and Vivian in 2006.

* * *

Saddle horses have been long associated with backcountry use in Waterton, and trail riding is one of the oldest recreational pursuits in the park. Unlike in Glacier, where saddle horse tours lasted several days and were a key attraction, in Waterton it remained primarily a day activity. The difference, in general, can be attributed to the small size of Waterton and number of relatively short trails. Backcountry lakes and camp sites are not difficult for hikers to reach under their own steam.

One of the first horse concessions in Waterton was run by the Morris family, which operated under the name of Morris Saddle Horse Co.

Mr. and Mrs. Jean Morris came to the park from Michigan via Pincher Station with five sons: Scotty, Cliff, Eugene, Billy and Clarence. The boys varied their duties between the saddle horse business and government employment. They ran a guiding business together from 1924 to 1928, until a variety of circumstances split the brothers. Cliff continued in the horse business until 1942.

It wasn't long before others got into the saddle horse business. While there were several outfits in the area which specialized in guiding hunters and sightseers, the park horse operators catered only to "dudes," visitors interested in sightseeing and sometimes fishing. Several horse concessions vied for customers at a central hitching rack in the town, east of today's Mormon church (Windflower and Clematis avenues).

At the central hitching rack wranglers were on hand to help visitors and to guide them on the trails, if requested. Each evening, the horses were taken out of the townsite to overnight quarters near the government compound and each morning they were returned to the hitching rack.

Rates were set by the government and varied according to time and distance. In 1930, a saddle horse could be rented for $4.50 a day and guided trips from the townsite ranged from $3 (to Bertha Lake return) to $9 (return to the head of Pass Creek).

Various residents of Twin Butte had horse concessions in the park.

George Riviere gave it a try in 1930 but sold out the next season after building a barn in the vicinity of Middle Waterton Lake. Jean Rankin, a Twin Butte spinster, bought out Riviere and took on Ed J. Schrempp as a partner. The Rankin and Schrempp business was known as the V Saddle Horse Co. A fire destroyed their stable in November 1937, but they rebuilt the following summer and Rankin continued to rent horses for years after Schrempp's departure in 1942.

Cliff Morris also left the park that year, selling to

The first horse rental concessions were located near what is today the government compound, across from Middle Waterton Lake. Eventually, stables were moved to other locations: on the Middle Lake, Red Rock Canyon and east of the park cemetery. The latter, Alpine Stables, was opened in 1969 by the Barrus family and is still in business.

S.J. Wacher, who operated under the name of Lakeside Saddle Horse Co.

The horse business had great appeal for visiting servicemen who came to Waterton during the Second World War. For many, it was their first opportunity to experience the mountains, as well as equine pleasures.

Meanwhile at Red Rock Canyon, a horse concession was operated by siblings Bessie and Don Vroom in 1940 and 1941. They kept their horses on the west side of the creek, near a log warden station, while the Vrooms lived in a tent in the nearby campground.

Following the Second World War, business ownership changed. After 20 years, Jean Rankin sold out to Andy Russell in 1951. Russell also bought the Wacher outfit and consolidated the business into the Skyline Pack Train and Saddle Horse Co.

His facility was located on Middle Waterton Lake within sight of the Prince of Wales Hotel. It included a cabin, a large barn, bunkhouse and commissary for the wranglers. Russell spent a few winters at the site but found it was an awful place: "God, that wind used to blow the snow down off the lake and, holy mackerel! I can remember 15 feet [4.6 metres] of snow in front of my barn."

When Russell took over the horse operation, the

Andy Russell

hitching rack in the town was eliminated so customers had to go to his barn to rent horses. He made a name for himself not only as a Waterton saddle horse operator, but also as an area guide, naturalist, lecturer and writer. He eventually went on to become a well-known conservationist, popular author and filmmaker.

Russell was born in Lethbridge in 1915 and raised 19 kilometres (12 miles) north of the park. He went to work for guide-outfitter Bert Riggall in 1936, eventually marrying the boss's daughter, Kathleen. From 1936 to 1960, Russell was a licensed guide in Waterton taking many famous individuals into the backcountry, including Viscount Alexander of Tunis, then Canada's governor general, in 1951. Russell left Waterton in 1957 to pursue broader interests outside the park, including the pack train business specializing in camera hunters and fishing parties in the summer, and big game hunters in the fall.

Dave Simpson, Russell's foreman for three years, filled the gap, renamed the outfit Timberline Saddle Horses and for a while was the sole saddle horse concessioner in Waterton.

After a few years absence, a saddle horse concession at Red Rock Canyon was seen by park authorities as desirable so visitors would have easy way to access more of the backcountry. A call for tenders

117

Those wishing to fish at Crypt Lake, 20 kilometres (13 miles) by trail from the townsite on the east side of Upper Waterton Lake, often chose to ride horses, which swam across the Narrows to reach the trail head. Riders, saddles and other gear were taken across in a boat.

went out. Simpson and partner Edward D. Burton submitted a bid based on their already established business near the townsite and were granted a five-year licence of occupation in 1960. They built a two-bedroom residence, without water, and a barn and corral for about 25 horses near Red Rock Canyon.

The location of the new Crandell campground, some distance from the old Red Rock campground where the horses were located, was expected to hurt the horse business. Permission to move the corral closer to the new campground was denied by officials.

In 1964, Simpson began negotiations to sell Timberline Saddle Horses to Dee Olsen of Leavitt, Alberta, whose silent partner was his brother-in-law, Dee Barrus of Spring Coulee. Olsen ran the stable closest to town while Barrus spent the next four

Dee Barrus

years running the Red Rock operation.

The last year horses were rented from the Red Rock Canyon location was 1967, and two years later even the warden's residence was removed. Although horses continue to be used in that area, they are trucked to the trail head and not allowed to graze overnight.

When a call for tenders for the saddle horse concession went out in late 1968, Dee Barrus was the successful bidder. It was the beginning of Alpine Stables, a multi-generational business.

"We built the stable building in 1969, stick by stick," said Lorna Barrus, Dee's wife.

A challenge for the Barruses was a change in requirements for pasturing horses. No longer were the rental horses allowed to graze on park land. Previously, each evening the horses were trailed to an area known as the "badlands," northeast of Blakiston

Creek, and rounded up each morning to be saddled at the stable. The new rules meant feed had to be brought in and the horses kept overnight at the stable.

Except for a brief period when the Barruses handed over operation of Alpine Stables to a potential buyer who failed to live up to an agreement, they have been "the" horse people in the park. Their daughter Deb Watson and her family have taken over the day-to-day management of the staff and horses.

The Barruses have seen many changes during their tenure in the park. At one time trail rides to Crypt Lake, on the east side of Upper Waterton Lake, were conducted by swimming the horses across the Narrows and transporting the people to the Bosporus by boat, where they saddled up. Horses could be corralled near the end of the trail or left overnight at the trail head. The Crypt Lake trail head corral was removed in 1975. Today, people wishing to ride to Crypt Lake must begin the trip from the Wishbone trail head, off Chief Mountain Highway, and return the same day.

At Cameron Lake, a small corral was available near the old warden's cabin (now under the management of the Alpine Club of Canada) to keep horses overnight after a trip over the Alderson-Carthew trail or to Wall Lake, British Columbia. Removal of the corral in the late 1990s ended that opportunity. Today, trucks and trailers are required to transport either animals or riders to and from Cameron Lake to begin that ride. Horses are no longer allowed on the Wall Lake trail.

The most dramatic event during the Barruses' tenure was the 2017 Kenow forest fire which burned the entire facility to the ground following an evacuation of all humans and domestic animals. By that time the facility was the property of the government, which

Timberline Saddle Horses was located near the north shore of Middle Waterton Lake. Owner Dave Simpson adjusts the bridle on a customer's horse.

was obliged to rebuild to fulfill its licence of occupation commitment to the concessioner, the Barruses. Due to environmental and wildlife concerns, the saddle horse operation did not fully resume until 2020.

* * *

Despite the challenges they face, Waterton's seasonal businesses still remain largely family operations, a credit to their entrepreneurial spirit. For returning visitors, there's comfort in knowing the owners and being recognized as a valued customer. The repeat business is part of what makes for the special experience that is a trip to Waterton.

Wind provides an additional hazard on Waterton's course and the views can be distracting, but there's something in the location that makes golfers want to return to better their scores.

Chapter 4

Golf Course
Breaking 100

Golfers who come to Waterton soon learn that playing the course is as much about the park experience as the game itself.

In a sport where every player is afforded silence while swinging or putting, the Waterton version of the game has the distraction of its magnificent scenery.

Here's a place where players can spot as many wild animals in four hours chasing after a little ball on groomed grass as they can see in twice that time on a mountain trail. If players are lucky, the roaming wildlife means a short pause in play; for the unlucky, it can mean abandoning a ball and making a quick retreat.

Then there is the wind, or occasionally the lack of it, creating conditions which result in different outcomes daily.

How Waterton came to have the first golf course built completely at the expense of the Canadian government for a national park is a story that begins more than a century ago, in 1921.

The announcement that Waterton was to have a golf course was a signal to southern Albertans that the park was being noticed in Ottawa and recognized as a popular tourist playground, one to rival other national parks. Until then, publicly funded amenities in Waterton were slim in comparison to the federal government largesse shown Banff and Jasper national parks to the north.

Building the course was a timely idea. With the First World War and the subsequent influenza pandemic over, Canadians were ready to get on with their lives. Both men and women embraced the game for its social as well as physical benefits.

The Parks Branch had already acquired some experience in running a golf course in Banff when it sent William E. Thomson, the golf professional there, to Waterton to find a site for the new course. Thomson spent two days during the spring of 1921 looking

William E. Thomson

at possible locations. He chose a bench on the south side of Crandell Mountain with a fine view of both mountains and lakes. Thomson was enthusiastic about the site, telling *The Lethbridge Herald* that, in his opinion, it would be one of the best courses in the country and would take a minimum of work to build.

The Scottish-born Thomson spoke from experience. Highly regarded by his bosses, he had designed the original nine holes of the Banff Springs Hotel golf course, was involved in its construction and had been the professional there since the course opened in 1911.

Banff's course was taken over by the Parks Branch in 1917, not returning to Canadian Pacific Railway control until 1927. Leaving course construction in Waterton to others, Thomson returned to Banff. He spent the better part of 40 years in that park, working as a course designer, teaching professional, club maker, greenskeeper and caddy master.

Shortly after Thomson's departure from Waterton, a crew of men and horses set to work on a 2,480-metre (2,712-yard), nine-hole golf course. Key among them was Edward H. "Teddy" Wagstaff, a man who proved to be the right person in the right place and time. While he is often credited with designing and building the course, Wagstaff was but one of many, though he was among the first involved.

English born, Teddy Wagstaff was a First World War veteran who had been hired as a clerk in the park superintendent's office in 1920. He had come to Canada in 1900 as a 13-year-old to work for his uncle in Gleichen, Alberta. He later moved to Calgary, where he found work as a carpenter until war broke out, when he enlisted in the 12th Mounted Rifles.

Wagstaff was sent overseas in 1915, where his regiment joined the fight along with the Fort Garry Horse, a Winnipeg-based cavalry regiment. During

Horse-drawn equipment was used to cut out the Waterton golf course from a mountain hillside locale.

a battle in France, Wagstaff saved a man's life. The story goes that during the height of the fighting, he heard someone call for help. A man he didn't know was badly wounded when his horse had been shot out from under him. Wagstaff scooped the man up and they rode double until Wagstaff's horse was also killed. Wounded himself, Wagstaff awoke in a field hospital with no recollection of how he got there. He hadn't even caught the name of his fellow soldier who he had rescued or learned his fate.

Wagstaff was promoted to corporal and stayed in the army until he was discharged in 1919. His return to Calgary was bittersweet. He was home, but his wife had left him and the hustle and bustle of postwar Calgary was a disturbing place for a shell-shocked veteran. He decided to apply for a clerical job far from the city, in Waterton.

According to his grandson Quenton Wagstaff, Teddy was ready to outline his qualifications for the Waterton job, but it was really a waste of breath. The unnamed interviewer said, "You don't know who I am, do you?" Wagstaff did not. The interviewer was the man whose life Wagstaff had saved in France. There was no question the job would go to anyone else.

Although Teddy Wagstaff was hired as a park

Edward H. "Teddy" Wagstaff served as a sergeant in the prewar militia before going overseas in the First World War.

clerk, in those days being a clerk didn't necessarily mean being tied to a desk. Many of those classified as "clerks" spent the bulk of their working hours outdoors. As a fellow who had many interests and talents, not the least of which was sports, Wagstaff knew golf and was soon involved in building the course Thomson had laid out. He became a sub-foreman during the course construction.

The golf course construction crew used horse-drawn hay mowers to cut swaths for fairways and, where necessary, cut away the brush by hand. They also built a road and parking lot. Tee boxes were built of baked clay. Each was equipped with a white wooden container for sand and water used by the player to form a temporary tee to elevate the ball. The yardage of each hole was painted on the container. Oiled sand "greens," typical of the time, completed the layout. The nine-hole links opened June 15, 1922.

True to form, Wagstaff organized what is believed to have been the first Waterton golf tournament with the help of Dr. G.A. Dubuc of Pincher Creek. The pair and about 30 invited players from clubs in Blairmore, Pincher Creek, Fort Macleod and Lethbridge participated in the Sunday, Aug. 12, 1923, event. Despite an exceptionally strong wind, the tournament began at 10:30 a.m. The competition was an 18-hole handicap, which meant playing the nine-hole course twice. The contingent from Blairmore in the Crowsnest Pass took top honours.

In the afternoon a two-ball foursome was played as was a ladies' competition and a single nine-hole competition. The tournament was reported to be one of the most successful of its kind in southern Alberta and every competitor strongly praised the beautiful, scenic course. Prizes were six golf balls for first place, four golf balls for second and two balls for third. With only a few exceptions, tournaments have been held annually for 100 years.

The course had its pluses and minuses. For players, the view of the mountains was excellent, but added to the difficulty of keeping one's eye on the ball. There was no shelter from the wind, which on some days provided an added if negative dimension to play. And although at the time it had neither water hazards nor bunkers, it was quite a challenging course.

Anglican Archdeacon Cecil "Swanny" Swanson, a park cabin owner and golfer, described the course as humbling: "The old golf course was a tricky nine-hole job with sand greens, made tolerable by a sweeper of matting. I once landed on the green in two—an Arnold Palmer feat—but it was in September and there was no upkeep of the facilities, so the sand greens were rough with deer and bear tracks plus some human footprints. I was down in 12 [strokes]—hard on one's power of expression!"

Teddy Wagstaff was appointed course professional and was, in effect, in charge. He sold tickets, accounted for the money, scheduled tee times when necessary and sold golf balls. He could also provide instruction or assistance to players. With his wide, friendly smile and natural ability to please, he quickly became a favourite with everyone—a true park ambassador.

In the early days of the golf course, respectable women wore either bloomers or skirts to play. The woman above was purposely posed going the wrong way on the first tee so the publicity photograph would show the yardage and direction. Below, an unidentified male golfer at the same tee box.

Early tournaments were started at the first hole and contestants played the course in numeric order, which sometimes caused bottlenecks and a bit of a wait for golfers.

When not playing host to visitors, Wagstaff worked with the grounds crew to ensure the course was maintained. The key challenges were the climate and geology. Since there was no irrigation system in the early days of the course, the men had to rely on rainfall, and since underlying the grass was porous alluvial gravel originally washed down from Mount Crandell, most of the rainfall was wicked away from the roots of the grass. Wagstaff earned widespread respect for his many skills and knowledge. A 1923 the newspaper reported, "Taking into consideration the course is only 12 months old . . . Teddie [sic] deserves lots of praise."

Wagstaff also played the game whenever possible, so fellow golfers were delighted to learn he carded the first hole-in-one on the course in August 1923, an honour befitting his position. Walter Jackson of Pincher Creek, whose father had just built a cabin in the townsite on Evergreen Avenue and who was a golfing regular, vouched for Wagstaff's feat on hole No. 2, in those days an 82-yard par 3.

The Lethbridge Herald made much of this achievement and with good humour noted that "there may be a lot of honour making this hole-in-one, but in Alberta it comes rather expensive as according to an old-fashioned custom which evidentially originates from Scotland, the performer has to buy his opponent a bottle of the best and Teddie [sic], like a true sport, is carrying out his end of the program to Jackson, as he says, 'What's expense compared to glory?'"

As for rushing out to pay his debt, Wagstaff didn't have to worry. Prohibition was in effect until May 1924. In fact, he couldn't even buy Jackson a cup of tea at the clubhouse since it was just being constructed by Cardston contractors Doug G. Oland and James C. Scott. No sooner was the clubhouse built when it was quickly enlarged, the work completed late in the summer of 1924.

The clubhouse contained dressing rooms and, as a concession to occasional nasty summer weather, a stone fireplace used when golf was out of the question. Sitting out inclement weather beside the fireplace became routine, with golfers turning to bridge as the game of choice. Jean Galbraith, Scottish-born wife of park clerk Hugh Galbraith, managed the facility, providing informal lunches and light snacks.

The success of the golf course was confirmed by the end of its second season. More than 700 golfers had played during the May-to-September season. It was a busy place on weekends, often patronized by visitors who came primarily for the Saturday night dance at the pavilion in the townsite and filled their days with golf. Restaurateurs and accommodation operators in the park benefitted, as well.

The Lethbridge Herald frequently praised the new course and began reporting the names and home towns of players, just as it did the names of those registered at various accommodations in Waterton. Exceptionally low scores were also published.

Blairmore champion hockey player Mel Rhynas was the first to set the amateur course record for two nine-hole rounds with a score of 81. But the newspaper also decried the fact most visitors were so occupied with either fishing or golfing they were totally ignorant of the 11 fine horse trails in the park. The golf bug had not only bitten, but it was infectious.

By 1925, Wagstaff had his crew undertaking maintenance projects and course improvements. A small tool shed and a registry office, which had been destroyed by high winter winds, were replaced, 11 sand traps installed and the fairways widened.

Wagstaff had found a niche working at the course each summer. He fit easily into the social life of park residents and was known as an excellent dance partner. This seemed like an all-round good place to live, so he took out a lease and built a cabin in the townsite.

His old carpentry skills came in handy and with the help of Waterton's premier "log man" and builder, Walter B. Foster, Wagstaff erected a five-room log house. By June 1925 when Oland & Scott Construction finished his stone fireplace, his cabin at the corner of Fountain Avenue

Teddy Wagstaff, left, was a hands-on fellow who personally saw to course play, tournament publicity and management, scheduling, refreshments and prizes. An excellent player, he was the first to make a hole-in-one at the course, for which he was sent a certificate from the Burke Golf Company of Ohio, a leading manufacturer of golf equipment starting in 1910.

125

The first starter's shack, above, was where golfers paid their fees and registered for play. Standing at the door is Teddy Wagstaff. The starting house was upgraded, below right, and a clubhouse, below left, was added in 1924, then quickly enlarged by Oland & Scott Construction.

and Cameron Falls Drive was completed. It was Wagstaff's first permanent home since 1915, when he had left to fight in the war in Europe.

Having his own accommodation worked out particularly well the winter of 1926 when he, like so many other local men, went to work as a carpenter building the Prince of Wales Hotel as part of Oland & Scott's crew. In later years during the off season, Wagstaff sometimes headed to warmer climes, where he could golf and learn more about the operation of other clubs. These winter expeditions paid off, and the Waterton course continued to get rave reviews.

In late 1927 the Great Northern Railway tried to lure him away to take over construction of its troubled golf course at Glacier Park Hotel in East Glacier Park, Montana. Wagstaff turned the railway down, much to the delight of his friends in Waterton.

Little by little, improvements were made to the Waterton golf course. In 1928, plans were implemented for a fence and better entrance gate to funnel patrons to a new registration office that was added to the clubhouse. By July 1929, a larger log-and-stone clubhouse, with a huge, open fireplace, was completed. Its glassed-in veranda was used as a tea room.

The course was so popular, the public wanted it to be expanded to 18 holes. In late 1929 the Associated Trade Boards of Southern Alberta asked Ottawa by

The golf course at "windy Waterton" was not the most appropriate place for women to wear dresses, so jodspurs became acceptable but not shorts. Men traditionally wore knickers and knee-high argyle socks. Below, long-time golfer Lawrence Hill of Lethbridge happened to keep a 1932 golf ticket that turned up decades later.

way of a written resolution to fund such a plan. The group told officials, "Another nine holes are deemed absolutely essential as the links are a great drawing card to holiday-makers and tourists."

The message was clear: there was economic benefit to the park in this venture, something that was not lost on local park officials.

But the request was ill-timed. The stock market crash that autumn and subsequent Depression made it impossible to immediately expand the course or replace all the greens with grass and install a watering system. The work already done that fall to prepare the greens for seeding had to be undone and the sand greens restored. It was a setback that was not corrected for many years.

Meanwhile, another sporting craze, miniature golf, was about to make its debut in Waterton. Miniature golf had taken the world by storm and by 1930 more

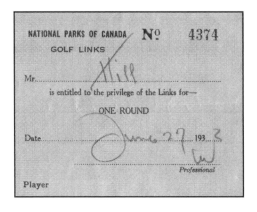

than 25,000 courses were operating indoors and out, in rural towns and on big city rooftops. Even the ocean liner *Ile de France*, hailed for its modern design and Art Deco features, had one. The miniature golf courses were known by names like Tom Thumb Golf, Pee Wee, Tiny Tim and Wee MacGregor.

Since a miniature golf facility didn't require a great investment by the owner or much golfing skill by the participants, it was a natural tourist attraction for the Waterton townsite. An unidentified businessman set up the Doo Dad 18-hole miniature course in late July 1930. It was located just south of the Crystal Swimming Pool at what today is 504 Cameron Falls Dr. (now Mountain Spirits liquor store). The new attraction immediately drew dozens of players and was an instant hit. "Everyone in the park is asking the other if he has played at the new course," *The Lethbridge Herald* reported.

127

Construction of a second nine holes to expand the course began in 1931, providing both additional challenge and striking views. Taken from the 13th hole, this photo shows northern portions of Glacier National Park in the distance.

This foursome of regional church ministers was a regular sight on the Waterton golf course, no doubt receiving divine support for tough lies.

The news item alerted officials in Ottawa to the existence of this new attraction and by September, acting superintendent William Cromarty was queried about it. Hidden away behind the pool, the Doo Dad might not have been obvious to Cromarty, who may have been too busy with other business to be aware of its existence.

In contrast to what the newspaper had reported, Cromarty told his superiors in Ottawa the course was used mostly by pool employees and suggested "it [was] best to issue a licence in case a charge was made to others desiring to play." It was tempest in a teapot. Whether the cost of the licence or the cost of improving the Doo Dad led to its downfall is not known. It was abandoned and did not reopen in 1931.

Despite the beginning of the Depression, business at the Waterton golf course was good.

Herbert Knight, appointed acting superintendent in 1930, noted that "golf course receipts increased by 85 per cent," adding, "the course has become so popular that at times there are as many as 14 players waiting for their turn to play."

Heavy use of the golf course came as visitation to

the park was climbing, thanks in part to popular attractions like the Prince of Wales Hotel and the dance pavilion on Waterton Avenue. In fact, for the past four years, Waterton had registered a larger percentage increase in visitors than any other western park.

Yet when it came time to allocate funds for unemployment relief programs, designed to build improvements in the park, Waterton received only $2,000 while Banff and Jasper parks split $31,000.

The Lethbridge Herald railed against the apparent injustice: "Surely in view of Waterton's growing popularity, its immense value as a magnet for American tourists and the consequent spending of an immense amount of foreign money throughout this part of the Dominion, it is entitled to a little more consideration than it has received from Ottawa."

The complaining paid off and in April 1931 it was announced the golf course would be extended to 18 holes as part of the relief work programs.

The fact that superintendent Knight was also an enthusiastic golfer and could personally vouch for the course's growing popularity—and the great job Wagstaff was doing—may have also had something to do with the federal government's largesse.

Knight and Wagstaff had a lot in common and had gotten to know each other in the five years before Knight's appointment as full-time superintendent, when Knight had served as acting superintendent during the winter months. Both men had been born in England and emigrated to Canada, served in the Great War and been wounded.

It was as much a sign of friendship as respect for the job that Wagstaff was doing that in 1931 Knight promoted Wagstaff to manager of the course, just as the course was about to be expanded.

Although the second nine was, in general, laid outside and around the existing nine, in fact, several of the original holes were also redesigned and realigned. A June 1932 newspaper story reported that the course would be ready for the season, and included a detailed description of each of the 18 holes, summing up the report with: "Southern Alberta golfers who have visited the course this season are loud in their praises of the new nine and are extending their congratulations to Supt. Knight and Teddy Wagstaff, the professional, who with other members of the park staff have cooperated in the layout and in the work of making the course playable so soon."

The praise and the predicted date of opening were off the mark. On July 19, 1932, the new nine were opened for one day and immediately closed by Knight "because of their rough condition."

William Thomson was summoned from Banff to do a thorough evaluation. By way of a praise, Thomson noted that Hole No. 13, the bane of most golfers' existence to this day, was "excellently located. No hazard construction is necessary as the natural grid is splendid for this purpose."

Rustic benches at tee areas were provided for players awaiting their turn. These ladies carried their minimal canvas club bags in the days before carts were common.

Thomson made many suggestions for improvement to the tune of $19,000, such as seeding of greens, but excluded the purchase of equipment at a time when the country was in economic crisis. Thomson also recommended an expenditure of $3,000 for completion of a water system.

It would be three seasons before the entire 18-holes were opened for play.

On July 1, 1935, the public was finally allowed

Rev. Samuel Middleton lines up his putt in preparation to complete his round while his teammates look on.

access to the new 5,178-metre (6,100-yard), par-71 layout with the promise from John S. Stewart, local member of Parliament, that $6,000 had been allocated for the finishing touches, including a system to bring water from nearby Pass Creek (now Blakiston Creek) that would be completed in the fall, and the possibility of grass greens.

Adelle and Jim Rackette were both enamoured of golf. She wrote a multi-year spoof of the antics of "The Chipputs," legendary gremlins who stole golf balls.

Not present to celebrate the improvements was Wagstaff. He'd stayed in Waterton long enough to see the course through its infancy and had managed it profitably.

In the spring of 1934 Wagstaff was offered an opportunity too good to be turned down: he could build and manage the Sugar City Golf Course in Raymond, Alberta, and have winter employment at the thriving sugar beet factory. His departure was noted sadly by Waterton golfers.

George Stewart, who had worked closely with Knight and Wagstaff in the building of second nine holes, stepped in as greenskeeper and foreman, a

job he would hold for nearly 30 years. James Rackette joined the course staff as a ticket seller through the 1940s. Both men were First World War veterans.

The golf course continued to be a work in progress as funds and staff allowed, with numerous small improvements until Canada went to war again, in 1939, the last year Knight was park superintendent. By 1940 only two grass greens were part of the course and players had access to neither showers nor lockers.

The challenge the Waterton course presented drew duffers from near and far. Among them was Blanche Walchli, the wife of Kalispell lawyer Hans. She was considered one of the best female golfers in Montana. Walchli carded a score of 44 on the par-35 first nine in Waterton, a feat that made the local paper. The story noted that had there not been a strong wind, her score would have been better. It is an excuse still used by Waterton golfers today.

During the Second World War, despite the shortages and rationing, Waterton continued to be a tourist destination and the golf course continued to operate, although to save on fuel for fairway mowers and the irrigation pump, only the inside nine holes were in play. Proceeds from the annual golf tournament were donated to the Queen's Canadian Fund for Air Raid Victims.

Unfortunately, the lack of money and manpower to maintain the golf course during the war years left their mark and could not, in Waterton's short growing season, be quickly put right after the war. The mowers for the greens had gone missing and the course was in very poor shape, with putting on five of the eight greens described as "impossible." Officials were quite aware of the deficiencies, having already begun discussions about the long-postponed new grass greens, a new clubhouse and other improvements.

Park superintendent Herbert A. DeVeber took up the matter with his Ottawa bosses in early 1947: "You will recall that plans were in hand for all-grass greens

prior to the outbreak of the war and it was thought then that this improvement alone would have a marked beneficial effect on the course's popularity."

The Lethbridge Herald editorialized that something had to be done to improve the existing course, and soon. "The setting for the course is ideal but unless the greens and fairways are kept up to high standard, there is bound to be criticism."

Senator William A. Buchanan of Lethbridge was among those on the receiving end of that criticism and he, too, appealed to bureaucrats in Ottawa to quickly get the course in better shape.

Enter Canada's best known golf architect, Stanley Thompson, who was hired by Ottawa (and no relation to William E. Thomson of Banff), 29 years after the course opened.

His view was grim: "I consider Waterton is more like a Scottish moorland course and I believe has some real latent character. The course should be re-laid out, choosing as far as possible lowland or valley fairways. The natural grass is the same throughout

Lonesome Lake, hidden from view from the highway, is best seen from the 18th tee box. These golfers were repositioned 180 degrees by the photographer to make the most of the background view.

the area and the fact that the existing route would not be used, would not add greatly to the cost."

His estimated cost to change the course layout, build grass tee boxes and grass greens was $33,000—a fortune, given that at the time greenskeepers, for example, were paid 90 cents an hour.

Stanley Thompson was among the most colourful characters in golf design history. Nicknamed the "Toronto Terror" for his proficiency as a player, Thompson had become a course architect in 1921 in Ontario and redesigned the world-famous Banff Springs Hotel and the Jasper Park Lodge courses. He was a founding member of the American Society of Golf Course Architects and gained a worldwide reputation as a genius of strategic design.

Thompson was described in a 1949 *Maclean's* magazine article as a ruddy, gregarious individual who "chews his way through 15 cigars a day" and at "215 pounds he looks like a greatly enlarged golf ball set on two tee-like legs."

His love of rye whisky was legendary. Waterton resident and park employee George Annand recalled being told to pick up Thompson at the Fort Macleod train station for one of Thompson's twice-yearly course inspections. Eager to talk golf with Thompson during the trip to the park, Annand was more than a little disappointed when Thompson stepped off the train roaring drunk and fell asleep in the car.

Stanley Thompson was as much renowned for his work as a golf course designer as he was for his penchant for cigars, ample dining and drinking.

Thompson was hired to review six national park courses, including Waterton's. His renewable annual contract called for a fee plus expenses to cover two visits a year while improvements were underway.

News that Thompson would be directing improvements to the course with government funds was well received by the public. *The Lethbridge Herald*'s editorial spoke for many when it said: "We can rest assured that the course will eventually be one of which we can all be proud."

As an alternate plan to improving Waterton's course, Thompson told officials they might consider building a nine-hole course elsewhere. "I think a good nine holes is much to be desired over a poor 18," he said.

The proposed new location, south of the existing course in the wooded section along the shore of Middle Waterton Lake, would have been well out of the wind and close to a good water supply. In addition, he suggested, guests of the Prince of Wales Hotel would have a vastly improved view if a course was constructed there.

Thompson, however, abandoned the idea of a new location. Relocating the course was a bold plan but, in retrospect, not that well thought out, given the subsequent history of high water and flooding in that place. Superintendent DeVeber expressed his relief in a letter to Ottawa: "It is gratifying to note that [Thompson] is now convinced that a 'very fine golf course' can be evolved from the existing location. The proposal to abandon the present course was not well received in southern Alberta."

Thompson's next plan incorporated 75 per cent of the existing fairways in a new layout, with tree and brush clearing to renovate all the fairways in 1951 and 1952, using park staff to do the work. It was a tribute to the early efforts of Teddy Wagstaff and Herbert Knight that so many of the original fairways were retained. And it was a feather in George Stewart's cap when Thompson reported he was "an excellent greenskeeper."

The appointment of Jim Atkinson as superintendent in June 1951 did not disrupt the golf course plans. Atkinson, a 30-year parks service man with a background in engineering, was keenly interested in the construction and closely monitored the work, both as an enthusiastic golfer and as a manager. The story is told that it was Atkinson who suggested construction of a small hill between the parallel ninth and 18th holes. Groundskeepers referred to it for years as "Mount Atkinson."

One of the most welcomed improvements was Thompson's plan for grass greens. By the end of the 1952 season, all 18 greens were laid with sod or seeded. A little behind schedule that year, Thompson arrived at the course in November for his annual inspection to discover not everything on his list had been completed due to lack of appropriations. His usual thorough report to Ottawa in December would be his last.

Thompson died suddenly in January 1953 of a hemorrhage. He'd left pages and pages of detailed instructions, however, as to what was needed to complete course improvements in Waterton, right down to the amount of fertilizer to be applied to the greens. The work would go on without him.

As the year progressed, it became obvious that 1953 was going to be a memorable one for the golf course. On June 24, an early morning fire destroyed the clubhouse.

John Haslam, shift engineer at the Prince of Wales Hotel, was driving to work from outside the park about 4:30 a.m. and noticed a building on fire at the golf course. "I drove to the fire to see what it was all about. I got a surprise to find no one was fighting the fire," he later told the police. He scrambled to alert the fire brigade, only to find the telephone office was closed, so he drove to the RCMP detachment to raise the alarm, but it was too late. The clubhouse was destroyed.

While the cause of the fire was not determined, the park superintendent lost no time letting his Ottawa superiors know of the fire. They, in turn, prepared for inexpensive, quickly built temporary quarters to accommodate golfers. Luckily, the ticket office and

The natural mixed forest and bush comprising the Waterton golf course attract wildlife through the summer and fall seasons, including deer, bears, elk, smaller animals and birds. During the early days of the 2017 Kenow forest fire, the course also provided ample space to land helicopters used to spot and fight the blaze.

When opened in 1955, this new club house provided change rooms, showers, lockers, restaurant, fireplace and indoor and outdoor dining, along with a pro shop and residence. A new pro shop and residence were added in 1966.

pro shop were not attached to the clubhouse and were undamaged. A budget of $40,000 was submitted to Ottawa, it being based on earlier discussions for a replacement building, and the expense was approved. The fire merely accelerated plans for a new clubhouse.

The new building was completed in May 1955. Its impressive decorative stonework was the effort of local mason Walter Foster. As was tradition, the new clubhouse included an interior brick fireplace, creating a homey atmosphere on chilly days. Dressing rooms complete with lockers and showers and a large restaurant space were included. Nearby was a small playground for children waiting for their parents to complete their rounds. The old ticket office building was salvaged and moved to Cameron Lake for use by the summer fish warden.

Within a few years, the Waterton golf course was being boldly promoted as one of the best in Western Canada and the connection with Stanley Thompson frequently touted. Thompson's contribution of developing a plan for multi-year improvements became the basis for a widely accepted myth that he had designed the entire course from the beginning.

While maintenance of the course, capital investments and revenue were the domain of the park and ultimately Ottawa, the pro shop and clubhouse

concessions were handled by private operators, such as Mrs. W.H. Matkin, who ran the tea room at the course in 1931.

Later, Arta Stewart, wife of greenskeeper George Stewart, ran the clubhouse until their retirement in 1963. The couple's accommodating service was appreciated, as visitor Harold Templeton of Lethbridge attested in a letter he wrote to Ottawa: "[They are] most gracious and untiring in their efforts to render an enjoyable service to the public."

There were many staff changes in the years that followed. Among those who headed operations was Harold Webb of Fort Macleod, who followed the Stewarts in 1963 and was awarded a concession to operate the clubhouse.

A new pro shop and staff residence were added to the clubhouse in 1966. And by 1974 Bill Hilton was the course pro and club house manager. Green fees continued to be set by the government.

The first step in a major shift in operations began in 1983, as park officials scrambled to balance their budget. Waterton was one of only three national park golf courses in Canada being run by the government. Park officials wanted private enterprise to take it over.

"A golf course is not unique to a national park and can be run just as well by the private sector," said Jim

Sheardon, director of information services for Parks Canada.

Aging buildings and course maintenance equipment were becoming a drain on the park budget. In the big picture of national parks, Waterton was seen as one of the lesser-used courses. Waterton superintendent Bernie Lieff implied that privatizing the entire operation was a way for Parks Canada to avoid new expenditures.

In February 1984, private operation became fact. Harry and Bill Wright of Edmonton won the bid to operate and maintain the course, clubhouse, food service, equipment rentals and sales for the next 10 years.

Bill Wright, a professional golfer since 1974, had played on the pro circuit in North America and Europe and was a member of the Canadian, U.S. and British professional golf associations. He was in charge of the pro shop and offered lessons. Harry Wright's expertise was in real estate sales and commercial development, and he took over the clubhouse and general operations. For the first time in the history of the park, a liquor licence was issued to the golf course and the soup and sandwich fare was broadened to include on-the-go selections as well as full meals.

In the summer of 1993, as the Wrights' lease neared its end, Parks Canada officials examined what capital improvements would be needed. They hoped to offer a longer lease so the lessee could finance improvements and still get a return on investment for both parties. Parks Canada officials also needed to set up a system to legally enforce the terms of a new agreement.

The arrival of new park superintendent Merv Syroteuk from Prince Albert National Park in 1992 was a turning point for the golf course operation. He quietly urged the Waterton Park Community Association (WPCA) to apply for the lease, as had been done at Prince Albert.

In the spring of 1994, the WPCA became the successful bidder for a 25-year golf course lease. In exchange for operation of the entire facility, the association agreed to make improvements according to a master plan developed and supervised by Parks Canada, which would receive a percentage of the revenues.

Teddy Wagstaff

In subsequent years, a number of changes were made to the course. The largest was a partnership with Parks Canada to provide for a lagoon system for treated waste water from the town's sewage. The waste water was used for irrigation rather than drawing water from Blakiston Creek. Consequently, green fees, membership fees and cart rental rates rose slowly but substantially.

Near the end of the WPCA lease, the Kenow Fire of 2017 destroyed both the private golf cart parking area near the practice green and a large maintenance complex which included a shop, a one-bedroom apartment and winter storage area for carts and turf equipment that had been completed in May 2000 at a cost of $325,000. That building was located below the No. 10 tee area and could be seen from the entrance road. It was insured and rebuilt at another site at the golf course where it could not be seen from the entrance road.

The lease held by the WPCA was to have expired in 2019 but was extended through the 2020 season. In the winter of 2020, Parks Canada made a public request for proposals which called for significant capital investment in the golf course. Much to the disappointment of the WPCA, it was not the successful respondent and a 25-year lease was awarded to Lakeland Golf Management (Alberta) Inc. Green fees and cart rentals fees rose yet again.

The golf course continues to be a popular and genuine asset to the park 100 years after it was first opened. The links that Teddy Wagstaff and the crew began, and many others have since maintained and improved, have stood the test of time. Only snow, sleet and dark of night keep Waterton golfers from their intended rounds.

The YMCA's Camp Inuspi was strongly supported by the residents of southern Alberta. Camp councillors met annually at the log dining hall for training prior to the opening each summer season.

Chapter 5

Summer Camps
The Memory Makers

Few Waterton visitors have had more fun at less expense—and with more lasting memories over the years—than those who attended summer group camps.

Fresh air and exercise were the obvious benefits of the summer camps, but much could be said for the spiritual and emotional growth of campers in the time spent away from home with their contemporaries.

"You can't really put into words the feeling a summer at camp leaves with one," wrote Don Maclean, a *Lethbridge Herald* columnist who was a multiple year camper as a youth. "Yes, it may be the experiences you remember, it may be the friends you make, it may just be the small taste of learning to live with one another that you cherish . . . but whatever it is that clings to the dark nooks and crannies of your mind, you're glad you went; you're glad you were part of it and somehow you wish—if only for an instant—you were going back again."

There were six fixed-roofed camps in Waterton: Kamp Kainai, Camp Inuspi, the Mothers Camp, Canyon Church Camp, Camp Columbus, and Tee-La-Daw. While each took a slightly different approach to supervised camping, they all focused on appreciation of the outdoors, some in a religious context, others in a secular way.

Prior to fixed-roofed camps there were several annual camp outings in Waterton, including the Young Men's Mutual Improvement Association of the Church of Jesus Christ of Latter-day Saints (LDS), which organized the Mutual Improvement Association Scouts starting in late 1911. It offered church-appropriate leisure and sports activities for its young men.

When this group became a recognized part of the Boy Scout movement a few years later, it gave LDS, or Mormon, boys the opportunity to participate in church-sanctioned Boy Scout troops of their own.

An annual father-son camp for Boy Scouts associated with the Mormon church proved to be one of the most popular camping events in Waterton. Lasting just three days once a summer, but never held on the Sabbath, the outings provided an opportunity for fathers and sons to get away from their homes and sample the great outdoors. They camped in tents in the Blakiston Valley, where nature and its wonders provided a perfect place to develop a bond of fellowship and comradeship during the all-male event. The camp was located on the north bank of Blakiston Creek, between Coppermine and Lost Horse creeks.

The first of these faith-based events, in 1929, drew 114 fathers and sons from Lethbridge, Raymond and Cardston, all three communities having large Mormon populations. As word spread, the following year more than 1,500 fathers and sons arrived in 300 automobiles from the same Mormon church stakes.

This was an astonishing number to camp at one location. A newspaper story described the camp as being "the greatest gathering of its kind in the history of the world." The environmental effects must have

The earliest group campers were Boy Scouts, who met in the Blakiston Valley but had no permanent buildings.

137

In the early 1930s, father-son camps sponsored by the Church of Jesus Christ of Latter-day Saints were held annually under canvas in the Blakiston Valley. At their largest, hundreds of Mormon boys and their dads attended.

been horrendous, but consideration was given to the location and depth of latrines and garbage pits as well as the weekend schedule of activities. The planning and organization had been done for the campers right down to which songs should be sung around the campfires.

In 1931, the LDS fathers-son participation was reduced to 170 campers, but by then the outing had been labelled by the newspaper as "a tradition." That year the campers hiked and learned about geology and flora. Sporting activities included baseball, horseshoe pitching and swimming. Dinner was to be ready at each campsite by 6 p.m., followed by campfire entertainment.

Despite the regular practice of camping in the park by the father-son group as well as other Boy Scout troops, both at Kamp Kootenai in the Blakiston Valley, they held no right to any particular site and had no reserved location. The Latter-day Saints campouts continued after the Second World War and into the 1950s; it is not known when they stopped camping as a group in the park.

Kainai Kottage

The first camp established in Waterton was in the townsite and under the supervision of Rev. Samuel H. Middleton, the Anglican minister and principal of St. Paul's Residential School on the Blood Tribe reserve. The camp was not only the first in the park, but also the first tied to a religious organization.

Middleton, just 22 years old, came to Alberta from England to work with Indigenous people in 1904, the year before Alberta became a province. He began his missionary efforts on the Piikani (then called Peigan) reserve at Brocket, later moving to the Blood reserve near Cardston, 56 kilometres (35 miles) east of Waterton. In 1912 he was appointed the principal of St. Paul's School, a position he held for the next 37 years, winning the admiration of many on and off the reserve.

Athletic and energetic, Middleton lost no time in exploring Waterton's beauty and was an outspoken advocate of the park. Over the course of decades of hiking, he came to know the front and backcountry as few others did and became interested in park events and developments. As early as 1910 he and his school staff brought some of the older students, both boys and girls, from St. Paul's to the park to camp for two to three weeks to enjoy God's handiwork.

When surveying of lots in Waterton began in 1910, Middleton realized development was coming and he resolved to get a piece of the place—for educational purposes—while he could. In August 1912 he applied for a townsite lease. His idea was to eventually construct a building, but in the meantime to use the property for the annual camp for his school's staff and students.

"To Indian children," Middleton wrote parks commissioner James B. Harkin in Ottawa, "such an excursion proves of inestimable benefit as the main point of our Indian education is to bring the Indian mind in contact with edifying and wholesome environments. No better place can be found than the Waterton Lakes."

Surprisingly, Harkin recommended to W.W. Cory, the deputy minister of the Department of Interior, that no lease be given to Middleton because of the "strong feelings around Banff against Indians being permitted in the parks." But Harkin did suggest a more flexible, if less permanent, arrangement: the residential school should be allowed to use a lot at no charge and be permitted to erect a building for the camp.

The decision was eventually reconsidered, and Middleton was able to obtain leases on three adjoining lakeshore lots in 1917 on what is now Waterton Avenue, where buildings were erected for $1,500. Before the buildings were completed and as a special concession to Middleton, tents that were prohibited on townsite leases elsewhere were permitted on the property for the duration of the children's summer camp.

The first building constructed for the camp was known as "Kainai Kottage," Kainai being the Blackfoot name for the Blood Tribe. In March 1921 a second building was erected for use as a dormitory for the children.

In 1921 for its first summer of operation, a group of eight Blackfoot girls ages 10 to 18 arrived at Kainai camp with Rev. Middleton and other chaperones. They came for a two-month stay, according to *Cal-*

Kainai Kottage was a fixed-roof facility operated under the auspices of the Anglican Church. It was the brainchild of Rev. Samuel H. Middleton, principal of St. Paul's Residential School on the Blood Tribe reserve near Cardston.

139

Groups of Indigenous boys and girls headed separately to Waterton to camp. The boys, in their army cadet uniforms, rode horses from their school to camp in the park, while the girls, in middies and bloomers, arrived by horse and wagon, and later by automobile, staying at the church-owned Kainai Kottage.

gary Herald reporter Sylvester C. Long Lance, who accompanied them.

The girls, dressed in middies and bloomers, climbed mountains, walked trails and played games during the day. At night, they sang at a blazing campfire accompanied by a portable pedal organ. The young campers occupied one of two adjacent lakeshore cabins, one for the girls, the other for the Middleton family and the chaperones.

The annual summer school outings, held separately for boys and girls, became a two-week summer tradition at the cottage.

For the boys, who were members of the school's army cadet corps, getting there was part of the event. Middleton organized and accompanied the cadets as they trooped from St. Paul's to Waterton on horseback and pitched tents in the campground, later using the camp buildings on the lakeshore. The St. Paul School's cadet corps was the oldest such group in the province and the only officially recognized Native cadet corps in Canada.

The girls got off easier, arriving at the park in the early years in horse-drawn wagons, later in motor vehicles, staying in the cabins when it was their group's turn.

Getting close to nature was an essential while in Waterton. Middleton was eager to share his love of the outdoors and he joined in the daytime activities. The children hiked, climbed, fished, camped overnight in the backcountry, and did as much chaper-

oned sightseeing as Middleton could work into each day.

From time to time, in the name of charity and goodwill, Middleton got excursion boat operators such as Les and Tom Morrow to take the group in their boat *Linnea* to spend a day in Montana's Glacier park, at the head of Upper Waterton Lake.

When the cottages weren't being used by the school children, various members of the Anglican ministry and school staff were invited to use them. By 1928 Waterton had its first place of worship, All-Saints Anglican Church, a 16-pew structure built by Oland & Scott Construction at the request of Middleton. It is not known whether the Indigenous campers attended services at the church but seems unlikely given the limited space in the building.

In 1945, park officials granted Middleton permission to erect another cottage on the lakeshore leases to accommodate more staff and Native children, but it was a phase in the school's activities which was nearing an end. Middleton retired from teaching in 1949 and the leases were transferred to the Calgary Anglican Diocese. With that, the enthusiasm for St. Paul's School camping in Waterton fell off.

In 1960, the original cottages were torn down and one three-bedroom Pan-Abode cottage, straddling two lots, was erected, thanks to the work of volunteers. It continued to serve as accommodation for visiting lay ministers and others until the All-Saints Anglican Church, on Windflower Avenue, was closed in 2007 after 79 years of use. All three residential leases on the lakeshore were purchased by private parties who built new residences on each, some as late as 2021.

Camp Inuspi

The most popular and best-known fixed-roof youth camp in Waterton was the Lethbridge YMCA's Camp Inuspi. Located on the eastern shore of Lower Waterton Lake (once known as Knight's Lake), it operated every summer for 35 years starting in 1934, becoming the largest camp of its type in southern Alberta.

What made Camp Inuspi successful and memorable was that it had the isolation necessary to get the full attention of campers and enough supervision to ensure learning in a fun setting. It became as dear to the hearts of its many campers as the park itself.

Camp Inuspi was not the YMCA's first attempt at camping in Waterton. Tent campouts were offered to Lethbridge boys in 1914 and 1922. It was not until the Depression, when community service clubs began to bloom in southern Alberta, that they got together with the YMCA to set up a permanent camp.

The YMCA's camp proposal was initiated in the spring of 1934 through Senator William A. Buchanan of Lethbridge. A request to park officials from Buchanan was no trifling matter. Besides being a senator, he was publisher of *The Lethbridge Herald* daily newspaper, happened to be cabin owner in Waterton, and was the park's major proponent in Parliament.

Senator and Lethbridge Herald *publisher William A. Buchanan, right, heartily endorsed the YMCA's Camp Inuspi and urged park authorities to allow its establishment.* Herald *managing editor Harold G. Long ensured readers were kept abreast of camp highlights.*

Buchanan was advised by Parks Branch commissioner J.B. Harkin that a camp in Waterton would be very much in keeping with park goals:

"I am pleased to advise you," Harkin said, "that the policy of the department is to encourage YMCA and other such camps in the national parks. The experiences with such camps in other parks have clearly demonstrated that these camps provide a means for a holiday in the parks for many boys and young men who would otherwise be unable to enjoy the benefits of such an outing."

With Harkin's approval, a small group of men arrived in Waterton in mid-April 1934 to select the site for the YMCA camp. Among them were Lethbridge lawyer A. Gladstone Virtue, who would later become a cabin owner in the park; Stan Sneyd, secretary of the 24-year-old YMCA in Lethbridge; Advance Lumber supervisor Don Hartman of Lethbridge; Jim Samson, the Y's boys work and physical director; and the owner of the nearby Shoderee Ranch, Russell H. Bennett, a wealthy and influential Minneapolis, Min-

Inuspi campers and their counsellors were assigned a service club-sponsored cabin for the duration of their session. The lad on the right front, Jack Snedden, eventually owned a cabin in the Waterton townsite.

nesota, businessman and a long-time devotee of the YMCA philosophy.

Together with park superintendent Herbert Knight, the group trudged over ground to find a suitable spot for a camp and followed up with the necessary paperwork. The 7.2-hectare (18-acre) site was made available for $1 per year for the first seven years.

YMCA staff and volunteers immediately got the ball rolling so a camp could be held under canvas that summer, just weeks away. There was no electricity at the camp site nor any buildings, but a rough layout was created and when the boys arrived, they slept in tents which the YMCA had found tucked away in its own storage space in Lethbridge.

Access to the site was such that campers had to load their personal effects, food and equipment and take a row boat across the lake to reach the spot on the east side of Knight's Lake. Later, truck access was

via a rough road off the new Chief Mountain Highway after it was completed in 1936.

However, until that route was open, Carl Ranson, assistant manager of the International Harvester Co., offered to transport the boys to Waterton from Lethbridge using a company truck that was big enough to take all the boys, their bedding and the camp supplies. On the designated day, the truck arrived at the Y in Lethbridge and all the kids and their baggage, together with groceries, pots and pans and extra tables were loaded in the truck and Ranson drove the group to Waterton. The first 35 boys arrived on Saturday, June 30, 1934.

A dedication was held on July 1, Dominion Day. The ceremony was well-attended and included speeches, prayers and songs, a flag raising, camp inspection and dinner for all. The aim of the camp, Russell Bennett told the gathering, was to assist in building better boyhood, to develop self-reliance, tolerance, rugged bodies and clear, alert minds. Moreover, he said, the camp would instill in the boys a love of nature and God.

The camp was named "Inuspi" (InÓspi), a Blackfoot name meaning "long hair" that had been given to Kootenai Brown (1839-1916), first forest ranger in charge of Waterton. In naming the camp, YMCA board chairman J.G. Hutchings noted: "Kootenai Brown was a man who loved the mountains; he loved all wildlife and the natural beauty of the country as the Creator had given it to man. He fought to keep this section in its natural state for the benefit of future generations. He was a great favourite with the Indians; they took him into their council and gave him a name. We believe, because of the historical setting, it is quite fitting to adopt this name for our camp."

Throughout its existence, the camp incorporated its version of Native skills, crafts and activities, and the camp logo featured an Indigenous man in full headdress.

Camp director Jim Samson arranged a packed program that first season for the boys, teaching swimming and boating, camp crafts and leading hikes, with the assistance of group leaders Stan Sneyd and George Swedish. Sneyd had several years of camping experience and Swedish was well versed in athletics. Fred Botsford, an old-timer from Lethbridge and holder of the honorary Indigenous name of Chief Putani, was in charge of teaching Native lore. The all-important meal preparation was covered by chef Walter Brunner, who had worked in the Lethbridge Y's dining room and doubled as an entertainer at evening campfire programs.

Jim Samson

Prepared to ward off parental concerns and campers' homesickness, Samson had brought along a two-way radio set, a heavy, bulky unit in those days, to receive and send messages, and keep in constant touch with Lethbridge. It was found superfluous the next season: the boys loved the camp from the start.

Samson's memoir notes that many of the campers had never been to the Waterton townsite. An impromptu hike was organized so the boys could take advantage of the heated waters of the Crystal Swimming Pool on Cameron Falls Drive. This impromptu idea cost the YMCA 15 cents per boy for admission, but YMCA gladly paid the fee.

As the boys hiked back, at the camp chef Brunner was preparing a big stew to serve on their arrival. "And I can assure you that at the end of the meal there wasn't enough stew left to feed a jack rabbit," Sampson recalled.

Eventually a permanent camp included log structures, sleeping cabins, cooking and mess areas, a hospital shack and other appropriate facilities. The

Camp Inuspi activities included swimming in adjacent Lower Watertron Lake, hiking, climbing, boating and arts and crafts. Visitors were allowed at the camp only on Sunday and Wednesday. Parents could purchase a meal for 50 cents.

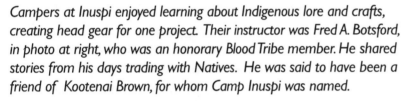

Campers at Inuspi enjoyed learning about Indigenous lore and crafts, creating head gear for one project. Their instructor was Fred A. Botsford, in photo at right, who was an honorary Blood Tribe member. He shared stories from his days trading with Natives. He was said to have been a friend of Kootenai Brown, for whom Camp Inuspi was named.

first building was an all-important five- by four-metre (16- by 12-foot) kitchen, erected in 1935. It housed cooking equipment and a hot water tank for proper cleanup. Doug G. Oland, one of the park's premier builders, erected the structure. The campers ate their meals in a large tent nearby.

Through the years the focus of camp life was the outdoors, with handicrafts thrown in on cool or rainy days, and campfire programs in the evenings. Good food, well prepared, was an essential part of every camp.

Mrs. Al Harris of Coalhurst, Alberta, who cooked at Camp Inuspi for several seasons, remembered she was amazed at the quantity of food the campers could put away, believing the kids must be hollow to their toes.

An active outdoor life creates huge appetites and when children came home a little heavier, it was a sign of a great camp. Good meals came at a price: periodic kitchen duty assigned to campers. It was as much a part of camp life as the discipline of cabin housekeeping.

For many, the camp experience was their first long period away from home, with plenty of pangs of homesickness. It was, though,

above all, an unforgettable time in the campers' lives.

Denny Ranson, nine years old in 1934, was among the boys to attend Camp Inuspi's first session. He fondly recalled camp life, especially the swimming: "We swam twice a day, once before lunch and once before dinner. The water was so cold when new guys came to camp, they were told if they could stay in the water for 45 minutes, they'd get free tuck [snacks] for the entire duration of their camp time. This amounted to two candy bars a day. Nobody but about two guys ever did it."

Despite all the early rhetoric implying that camping at Inuspi was for boys, from the second season onward, sessions for girls were part of the schedule. The first of these was supervised by Jim Samson's wife, Marie Lovering Samson, and her assistant Agnes Davidson, both school teachers.

In 1936 the Y began an annual Lethbridge fundraising drive that continued for more than 30 years. There was no end to the list of needed improvements to the camp. The initial plan, to be completed as money allowed, was to build sleeping quarters for the campers and eventually a permanent kitchen-dining hall and activity area.

The Kiwanis Club, already sponsoring a camp for

underprivileged mothers in Waterton townsite, came forward in May with the gift of a cabin for Camp Inuspi. Eventually, nine sleeping cabins were built, thanks to the efforts of the Kinsmen Club, the Rotary Club, the Gyro Club and *The Lethbridge Herald*. A large craft and theatre cabin was built by the YMCA's Red Triangle Hostess Club. And a three-bed emergency hospital was made possible by the combined efforts of several clubs. Camp Inuspi became a symbol of what a community could accomplish by working together.

With the camp off to an excellent start, in July 1937 Samson announced he was moving to London, Ontario. *The Lethbridge Herald* praised Samson and showed no enthusiasm for his departure: "As director of Camp Inuspi, Samson achieved an enviable regard and increased both activity and attendance at the camp."

Ranson vividly recalled Samson not only as a key figure, but also one who was much admired. "He was one of the greatest guys I ever knew. He taught us values we didn't even know we were learning and was more like a second father to us. He touched a lot of young men's lives."

George Swedish, who had joined the Y in 1930, credited Samson for coming up with the idea for the camp. In an interview years later, Swedish recalled that he and a fellow hiker had found a hidden valley above Inuspi at the head of Sofa Creek.

"It was about one-half mile by three-quarters of a mile with a creek that would disappear in and out of the rock. We built a cairn there and dubbed it Samson Valley." Although the valley is not designated on topographical maps, it became a well-known destination to generations of Camp Inuspi hikers and other Waterton aficionados.

In 1938, a new, hipped-roof log dining hall was built, in large measure thanks to a donation from Russell Bennett. It was dedicated on July 18 by Rev. Middleton, rector of Waterton's All-Saints Anglican Church. Among those present were YMCA officials and guests, including Senator Buchanan, and the campers. Carl Ranson, Denny's father and one of the founders of the camp, spoke briefly at the ceremony, noting that Camp Inuspi was unsurpassed in the West.

As usual, *The Lethbridge Herald* ensured the event received full coverage. In fact, because the publisher was among the initial supporters and so many children attending Camp Inuspi lived in Lethbridge, no camp in Waterton received more newspaper coverage.

Apart from the normal equipment and buildings for housing and feeding campers, there was one

Since kids will be kids, a "hospital hut" and nurse, above left, were a must at Camp Inuspi. At right is the camp's first dining hall, and in the distance Vimy Peak—an inspiring view highlighted every day by the morning sun.

special requirement at Inuspi: the camp bell. As camp counsellor Allan Little would later note, it was "the camp clock." It was used to wake campers and indicate every change of events throughout the day. And in the case of a roving bear or cougar, the ringing of the bell signalled an alert. It was a camp rule: the ringing of the bell was not to be ignored.

Camp Inuspi would, at different times, have two bells: a small one from a locomotive and a larger one from a school. The Canadian Pacific Railway donated the locomotive bell. It was placed on a tall pole outside the dining hall.

Some years later a replacement bell was installed, a "gift" from the Lethbridge School Board. Walter Harris, general secretary of the Y, wrote to the board noting a bell could do what a triangle, a siren or the power of the human lung could not—get campers' attention and response. When he requested the school board consider giving the camp the Central School's bell, as it hadn't been used in years, he caused quite a stir.

"I didn't even know there was a bell there," said school board trustee Gilbert C. Paterson. Undecided whether the bell should be donated or loaned, Paterson said, "We'll loan it to them and forget they have it." The only caveat was the YMCA had to pay for removal and transportation of the bell. The larger bell was procured, mounted in a hanger and installed on a stone wall at the camp.

Camp Inuspi created its own pool of leaders. Many were camp alumni too old to attend, but just the right age to serve as counsellors in training, later graduating to full-fledged counsellors. They knew the routine and the importance of such camp traditions as the campfire council, held every Friday to initiate new campers into the "tribe of Inuspi."

At the council, blankets were worn Native fashion and each camper pledged loyalty to Inuspi and to each other while friendship sticks were held in the flames of the fire. Counsellors would then supervise leg wrestling competitions, talk fests and nail driving contests.

The authenticity of these Native-inspired activities was aided by Fred Albert "Gramps" Botsford, who had worked at a trading post near Calgary and as a fur trader in northern Alberta. He had befriended and earned the respect of many Indigenous people in the area and was made an honorary member of the Blood Tribe.

The camp bell at Inuspi was the universal signal to campers to pay heed, whether it was to mark meal times, participate in new activities or announce emergencies. On a calm day it could be heard for miles.

Botsford had arrived in Lethbridge in 1914 and was said to have been a friend of Kootenai Brown. As a long-time member of the YMCA, his participation at Camp Inuspi each summer was eagerly sought and he shared Native lore with campers until 1957, when he was 77 years old.

Another camping custom was the "snipe hunt," held whenever "the snipe began to flock" and whenever mischievous older campers wanted to pursue this mythical bird at the expense of younger, gullible newcomers. Despite years of expeditions in search of snipe, obviously no successes were ever recorded.

Development of Inuspi from vacant, difficult-to-access parkland to a well-equipped camp was no easy task and the Y was faced with many and varied financial problems. One of its greatest benefactors was Russell Bennett. Learning in 1941 that the camp would find it difficult to operate under wartime restrictions, Bennett gave the camp $450, which not only provided an outing for many needy girls and boys, but also cleared an accumulated construction deficit.

The camp not only continued to operate through the war but thrived. By 1944, financial assistance came from all the local service clubs, plus *The Lethbridge Herald*, the Sick's Brewery, the Stevens Memorial Fund, T. Eaton department store and the YMCA's Red Triangle Hostess Club. The money provided for

The July 1949 fire at Camp Inuspi destroyed the dining hall, but public support from residents and businesses across southern Alberta ensured funds were collected and a new hall built at a nearby site.

two new sleeping cabins, a directors' cabin, a craft shop, a water storage and supply system, an electric fence and several additional boats. By this time the camp could accommodate 80 youngsters per session, with hundreds attending each summer.

For $8.50 a week, a boy at least 10 years of age could stay at Inuspi for up to three weeks and a girl, the same age, up to two weeks. During the war, campers were required to bring along their ration coupon books to comply with government regulations.

The postwar success of Camp Inuspi hit a major bump on Saturday, July 16, 1949. Campers, all boys, were jarred awake at 2:40 a.m. by a fire alarm. It took 25 minutes for volunteer firefighters in Waterton townsite to wake up and rush equipment 10.5 kilometres (six and a half miles) to the camp, by which time the buildings were engulfed in flames. Not surprisingly, a strong wind was blowing and it took firefighters over three hours to bring the blaze under control. In the end, the kitchen, dining lounge and ice house were lost. Damage was estimated at $9,000, only part of which was covered by insurance. Oddly, the fire was believed to have started in the ice house.

Russell Bennett

Fortunately, no one was injured. Camp director Bert Stretton had gathered the boys near the lakeshore to wait out the firefighting effort. When daylight broke, although most of the camp's food had been destroyed, the boys were given a slim breakfast by cook Bobbie Steadman, sharing three rings of bologna that had been saved and supplemented with bread and jam sandwiches brought from town. The campers then climbed on a bus to return to Lethbridge.

Long-time Waterton folks still speak of the fire at Camp Inuspi, and it has become something of an insider's legend that has been handed down from one generation to the next, with numerous variations that range from stories of witnessing the fire to the destruction and immediate demise of the camp.

The story of the camp's resurrection, however, is one of fact and one of the proudest moments in its history.

The YMCA's board of directors, stunned by news of the fire, held an emergency meeting two days later and planned a visit to the camp on the weekend. It was decided not to cancel the balance of the camp sessions that summer, as a large percentage of those campers were underprivileged children. The Y turned the newly erected and undamaged handicraft hut into a dining room and gratefully accepted use of a modern trailer kitchen along with a large marquee tent offered by the General Construction Co. of Lethbridge, which was working in the park.

Within days of the fire, cash and donations of material began to flow from Lethbridge and district residents, a sign of the respect the camp had garnered across southern Alberta. Workers from the General Construction Co. came en masse to the camp to build shelves and storage places without which the approaching girls' camp would have been impossible.

The new Canyon Church Camp gave $50, T. Eaton department store gave $100 and Eaton's employees added $25, Advance Lumber gave $75 worth of wood, Lethbridge Farm Equipment donated $25, and Southern Stationers sponsored a Camp Inuspi rebuilding fund contest. Even the Lethbridge Motorcycle Club arranged to put on a public show in support of the fund. Within a month, the fund totaled $3,097.41 and more was to come. Once again, Camp Inuspi was indebted to its southern Alberta supporters.

In May 1950, Oland Construction was chosen to rebuild the dining lodge and kitchen at a cost of $11,000. Twice as large as the former dining hall, the new timber, glass and stone building had seating for 200 campers with large stone fireplaces at both ends of the building built by Walter B. Foster and his son Rob. It was situated on a clearing in the trees high above the old location, giving campers a panoramic view of the lake and mountains. Summer camps continued during the construction period using temporary facilities.

As a personal donation, Doug G. Oland provided a 2,270-litre (500-gallon) water tank for the camp and Lethbridge architect George Robins, who had attended the very first camp in 1934, drew the building plans free of charge. The new facility was completed in time for a ceremony on Labour Day 1950.

Camp Inuspi continued to figure large in the lives of the young people who attended. Chester Robins, a camp committee member, was asked how the boys

Following the 1949 fire that destroyed the dining hall at Camp Inuspi, a public display was created in Lethbridge to help potential donors understand the camp's plan for a new layout. Fred Botsford attended the display.

The public was invited to visit the new main building at Camp Inuspi, which featured space for indoor activities when the weather was inclement. It was built by Oland Construction, with fireplaces at both ends of the lodge. The fireplaces were built by local contractor Walter B. Foster and his son Rob. The hall was a major improvement to camp facilities.

liked the camp. "Well, when you come down to Inuspi with them on the bus," he said, "you can hardly hear yourself think. But when you're going back to the city with them, it's hard to find a boy to talk to. They're nearly all homesick—for Inuspi."

With the new facilities came organizational changes. For the first time the YMCA offered a week of camping to adults, those 19 years of age and older. At the end of the summer of 1951, the camp had seen its largest attendance since it was opened: some 160 boys totalling 214 camper weeks, and 200 girls totalling 295 camper weeks.

Inuspi made front page news again on July 21, 1955, when two campers, Duane Clayton, 11, and Gayland Erickson, 12, both of Warner, Alberta, were attacked by a bear that broke into their sleeping cabin in the early morning. Both boys were admitted to hospital in Cardston and treated for head lacerations. Five other boys in the cabin were unharmed and were credited with driving off the bear. A park warden was posted at the camp and the bear, later determined to have been suffering from an undisclosed disease, was killed the following day.

Throughout the rest of the 1950s and 1960s, many improvements were made to the camp. It was ranked among the top camps in Canada for leadership, location and programs, and was featured in the nationally distributed *Weekend Magazine*, a newspaper supplement. Appropriately, it was professional photogra-

pher Denny Ranson, whose mother owned a summer residence in the park and who had been an Inuspi camper himself as a youth, who took the photos for the magazine, one of which featured his nephew, Bob Worthington.

Then it was over. Without warning to the public, Camp Inuspi did not open in 1969. The fate of the camp only became public on April 20, 1971: the lease was surrendered and the buildings were sold to the federal government for $18,000.

The Lethbridge Herald quoted Ken Spence, executive director of the local YMCA, as saying the sale was made in accordance "with a new government policy to get rid of private enterprise in the national parks." In fact, the policy was not aimed at private enterprise so much as outlying facilities, but Spence's bitterness was widely shared. The personal pleas of southern Albertans hoping to persuade Ottawa officials to make an exception fell on deaf ears.

A week later, another newspaper article noted that the government's policy for national parks no longer favoured leasing land to organizations such as youth groups, churches and clubs. This was a complete reversal of the park philosophy that had launched the camp 34 years earlier. Now, the report noted, only government-owned facilities would be made available to groups.

The Lethbridge YMCA began looking for alternative camping venues. As Ken Spence acknowledged in 1973, residential camping like the defunct YMCA Camp Inuspi appeared to be a thing of the past. Family and wilderness camps were the future.

From 1971 to 1978, under federal ownership, the camp facilities housed the Conservation Corps, a youth employment initiative. The last of the buildings was moved off the site in the summer of 1981, with two of them going to Yarrow Creek, where they were used for warden patrol and warden cabin-storage sheds until being destroyed in 2015.

The road to Camp Inuspi from the Chief Mountain Highway reverted to a trail in 1981 and is now known as Wishbone Trail.

For a few years the YMCA held camps at Westcastle, west of Pincher Creek, but would have to wait until 1983 to return to Waterton, leasing space and briefly sharing time at Canyon Church Camp.

Mothers' Camp

Established in 1930, the Mothers' Camp was one of only two camps in the townsite, but the words "roughing it" hardly applied. The camp was the first major project of the then year-old Kiwanis Club of Lethbridge and was intended for underprivileged mothers and their young children.

With the effects of the Depression taking hold in southern Alberta, the idea of a camp in Waterton appealed to the members of the service club because it gave mothers who would ordinarily not get a vacation a holiday in a "scenic wonderland."

Dr. Bob Lynn, a charter member of the Lethbridge Kiwanis Club, was credited with the idea. He told *The Lethbridge Herald* "that the club could do nothing more thoughtful or fitting in making a contribution to the community service than to relieve groups of deserving mothers from the cares and humdrum of home and family for a week or 10 days by giving mothers an outing at Waterton."

"Inglenook" cabin on Mount View Road was the site of the Lethbridge Kiwanis Club's highly successful Mothers' Camp, which was expanded to an adjacent, larger cabin named "Inglemere."

Various Kiwanis members were well acquainted with the park, being either cabin owners or regular visitors. Les Allen, a Lethbridge dentist and park cabin owner, scouted the townsite, recommending that the club lease a two-year-old cabin owned by Mary Mason, wife of Lethbridge painter John Alfred Mason who worked for the park in the summer.

Mrs. Mason's "Inglenook" cabin was located on the western portion of what is now the site of Bear Mountain Motel (formerly the El Cortez Motel). She rented the cabin to the Kiwanis club for $150 for the month of July. The club hired her as camp matron at the rate of $13.75 a week.

Not only was "Inglenook" new, but it was also conveniently situated close to Emerald Bay and the lakeshore trail, and was a leisurely walk from the children's playground, tennis courts and Cameron Falls.

A committee of three, comprising Gordon Porter, Fred Becker and Jesse Bigelow, was appointed to devise ways of raising the necessary money for the camp. Eager to get the project underway, club members decided to organize a "tag day," a downtown sidewalk solicitation in which donors were given a tag to pin on and identify them as contributors. A common fundraising event of the time, the tag day netted $1,100, breaking all previous records in Lethbridge, then a city of 14,000 people.

The cost for the club to operate the camp was about $8.70 per guest per week, which included all expenses except transportation to and from the park. Throughout the life of the camp, the operating cost averaged near this figure and the Kiwanians continued to solicit public donations, appropriately by holding a tag day on or near Mother's Day.

Guests at the camp were selected with the help of the Nursing Mission, the Lady Kiwanians and other institutions. Each selected mother could be accompanied by one child up to the age of 10.

The Lethbridge Herald made a special effort to cover the first week-long camp, which began July 13, 1930: "It was a happy day for the Kiwanians of the city for it saw the realization of plans that have been maturing for months. Six mothers and as many eager little tots are now at 'Inglenook' as guests of the club and are they enjoying it? One appreciative mother

Children attending the Mothers' Camp only had to step out the cabin door to find wildlife in Waterton, as deer frequent the townsite. Feeding wildlife is now forbidden.

exclaimed, 'It doesn't really seem possible that we are all to stay here a week with nothing to do but enjoy ourselves in these wonderful mountains. It is all too glorious to be true!'

Anna Tilley

"Miss [Anna] Tilley and the staff of the Nursing Mission entertained the Kiwanis mothers and their kiddies at breakfast [in Lethbridge], taking a few minutes to tell club members of the value of their efforts: 'You Kiwanians cannot know fully what a wonderful thing you have done by making it possible for some of our city mothers who could not otherwise get away from home ties and the cares and responsibilities of their families to spend a holiday in the mountains. . . . The benefit these mothers will receive cannot be told—it will give them a new inspiration, a new hope, a new grip on life—for it will place them in an entirely new and beautiful and wholesome environment.' "

After a hearty morning meal, the club men had their cars waiting to whisk the mothers and children away—away from the daily routine of home and family life for a glorious week's holiday. Seven cars carried the party safely to Waterton.

Mary Mason served as matron every year the camp was held. She settled the mothers and children into their bright, clean and cheerful accommodations and had lunch ready soon after.

The cabin's two large bedrooms, a screened sleeping porch divided with curtains for privacy, and a living room furnished with Windsor couches that easily converted into beds, providing ample sleeping space for a dozen or more. The Victrola record player in the living room was an added touch, and a small library was available. The guests were not assigned any "camp" duties except to make the most of their mountain rest. For many, it was the first such opportunity in their lives.

"There are no rules—it is just a happy home for tired mothers where cares drop away and the spicy smell of the pine, lovely lakes and peaceful mountains mingle their healing powers for the contentment of weary minds and lend refreshment to tired souls, and to carefree happiness to the tiny tots accompanying their mothers," *The Lethbridge Herald* assured its readers.

The Kiwanis Club was thrilled with the camp's success and at a September 1930 luncheon, Kiwanians showered Mary Mason with praise, flowers and gifts. By the following spring the Masons had built a second cabin one door to the west, called "Inglemere," with room for 14 people. The camp moved to this larger, newer cabin for six weeks in 1931. As an added feature, camp guests were given a complimentary ride on the excursion boat *Motor Vessel International*, which carried passengers to the head of Upper Waterton Lake.

Les Allen became chairman of the Mothers' Camp, telling club members at a November 1931 meeting that he considered it "our excuse for existence as a club and we should go wholeheartedly into the matter of the successful conducting of the activity."

Focusing on mothers who needed to convalesce after illnesses, the Kiwanis Club's camp was ideal.

"I had never had a holiday since coming from England years ago," one mother told a reporter. ". . . I thought Canada was a flat, dull place with little natural beauty until the Kiwanians kindly took me to their Mothers' Camp at Waterton. There I had my first holiday in Canada, and it was glorious up there in the mountains. It came as a blessing to me."

The Kiwanis Club in Lethbridge worked hard to raise funds to operate its Mothers' Camp.

The camp was a summer ritual until 1938, when the last group was hosted. By then, an estimated 700 mothers and their children had been guests of the club. In 1939, the club felt it had fairly well exhausted local deserving cases and put its efforts into special sponsorships of children at Camp Inuspi, and helping to build new facilities there, later assisting other camps in the park.

Mary Mason, who was widowed in 1937, sold "Inglemere" in 1941 and "Inglenook" in 1952.

Canyon Church Camp

Canyon Church Camp, located in the Blakiston Valley near Red Rock Canyon, began in 1944 as a permanent camp but its origins are tied to a church-run group for boys founded in 1939—the New Dayton Trail Rangers.

The Rangers was started by John Mayell of New Dayton, Alberta, and his assistant, Emanuel Heuer, a United Church minister. It was made up of boys between the ages of 12 and 16. The two men worked out a program that included a Tuxis Parliament, a longstanding, Christian-based boy's educational activity which included debate, as well as skiing, tobogganing, hiking and camping.

In July 1940 the New Dayton Trail Rangers, together with the Boy Scouts of Warner and Milk River, Alberta, pitched their tents along Pass Creek (now Blakiston Creek) on the site of what is now the church camp. This location was some distance from the campsite normally used by Boy Scouts. Later that summer it provided a place for a group of Canadian Girls in Training from the same three towns to use all the tents and equipment.

When he returned to the site on the 50th anniversary of that camp, Heuer recalled how it started: "I took three boys from Warner and New Dayton [Bill Combs, Bill Norris and Rex McKenzie] and we left home at 5 a.m. to spend the day to look for a campsite. The wardens told us to look for water and wood."

The first place they found turned out to be the best of several they considered. For 10 days, the 35 boys—under the supervision of Heuer, Johnny Mayell, Grant Carnine and George Fyfe—got a taste of camping in the mountains. The camp was so memorable and popular to these young prairie residents that the Waterton outings continued for several years. By then, it was apparent a permanent camp would be desirable.

Since a large organization had a better chance of obtaining a lease for a camp, as well as raising funds needed to bring it to fruition, Rev. Heuer suggested to the Lethbridge Presbytery of the United Church of Canada in 1944 that it submit an application to the park. The history of United Church youth camps in Western Canada was a long one, with the first founded in Saskatchewan in 1905.

In making his recommendation to Ottawa that a lease be approved, and to expedite the process, park superintendent Herbert A. DeVeber had drawn a site plan in July 1943 and attached it to the paperwork.

Ottawa readily approved the camp, confident the United Church would be able to live up to its commitment. Government officials initially provided an annual lease, promising to issue a long-term lease on the 0.8-hectare (two-acre) site once buildings were constructed to their satisfaction.

Although members of the presbytery were worried that wartime restrictions on building materials would delay construction of the Waterton camp, they

Canyon Church Camp's cabins featured bunk beds and little else. Below, the main lodge at the camp, which has plenty room for indoor activities.

were able to obtain enough in the summer of 1944 to build a dining hall-kitchen, one sleeping cabin and an outhouse.

Much of the labour was volunteer, under the direction of Carl Carlson, a long-time local builder. According to Mary Saruwatari, a group from Taber, Alberta, including Japanese Canadians relocated from British Columbia, helped build the camp and were paid 25 cents an hour. With the main dining hall accommodating 80 youngsters at one sitting, it was just the right size not only for meals, but also for indoor activities during inclement weather.

In the humour that only a camp can provide, the outhouse became known as "Mr. Brown," some would say for Kootenai Brown, others for the colour of the building, with the most polite simply refusing to say. The outhouse was universally hated by campers, who normally had access to flush toilets.

Borrowing tents and other equipment, church leaders were able to schedule three 10-day sessions that first summer, one for boys and two for girls. The first session began July 17, 1944, under the direction of Rev. W.J. Collett of Claresholm, Alberta. Fees were $1 a day plus $3 for transportation. The children came from throughout the southern part of the province and while the camp was open to youngsters of all denominations, over the years its brochures emphasized the "Christian character building" role of the camp.

Annual pre-season volunteer work parties ensured the Canyon Church Camp facilities were well maintained.

To finance the building program, United Church congregations in the Lethbridge area were canvassed and raised $3,200 for the camp, but more money was needed for additional buildings. Even before the first summer sessions were completed, plans for next year's improvements and future session schedules were underway. Most of the building plans for 1945, however, had to be held in abeyance when the Controller of Wartime Construction refused to issue a licence, since the work was not considered "essential." Only one additional sleeping cabin was permitted. Enthusiasm was in great supply, even if building materials were not.

The camp grew gradually as money and materials became available. By September 1950, nine sleeping cabins and a modern shower-toilet house, ablution shelter and an insulated cooling house had been built. A rustic but pleasing outdoor chapel was also a part of the facilities, and in the years to come would be the site for not only religious services, but also weddings and baptisms. Paige Allison Burns, daughter of camp nurse Dianne Burns of Pincher Creek, was the first to be baptized at the outdoor chapel, in August 1971.

Each camper was required to bring a mattress casing or tick (straw was provided as were bed springs), warm bedding (at least three blankets), rubber-soled shoes, wool socks, slacks, a heavy sweater, bathing suit, sports equipment, two towels, soap, tooth brush,

comb, Bible, pencil, notebook and hiking boots. Sessions for Canadian Girls in Training and Explorers required an extra middy to wear for Sunday services at the chapel.

There was no end of activities for the campers, with Crandell Lake just 1.6 kilometres (one mile) distant for a hike and a swim. Like the other camps, friendships were formed and challenges met in a setting that was nothing like home. Many campers would return year after year and as was the case at Camp Inuspi, some participants returned to become counsellors. That the campers might return home not only happy but "many pounds heavier" was considered a real benefit of the camp, and was noted in a camp song titled *Wind*:

> *Let's give a cheer for the cooks in the kitchen*
> *We thank them for the food they been fixin'*
> *We hear the bell so let's get at 'er*
> *We'll all go home at least 10 pounds fatter*

When the kids went home a little heavier, it was due primarily to the work of Kate Parry of Taber, who began as the camp cook in 1944 and continued in that position for the next 20 consecutive summers. She was assisted for years by Mrs. M. Meikle.

If an army runs on its stomach, so too does a camp, and those having to rough it should not be the cooks. "They are wonderful cooks, and it is mostly on their account that this year we installed a propane range, propane refrigerator and made improvements that the cooks would appreciate," Rev. A.E. King of Southminster United Church in Lethbridge, and a camp director, told *The Lethbridge Herald* in 1952.

The cooks did indeed appreciate the improve-

A rustic outdoor vespers area, above left, was set apart from other buildings to take advantage of nature's offerings. The Kate Perry Lodge, above, contained numerous wooden tables for every purpose under the sun, including meals, crafts and presentations. A small infirmary, below, was also built at Canyon Chuch Camp.

The Canyon Church Camp's cooks made efficient use of the limited available kitchen space. Campers were expected to participate in cleaning up after meals.

ments. Parry recalled the years when camp conditions were not exactly "homey," as she put it: milk was kept in tubs of ice and meat was put in waterproof bags in the river.

Having cooked the meals for so many boys and girls over the years, it was appropriate that in 1963 the dining-recreation hall be named for Kate Parry. More than 200 people attended the dedication. Her photo hung for many years in the dining hall alongside that of Queen Elizabeth II.

Children weren't the only ones to attend the camp. As an experiment, in 1951 an adult family camp was scheduled for late August. It was created so children who were too young to go to camp by themselves could attend with their parents. It was successful enough to be continued for several years.

Kate Parry

In 1971, two other variations on the youth camps were attempted. One was the introduction of a week-long camp for seniors. Very loosely structured, it included an opportunity for companionship, handicrafts and enjoying the mountains. Due to the number of amateur musicians in attendance, those who didn't want to go for group walks were entertained by their fellow campers. Among them was Harriet McDonald, who played the piano and whose audience described her music as "fantastic."

The first seniors' session, attended by 14 people, was well received. One male guest told *The Lethbridge Herald*, "This is the first Sunday in about four years that I haven't been lonely."

The seniors' camps continued through the decade.

Another variation at the camp saw the arrival of patients from homes for the mentally ill in Claresholm and Raymond, Alberta. Some had never been out of their institutions. Others were outpatients recommended by the Lethbridge Municipal Hospital. They could leave behind the rules and participate in a Gay Nineties carnival, painting, games, dancing, a song-writing contest and hikes. This camp was also held several successive years.

For five years starting in 1983, Canyon Church Camp was managed by the YMCA. Steve Rocque, director of young peoples' programs at the Y, told *The Lethbridge Herald* that the church found the administrative duties too difficult and asked the YMCA to take over. "We jumped at the opportunity to get back into this area," Rocque said.

The United Church continued to book camp sessions for its youths, using the services of the YMCA which, in turn, ran two sessions of its own. It was the first time since it had sold Camp Inuspi that the YMCA was able to offer camping in Waterton.

Management of the Canyon Church Camp reverted to the United Church in 1988, but for several years the YMCA continued to rent scheduled weeks, as did the Lions International Youth, the Artists Club of Fort Macleod, Mennonite Youth, and on one weekend in June, Canadian Girls in Training.

Supported by South Alberta and Foothills Presbyteries of the United Church, the camp is administered by a 15-person board whose goal is to make camping financially available to young people. As a member of the United Church Camping Association, Canyon Church Camp is required to adhere to the accreditation standards of the Alberta Camping Association and is the only youth camp in Waterton so recognized. It can accommodate 97 campers and staff in each session. For its own sessions, the United Church aims to nurture "Christian faith through fun and fellowship in God's outdoors," with a focus on hiking.

The Canyon Church Camp, the youngest among its United Church camp peers, is now the oldest surviving youth camp in Waterton. That may be because it wasn't until 1953 that officials in Ottawa insisted the Church Camp Association sign a long-term lease for the land, which it had occupied for eight years. Due to the delayed signing, the original lease didn't expire until March 1975, by which time the government's policy toward existing camps had been amended, thus avoiding the fate of Camp Inuspi.

Fifty per cent of the camp area was devastated by the 2017 Kenow forest fire, despite park crews' best efforts to prevent damage. The Kate Perry Lodge, the bear shed, the custodian cabin, the boys' bathroom, and Cabins 1, 2, and 3 all survived the fire. Unfortunately, lost to the fire were the craft shack, medic's cabin, most of the staff cabins, Cabins 4 to 7, the girl's washrooms and the outdoor vespers area.

When the extent of the damage was known, southern Albertans swung into action to raise funds for rebuilding of the camp, much to the elation of the camp committee. It took until 2021 to obtain Parks Canada's approval to begin rebuilding, as well as that of the United Church itself.

The first step, planned for 2022, was to improve the sewer system, which was unaffected by the fire but was, nevertheless, needed.

Camp Tee-La-Daw

Seeing the success of Canyon Church Camp, Leroy Rollins of Cardston, a member of the Church of Jesus Christ of Latter-day Saints, expressed interest in 1950 in building a camp near Red Rock Canyon "along the order of that built by the United Church."

Park officials moved slowly on this inquiry and when the former residence of the chief park warden on the southwest shore of Lower Waterton Lake was suggested by the church, park administrators balked. They said they might need the location, known as the Cedar Cabin site. In 1953, park officials reconsidered, demolished the crumbling cabin and the Mormon church received a short-term lease for a camp on the site.

The all-girls camp, the only one in the park, was a project of the Taylor stake of the LDS church in Raymond and the culmination of six years' planning and fundraising.

Fifty girls and supervisors could be accommodated in the two large camp buildings, which cost $13,000. The dormitory-recreation building was designed with adjoining shower and locker rooms, and

Having received approval for the design of camp Tee-La-Daw, Mormons hold a brief sod-turning ceremony to mark the beginning of construction, most of which was done by volunteers from the Taylor stake in Raymond, Alberta.

Girls Camp Opened
July 31, 1954

Dedicated camp committee members, from left, Bertha Stone, Dorothy Dahl, Zina Anderson, president Zettella Taylor, Phoebe Dahl, Elenor Hudson and Maria Strong were from the Taylor stake of the Mormon Church.

Fire claimed Camp Tee-La-Daw in May 1970, the cause never determined. The camp was not rebuilt due to changes in park rules related to outlying developments.

the beds could be folded against the wall to provide plenty of space for indoor recreation when necessary. The other building contained the dining room and a kitchen equipped with a coal and wood cooking range, with double sinks built on either side of an island.

The camp buildings were laid out in an "L" configuration, which provided space for an outdoor amphitheatre, equipped with stage and floodlights for after-dark activities. An outdoor fireplace backed onto the fireplace in the recreation building. Built by local stone mason Walter B. "Waddy" Foster, the fireplace allowed the girls to stay outside but close to the camp for evening events. As at other camps, mornings always started with a flag-raising ceremony.

Located close to the incoming power line for the park, electricity for the camp was then provided by Calgary Power and water was supplied from a well with a pressure tank system. The buildings, just below Knight's Hill, were so well hidden from view of the road that for many years visitors were unaware of their presence.

The opening ceremony for what became known as Camp Tee-La-Daw was held Aug. 3, 1954. The name was said to have been given in honour of Mrs. Frank Taylor under whose leadership the camp was built. As a child in Utah, she was given the sobriquet by an old Swedish gentleman. It was a nickname that stuck with her as she grew up. It was not until she was an adult that she said she learned Tee-La-Daw was Swedish for "little girl."

Although most of the summer was over by the time the camp opened in 1954, six groups comprising a total of 44 girls camped for three days each during the first season. All the camp work, including the cooking and cleanup, was done by the girls under adult supervision. In subsequent years, the camp operated for two full months, for girls 12 and up. By 1960, two sessions were added for married women.

Camp Tee-La-Daw met its end in a fire on Tuesday, May 19, 1970, just after replacement furniture had been moved in and the six-person board of directors had checked the buildings. Volunteer firefighters, park wardens and maintenance staff rushed to the camp from the townsite, doing their best over two hours to extinguish the fire. It was a lost cause and the camp burned to the ground.

Mop-up activities carried on through early evening. About 0.8 hectares (two acres) of nearby mixed forest were also consumed. The cause of the fire was not determined, and the building was only partially insured. The fire's devastation ended plans for that summer's camp.

The Taylor stake decided not to rebuild, given the federal government's plans to disallow private camp ownership as announced in its new master plan a year later. The lease was surrendered, the land reclaimed and the site was later restored to a natural state.

Camp Columbus

Close on the heels of the Mormons establishing Camp Tee-La-Daw, members of the Catholic Church began to sound out park officials about a camp.

In 1954, Danny Gilborn, Gene Cody and Joe Hovan, members of the Knights of Columbus in Milk River, Alberta, began making inquiries. When the Knights applied for permission for a camp lease, the group requested one of four locations: two were on Pass Creek; one along Upper Waterton Lake; and one along Middle Waterton Lake, opposite Vimy Peak. Park officials refused the Upper Lake location in no uncertain terms, settling in 1956 on the Middle Lake site.

Estimated to cost $25,000, Camp Columbus was to have one large camp building in a "U" configuration to include sleeping quarters, toilets and showers, a dining-recreation area and the kitchen. From a maintenance point of view, the layout was ideal: there was just one building to paint and keep up. According to the newspaper announcement, the camp would "compare favourably with any now in southern Alberta."

"Who would like to ring the bell?" was a favourite question asked of new arrivals at Camp Columbus. The chosen volunteer was greeted with a surprise when he or she gave the rope a tug.

The camp occupied about two hectares (five acres). The facility could accommodate about 250 children between the ages of nine and 16 each summer.

The Knights of Columbus got behind the camp project in a big way, drawing on the financial and volunteer support of councils from Lethbridge, Pincher Creek and Milk River. As well, it began a house-to-house canvas of Catholics in the area and sold tickets for a draw to raise money for the camp.

By May 1956, the plans and specifications for the building had been approved and construction began, with the hope it would be ready by July. In fact, it would take a year for Sieben and Schamber, general contractors from Milk River, to complete the work.

On July 1, 1957, Gene Cody of Milk River, chairman of the camp construction committee, cut the ribbon to open Camp Columbus and the celebration, which included Dominion Day events, was kicked off with a flag raising while the Milk River band played *O Canada*. Throughout the afternoon, visitors took part in bingo, races and other outdoor games. Leonard Knapik of Cowley, Alberta, recalled serving barbecued beef to 1,200 people that day.

One week later, the camp began its first 10-day session with camp manager Bruce Field supervising the boys and Mary Stadnicki, matron for the girls' session. Administration of the camp was under the direction of U.J. Pittman of Lethbridge, with Victor Pittman of Warner in change of registration and information. The board of directors was made up of church members from 14 area parishes.

In 1961, arrangements were made by St. Augustine's Anglican Church in Lethbridge to rent Camp Columbus for two weeks in August. The Anglicans continued to rent the camp each August for the next several years. Like Canyon Church Camp, those in charge saw merit in sharing.

Here, as at other camps, hijinks were a normal part of the summer events. Mariette Moroz of Lethbridge, who cooked at the camp for three seasons in the 1970s, remembered Sundays as being an arrival day for one group and departure day for another. The coming and going each had its own traditions.

"When a new group would arrive," Moroz said, "we'd all gather under the [upturned] camp bell and then ask, 'Who would like to ring the bell?' "

The returning campers would know why the bell was turned upward: it was filled with water and the first eager newcomer to volunteer to ring the bell would get drenched, much to the laughter of all on hand.

The evening before departing, the campers would hold a kind of kangaroo court, complete with invented "misdemeanours." The "punishments," carried out for the pleasure of all, might involve something silly like trying to eat popcorn without hands and similar stunts. It was all in fun and became cherished camp memories.

There were times when more serious punishments were enforced under camper self-rule. To let someone know his or her behaviour or attitude didn't meet with general approval, the kids sometimes ran the offending camper's underwear up the flag pole, a humiliation for all to see.

Moroz, mother of three sons, had considerable additional experience with youngsters as a school bus driver and was well acquainted with the things kids will do. In fact, sometimes she would help them, such as when a group put Cornflakes in the camp director's sleeping bag, everyone listening with anticipation for his discovery of the dirty deed.

Feeding the 48 youngsters three times a day was a major responsibility. As the camp cook, Moroz was on her own unless one of her sons, who came to camp with her, or one of the other children volunteered. "If they were peeling potatoes," she said, "you'd have to watch them closely or there'd be no potatoes left." They would peel the spuds down to nothing.

Camp Columbus was missed by the 2017 Kenow forest fire that swept through Waterton, but was forced to close during the COVID-19 epidemic. This well-maintained facility was built in 1957 and is close enough to the townsite and adjacent trailheads to get campers out and about.

A ball game requires little by way of equipment while teaching campers the spirit of sportsmanship and the importance of keeping their eyes on the ball.

The worst part of being the camp cook, Moroz said, was getting up at 5:30 every morning to prepare for the day, which started for the kids at 7:30 a.m. She had only one day a week off, when the entire group went for an overnight outing, and that was only if the weather permitted. The meal for the outing was prepared before the kids left: foil packets frozen to keep them from spoiling and easy to cook over a camp fire.

"The best part of the day," she recalled, "was when the kids had all gone to bed and the counsellors and I would sit by the fireplace, have a glass of wine and think about the day." Even then, the counsellors would be attuned to the giggles and talking in the sleeping area and have to shout a reminder to "Go to sleep!"

Only once in three summers does Moroz recall a bear causing problems at the camp. The first clue was when a group in the kitchen heard breathing, snorting and then scratching. "We all ran from the windows. The girls just screamed and screamed," she said. The youngsters thought the bear was going to break into the building.

Campers at Columbus had easy access to Middle Waterton Lake for canoeing and learning the finer points of water safety, but after the Olympic-sized, heated swimming pool opened in 1960 in the townsite, just a few miles distant, attendees could hike to the pool, take lessons and swim in relative luxury.

For many years Columbus's faded blue van was a common sight in Waterton, a reminder to park residents and knowledgeable visitors of the camp's existence. The van was frequently seen parked at the Waterton Lakes Resort, where campers used the indoor pool after the outdoor one was removed, as well as at trail heads when it dropped off the kids. Duffers also became aware of Columbus as on a calm day the camp bell could be heard from the golf course early in the morning as it cut the clean mountain air calling children from their beds.

The activities at Camp Columbus were seldom reported in the local media over the years, with one exception. On July 25, 1973, five boys became separated from their group of 23 while on a two-night outing, resulting in the death of 12-year-old Arthur Joseph Cordiero of Lethbridge who was found at the bottom of a cliff on Mount Lineham. The accident and subsequent inquest cast a terrible pall over the campers and counsellors that summer.

It was only a fluke of nature—or perhaps divine intervention—that the 2017 Kenow forest fire did not reach Camp Columbus while it destroyed the nearby Alpine Stables. Health regulations to combat the COVID-19 epidemic however, closed the camp for several seasons.

The camp philosophy, simply expressed on its website, remains as true today as it was when written: "The camp program is one that emphasizes Christian Spirit, concern for our fragile environment and co-operation with others, while still allowing the campers to maintain their own special and unique individuality."

* * *

Today, only Canyon Church Camp and Camp Columbus continue to own facilities in Waterton. The effects of the Kenow forest fire and the subsequent COVID-19 epidemic have temporarily brought camp activities to a halt, but it is hoped a camp schedule will resume in the not-too-distant future.

For the thousands who were fortunate enough to attend any one of the six camps over the years, the other camps will live on, if only in memories.

The owners of some 300 Airstream trailers visited Waterton in 1962 as one stop on a tour of the western United States and Canada organized by the famous Wally Byam Caravan Club. The members of the club, named for the founder of the company that builds Airstream recreational trailers, parked their rigs at an overflow campground about 3.2 kilometres (two miles) from Waterton townsite.

Chapter 6

Gone But Not Forgotten

Slightly Ahead of Their Time

When Edward Leighton of Los Angeles, California, found a spot to camp in Waterton in August 1923, a year before a formal campground in the townsite was opened, he made history.

The modified REO caravan he was driving was the first motorized recreational vehicle to enter the park. Vacationers had likely used horse-drawn caravans previously in Waterton, but never had a conveyance adapted to leisure travel been mechanically powered.

Leighton, a prominent agricultural attorney, had purchased an REO chassis with engine and then paid further to have it made into a "palace on wheels" for himself, his wife Kathryn and their son, Edward Jr.

It contained all the comforts of home including hot and cold water, cooking facilities, sleeping places and a radio set, then a novel technology.

The body of the vehicle was built of thick steel, with sides that unfolded to form two bedrooms, each with a full-sized mattress and springs. The main body of the vehicle was a combination sitting room and kitchen, with every space utilized to maximize storage and utility. By touching a spring on one of the sides of the vehicle, a writing table dropped down, equipped with pens, paper and ink. On the right side, another button exposed a proper wash basin with taps offering hot and cold water.

On the left side of the caravan was an oven with a heat regulator for baking. There was a fully stocked medicine chest and a boudoir cupboard completely furnished for Edward's wife, Kathryn. Comfortably sized dining and card tables and three richly upholstered swing chairs provided the seating.

The RV had electric lighting, was specially heated for chilly nights, while vacuum cleaners kept the house on wheels free from dust and dirt. Evenings were made enjoyable by listening to concerts on the radio that

The chassis of an REO Speedwagon, above, was the basis of the first gasoline-powered recreational vehicle to arrive in Waterton, in August 1923.

were broadcast from Los Angeles, San Francisco and other centres such as Calgary, where the radio craze sweeping North America had seen two stations, CFAC and CFCN, established in mid-1922.

The Leighton family had travelled about 5,600 kilometres (3,500 miles) before reaching Waterton, arriving from Banff.

The family intended to spend a few days in the park so Kathryn Leighton, well on her way to artistic fame, could paint one or two works featuring Waterton. She became renowned for her western landscape paintings and for portraits of Indigenous people such as the Blackfeet, whom she was later commissioned by Great Northern Railway president Louis W. Hill to paint.

Kathryn Leighton

While Edward Leighton's REO caravan was, at $5,000, expensive to build—by comparison, the cost of a new Ford Model T runabout was $364—he was convinced that it was a long-lasting, money-saving proposition. The fact others would follow in his path in all manner of recreational vehicles shows he was on to something.

Have Unit Will Travel

Fast forward to August 1962, when the Wally Byam Airstream Caravan arrived in Waterton.

A 20-hectare (five- acre) site known as the overflow campsite, near Camp Columbus, became the temporary locale for the caravan's 300 light-weight Airstream trailers. Business in Waterton was said to have boomed as caravan participants, identifiable by the dark blue berets they all wore, swarmed the townsite to purchase food and other supplies.

Described as "the friendliest group of people one could hope to meet anywhere," the 481 Airstream trailer owners had been on the road for about six weeks, having started from Auburn, Washington.

Airstream trailers, still manufactured today, were introduced in the 1930s and quickly became known for their distinctive, rounded shape and polished aluminum exterior, plus an interior that lacked for nothing. They carried their own water supply, complete with a pressure pump, a sewage storage tank, a dual electrical system, stove, refrigerator, and had a full bathroom. They also featured custom-built furniture that fit the curved walls of the units.

Each trailer cost an average of $4,000 in 1962 and weighed about 1,360 kilograms (3,000 pounds). Today an Airstream trailer can cost up to $170,000, depending on the model.

The caravan expedition was known to be excep-tionally well planned by its directors. Programs were arranged for participants, menus of local cafés were posted, tourist brochures were brought into the camp, and a company-paid mechanic was available with a supply of spare parts.

While in Waterton, a charter sightseeing boat was booked for the caravanners, as were golf tee times and saddlehorses. In fact, help was offered with any activities in which the members were interested.

The gleaming aluminum trailers at the overflow campground were said to be "an awe-inspiring sight." Waterton was the last stop for the group.

At the time the Byam Air Stream clubs had a membership of about 7,000 members throughout the United States and Canada.

Don't Leave Home Without It

A tourist arriving at the townsite campground in early September 2013 had everyone wondering what would be next when his RV pulled in with a trailer loaded with two kayaks, two bikes, assorted storage containers—and a helicopter. Later inspection by curious Waterton residents showed no one at the campsite so it was never discovered where the people were from or why they were towing a helicopter. It was, without question, one of the most unusual sights at the campground that season and subject to much speculation.

A boat or trailer with bicycles or motorcycles are not unusual items for campers to haul behind their vehicles, but few people in Waterton had ever seen, until September 2013, a helicopter towed as a needed vacation accessory.

Part of the fun attending the Glacier-Waterton Hamfest is checking out the equipment used by fellow amateur radio enthusiasts. Here, participants at the 1950 hamfest delight in examining a display set up on a picnic table.

Glacier-Waterton International Hamfest

The oldest continuous amateur radio enthusiasts' convention in the world is said to be the Glacier-Waterton International Hamfest—a tribute to the dedication of those who organize and attend it.

It arose from a meeting of several Montana amateur short-wave radio operators (a.k.a. hams) in 1934 at the Two Medicine Lake campground on the east side of Glacier National Park.

The men, who were generally isolated in their "ham shacks" and seldom if ever met in person, had such a good time they vowed to return the following year and in the meantime spread word of the event over their network, or "net." More enthusiasts soon joined them at the gatherings, upholding the common values of all hams to promote "fellowship, goodwill and mutual help for fans of this fascinating hobby."

That fascination with a technology that let enthusiasts talk to others anywhere in the world wasn't limited to south of the border and interested Alberta hams were invited to attend the Two Medicine gathering in 1937, for the first time making the get-together an international affair. Of the 71 licensed operators at the following year's hamfest, five were Albertans—two from Blackie and one each from Strathmore, Glenwood and Lethbridge.

There was discussion of holding the hamfest in Waterton in 1940, but the start of the Second World War nixed that plan. With the outbreak of hostilities, Canadian amateur radio operators were ordered by the government to dismantle their sets to prevent them from sending information to foreign countries without the approval of the censor board.

During the war many members of the Southern Alberta Amateur Radio Club joined the armed forces, providing the military their valuable experience.

The end of the war provided an opportunity for those new to amateur radio to get a foot in the door when the Canadian War Assets Corp. sold surplus parts and even complete radios for nominal sums. After years of waiting, Canadian hams scurried about buying tubes and other parts to resurrect their rigs.

Dr. Joseph "Doc" Dobry of Cardston, centre, helped make the Glacier hamfest an international affair, bringing it to Waterton. Below, his personalized automobile license plate featuring his call sign is a valued family heirloom.

Back on the air and with rubber and gasoline rationing now at an end, Canadian hams returned to the Glacier gatherings.

Dr. Joseph J. Dobry of Cardston, a Waterton cabin owner and a ham since age 13 (VE6DR), attended the 1946 event and proposed the name of the gathering be changed to "Glacier-Waterton International Peace Park Hamfest." His suggestion was accepted by the members.

In the spirit of the new name, Dobry was charged with organizing the event in Waterton for two days in July 1947, an assignment he willingly accepted.

In all, 150 members and their families attended the Waterton gathering, coming from all over the United States and western Canada.

Park superintendent Herbert A. DeVeber, himself a ham (VE6NL), formally welcomed the participants, and the national director of the American Red Cross spoke to the gathering on the subject of radio amateurs providing help to the Red Cross during disasters.

Dobry arranged a memorable program for the Waterton gathering. It included a bonfire, sing-song and gab fest, or in ham parlance a rag chewing. An excursion on the *Motor Vessel International* took convention attendees to Goat Haunt, Montana, at the head of Upper Waterton Lake. When they returned, they topped off the evening at the Saturday night dance in the pavilion on Waterton Avenue. The next day, after a business meeting to elect officers, the hamfest wound up with a picnic at Cameron Lake.

From then on, the hamfest was held two years in Glacier followed by one year in Waterton, a pattern that was repeated for the most part over the next 40 years.

What was done at each hamfest varied slightly but included variety enough to interest everyone as from early on spouses and children also attended the gatherings. There were "wiener busts," open air square dancing to live music, technical discussions, the showing of films, special speakers, an equipment sale, bingo, ball games and much more.

Wives, whether hams in their own right or not, were encouraged to be a part of the activities. The 1954 program included a special note just for them. Wives, known in the lexicon of hams as MYLs (My Young Lady), were told: "Do not wait for an invitation or an introduction. MYLs, this is your Hamfest as well as the OMs (Old Men). Step forward, there are other 'radio widows' just as anxious to meeting someone as you are." It was pure Canadian hospitality without an ounce of guile.

The Glacier-Waterton hamfest became so popular that by 1961, the 27th event, some 840 people, 216 of whom were hams, registered for the largest meeting in the group's history.

In Waterton so many hams attended that an overflow site near Camp Columbus was used as their primary gathering spot to handle the multitude. They have also gathered a few times at the Belly River campground, which had space for group camping.

There have been some departures in the venues in more recent years in an effort to accommodate all the hams, and due to a change in park policies related to group camping. Apart from meeting in Glacier and Waterton, the group has also stayed in Crowsnest Pass, Alberta (1977), Fort Macleod (1980), and the Homestead Campground adjacent to Waterton, (1986).

Since 1987, the group has quit meeting in Canada and gathers annually at Glacier Meadow RV Park (originally known as Three Forks Campground) in Essex, Montana, on Glacier's southern boundary. Canadians are still welcome and attend.

The continued appeal of the Glacier-Waterton International Hamfest is a reflection of the partici-pants' love of their hobby, their volunteerism in times of need and of peace, and hamdom's commitment to fostering international goodwill.

From Champs to Tourism Stars

When William Rodney became Waterton's first summer technical officer in 1948, he was handed a big job. In effect, he became a seasonal park inter-preter, a public relations man, and an organizer the likes of which has not since been entrusted to just one person.

That summer he announced a tennis tourna-ment would be held in the park, which then had four courts on Cameron Falls Drive. By way of a newspa-per announcement, he invited all comers to partici-pate.

Enid Dowdle of Cardston and Harry Wismer of Vulcan, Alberta, were a team in the mixed doubles and won their division, but little did they know their

Harry Wismer and Enid Dowdle make the traditional leap over the net after winning the mixed doubles tennis tournament in Waterton in 1948. The photo was used in major North American magazines to promote tourism in Canada.

images would appear in a full-page colour advertisement early in 1949 in *Life* and nine other magazines promoting tourism to Canada. The two players were shown leaping over a tennis court net, with the Prince of Wales Hotel in the background. It was a classic tennis champions photograph.

Enid Dowdle later became Mrs. Pepper and in 1982 was inducted into the Alberta Sports Hall of Fame in the multi-sports division. In 1987 she was named Cardston's female athlete of the century. Harry Wismer went on to complete his education and marry a Vancouver woman in 1950. They made their home in Winnipeg, where he worked for an insurance company.

And William Rodney went on to write an outstanding biography of John George "Kootenai" Brown (Waterton's first forest ranger-in-charge), teach at a Royal Rhodes Military College in Victoria, British Columbia, and become a fellow of the Royal Historical Society.

William Rodney

The Brown Dilemma

Nearly 81 years after it was built and unveiled before a crowd of visitors and distinguished guests, the John George "Kootenai" Brown stone cairn was dismantled and put into storage without so much as a peep from park visitors or residents.

The cairn had been built in 1936 at the eastern end of Cameron Falls Drive by A.H. "Pop" Harwood, then Waterton's postmaster. Harwood was one member of a committee of local citizens, some of whom had known Kootenai Brown and wanted to honour his memory. Other committee members were Rev. S.H. Middleton of Waterton's All-Saints Anglican Church; Senator W.A. Buchanan of Lethbridge; former Lethbridge member of Parliament Brig.-Gen. J.S. Stewart; Waterton businessman Ernie Haug Sr.; and local rancher Russell H. Bennett.

The unveiling of the cairn on July 5, 1936, was held in conjunction with the celebration of Waterton as the Canadian section of the world's first international peace park, which had been declared in 1932. Heading the list of dignitaries in attendance at the cairn ceremony was Alberta's Lt.-Gov. W.L. Walsh .

During his address at the dedication, Middleton emphasized the historic character of the cairn, it being the fulfilment of an obligation of 20 years' standing. Kootenai Brown had died in 1916. He also noted the credit due to Waterton's citizens for their co-operation in erecting the monument.

Lt.-Gov. Walsh then unveiled the cairn, which was dedicated with a prayer led by Anglican Bishop Louis R. Sherman of Calgary, followed by a speech from Senator Buchanan, who compared Brown's life with those of other adventurers.

Dignitaries solemnize, above, a cairn for Waterton pioneer John George "Kootenai" Brown, in photo at right, at the cairn's unveiling before hundreds of spectators in July 1936 in a vacant lot on Waterton Avenue.

The audience of 300, which included a Boy Scout troop, a band and RCMP officers, then heard from Russell Bennett of the Shoderee Ranch, who recalled his first meeting with Brown, followed by superintendent Bert Knight, who gave an outline of Brown's life.

As was the tradition with commemorative cairns, this one was hollow and contained items of significance to the occasion. Since both Middleton and Harwood had known Brown, they had two bottles of whiskey and at least one can of tobacco placed inside the cairn before it was sealed.

Unfortunately, the site was inundated in the 1964 and 1975 floods and the objects were damaged. In 1985, street improvements necessitated moving the 23-tonne (51,520 pound) cairn by crane from its original site to near the marina, and the glass bottles may have been damaged at that time.

With the removal of the Peace Park Pavilion east of the marina on the lakeshore, and its replacement with a new Peace Park Plaza, the cairn was disassembled.

The main reason cited for the removal was errors that appeared on the plaque, which read:

"In memory of John George "Kootenai" Brown
Frontiersman Pioneer Gentleman
Arrived at Waterton Lakes 1868,
and thus became first White Settler.
First Superintendent of Waterton
National Park 1910-1914.
Born in England October 10, 1839
Died at Waterton Park July 16, 1916.
Erected by His Friends of Pioneer Days"

In fact, Brown had become Waterton's first permanent European settler in 1878, not 1868, and was appointed "forest ranger in charge," not superintendent. Finally, he was born in Ireland, not England.

Also a factor in the cairn's removal was the plaque was in English only, with no translation into French, Canada's other official language.

Nevertheless, no action was taken to revise the plaque, which remained on display until the summer of 2017, when the cairn was dismantled stone by stone—each one numbered in the event it was rebuilt—and placed in storage. Ben Hofer, a park employee trained for this kind of work, was responsible for taking down the cairn.

The Kootenai Brown cairn was moved in 1985 from its original site on Waterton Avenue to near the Peace Park Pavilion. The original site became a parking lot.

Park officials report the plaque will be revised and the cairn rebuilt at the Brown family gravesite, near Lower Waterton Lake, where Kootenai Brown and his two successive wives, Olivia and Isabella, are buried.

Olivia Brown died in 1884 and Isabella died in 1935, but the graves were unmarked until 2006. That changed thanks in part to the urging of park visitor Neville Calvert of Fort Saskatchewan, Alberta.

The Waterton Natural History Association took the matter in hand, accepted donations and had headstones made for the two women, who are buried on either side of Kootenai Brown.

One of the association's directors told the gathering at the unveiling of the headstones, "Although many tales have been told—some conflicting—little is known about these two women who made Kootenai Brown's various cabins a home."

Specially trained park employee Ben Hofer, photo at left, disassembles the Kootenai Brown cairn near the marina, numbering and saving each stone for future reconstruction. Photo at right, park staff from left: Byron Pierson, Wes Neilson and Les Lund installed headstones on previously unmarked graves of Brown's two wives, Olivia and Isabella.

Olivia's burial in 1884 had been private affair as were most remote pioneer interments in those days, but Isabella's funeral in April 1935 was held in the park's first Catholic church, then located near the corner of Windflower and Harebell avenues. It was said to have been attended by everyone in Waterton, a measure of regard local people had for her.

"We hope by installing these grave makers, we will show a woman's place is right there when history is being made," said the director of the Waterton Natural History Association.

After the ceremony, park employees Locke Marshall, Byron Pierson, Wes Neilson and Les Lund installed the headstones.

Bureaucracies within a bureaucracy

Years ago, Waterton Lakes National Park was home to three federal bureaucracies which co-operated with the nation's park service but were outside the park's jurisdiction: the Royal Canadian Mounted Police, the post office, and the fish hatchery, each in separate quarters.

The RCMP continues today to provide police service in Waterton from the same building since 1928. The post office and the fish hatchery have seen less consistency.

Essential service: the post office

The first post office was a tiny structure in Oil City, six kilometres (3.7 miles) west of Waterton townsite in the Akamina Valley. John Lineham, who was in part responsible for the exploratory drilling that put a name to that location, was named postmaster. This facility, such as it was, served between 1905 and 1907.

When that post office closed due to lack of need, the oil exploration boom having fizzled, a new post office was located from 1908 to 1916 at Waterton Mills near the Maskinonge. Again, it was at the time outside the park boundary. While mill owner Henry Hanson was the official postmaster, it was his wife who reputedly handled all of the work. In 1914 that location became part of Waterton as the park's boundaries were expanded.

The third post office was located in the Hazzard Hotel, site of today's Bayshore Inn, on a seasonal basis from about 1915 to early 1918, and then year-round for the balance of 1918 and 1919. Jack Hazzard was the postmaster, followed by Carl J. Danielson for one year.

The post office operation was moved in July 1919 to the residence of Arthur H. "Pop" Harwood, on the entrance road across from Linnet Lake. When he

Pop Harwood's home on the entrance road near Linnet Lake, above, served as Waterton's post office from 1919 to 1928, but was relocated when he built a new residence-post office in the townsite, below, at Fountain and Fir Grove.

built a new home within the townsite on the corner of Fountain Avenue and Fir Grove Street in 1928, it included the post office. That site served until 1952, when Harwood retired.

Ollie Tidball, a First World War veteran, replaced Harwood as postmaster and had Oland Construction of Lethbridge build a new structure on Windflower Avenue, across Fountain Avenue from Harwood's location. The new post office had living quarters as well as office space in a dedicated building and met all the requirements of the federal government as well as the national building code.

When Tidball retired, his wife Nellie became acting postmaster for a few months. The parks department then started discussions in 1966 to purchase the building from him. Erected at a cost of $18,000, Tidball sold it to the park for $21,500. The purchase paved the way for Parks Canada to rent the residential portion of the building to either post office staff or park employees.

The next postmaster was 43-year-old Lars Brandvold, who moved to Waterton from Fort Macleod in 1955. A single man, Brandvold served one year as acting postmaster in 1960 and was promoted to full postmaster in late 1961, working in that capacity for the next 22 years, retiring in December 1976. Brandvold was the only Waterton postmaster to serve in the Second World War.

During Brandvold's tenure, his assistant was Nina Neville, who lived outside the park with her family. When Brandvold retired, Neville applied for the job and was appointed, officially becoming the first female postmaster in Waterton's history. Neville worked at the post office until January 1998.

Jennifer Schaffer of Cardston served after Neville, but her record was sporadic, and she had to be substituted by others during three pregnancies. Schaffer was the first Waterton postmaster to meet federal requirements as an English and French speaker. By

1981 the post office had become a Crown corporation and was a separate entity from Parks Canada.

In 2008, Bristol Clark Lawson became the ninth postmaster in 103 years, taking over from Schaffer and became the second bilingual postmaster.

There were startling changes to the post office facility beginning in the spring of 2017.

With the demolition of the park-owned post office building due to construction of a second staff housing building on Windflower Avenue, new quarters had to be found.

Although it was tiny by comparison, the new location was on Fountain Avenue in the north end of the Community Hall, which was renovated to accommodate installation of the postal lock boxes, a sales counter and loading area.

The relocation was effective March 31, 2017.

The sigh of relief from residents, who feared a closure, could be heard throughout the park.

A new post office, above, was built on the southeast corner of Windflower and Fountain avenues in 1952. A new location, in the renovated Community Hall on Fountain Avenue, below, is the current site of the post office.

The Birth and Death of the Fish Hatchery

Unknown to most Waterton devotees today is the fact that for over 30 years the park had two separate men serving at the same time as superintendent. One looked after the park in general and the other oversaw the specialized operation of the fish hatchery. Each man had separate offices, the former in the townsite, the latter on Highway 6, not far from the old park registration office.

The origin of the need for a second superintendent began in 1927 when the federal government decided it would be advantageous for Waterton to have its own fish hatchery. It eventually would be not only for stocking park lakes and rivers, but some other southern Alberta waters.

The Department of Marine and Fisheries issued a call for tenders to build a hatchery and residence in 1927. The successful bid went to Oland & Scott Construction, the Cardston firm that had just completed the Prince of Wales Hotel, among other local buildings.

From the start, the fish hatchery grounds were intended to be both utilitarian and invitingly attractive. They featured the use of fieldstone as well as decorative, eyebrow dormers and a half-timbered porch on major buildings, in keeping with the rustic architectural theme of other public buildings in the townsite.

The first superintendent of the hatchery was 34-year-old Gerald E. Bailey. English by birth, he had moved to Manitoba in 1911, spending the prewar years travelling and working in various parts of Canada and the United States. When the First World War began in 1914, Bailey chose to join Britain's Royal Flying Corps.

The fish … 6, not far from the junction with the entry road into Waterton. Well land-scaped a… eral public fundraisers during the Second World War.

When E… he returned … ing a job at the Banff fish hatchery in 1923 where he learned the finer points of aquaculture. He transferred to Waterton's new hatchery as its first superintendent in 1928. In 1931 hatchery operations were placed under the Parks Branch, but the position and title of hatchery superintendent were retained

Gerald Bailey examines hatchlings in a jar.

Although not residing in the townsite, Bailey, his wife Helen and his son Reggie soon became a part of the community and were well known among locals. In 1928 Bailey was a member of the All-Saints Anglican Church ways and means committee. Reggie, who had an impressive singing voice, often performed at public events. And Helen joined the local war effort to raise money for the Queen Elizabeth's Fund in August 1941, hosting a tea party at the hatchery and helping with a major barbecue in the townsite.

Over a period of years, Bailey worked diligently in his spare time improving the Waterton hatchery grounds until the facility was a showplace. In later years, the park's grounds crew was assigned to maintain the lawns and plants.

Throughout the life of the hatchery, visitors were encouraged to tour the facility and enter comments in a registration book. Visitors could stand on a picturesque foot bridge and gaze into the shallow depths of the shaded pools to watch the fish below. By all accounts, people came by the thousands and were "delighted with the beauty of the grounds and the many interesting and educational features of the hatchery."

William Cable, a former British soldier who

Townsite resident Betty Meads and a young companion visit the fish rearing ponds south of Cameron Falls.

started at the hatchery in 1929, worked with Bailey for 12 years. Cable was promoted in 1941 to become the first superintendent of the new Jasper National Park hatchery. He worked at that facility for the next 18 years, until his retirement.

Following Cable's promotion, Bailey continued as Waterton's hatchery head, assisted by local man Ken Goble, who was appointed hatchery assistant in 1948, later becoming the fishery technician at the townsite fish-rearing ponds, near Cameron Falls.

Bailey was transferred back to the Banff hatchery in May 1952 and retired there in 1957. He was credited not only with extensive fisheries work in rearing and planting fish throughout southern Alberta, but also with a keen understanding of this occupational specialty, advising his Ottawa superiors of the Waterton hatchery's advances.

Bailey's Waterton position was assigned in 1952 to Art Colbeck, a Second World War veteran. It was under Colbeck's watch in April 1956 that *True Magazine* listed Waterton as one of the 12 top fishing loca-

William Cable

Art Colbeck

Ken Goble

tions in Canada. Colbeck worked at the Waterton facility until 1960, assisted by Ken Goble.

During their time in Waterton, Art Colbeck and his wife Nancy were active in the Lion's Club, the local square-dancing group, dramatic productions, and son Dave was a patrol leader in the Waterton Boy Scout troop. Art later became hatchery superintendent in Jasper, where he served for eight years.

Meanwhile in Waterton, Goble continued his duties during the summers at the fish ponds near Cameron Falls, retiring in 1971.

The Colbeck's descendants continue to maintain their association with Waterton through the United Church in the townsite and its Canyon Church Camp in the Blakiston Valley.

Based on evidence of fish diseases in hatcheries caused by the importation of stock from eastern Canada, the Waterton facility was closed in 1960 and consolidated with hatchery operations in Jasper. The focus on fish turned to the existing species in park waters.

In the years that followed, fish management was

addressed much differently through new scientific practices, such as revising fishing regulations to reduce catch limits to help native species prosper.

During operation of the hatchery in Waterton, more than 15 million fish were planted in the park waters and surrounding areas, first transported by horseback in ice-cooled milk cans and later in plastic bags.

The fish ponds near Cameron Falls closed in 1973 after 35 years of summer use and were removed in 1976.

The hatchery building was torn down with little ado but the two residences next to the hatchery building were used to accommodate other park staff. One residence was destroyed by fire in 1961 and replaced early in 1962. In the spring of 2007, all buildings were removed, and the site restored to natural vegetation.

Waterton's First Church

When the wrecking crew arrived in Waterton on July 7, 2014, to tear down the All-Saints Anglican Church, they had no idea they would be demolishing an 86-year-old structure that was near and dear to generations of local people and an important part of park history. But seven years of disuse and lack of maintenance had done their worst, and without a congregation and money, there was nothing that would save it. The church was quickly and unceremoniously flattened.

All-Saints Anglican Church was built by Oland & Scott Construction in two stages: in the fall of 1927 and the spring of 1928, with work suspended over the winter of 1927-28 as the construction company completed additions to the Prince of Wales Hotel.

Construction of the church, which was designed by the architectural division of Canada's national parks branch in Ottawa, was entirely funded by donations, with $823.15 raised by public subscription, including the ladies auxiliary which held several fundraisers.

All-Saints Anglican Church was dedicated on July 26, 1928, by Calgary diocese Bishop R.L. Sherman, assisted by Rev. Samuel H. Middleton, Archdeacon Cecil Swanson, who was a new Waterton cabin owner, and Rev. Neville Blunt of St. John's Anglican Church in Cardston.

Bishop Sherman gave the honour of formally naming the church to Middleton, who chose All-Saints after his family's church in Berton-on-Trent, England.

With the dedication, the 16-pew All-Saints became Waterton's first church.

A major contributor to the church was Great Northern Railway chairman Louis W. Hill, whose

All-Saints Anglican Church, locally known as the "little brown church," opened in 1928. In later years the exterior of the church was reinforced and painted white.

The Anglican church in Waterton, simple and tiny, served the faithful for decades. American tourists were advised that Anglican and Episcopal services were similar, and the church welcomed one and all.

company had the year before opened the Prince of Wales Hotel. Middleton had assisted in the hotel project by orchestrating the painting of pictographs by members of the Blood Tribe which adorned the lobby walls and were used as lobby lamp shades.

When Middleton asked Hill about contributing toward the cost of the new church, Hill showed his gratitude for Middleton's help with the hotel and responded with a $500 donation.

The night of the dedication Louis Hill, who was staying in his new hotel to the north across the lake, was said to have come to the ceremony after which he remarked: "There on the hill is the big show; here is the jewel." It was a striking salute.

The first couple married in All-Saints was Ruby Elaine Campbell and Alexander Aitken on Aug. 6, 1929. The bride was the sister of Winnie Frache who, with her husband, owned a cabin on Evergreen Avenue.

Over the years the church became a community repository for Waterton-related items not necessarily with any church connection, including three flags, two Second World War honour rolls, a Coventry cross, a commemorative Holy Bible, and a bishop's chair.

The two honour rolls originated in 1943. An article appeared in *The Lethbridge Herald* explained how the Department of National Defence was prepared to provide a specially designed "honour roll" form for use in industry, churches, schools and the like to recognize the "loyal men and women who have volunteered for active service in the Armed Forces of Canada."

Leaders of All-Saints Anglican Church decided to take advantage of the offer, acquiring two of the scrolls designed by A.J. Carson, a member of the prestigious Royal Canadian Academy of Arts as well as a member of the Group of Seven. It was intended to symbolize in authentic heraldic form "the historic majesty of the British Empire," incorporating the flags of the navy, army and air force in brilliant hues of red, blue, green, yellow, buff and gold. Six sizes of forms were available.

Waterton ordered two copies in the 29.2- by 52-centimetre (11.5- by 20.5-inch) size to accommodate the 49 names of those on active service.

Instructions with the scrolls outlined specifications for the style of lettering for the names, that had to be written "by some competent artist or draftsman."

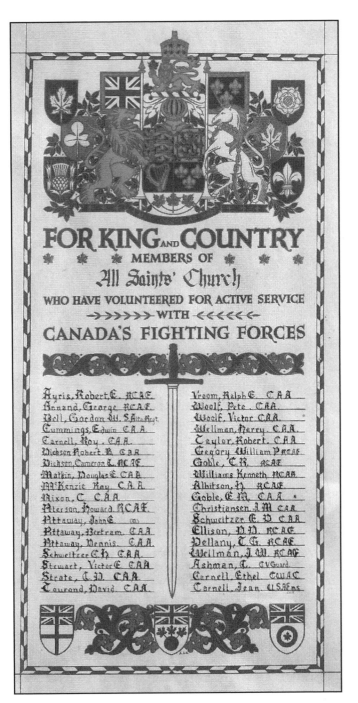

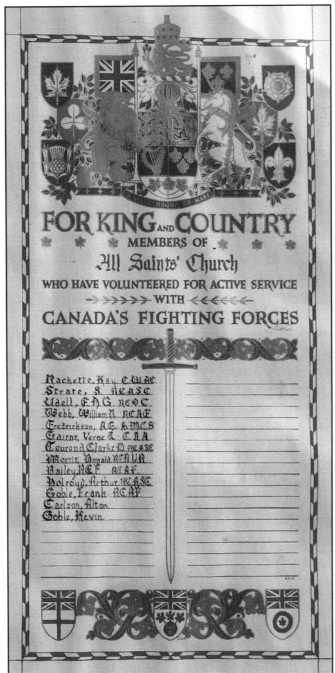

Special blank honour roll scrolls in various sizes were made available to towns and cities all over Canada to list the names of those who volunteered to serve during the Second World War. These colourful Waterton scrolls, 20.5 by 52 centimetres (11.5 by 20.5 inches), were hand-lettered, framed and displayed at All-Saints Church.

Finding a qualified artist to letter the scrolls was not difficult. Middleton assigned his talented and artistic daughter-in-law Lilly Elvira Middleton to the task of applying the names in calligraphy. With no way of verifying the spelling of each name or full initials, Mrs. Middleton did her best.

The Remembrance Day Service of 1944, held on the first Sunday of November, was dedication day for the Honour Roll, which remained in the church for the next 70 years until the building was demolished. Although a number of the people whose names appear on the roll were not members of the Anglican Church, the list symbolized all of Waterton's service members regardless of their religious affiliation.

At one time All Saints—known informally as "the little brown church" for its simple, unadorned exterior paint colour—was supported by a strong congregation willing and eager to serve as volunteers.

Among the volunteers were Hugh and Jean Galbraith. A park clerk, Hugh played the church organ from 1928 to 1939 and his wife Jean served as the children's Sunday school superintendent. Other volunteers were fish hatchery superintendent Gerald Bailey and carpenter Harry Reeves, both church wardens. After the Galbraiths moved to the coast, Helen Gregory, who lived on Evergreen Avenue, was the organist for many years and donated the bishop's chair.

Middleton served as minister until 1951, when he retired.

A decade later, in 1962, the church was renovated. It was moved onto a new foundation and an addition was put on the south entrance of the building, which served as a shelter from the prevailing south wind. Buttresses were also added to strengthen the building.

Apart from this work, architecturally the church changed very little, remaining without much adornment: the altar was simple, there was a minimum of interior woodwork, and the original pump organ remained in use for many years.

The church was closed in the fall of 2007 due to structural deficiencies and a dwindling congregation. Its time had come.

As for the artifacts that had been collected over the years, arrangements were reported being made to donate them to a museum.

Above the Clouds

Hiking and scrambling to the top of area peaks are popular pastimes in Waterton, and have been from the earliest days.

In 1915, visitor Lula Nielsen joined Anglican Rev. S.H. Middleton and Leo Coombs to climb Mount Cleveland, the tallest mountain in what is now Waterton-Glacier International Peace Park.

Middleton led the climb, scouting the route for problems and blowing a whistle to signal to Nielsen and Coombs that it was safe to follow. It was a hard climb over fallen timber, but they forged on, determined to reach the summit.

"The last 15 minutes were wonderful," Nielsen recalled. "We were standing on the top of the world."

"It was a landmark in my career," she said. "It was at this time I realized the greatest things in the world can't be bought but must be won step by step by my

All-Saints Anglican Church was demolished in 2014 and the lot quickly cleared of debris.

own efforts. I learned to love Waterton. . . . I am thankful I earned every step of the way up Mount Cleveland. This calm, lovely quiet had this day opened up to me the meaning of life."

Eleven years later in April 1926, Waterton resident and outdoor enthusiast Walter B. "Waddy" Foster tried to capture Nielsen's elation when he formed the Rocky Mountains Club.

He drew up a club constitution with seven aims:
• To awaken more intelligent interest in our national parks.
• To explore and make note of the territory.
• To create a spirit of camaraderie and adventure in each park community by joining together in local hikes over existing trails or other accessible territory.
• To bring to the attention of the people the educational value of the national parks.
• To encourage the preservation and propagation of game, fish and valuable fur-bearing animals.
• To conscientiously assist the parks service in preventing forest fires.
• To extend a spirit of international co-operation and good fellowship to all lovers of the great outdoors.

Foster became president and immediately rallied support from community members, including businessman Nahor Dilatush, postmaster Arthur Harwood and hotelier Eddie Poulin, among others.

Rev. Samuel Middleton, left, and Lula Nielsen eat lunch atop Mount Cleveland, the tallest peak in the peace park. Enthusiasm for summitting park mountains was behind the formation of the local Rocky Mountains Club in 1926.

He also made J.C. Campbell and J.B. Harkin honorary presidents. Campbell was the director of publicity for Canada's national parks, while Harkin was his boss, commissioner of national parks. The club was immediately elevated from local to national with their involvement.

Meanwhile, Foster was already working on a building adjacent to the Waterton superintendent's office that he hoped would be the club's headquarters.

Through its fees, $4 for the first year and $2 each year thereafter, the club was able to advertise itself and organize hiking and camping trips, resulting in increased membership.

Foster later tried to fulfill the goal of the club being international by including Stephen T. Mather, director of the U.S. National Park Service, and Great Northern Railway boss Louis W. Hill as honorary presidents.

Unfortunately, the Great Depression of the 1930s took a toll on the club as recreation came second to simply surviving, and by the time the Second World War began in 1939 the club had stopped holding summer camps.

All that remained was the name, Rocky Mountains Club, and the warm glow of having been named one of its 17 honorary life members, the last two of whom were Reg Bailey, son of Gerald Bailey, the fish hatchery superintendent, and Jeff Banks-Smith of the flight training facility at Pearce, Alberta.

This pair received appointments because together they had climbed Mount Alderson, at 2,692 metres (8,832 feet), and found a cairn that Foster built on the peak in 1931. Hidden in the 1.5-metre (five-foot) high pile of rocks was a glass bottle and a notebook in which climbers could write their names.

It was a last hurrah and with that, the club dissolved into just a memory.

Waterton townsite sits on an alluvial fan created by Cameron Creek, on the far centre right, flowing over Cameron Falls and into Upper Waterton Lake. Primarily a summer community, Waterton Park—the official name of the townsite—is more than a century old. The original survey was done in 1910, with the first leasing of lots the following year.

Chapter 7

Buildings
With Sticks and Stones

The townsite is where the action is in Waterton. It's the focal point of businesses and creature comforts for visitors, home to year-round and seasonal residents, and the place where people congregate to socialize. It's small, it's quaint and surprising to many after a long absence, the changes are sometimes subtle yet steady. Since many buildings are original, there's a welcoming familiarity.

The official name for the townsite is Waterton Park, although it was sometimes referred to as the "visitor service centre" by its caretakers, Parks Canada.

The stage for development of the townsite was set in 1911, when the government invited the public to apply to lease lots. The townsite was originally surveyed in 1910 and three times thereafter with additions until 1924, when there was no land left to survey. An original, large subdivision on Middle Waterton Lake was largely never opened for leasing while another, on Lower Waterton Lake, was surveyed but later withdrawn as an unsuitable location.

Those who wanted a lot applied on the understanding they would have to build within a specific time and to a minimum value. When that was done to the satisfaction of the government, the applicant received a 42-year renewable lease. Building lots were offered a few at a time so monitoring building progress was not unduly difficult for park officials.

"Property" in Waterton, like other western national parks with leased land, takes on slightly different criteria than in non-park locations. Property is a composite of public and private. The leased lot is owned by the Crown and the improvements (the buildings) are owned by the lessee. Information on lot ownership is strictly a federal responsibility and is not listed in the provincial land titles office.

Until about the beginning of the Second World War, the architectural division of the Parks Branch in Ottawa provided drawings for the buildings based on input from the applicant.

William Cromarty, who served as summer superintendent in Waterton and winter head of the architectural division from 1925 to 1930, supervised the completion of many of these plans during Waterton's first building boom.

Cromarty was a trained architect who practised in England before emigrating to Canada about 1911. He worked in Edmonton, taught at the University of Alberta, then moved to Ottawa to work at the Federal Commission of Conservation. The commission was merged into the National Parks Branch in 1921 and Cromarty began his upward rise in the parks' bureaucracy.

Cromarty's familiarity with Waterton's physical environment, the lot locations and the people were major factors in his successful application of common sense to good design. Through him, it was government supervision that ensured the buildings were appropriate in size, location and appearance. At the same time, it was Cromarty's oversight that ensured that no two privately owned buildings were alike.

It was no easy proposition building in Waterton in the early years. Poor roads made transportation of material difficult and the choice of material was determined by transportation. You'll see no brick buildings here, although there are a number of newer ones of concrete block construction. The use of bricks was confined to fireplaces and chimneys. Local field stone was abundant, as were pine logs. Later, milled lumber and stucco were used

Despite the obstacles there was, at the outset, no shortage of people who wanted a residence in the park. However, it is rare today that an original lease remains in a family line. After an initial burst of building, many lessees sold out. In many cases it was the second round of lessees who saw the value in holding on to the property.

Owning a residence in Waterton was not a show of wealth; it was a personal reward that has become a tangible part of family tradition. Memories and experiences of childhood are tied to this spectacular place of simple pleasures. While the rustic but aging residences are giving way, by necessity, to replacements, the new "residences" are more in tune with a different lifestyle, with emphasis on convenience. Commercial buildings, whether new or renovated, have been adapted to functional practicality.

Being a lessee—either residential or commercial—has not been all sweetness and light. Beginning in the late 1960s and gradually increasing over the latter part of the 20th century, politicians viewed lessees as speculators who were making profits by selling at ever-increasing prices.

Those who held on to their places became nervous as the federal government began exerting its authority, without public consultation. But lessees can be a tenacious bunch and they fought valiantly against bureaucrats and politicians who would try to renege on long-standing leases.

What the government never understood about lessees in Waterton was their places were more than real estate with improvements.

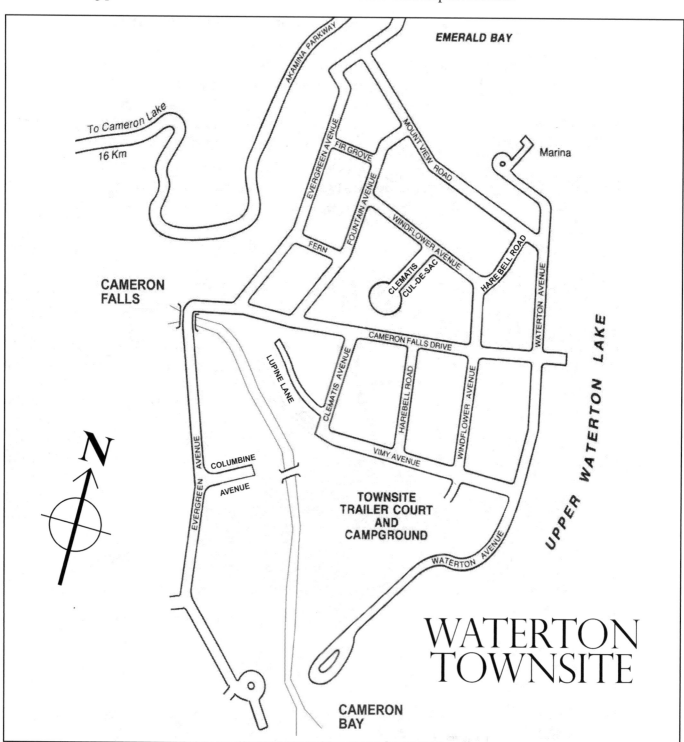

Residences on Cameron Falls Drive

Cameron Falls Drive has a jumbled past. Originally called Avenue A, it was created by the second survey of the townsite in 1919. It comprised today's Fountain Avenue and then headed west to the falls. Another survey, in 1924, extended the street east from what is now the Fountain Avenue intersection, ending at the lakeshore.

For many years the portion of Evergreen Avenue which begins at Cameron Falls and ends in a turn-around near *the mouth of Cameron Creek was called Cameron Falls Drive because it crossed the lower end of the creek and was part of a loop that connected with Waterton Avenue.*

When the automobile bridge near the mouth of Cameron Creek was replaced by a foot bridge after the flood of 1975, the loop was broken and that section was renamed Evergreen Avenue.

101 Cameron Falls Dr.

First lessee: Dewitt Talmadge Johnson

"Kerr Cabin Grandview"

Original residence replaced

Dewitt Talmadge Johnson of Fort Macleod had the first residence on this site built in 1921 by Art Auger and made major improvements to it in 1924. Johnson was a Waterton business pioneer, having built both the Tourist Café and a garage, both on Waterton Avenue.

Late in the 1920s Johnson developed a regional bus and trucking business in southern Alberta which served Waterton, and later operated Alberta-Montana bus lines and Johnson Transport. He proposed to build a 25-room hotel at Cameron Lake in 1947 but withdrew his offer when the government imposed too many restrictions.

Johnson was a bachelor who kept his residence long after he sold his park businesses. His widowed mother Julia often came to stay for the entire summer, with frequent visits from his sister Luella Dixon and her husband Lawrence, all of Fort Macleod.

Johnson died unexpectedly in 1949, leaving the residence to family members who sold it in the early 1970s to a Mr. Terry, who had the residence renovated inside and out, giving it a new look. It was sold in 1982 to Phil and Glenda Morrison of New Dayton, Alberta. Their daughter Cathy worked in the park for

many years, eventually opening her own ice cream business in the theatre and later a coffee shop at the same location before opening the Larkspur Coffee shop (now Waterton Park Café) on main street.

The house changed hands again in 2005. A new residence was completed in 2019 by Gero Construction of Pincher Creek. The old cabin was not demolished but sold and moved to Rochon Sands Provincial Park on Buffalo Lake, east of Red Deer.

The owners kept the original name "Grandview" as well as adding their own.

102 Cameron Falls Dr.

First lessee: Jean Rankin

"Fir bank"

Builder: Harry Cummings

Jean Rankin, a 53-year-old single business woman from the Twin Butte district, applied for the lease on this property in 1931. At the same time, she had started a saddle horse company in the park with E.J. Schrempp.

The residence was begun in the fall of 1932 by Harry Cummings, a local carpenter who worked for the park during the summer and took on private jobs during the balance of the year. Rankin moved into this house in January 1933. When she died in 1960 at the age of 83, Rankin was still widely known among the region's horse enthusiasts.

The new owner, Orene Strate, who grew up in the park and was the son of Theresa and Delance Strate, transferred the lease to his sister Helen Strate and her husband Marion Woolf. The couple, both of whom worked for the park at one point, undertook substantial renovations to make the house suitable for their family of five. Helen had been raised in the park along with seven siblings. Marion worked for the park as a mechanic for 34 years and Helen worked briefly in the superintendent's office. They are both buried in the park cemetery.

The residence remains in the family.

103 Cameron Falls Dr.

First lessee: Eleanor DeLong

"Rockwood"

Builder: Oland & Scott

Eleanor Tricker DeLong applied for this lease in her own name in 1924. Women often took advantage of the opportunity to become leaseholders and De-Long was one of the first to do so.

She and her husband Harold hired Oland & Scott Construction to build the residence, which was completed in the spring of 1926.

When the new Waterton Dance Pavilion opened on May 18, 1926, the DeLongs led the first dance.

Ontario-born Harold came to Alberta in 1907 and spent his entire career working for Plunkett and Savage, a wholesale grocery and produce supplier, becoming widely known throughout southern Alberta. He died from injuries he received in an automobile accident in Spring Coulee, Alberta, in November 1932. He was 44 years old.

Eleanor continued to use the residence, entertaining friends, and renting it from time to time to Lethbridge residents. A world traveller, she was one of only three people associated with Waterton to attend the coronation of Queen Elizabeth II in 1953.

The residence was sold in the 1950s to Roy Campbell of Burdett, Alberta, and continues to be owned by his descendants.

105 Cameron Falls Dr.

First lessee: E.H. Wagstaff

"Graystone Manor"

Original residence replaced

Waterton's first golf pro, E.H. "Teddy" Wagstaff, helped build his own 7.2- by 9.6-metre (24- by 32-foot) residence near the rear of this lot using logs cut in the park. The residence featured an open fireplace with stone chimney built by Oland & Scott and was completed in 1925.

Wagstaff, whose job at the golf course was seasonal, fell into financial difficulty and was forced to sell the property in December 1930 to Augustus Leather, a prominent Fort Macleod businessman. In 1946 the residence was sold to Colin Hedderick of Pincher Creek who, in turn, sold it to Dr. John Pohl of Minneapolis, Minnesota, in 1959. Pohl replaced the crumbling log residence with the present two-storey house. It was one of the first Waterton residences to utilize concrete blocks. The Douglas fir trees at the front are among the oldest and largest in the townsite.

The house, designed by architects McEnary & Krafft of Minneapolis as a no-maintenance structure, was completed in 1964. It was avant-garde for its day, furnished with the latest labour-saving appliances: an elec-

tric stove, washer and dryer, and dishwasher. While it has provision for an elevator, one was never installed. Its startling, unpainted concrete block construction caused locals to dub it "The Bunker." The residence changed hands in 2006 and was given its name by new owners.

---

202 Cameron Falls Dr.

First lessee: Edward Johnson

"Parkinson"

Original residence replaced

Edward Johnson was a carpenter who worked for the government in the summer and as a private contractor at other times. He built the first residence on this lot on speculation and acquired the lease on April 1, 1931.

Beginning in 1937, a series of people owned the original residence, the last of whom was Stan Kretz, a boatman. Construction of the Johnson building was of a dubious nature because it was not properly secured to the triangular lot, which was below the street level but faced Cameron Falls Drive. The structure was linked to the street by a wooden ramp. The residence stood until the flood of 1964, when Cameron Creek broke through its banks, cutting a temporary course through Lupine Lane. The building was carried half a block to the east and smashed to pieces.

Well-known Lethbridge businessman John Deak purchased the lease in 1965 and had the current residence built by Dorigatti Construction Ltd. of Lethbridge. The front of the residence faces Lupine Lane but it has a Cameron Falls Drive address which was assigned years later. Nonetheless, the residence is very much a part of the Lupine Lane "neighbourhood." It is still owned by a family member.

206 Cameron Falls Dr.

First lessee: Sara Cummings

Original residence replaced

Sara Cummings applied for this lease in 1928 but she died before a residence could be completed. Her husband Harry, a building contractor, inherited the lease and completed the residence in 1930.

Cummings was a carpenter who worked for the government in the summer and found winter jobs working on the Prince of Wales Hotel, the Ballinacor Hotel and built several residences for customers.

Looking for a way to find a better life for his son, Harry set fire to the house in November 1939 to claim the insurance money. Overcome with remorse, two months later Cummings pleaded guilty to arson and was sent to jail for six months. He moved to Cranbrook, British Columbia, where he died in 1945. With land rent in arrears, the lease was cancelled in 1947.

The government built the existing residence in 1951 for Bob Hand, chief park warden. He and his wife had four children and the family lived in the three-bedroom residence until 1956.

It continues to be used for Parks Canada staff accommodation.

302 Cameron Falls Dr.

First lessee: Hugh Thompson Galbraith

"Putney House"

This is one of the larger original residences and was erected in 1931 for Hugh Galbraith, a park clerk from 1919 to 1941. His wife Jean Clark owned another residence on Evergreen Avenue which was sold to build this one. In 1943, Charles Leonard Wesley of New Dayton, Alberta, bought the residence, but sold it in 1947 to Ada Kemmis, the owner of Kilmorey Lodge. It was she who gave the house its name, having been born in Putney, just outside London, England.

The Sommerfields, from the Crowsnest Pass, owned the residence for a few years before it was sold to Waterton Inter-Nation Shoreline Cruise Co. for staff housing.

304 Cameron Falls Dr.

First lessee: Garnet P. Clark

"Casa Jose"

Original residence replaced

Garnet Clark was an agent for Imperial Oil in Warner, Alberta, in 1930 when the original residence was started. For a variety of reasons, the residence was not completed to the superintendent's satisfaction until 1942, when the lease was finally issued.

The original residence was named "Ja-Ge-Lo" for Garnet and Eva Clark's three children: James, Gertrude and Lois.

Beattie C. Lillie, a Warner farmer, bought the residence but kept it for only one summer. His wife Edith bought another residence a few years later, at 106 Harebell Rd. Meanwhile, this lease was sold in 1946 to Harold Hutchinson, also a Warner farmer.

The original residence on this site was torn down in 1987 and replaced by a modern house suitable for year-round occupancy.

A small outbuilding on the property is a reminder of the matching original residence.

The lease is owned by Hutchinson's descendants.

306 Cameron Falls Dr.

First lessee: Fred K. Houston

"Otherone House"

Builders: Carlson & Hagglund

Fred Houston applied for this lease in 1929. At the time he was working as a mining engineer in Seattle, Washington, and he soon became one of the first U.S. citizens to hold a lease in Waterton when the house was completed in 1932 by local builders Carl Carlson and Erik Hagglund.

Due to the nature of his job, Houston travelled all over the world but insisted that Waterton was the only place he would ever take a vacation, looking forward to the day when he could retire and spend the entire summer in the park. The residence remained in the family until 1980, when it was purchased by the Cruickshank family of Lethbridge which has a business in the park.

Under the new ownership, it was renovated by original builder Carlson's grandson, Gavin MacKay, and his business partner Dean Haslam, who had grown up in the park.

308 Cameron Falls Dr.

"Palmer House"

First lessee: Nahor W. Dilatush

This was the first residential property of several leased by Waterton businessman Nahor W. Dilatush, who had the residence built in 1932. Over the years, the Dilatushes held many leases, both residential and commercial.

This property was sold early in 1942 to Anna Wesley of New Dayton, Alberta. She sold it in 1945 to Ellen Giddie, who gave the home its original name, "Devonia Cottage."

She was married to Jack Giddie, a First World War veteran and park warden who retired in 1946. The couple moved to Victoria, British Columbia, in 1959.

The new owner, Delbert Palmer of Lethbridge, renamed the residence "Palmer House," a play on his name and that of the famous Chicago hotel. Del,

a university professor, was an active participant in leaseholder affairs in his later years. He was the son of Asael Palmer, one of Canada's pre-eminent agricultural innovators.

The residence remains in the family.

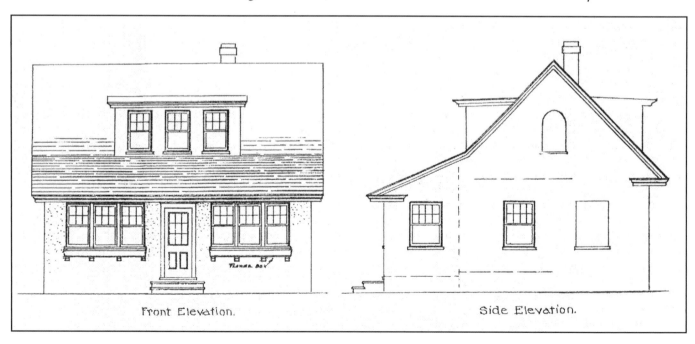

Front Elevation.

Side Elevation.

Residences on Clematis Avenue

Named for a delicate, blue wildflower, this avenue was constructed in 1953, when these lots were first offered for leasing. It has become one of the most altered routes in the townsite. Development of swimming pool in 1960 altered Clematis Avenue, which had originally been built to connect with Cameron Falls Drive.

In the late 1980s, the Waterton Recreation and Cul-

tural Society requested the area in front of the school building be redeveloped into a multi-use playing field and contributed to the cost of the change. The demise of the swimming pool in 1995 saw the subsequent construction of The Lodge at Waterton Lakes, which sited its lobby on Clematis when it became a cul-de-sac, ending immediately east of the United Church.

104 Clematis Cul-de-sac

First lessee: Federal goverment

Phase 1 Staff Housing

Phase 1 of Parks Canada employee housing in the townsite began in 2016 with this building. The one-and-a-half storey, 10-suite, 22-bed building was completed in May 2017. It has a wood frame, "Alpine cottage" motif with a full concrete basement. Occupants may park vehicles in a dedicated lot across Windflower Avenue to the north. The staff housing plan enabled removal of an existing bunkhouse at Compound Road which had reached the end of usefulness and was unsuitable for winter use.

203 Clematis Ave.

First lessee: Francis Bernard Frey

Frank Frey, manager of the Pincher Creek Co-operative Association, took out an interim lease on this lot in 1954. He chose to erect a Pan-Abode structure, a new Canadian concept in residential construction. Pan-Abode proved to be a boon to owners in rural areas like Waterton because the residences were easy to assemble and constructed of durable, western red cedar. This residence was completed in 1956.

The lease changed hands in 1960, when it was purchased by Van Christou, a Lethbridge dentist, who expressed his extreme unhappiness in writing when he learned that during the 1964 flood his lot was the site of the altered path of Cameron Creek, which overran its banks. The structure was inundated.

Bart and Shirley Kesler later bought the residence.

After Bart retired from the Lethbridge Research Station where he specialized in rangeland management, the couple was able to take full advantage of their Waterton property in the summer to explore the park.

The residence remains in the family.

204 Clematis Ave.

First lessee: Marvin Carl Culler

"Sneak Inn" (Don't Crawl)

Like numerous others in rural southern Alberta, Marvin and Alice Culler were strongly attracted to Waterton for its beauty and outdoor activities. Marvin Carl Culler, who farmed near Wrentham, north of Warner, Alberta, applied for this lease in 1946. So determined were the Cullers to come to Waterton during construction of their house that for two summers they rented the "Bide A Wee" residence on Fountain Avenue which was then owned by Ernie Haug, Sr.

Erection of their residence was no simple task given the postwar shortage of building materials, but they persevered and by 1948 the lease was finalized. Hosting friends at the new residence was routine, as one and all joined in both front and backcountry activities.

During the June 1964 flood, the raging water and associated debris that flowed over Cameron Falls to the west found their way into this residence and others nearby, requiring extensive cleanup.

The residence continues to be owned and enjoyed by family members.

205 Clematis Ave.

First lessee: Cy Redfern

"Red Fern"

Cy Redfern, a Second World War flight lieutenant, was awarded the distinguished Air Force Cross by King George VI in 1945. He went on to become a successful Lethbridge auto parts dealer for Baalim Motors and married the boss's daughter, Gladys.

The Redferns built this residence in 1951 next door to one owned by Gladys's sister, Barbara McCulloch. Both women and their siblings had a life-long acquaintance with the park. Their parents, Art and Gladys Irene Baalim, owned a residence on Fountain Avenue which they purchased in 1929.

Long-time and successful fishermen, the Redferns and Baalims were often seen out on the lake in the inboard motorboat *Cecily*. Redfern descendants continue to own the residence.

206 Clematis Ave.

First lessee: Earl Pingree Tanner, Sr.

Earl Tanner, general manager of Tanner Supplies Ltd. in Magrath, Alberta, took out an interim lease on this lot in 1955 but died before he could erect a residence. His wife Vinessa, after much wrangling with officials, was finally able to have this Pan-Abode residence built in 1959. It was advertised for sale in 1968. Like most residences at that time, it was offered "fully equipped," which usually meant it included not only furniture, but also linens, pots, pans and dishes.

The residence was owned by Verna Hembroff of Lethbridge from about 1970 until 1999 and was then sold to others.

207 Clematis Ave.   "The Olivers"

First lessee: Barbara Baalim McCulloch

This was the last lot to be leased on this block because it needed some ground levelling before construction could begin. A call for tenders was made on this lot in 1954. The only bid received was that of Barbara "Babb" Irene Baalim McCulloch, who offered $175. Babb and her husband Bart had their residence completed within two years. It was one of the last of the larger residences allowed in those years. Howard Oliver of Lethbridge, who became the head of Barons Oil, purchased the residence in 1968 and it remains in the family.

208 Clematis Ave.

"Sitka Wildwood"

First lessee: Owen Spencer McClung

Owen McClung was a Cardston painter who had the residence built simply so he could resell it.

Originally, the attached section on the north end of the residence was to have been a garage, but while it was still under construction, McClung had a prospective buyer who was interesting in making the deal only if he didn't install the garage doors and would substitute a door and window. Although McClung complied with the request, the buyer reneged. In 1948, just one year after this residence was completed, Ida McClain bought it.

It was first named by Maxine McClain, who acquired the lease in 1957, calling it "Topanga," after a beloved California canyon she knew well.

The residence was sold to a member of another long-time Waterton family in 2011 and renamed.

Residences on Columbine Avenue

This short, dead-end street, named for another park wildflower, was the site of the very last new lots offered for leasing. The lots backed onto the government-operated fish rearing ponds, a popular tourist attraction, and faced the new trailer camping grounds to the south. The lots were opened to leasing in 1954 as replacement sites following a snow slide on Bertha Peak. Park officials had to move a camp kitchen and comfort station to make room for the new residences.

---

101 Columbine Ave.

First lessee: Stan Peszat

Stan Peszat, owner of Stan's Men's Wear in downtown Lethbridge, applied for this lease in 1954. Regulations of the day called for the issuance of an "interim" lease, which led to a full lease once the conditions were met. Peszat received his lease in August 1958, less than a year before the government called a halt to issuing additional new leases. An expert tailor and a member of many Lethbridge service clubs, Peszat was well known in the region. He died in July 1974. The residence remained in the family until 2015, when a new owner took possession.

103 Columbine Ave.

First lessee: Elsie Ranson

Carl and Elsie Ranson began bringing their family to Waterton in 1929. Carl commuted from Lethbridge, where he worked as assistant manager at International Harvester Co. while Elsie tented with their children Margaret, Bud, Bob, Waldo and Denny. Carl and Elsie moved to Edmonton in 1946 where he died four years later. When an opportunity arose in 1956, Elsie applied and got one of the last available park leases. The residence was finished in 1958 and has been in family hands since.

105 Columbine Ave.

First lessee: Leigh Kuschel

"The Spackmans"

Leigh Kuschel obtained this lease in October 1954, when his residence at the south end of Evergreen Avenue was partially demolished by an April snow slide. It was rebuilt and moved to this location.

Kuschel and his mother Flora were well known by Waterton visitors as the proprietors of the Waterton Lakes Hotel and Chalets. He was the first residence owner to apply for permission to install a swimming pool, a six- by nine-metre (20- by 30-foot) fiberglass unit. This 1957 request was flatly turned down because regulations stated that water use was restricted to domestic, business and railway purposes. Kuschel sold his residence in 1957 and it was sold again to Gordon Hamilton of Claresholm, Alberta. Sara Spackman Tanner, wife of N. Eldon Tanner, acquired the residence in 1966 and it has been in family ownership since.

107 Columbine Ave.

First lessee: John Hunt   Builder: Yanosik Construction Ltd.

Doctor John, as he was called, and his wife Leone had this residence built in 1957. A well-known Lethbridge physician, John Hunt was born and raised in Foremost, Alberta. He and two of his nine siblings had residences in the park, and each has been retained by family members. Leone, a registered nurse, was a pioneer among Trans-Canada Air Lines stewardesses prior to her marriage. She became head stewardess for Western Canada. The airline, with operations in Lethbridge, was the forerunner of Air Canada.

The concrete block residence was erected at the beginning of a period when this building material was finding favour in both residential and commercial construction in the park. This residence continues to be owned by family members.

---

109 Columbine Ave.

First lessee: John Henry Willie

John Willie, like his neighbour Leigh Kuschel, was forced by nature to move. He had originally located this residence on two lots on Evergreen Avenue (now a road access). A second snow slide, which followed the one that damaged Leigh Kuschel's in the spring of 1954, hit Willie's residence, fortunately while the family was in Lethbridge for medical attention. The situation alerted park officials to the wisdom of excluding his original site from occupation when 7.2 metres (nearly 24 feet) of snow fell that winter.

Willie, who owned the Lethbridge Woodworking Co., was able to do his own repairs on the residence. Chester Sarka, a moving contractor from Picture Butte, Alberta, was hired to move both the Kuschel and Willie residences to new locations in the fall of 1954.

The residence was later sold to the Lomas family of Lethbridge which in turn sold it in 2005.

New owners have since made major renovations to the residence.

Residences on Evergreen Avenue

Evergreen Avenue has had various names, both official and unofficial. It was originally called Avenue B or "the backstreet" by locals and ended at the falls. It was renamed Evergreen in 1925 but was often referred to as Pine. After the 1975 flood, when the lower bridge near the mouth of Cameron Creek was removed and it was no longer possible to make a circle drive from Cameron Falls to the lake and back, the entire distance was named Evergreen. This is the longest residential street in town.

During the 1920s and 1930s this street was where most park employees and other year-round residents lived. Although the area has limited mountain views, it is more protected from snow.

In the 1970s, a brief attempt was made to stop through traffic from using the northern portion of the avenue. Heavy planters blocked the route, drawing the ire of vigilantes who knocked them over. The experiment was deemed a failure and the street was reopened. Standard stop signs proved ineffective and in 2021, oversized stops signs were painted on the street to slow traffic.

110 Evergreen Ave.

First lessee: Government

"Superintendent's House"

Builder: Lethbridge Construction Co. Ltd.

This 1956 ranch-style house was the second government-owned residence built specifically for the park superintendent. The first, built in 1919 for George Ace Bevan, was several lots to the south. Jim H. Atkinson and his wife were the first to occupy the new, three-bedroom house.

Atkinson, the ninth man to head Waterton, was superintendent for five and a half years, ending in 1957 when he was transferred to Nova Scotia.

The house was built for $25,000 on two vacant lots then considered a prime location.

It was, however, not an idyllic place to live in the summer. Every car entering or leaving the town passes this residence. The yard was usually neatly landscaped, a job that normally fell to park employees.

The attractive yard made it immediately noticeable in August 1956, when a bear chose to put on a show for the day, causing a "bear jam" of 30 cars and three buses.

Visitors watched in amusement as a black bear sat on the front lawn spinning the wheel of an overturned wheelbarrow.

He then lumbered over to the lawn sprinkler, picked it up and gave himself a refreshing shower, much to the delight of the crowd.

The days of a resident superintendent are long since over. Terms of employment no longer require the superintendent to live in the park, but the residence is reserved for his or her use.

The original residence for the superintendent was across Evergreen Avenue from the Kilmorey Lodge.

120 Evergreen Ave.

First lessee: Cyril F. Jackson

"Lost Horse Trailhouse"

Original residence replaced

Cyril Jackson, who had the first residence built on this lot in 1921, was one of the Jackson Brothers who ran a Pincher Creek hardware store. Since he owned both an automobile and a residence, Jackson often brought friends to stay in Waterton. After his retirement, he moved to the West Coast and transferred the residence to his niece-by-marriage, Frances Jackson, in 1952.

After Cyril moved on, Frances' husband, John R. Jackson, continued to operate the Pincher Creek hardware store, which was renowned for its excellent stock in such a small, main street building. John was an active member of his community, serving as mayor of Pincher Creek from 1956 to 1959 and later was head of the police commission.

The lease changed hands in 2006 following the death of Frances and a new residence, designed by the architectural firm of Ferrari Westwood Babits of Lethbridge, was erected on the lot in 2012.

122 Evergreen Ave.

First lessee: Albert Lorenzo Wood

"Bertch Wood"

"Bert" Wood was a partner in Smith and Wood's, a general store in Taber, Alberta, when he had this residence built in 1921. His partner, Byard Smith, had built a residence in the park four years before. In 1927, Wood moved to Hillspring, Alberta, with his wife Eva and six children. Although Hillspring was very much closer to the park, it was the opportunity to buy a new store that motivated Wood. He bought the general store from N. Eldon Tanner and renamed it Wood's Cash Store.

After a hard week at the store, fishing was a much sought-after getaway and Wood did his share of that with family and friends. They often rowed a boat all the way to the head of Upper Waterton Lake so they could walk into Glacier's Kootenai Lakes for eastern brook trout.

The residence's name is a combination of Bert, Wood and birch, the species of tree which grows around the residence. Its local stone fireplace is a near duplicate of others of the same age built by local stonemason and log builder Walter B. Foster.

124 Evergreen Ave.

First lessee: Robert H. Anderson

"Niven"

Irish-born Robert Anderson, like his Waterton neighbour Bert Wood, was a successful merchant in Taber, Alberta. One of that town's pioneers, Anderson was selling clothing by 1906. He was just 41 when he had this residence built in 1921 for his wife Marion and six children.

If all the Andersons and the Woods were present in the park at the same time, the neighbourhood must have seemed awash in kids.

Anderson's children followed their father into the clothing business and were well known in their hometown for their dedication to Taber's Knox United Church.

Marion and the children spent summers in the park and at least one daughter, Margaret Elizabeth, worked in a curio shop for three summers and then joined her father in Anderson Clothing.

The residence, which remained in the Anderson family until 1977, was sold to long-timers Bob and Mary Niven of Lethbridge.

The residence is now owned by their descendants.

126 Evergreen Ave.

First lessee: Stephen Harwood

Steve Harwood moved to the park as a boy with his father Arthur "Pop" Harwood following the death of Mrs. Harwood. When he was 29 years old, Harwood applied for this lot after two previous applicants failed to meet the building requirements.

The house was completed by the time Harwood married Marjorie Thompson in 1932. Marjorie taught at St. Paul's Residential School two years before, under the supervision of Anglican minister Rev. S.H. Middleton, who himself had a park residence and was in charge of the now defunct All-Saints Anglican Church.

As a 16-year-old, Harwood lost his left arm when a shotgun accidentally discharged near him but like many amputees, he was proficient at a variety of tasks, including photography. He worked as a mail truck driver and later went to work for the park. He retired in 1965. He and Marjorie moved to Pincher Creek in 1969. The couple is buried in the park cemetery.

The residence has since had four subsequent owners and is once again a year-round residence.

128 Evergreen Ave.

First lessee: Walter B. Foster

Builder: Walter B. Foster

Among the first applicants for this large, prominent lot was the Anglican Church, but officials withdrew their application in 1927 after they determined most of the lot was on a hillside, making it not as appealing as they hoped.

Walter B. Foster, a First World War veteran and well-known in Waterton as a stone mason and log builder, applied for the site. The wood-frame structure is clad with local stone, a one-of-a-kind residence with a true street presence, locally known as "The Stone House."

By the fall of 1930, Foster and his wife Eda were able to move into their new house, but it took Foster four more years to complete, since he had a number of other residences underway at the same time.

The Fosters continued to live in this house until 1951, raising three children, Gladys, Robert and Alan, who all attended the Waterton School at one point.

The residence was sold in 1951 to Peter Oscar Enerson, a Lethbridge car dealer since 1948. He was killed in a private plane crash northeast of Lethbridge in a spring snowstorm in 1953. Enerson's daughter Pat acquired the lease late in 1961. She was married to Fred Weatherup, who later purchased the Bayshore Inn. The residence stayed in the extended Enerson family until 1996, when it was sold.

129 Evergreen Ave.

First lessee: Jean Clark Galbraith

Original residence replaced

The original residence on this lot was built in 1926 for Jean Galbraith, who bought the plans from the Canadian Aladdin Co. Ltd. A Scottish immigrant, she married Hugh Galbraith, also from Scotland, who worked as a clerk in the superintendent's office for many years.

The couple had one child, Clark.

She sold the residence in 1931 to "Granny Brown" (Urvilla Isabel Brown), the 80-year-old mother-in-law of Tom Morrow, who was a long-time boatman in Waterton. Then the Galbraiths had another residence built on Cameron Falls Drive.

After Brown's death in 1934, Etta Platt, a talented artisan, bought the residence, selling it in 1955 to park businessman George Baker.

The building was demolished in 1964 and was replaced by a modern, year-round home for Baker's son and daughter-in-law, Rae and Shirley Baker.

130 Evergreen Ave.

First lessee: Jack Hazzard

Original residence replaced

Jack Hazzard applied for the lease on this property in 1926 after selling the Hazzard Hotel on Waterton Avenue, which was the first fixed-roof accommodation in the townsite. The residence he had built on this lot was his only home in the townsite. When he sold his share of an Akamina sawmill business to Carl Carlson in 1929, he also sold this residence.

Ernest and Mary Ann Wright purchased it and it became the first of three residences the Wrights owned. They sold the lease in 1940 and it changed hands several times over the next 27 years.

It was purchased by the government for $4,000 in 1967 and replaced in 1968 by Weston Brothers, a Cardston contractor which built a three-bedroom residence for the park operations manager.

It was later reconfigured into two separate living units.

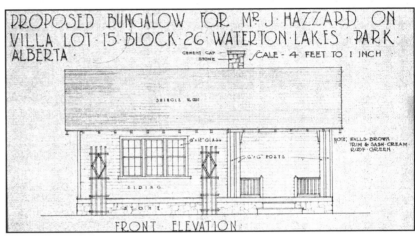

131 Evergreen Ave.

First lessee: S.L. Dickson

Original residence replaced

The first residence built on this lot was erected in 1929 for Silas Dickson, a park labourer who lived in Waterton until 1951. He sold the lease to Ollie Tidball, a First World War veteran. Tidball, Waterton's postmaster, lived there until 1952, when he moved to the new post office and residence that he had Oland Construction build on Windflower Avenue (non-extant as of 2018).

After 10 years as postmaster, Tidball moved back to his original residence at this site since by then the post office building had become the property of the park by previous agreement. He then worked as a seasonal government employee, primarily in charge of the park gate. He was an active community member involved in the Waterton Park Lions Club and its annual golf tournament, and served as secretary-treasurer of the Waterton School Board for several years. The next owners of this property were Ernie and Maxine Haug. Ernie, then a park employee, had grown up in Waterton. The residence was sold to the government for $7,500 and torn down in 1975. A new house for staff was erected on the site.

132 Evergreen Ave.

First lessee: Cliff J. Morris

"Trail's End"

Original residence replaced

Cliff J. Morris was born in Michigan in 1895 and moved to Alberta with his parents, Jean and Malvina Morris, as a youngster. He was drafted for service in the Canadian Expeditionary Force late in the First World War and was promptly sent to Russia, where he served in the Northern Russia Mobile Force, Dog Sled Detachment. Upon his discharge he moved to Waterton, where he was reunited with his parents and brothers and began building a $1,500 residence that took several years to complete. The first residence was similar to one located at 305 Evergreen Ave. and was faced entirely with stucco.

Morris and his brothers built the first Catholic church in the park, but they were not known for the longevity of their structures. The church was later declared unsound and demolished. During the Depression, Cliff Morris sought work as a driller in the gold mines of South Africa but returned to Waterton after two years to resume renting horses.

In 1942 he sold the business and his residence. The latter was sold to Ada Kemmis, hotelier and businesswoman. Although the original residence has been replaced, the name "Trails End" remains. The property continues to be owned by Kemmis's descendants.

133 Evergreen Ave.

First lessee: David V. Tourond

David Tourond, a park labourer and First World War veteran, had this residence built in 1930, but sold it the following year to Jean Stratton of Cardston whose husband had died in the Battle of Vimy Ridge in 1917. Jean Stratton died in 1943 and rather than leaving the residence to her five children, she left it to her caregiver, Elizabeth Bishop. It was not the only time such a disposition of a residence created hard feelings in a family.

They contested the gift but lost in court.

In 1948 George Baker, who lived across the street, bought the property for use as a rental.

It continues to be owned by Baker's descendants, who have renovated it more than once and improved the streetscape.

134 Evergreen Ave.

First lessee: Joseph C. Shaw

"The White House"

Builder: Oland & Scott

This residence was started in 1928 for Joseph C. Shaw, a Cardston plasterer who worked on many residences and business structures in the park. The Depression took its toll and the builders had to take over the ownership, completing the residence in 1931. That year, businesswoman Hannah Carnell Presley purchased the building from them. It soon became known as "The White House," not to be confused with another residence on Mount View Road with the same name that was joined to the Kilmorey Lodge.

With many other rental properties to oversee and an ailing husband, James, who was both a Boer War and a First World War veteran, Mrs. Presley transferred the house to her five sons in 1938.

It has since changed hands numerous times, including to Lethbridge businessman John Haibeck and later Dr. Duncan and Patricia Brown, among others, and has undergone major and striking renovations and landscaping improvements.

135 Evergreen Ave.

First lessee: William Joseph Carnell

Original residence replaced

The first applicant for this lease was John C. Auger, a local carpenter who died before he could complete the residence and obtain the lease. William Carnell acquired the lease for this property in June 1933. Carnell, who was also a Waterton contractor, died in 1946, leaving the property to his mother, Hannah Carnell Presley. As she had done across the street at 134 Evergreen, she turned the residence into a four-suite rooming house. In 1966 the government purchased the property and built the existing four-bedroom house in 1967 for the park's maintenance supervisor.

136 Evergreen Ave.

First lessee: George Baker

This 1928 residence was the second home built for George Baker. His first house was across from Linnet Lake.

He married Betty Annand Nixon in 1935 and together they raised two sons, Alf and Rae.

This residence, remodelled and enlarged over the years, was home for his family throughout his life.

A businessman of some importance in the park because of his various holdings and "can do" spirit, he also did work for the Great Northern Railway, which owned the Prince of Wales Hotel, and was an essential local contact for that St. Paul, Minnesota-based company.

The residence remains in the family.

George and Betty are buried in the Waterton cemetery.

---

201 Evergreen Ave.

First lessee: Harry B. Stacpoole

Original residence replaced

This lot was first developed in April 1922 by Harry Stacpoole, a Cardston physician and pharmacist. His wife, Mary Elizabeth, had another residence on Mount View Road at the same time. This lot changed hands four times between 1945 and 1951 before Charles and Gladys Patching of Lethbridge purchased it.

Southern Alberta farmers, the Patchings had come to know the park as campers during the 1930s. By the time they purchased the residence, Charles had been retired for five years and soon became a regular volunteer at Canyon Church Camp. They kept the residence for 11 years.

It was replaced in 1962 with this modern house built for Anne C. Luchia, who later shared it with her daughter and son-in-law, Vilma and Larry E. Markus. Larry became the park electrician. When he was transferred to another park, the residence was sold in

1969 to businessman Doug Allison and his wife Sophie, a former school teacher who was the daughter of Rev. S.H. Middleton.

The Allisons sold the residence to Jim and Meredith Hodges about 1984 who in turn sold it to Waterton long-timer Paul Madge in 1985.

The residence is now owned by a son.

202 Evergreen Ave.

First lessee: Agnes W. Ford

This residence, originally named "Rambler's Rest," was completed in the fall of 1927. It was owned by Agnes Ford, wife of Cpl. Andy Ford, who was the park's first full-time and most popular RCMP officer. The couple had two daughters, June and Betty, who attended school in Waterton. The Fords were transferred to Banff in 1933 and the residence was rented. It is situated such that it is one of the only residences on this street to have a full view of Vimy Peak. When the lease was purchased in 1944 by June and Slim Udal, the name was changed to "Victoria Cottage," reflecting their association with Victoria, British Columbia, their winter home.

Slim, a boatman in the park, died in 1958 and is buried in the Waterton cemetery.

June sold the residence in 1963 to Nel and Bob Parsons of Lethbridge, who were Waterton enthusiasts.

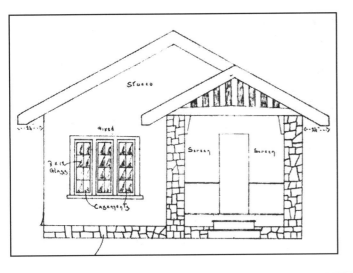

203 Evergreen Ave.

First lessee: Sadie Dayman

Original residence replaced

The application for the first lease of this property was made in 1928 by Sadie Dayman, wife of Art Dayman, the park mechanic. Sadie was not able to meet all of the requirements of building a residence here until 1934, an unusually long time for park officials, which may have tested their patience in this difficult economic time. The two-bedroom, 7.9- by 7.3-metre (26- by 24-foot) residence was slow to be completed, given the size. When Sadie died in 1947, Art inherited the lease and when he died in 1955, he left the residence to his housekeeper, Violet O'Bray. She sold the property to the government in 1967.

A park staff residence was erected sometime later and remains in use.

204 Evergreen Ave.

First lessee: Hannah Carnell Presley

"Green Gables"

This residence was built in 1926 for Hannah Carnell Presley and her husband James, who rented rooms to visitors both in this residence and in the two others Mrs. Presley owned. This residence was known as "Green Gables." A portion of the residence was rented to the school district for classes until the one-room school on Fountain Avenue was enlarged in 1929.

The widow of Patrick Carnell Sr. and mother of eight children, Hannah married Presley in 1922. Two of her sons, Pat Jr. and Charles, later had businesses in the park.

James Presley, a veteran of both the Boer War and the First World War, worked for the government at a variety of jobs, including labourer, seasonal park warden at Cameron Lake, and campground caretaker at Red Rock Canyon, then worked for one season at the Cameron Lake Auto Bungalows.

After James's death in 1944, Hannah continued to operate "Green Gables" as a rooming house until 1962. She died in 1966.

205 Evergreen Ave.

First lessee: Neil A. MacLean

Original residence replaced

Dance hall operator Neil "Pat" MacLean applied for this lot in 1931 and had the residence erected in 1933-34, just as the dance hall business was beginning to flourish. After a mysterious fire destroyed the dance hall and in need of additional money, MacLean sold the residence in 1939 to Art Dayman, a park employee. Dayman's wife Sadie owned the residence next door at 203.

This property saw a succession of lessees over the next 18 years. One was George B. Allred, who operated the Waterton Auto Bungalows and who owned another residence on Cameron Falls Drive.

In 1957, Alf and Ella Baker, son and daughter-in-law of George and Betty Baker, purchased the lease, demolished the original residence and had a new house erected where they raised their five children.

The lease changed hands in 2015.

206 Evergreen Ave.   "Argyle"

First lessee: Archie MacLean

Archie MacLean, a Pincher Creek farmer, was best known in Waterton for his association with the dance hall that was operated by his sons Pat and Slim MacLean. Archie and his wife Bonnie had the residence built in 1926, shortly after the Waterton Dance Pavilion was constructed on Waterton Avenue.

Archie was said to have held the mortgage on the dance hall but was involved only marginally in the business. This residence was sometimes used to house the members of dance hall orchestra until it was sold in 1943 to Hannah Carnell Presley.

She subsequently had an addition made to the front of the residence, making it nearly unrecognizable from the original structure. She owned several other properties on Evergreen Avenue which she rented to the public.

This residence was rented year-round for years to Gladys Foster Prince and her husband Lyle, who raised their children there.

A number of owners followed, the latest taking ownership in 2010.

207 Evergreen Ave.   "Razia's Cabin"

First lessee: Robert Oldroyd   Original residence replaced

The manager of the Pioneer Lumber Co. in Carmangay, Alberta, Robert Oldroyd had a residence built here in 1922. Oldroyd and his wife Estella sold the lease in 1927 and bought another residence near Cameron Falls in 1931.

Mary Cooper of Barons, Alberta, owned the lease until 1953, when Delance Strate, a long-time park resident and employee, obtained the property.

The original residence was replaced by businessman Paul Shaw and was sold in the 1980s to Rick and Mary Kratz, who owned and operated the Bayshore Inn.

As a corporate holding, it went to the new owners with the sale of the Bayshore Inn in 1991 and became known as "Razia's Cabin."

208 Evergreen Ave.
First lessee: Samuel Edward Jones

"Cronkhite"

Samuel Jones of Cardston was a Canadian Pacific Railway conductor in October 1923 when he applied for this lot and hired Cardston builders Oland & Scott to erect the residence.

Two years before, Jones was the victim of Canada's last great train robbery, which occurred in the Crowsnest Pass. He narrowly escaped death. It took several years to track down the robbers. When the CPR transferred Jones to Medicine Hat, he sold the property to Mr. and Mrs. Ed Goble in 1936.

Ed Goble had come to Waterton in 1926 with his father and brother Ken to work on the Prince of Wales Hotel. One of six children of Oliver and Arletta Goble, Ed married local girl Nellie Hunter, daughter of Cal and Elenora Hunter.

When Ed died, Nellie sold the residence in 1943 to Goldie Cronkhite. She and husband Otto were farmers and lived in New Dayton, Alberta.

A soldier in a First World War RCMP cavalry unit in France and Belgium, Otto never lost his enthusiasm for horses, especially if it involved fishing in Waterton's high-country lakes.

The residence remains in the family.

209 Evergreen Ave.
First lessee: Lula Nielson

"Loch Mhor"
Original residence replaced

Lula Nielson, a Cardston businesswoman, obtained this lease in 1922. Estella and Robert Oldroyd of Carmangay, Alberta, Nielson's sister and brother-in-law, had the residence next door. Unable to keep up the lease payments and becoming years in arrears, in 1931 Nielson sold to George N. Giles, a physician in Milk River, Alberta, who kept the residence for 20 years before selling it.

It changed hands two more times and was bought in 1956 by C.W. Boulton, who kept it for the next 40 years. The residence was sold, demolished and replaced in 1996.

The next residence on this site was named "Glenmohr," reflecting a Scottish heritage. When it was discovered the residence's name was incorrectly spelled, it was renamed in 2011 for a body of water in the Scottish Highlands. It means "big lake" apropos of Upper Waterton Lake. The residence was built by Gero Construction of Pincher Creek.

210 Evergreen Ave.

First lessee: Fred J. Coates

Builder: Oland & Scott

This is one of only a few residences, albeit modernized, that has been in the same family since the original lease was signed. It was built in 1929.

Fred Coates, one-time mayor of Milk River, Alberta, was an extremely active businessman who was involved in several endeavours simultaneously, including a mercantile business, an Imperial Oil agency, a radio repair and service shop, a plumbing supply business, life insurance, a land agency and undertaking business. His wife Faye and their two children spent summers at the residence and Fred joined them for weekends and holidays. The Coates family was outdoors oriented and hiked, fished, swam and golfed together. Fred died early in 1939 at the age of 53.

A stone fountain was erected on the property line between this property and 208 Evergreen but is no longer operational.

The residence remains in the family.

212 Evergreen Ave.

First lessee: James B. Taylor

Original residence replaced

James Taylor was a Pincher Creek farmer who applied to lease this lot in 1922. The original residence was sold several times before the 1950s, when it was named "The Pines" by owner Clarence J. Bundy. Bundy was the agent for the Canadian Pacific Railway at Pincher Station, north of the town of Pincher Creek, until his retirement in 1957.

His wife Freda Graham Bundy was a well-respected and widely known writer of magazine and newspaper articles, as well as novels. Both Bundys, themselves amateur artists, were good friends of Group of Seven artist A.Y. Jackson, who they invited to the residence to sketch and paint in the park.

The lease was transferred to Thomas Alfred and Amy Spackman in 1962 and has been in that family since. The original structure was demolished and replaced with a modular house in 1988.

214 Evergreen Ave.

First lessee: Walter B. Foster

"Westbrooks"

Builder: Walter B. Foster

This was one of the first residences with a stone fireplace built by Walter Foster, who completed it in 1923.

The log construction was said to be so precise that "even a cigarette paper cannot be placed between the joints." Every log saddle was cut by hand and drew favourable comments from tourists who came to examine the work. It was described as one of "the finest houses at Waterton Park."

In 1925 Foster sold the house, dubbed "Sun Butte Lodge," to his friend Thomas D. Morrow of Spring Coulee, Alberta, who operated a boat business in the park with his brother Les Morrow. For a few years Tom, his wife Kate and their five children lived here year-round.

After Tom's death, Kate Morrow sold the residence in 1952 to James and Harold Westbrook, who had already done some renovations to it. The Westbrooks were long-time and well-known barbers in Lethbridge.

The residence remains in the family and has been renamed, with the original sign, "Sun Butte Lodge," moved to above the door of the adjacent garage.

302 Evergreen Ave.

First lessee: William Stewart

"Braeside"

Scottish-born William Stewart came to the park in 1927 to work at the Prince of Wales Hotel, driving the luggage truck. In 1929 he married Alice Bowden, the assistant pastry chef at the hotel, and in 1930 this residence was completed. A cement finisher by trade, Stewart worked for the park and helped to construct the sea wall along Emerald Bay, an anti-erosion project. The Stewarts and their small son moved to the coast in 1937 but were not able to sell the residence until 1943.

It was purchased by Grace M. Morrison, wife of Gordon Morrison, who was part-owner of a park rowboat business. The residence has changed hands several times since 1958 and was once owned by the Art Burch family, which also owned and operated the *Motor Vessel International.*

More recently, the residence was used for staff housing by owners of the Kilmorey Lodge. "Braeside" is Gaelic for slope of the mountain.

303 Evergreen Ave.

First lessee: Alwin Oscar Frache

Construction of this residence for Alwin Frache began in July 1927, but it was such a wet summer that it was impossible to get material to the site to complete the work. By the following spring, the $1,750 residence was finished and occupied in July 1928. While Jack Hazzard had submitted a bid for the construction, it is not known who built it.

Alwin Frache and his brothers ran a greenhouse business in Grand Forks, British Columbia, during the late 1800s. In 1908, they built a greenhouse in Lethbridge, which grew into a large wholesale enterprise.

Alwin and Winnie Frache had three children. Their eldest, Don, became a successful landscape, portrait and mural painter. The younger son, Warren, worked in the greenhouse-floral business. Daughter Elayne married John Deak, who became company owner.

The residence was sold outside the family in 1995 and underwent extensive interior renovations.

304 Evergreen Ave.

First lessee: Peter Gairns

Peter Gairns was a Scottish immigrant who moved to Lethbridge in 1905, the year Alberta became a province, worked there as a teamster and then spent four years in France as a member of the Canadian Expeditionary Force during the First World War, being wounded in action. He homesteaded in the Twin Butte area and then moved to Waterton, where he married Florence Haynes and built this house in 1927. Known as "Grub hoe Pete" for his diligent trail maintenance, Gairns worked in the park for 41 years in several capacities, including mail carrier, labourer, golf course groundskeeper and temporary park warden during the Second World War.

He retired in 1962. His wife Florence, who had considerable experience running Mom's Kitchen in Lundbreck, Alberta, became the cook at the YMCA Camp Inuspi in the 1940s.

They sold the residence in 1970 to John Shigetake "Shig" Shimamura, a park painter, one of whose descendants still owns it. Shig and his wife, Hamagi, are buried in the park cemetery.

305 Evergreen Ave.

First lessee: George Stewart

"Glen Elg"

Builder: George Stewart

Scottish-born George "Geordie" Stewart came to Canada, after serving in the First World War, to visit his uncle William Stewart (302 Evergreen) and then moved to Waterton in 1921. He finished this residence in 1930 at a cost of $1,200, two years after he applied for the lot. George and his wife Arta (née Smith) were well-known for their long-time work at the golf course.

George was on the crew that built the first nine holes, became a groundskeeper and spent 42 years at the course.

He and Arta, who were very active in the community, operated the clubhouse from 1955 to 1963. They retired in 1964 and left the park but retained the residence until 1966.

It was purchased by Ernest Wesley Nottingham in 1967. He sold it in 1969 to NeWana Holt, who owned the Itussiststukiopi Coin Op Launderette.

The residence has since been sold at least twice.

306 Evergreen Ave.

First lessee: John Fleming Auger

Builder: Art E. Auger

This residence was built in 1928 by Art E. Auger, son of the lessee who worked for many years as a carpenter building and renovating residences on contract. A bit of a rebel, Art Auger ran up against park authorities who threatened to cancel his lease and take the residence for failure to pay his land rent during the Depression. While many lessees were somewhat in arrears, Auger was five years behind in his land rent and would not even respond to numerous written requests. Auger stood firm and officials backed down.

When he died in 1948 of a heart attack while painting the residence and without a will, ownership details became excruciatingly complicated. Finally, this residence was purchased in 1957 by Leonard Zorn, a First World War veteran and the park electrician, after he had rented the residence for several years.

Zorn had come to the park in 1928 and worked one summer for Baker's Park Transport Co., then came back in 1937 when he went to work for the government. He and his wife Mildred raised four daughters here. Zorn retired in 1961 after 22 years with the park.

The residence has since changed hands and has been enlarged.

307 Evergreen Ave.
First lessee: Bert Barnes

Bert Barnes, who was a private with the East Kent Regiment during the First World War, came to Waterton in the early 1920s, filling a variety of jobs. He worked on Oland & Scott's crew helping to build both the dance hall and the Prince of Wales Hotel before he became a seasonal park warden and then a full-time warden.

Barnes built a residence on this site in 1929, but he lived at the Belly River warden station, so he rented the cabin for classroom use and then to visitors. Mary Ann and Ernest Wright of Lethbridge purchased the lease in 1943. With building supplies exceedingly tight during wartime, the Wrights planned to tear down the residence and use the lumber for a building in Lethbridge.

Instead, it was sold to Pat Carnell Jr. in 1945. Carnell and his wife Vella chose to paint the residence a distinctive pink.

"Fern Lodge"
Original residence replaced

It was sold in 1970 to Orson Bingham who retained the colour and named the residence "Wild Rose."

It was sold again in 1997, demolished in 2000, replaced with this log structure and renamed.

308 Evergreen Ave.
First lessee: Delance Strate

The residence that was built on this lot burned to the ground on Nov. 4, 2019. The cause, according to authorities, was not determined.

It was home to Delance Strate, who grew up in Hillspring, Alberta, and who had a long association with the park. The Strate brothers had one of the first butcher shops in the town. He worked on most of the road projects in the park, as a blacksmith or machine operator, and met his future wife Theressa when she worked as a waitress at Harry C. Lee's tea room, formerly the steamboat *Gertrude*. Delance was the only man to personally have known every superintendent in the first 90 years of the park.

The couple raised a family of eight and spent nearly all their lives in Waterton. This residence was started in 1931 but took several years to complete. Strate began working for the park in 1932 and retired nearly 30 years later as the maintenance supervisor, then went to work at the Prince of Wales Hotel in the powerhouse.

"Birchdale"
Original residence destroyed by fire

Cecilie "Squish" Swanson Parke, a long-time Waterton regular, purchased the residence in 1986 and lived in it year-round until 1994, when it was sold to Beth Russell-Towe, who lived there and later rented it to people who worked in the park.

The lease has been sold to another lessee who, at this writing, is awaiting approval of building plans.

310 Evergreen Ave.

First lessee: J. Percy Gregory

This residence, built in 1953, replaced the original 1927 building of the same name built by Percy and Helen Gregory. Percy Gregory, foreman of construction on the Akamina Highway, had moved to the park in 1925 from a ranch near Twin Butte, Alberta. Despite holding a good job, Gregory, like his neighbour Art Auger, refused to pay his land rent during the Depression and went into arrears for five years. Due to the debt, officials chose to cancel Helen Gregory's agreement on the lot next door (308 Evergreen) because they felt she would not be able to comply with the building obligation. Finally in 1936, Gregory cleared his debt and was promoted to general foreman of park crews. Both Gregorys were active in the community.

Percy died in 1949 and Helen and their daughter moved to Fort Macleod, selling the residence to Rudy Kotkas, a farmer from Barons, Alberta, who replaced it.

While the new residence was being built, the fam-

"Akamina Cottage"

Original residence replaced

ily lived in the garage during the summer.

The residence, with its original name, remains in the Kotkas family. At one time before the Akamina Parkway was built, the trail to the Akamina Pass ran behind the residences on this side of the street due to the difficulty manoeuvring past the "Devil's Point" formation, which eventually was cut out of the route.

312, 314, 316 Evergreen Ave.

First lessee: Government

Before these residences were constructed, the only government-owned house in the townsite was the park superintendent's. Single men could reside in the park bunkhouse, but married men had to find their own accommodations. Some applied for leases and built homes; others rented.

These three lots were set aside specifically for park needs and were vacant until these houses were constructed. They were originally assigned to staff according to their job position.

The one at 312 was known as the "accountant's house." It was finished Jan. 31, 1948. The residence was later taken out of use due to mould and asbestos. The house at 314 was completed early in 1950, as the revenue clerk's residence, and the house at 316, the maintenance officer's residence, was completed in 1948. Both 314 and 316 have been renovated.

402 Evergreen Ave.   "Johansen"

First lessee: Clara Pitcher

Lula Nielson, one of the park's most feisty and independent single women, applied for this lot in 1923. Although she was unable to fulfill her building obligation and had to surrender the lot, she never let go of her desire to get it back. Two years later, Nielson's married sister, Estella Oldroyd of Woolford, Alberta, applied for the lease but couldn't build, either.

The next applicant was Clara Pitcher, a bookkeeper from Woolford who had the residence built in 1928. Estella and Robert Oldroyd bought the property in 1931, but times were tough, and they sublet it to Lenore Costello, who turned it into a tourist rooming house with a restaurant in conjunction with the residence next door. The Oldroyds transferred the lease to Lula Nielson in 1944. Nielson travelled the world and brought home many archeological artifacts which she displayed in the residence.

The residence is owned by members of her extended family.

---

404 Evergreen Ave.   "The Tavern"

First lessee: Doug Oland   Builder: Oland & Scott

This residence had been started in 1927, when Oland & Scott were finishing the Prince of Wales Hotel, but trucks to bring the building materials were seconded to the larger job, so the completion of this residence was delayed until June 1928. Like other lots chosen along this bench, considerable brush cutting was required before work could be started. The lane at the back of the lots was not built until 1931, which only added to the builders' problems.

This was one of the residences Oland & Scott built on speculation, something that was not encouraged but could not be prevented if all the rules were followed. Oland sold the residence to local magistrate and First World War veteran C.F. Reilly in 1931 and he sublet it to his sister, Lenore Costello, who rented rooms and served meals in conjunction with the residence next door.

Mrs. Costello named her tourist accommodation "The Tavern," but no alcohol was served to guests.

Eddie Bell, a park employee, purchased the lease in 1935 and made it his home until 1959. He was one of the park's most ardent stream fishermen.

When Bell left the park, he sold the residence to J.T.C. "Todd" Haibeck, who was head of HaiCo Manufacturing Ltd. He was inducted by the Blood Tribe into the Kainai Chieftainship in July 1970 and given the name Eagle Head.

The residence was purchased by new owners late in 2012.

406 Evergreen Ave.

First lessee: John Achtem

"House of Hurlburt"

John Achtem, proprietor of The Arcade in Lethbridge, was the fifth applicant for this lot, but the only one able to fulfill his obligation to build. The first application was made in 1923 by Mark C. Rogers, who was building a hotel in the park; the second was made in 1925 by Hal Lyon, a drugstore owner in Gravity, Iowa; the third was made in 1928 by John Dow, a Lethbridge telephone engineer; and the fourth was Cecile Carlson, wife of builder Carl Carlson, in 1930.

Achtem, who applied for the vacant lot in 1945, finished the $1,200 residence in 1947 and then promptly sold it to Henry J. Neufeld, a southern Alberta rancher.

Some years later, long after Ken Hurlburt of Fort Macleod acquired the lease, he recalled the deal was made based on a handshake and included everything: the sheets on the bed and the food in the cupboard. It was not until months later that money changed hands.

The residence has been in the Hurlburt family since 1968.

410 Evergreen Ave.

First lessee: Francis R.K. Hewlett

"Windfall"

Original residence destroyed by fire

The original residence on this site had two names over the years: "Hewlett House" and "Paha Taha Teepee." For the first several decades of ownership, this property was beset with legal problems. Originally this lot and the one next door were held by Francis Hewlett, a southern Alberta wool broker who had

his residence built on this lot in 1924. Hewlett was unable to pay for the residence and Oland & Scott Construction placed a lien on it. Since the residence overlapped onto the adjacent lot, a fact that was unnoticed for several decades, it caused problems that were only resolved by redrawing lot lines.

The residence was sold in 1936 to John Smith, manager of the Cardston Loan Co. who rented it to visitors, but he was beset with problems related to the lease transfer.

Doug G. Oland and his daughter, Mary O'Brien, owned the lease for a time, but sold it to a Lethbridge businessman in 1963. The final legal battle occurred when the house burned to the ground in June 1995 and park officials refused to allow the owner to rebuild to its original size due to a change in regulations.

The lease was sold, and a new residence built in 1998.

412 Evergreen Ave.

First lessee: Francis R.K. Hewlett   Original residence replaced

This residence was built in 1991, but cleverly incorporated some of the stone features of the original, which was built in 1924. Like the residence next door, a lien was placed on the original building for default of payment, and it was picked up by John S. Smith, who in turn sold it back to Doug G. Oland in 1940. He sold the residence in 1941 to First World War veteran Gladstone Virtue, a Lethbridge lawyer known as an avid fly fisherman and trail rider.

Gladstone's wife Marion spent the entire summer here each year with her children and together they rode horses, hiked, fished, swam and played golf, making many friends both in the park and areas adjacent.

The residence continues to be owned by family members.

414 Evergreen Ave.

First lessee: Joseph E. Carson   Builder: Lethbridge Woodworking Co.

This lot had an exceptionally long list of applicants who, for various reasons, were unable to fulfill their building obligations. Starting in 1923, there were eight applicants before Joseph Edward Carson, a Lethbridge dental surgeon, had an $11,000 residence built in September 1952. Carson originally had a residence at the end of the street, close to the present-day turn-around.

When a snow slide hit the vacant lot in 1951, he requested a lot exchange. Park authorities agreed and he was assigned this lot. Plans for his residence were drawn by John Willie's Lethbridge Woodworking Co. Willie built several residences in Waterton, including one for himself.

This lot was later sold to Dr. Brian O. Black, a Lethbridge radiologist. His descendants continue to own the residence.

416 Evergreen Ave.

First lessee: William A. Fraser

Original residence replaced

William A. Fraser was a well-known Pincher Creek merchant who applied for this lot in 1930. He and his wife Katherine owned two other residences, both of which were on Fountain Avenue. Fraser ran an impressive dry goods store in the Stanley Hotel until 1931.

Fraser sold his residence in 1936 to Dr. Jesse Bigelow, who co-founded the Bigelow Fowler Clinic in Lethbridge. Bigelow's partner, Dr. Douglas Fowler, had a residence on Mount View Road.

Bigelow was also a charter member of the Kiwanis Club in Lethbridge which created the Waterton Mothers' Camp. He owned the residence until his death in 1989.

The lease was sold, the residence demolished and this one built in 1999.

418 Evergreen Ave.

First lessee: Erik Hagglund

Builder: Erik Hagglund

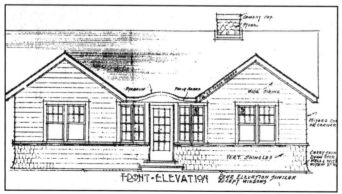

Mabel Lineham, sister-in-law of pioneer oilman and entrepreneur John Lineham, applied for this lease in 1923 but failed to meet her obligations and surrendered her application. In 1930 Blairmore, Alberta, miner Erik Hagglund built this residence and moved his family to Waterton. They lived in the house until 1937.

For many decades to follow the Hagglund family was closely associated with construction and tourist services in the park.

Both Erik and Olga Hagglund are buried in the Waterton cemetery.

The residence was so admired by local resident and fellow builder Carl Carlson that he requested the permission of park authorities to build a house just like it on the lakeshore. His request was denied.

The residence was sold to Charles Sartoris, a Blairmore businessman who kept it until 1941, when it was sold to William Standige, a former RCMP officer in Hilda, Alberta.

In 1947, it was purchased by Ethel Freel and has been in her family since.

504 Evergreen Ave.

First lessee: W.C.L. Cooper

Original residence replaced

W.C.L. Cooper of Barons, Alberta, was a partner in Murray and Cooper, general merchants, and his wife Mary was a former school teacher when they had a residence built here by Oland & Scott in 1923 using a new style of economical construction. A 1937 snowslide just missed Cooper's property. He died in 1940 and his widow Mary sold the lease in 1946 to Harold Turner, also of Barons, who sold it nine years later to Elmer D. McNellis.

McNellis was not so lucky when, years later, the residence received major damage from an avalanche. Another residence next door, owned by John Willie, was so badly damaged it was removed, the lot withdrawn from leasing and was turned into a road allowance.

The original Cooper building was sold in 1946 and changed hands two more times, until the lease was purchased in 1962 by Lethbridge dentist Dr. D.A. Rylands. The old structure, which stayed in family ownership, was removed in August 2018 and a larger one, designed by Simple Architecture of Calgary and built by Erickson and Sons of Cowley, Alberta, was completed in 2021.

---

508 Evergreen Ave.

First lessee: Walter B. Foster

"Sun Dance Lodge"

Builder: Walter B. Foster

This residence was Walter Foster's second major log building in town (after "Sun Butte Lodge" at 214 Evergreen) and was built in 1926-27 with the intention that it would be an even finer building than his first. The lack of access to the back of the property at the time was solved by a front-facing garage under the building. When it was completed, the residence was valued at $1,500. Five years after it was finished, local businessman Nahor Dilatush bought the residence and used it as a rental. It was later owned by several members of the Baker family and was then purchased by Fred and Elizabeth Meads, who owned several other residences.

It changed hands several times since, with the Pruegger family, long-time Lethbridge music store owners, among the best known of the people who leased the property.

They had it for many years, selling it in 1967. It has subsequently had three different owners.

512 Evergreen Ave.

First lessee: J.T.C. Haibeck

The original residence was built for Todd Haibeck in 1946. Haibeck sold the residence to Violet Faye Broder two years later and she subsequently got in a lot of trouble with park authorities. Broder destroyed 26 trees and damaged another 16 on the property and was threatened with charges because of her violation of the National Parks Act, which carried a maximum fine of $500. The matter was settled out of court when it was discovered that a warden had allowed her to proceed without a work permit. She sold the property in 1953 to Frank Bond, a veteran of the First World War turned farmer in Coaldale, Alberta.

It wasn't the last time someone associated with this lot would be taken to task under the National Parks Act.

When park engineer Ken Slovack owned the residence in 1979, a bear tried to break into the house while his family was inside. He shot and killed the bear, was taken to court, but was found not guilty because his actions were deemed self-defence. He kept his job with the park.

The house was sold in 1989.

---

516 Evergreen Ave.   "Thompson"

First lessee: Ralph and Harlan Thompson

The Thompson brothers were the sons of William and Clara Thompson, pioneer business people in Spring Coulee, Alberta. The brothers had this log residence built in 1923 on two adjacent lots with the residence on one lot and the driveway on the other. This was a practice that was later prohibited. Harlan became an award-winning writer of boys' fiction after a workplace accident required extended recuperation. He moved to California and wrote more than a dozen books under his own name and the pseudonym Stephen Holt, occasionally using Waterton for a setting. His first book, *Wild Palomino*, was an instant bestseller in its field. He continued to spend summers in Waterton for the rest of his life.

The residence continues to be owned by family members.

602 Evergreen Ave.

First lessee: Lilly Elvira Middleton

Lilly Middleton was the daughter-in-law of Rev. S.H. Middleton, a long-time Waterton visitor and himself a lessee. The residence was completed in 1948 and sold to William Betts in 1949.

Born and raised on a farm north of the park, Lilly Middleton became a teacher at several schools, one of which was the St. Paul's Residential School on the Blood Tribe reserve. Lilly was a talented artist who completed the war honour roll scrolls that hung in Waterton's Anglican church. She married Charles Middleton, who worked for the federal government, and lived in several places in Alberta and Manitoba before returning to Fort Macleod. She taught school for two years in Waterton. The Middletons are buried in the Waterton cemetery.

The residence was purchased in 1955 by Herbert M. Turner, a First World War veteran and well-known Lethbridge merchant who operated Bert & Mac's Cycle and Radio. In 1966 the residence was transferred to his daughter, Mary Yvonne Hohm, who kept it until 2014, when it was sold.

604 Evergreen Ave.

First lessee: N. Eldon Tanner

"Ain Karim"

Builder: Remington Construction

This residence was built in 1949 for N. Eldon Tanner, an influential leader in the hierarchy of the Church of Jesus Christ of Latter-day Saints. Tanner had an impressive career as a member of the Alberta legislative assembly, where he became the provincial minister in charge of lands and was responsible for encouraging petroleum exploration. He then became head of TransCanada Pipelines, but when he moved to Utah for his church, he no longer wanted the residence.

It was sold in 1951 and it was later purchased as a retreat for the Sisters of Saint Martha, a Catholic order. "Ain Karim" is the name of the village believed to be the birthplace of John the Baptist.

The Sisters of St. Martha first came to Lethbridge in 1929 from their motherhouse in Antigonish, Nova Scotia. On arrival they built the St. Michael's hospital, now known as St. Michael's Health Centre.

When the order returned to Nova Scotia in 2019, the residence was sold to owners who were long-time Waterton aficionados.

606 Evergreen Ave.

First lessee: Wesley B. Eddy

Wesley Eddy was a barber from Creston, British Columbia, who had this residence completed by July 1931. There was some confusion as to the ownership when H.H. Bossenberry claimed to own the residence and produced a bill of sale plus multiple rent receipts. It is not clear how the matter was resolved, but the property was transferred to Robert and Beryl Shaw in January 1946.

Shaw was a garage and auto dealer in Cardston who went into the trucking business before becoming town foreman. He retired in 1971. Shaw's greatest pleasure was roaming the mountain trails on his saddle horses. Walter B. Foster built the residence's stone fireplace. The residence is believed to remain in the Shaw family.

---

608 Evergreen Ave.

First lessee: D.C. and H.D. Remington

This residence is the only instance of architectural duplication of a private residence in the townsite. It has the same lines as the residence at 304 Fountain Ave. built by Doug G. Oland.

"Ya-Ha-Tinda"

Builder: Remington Construction

The original plans were to build a frame house on this lot, but Don Remington found that inappropriate. "I have a preference for rustic houses in a place like Waterton," he said. The residence was completed in 1954 at a cost of $8,000 using specially milled logs from Montana which used a "spline cut," simplifying construction. The residence changed hands and was sold to a U.S. resident, but the residence name was unchanged.

Ya-Ha-Tinda, translated from a Stoney Nation placename, means "the little prairie in the mountains."

610 Evergreen Ave.

First lessee: Geddes Bissett

Original residence replaced

The name of the original residence was "Greenbrier." Built in 1933, it was owned by Geddes Bissett, who was a grocery store manager in Lethbridge. He sold the residence in 1941 to John Jacob, a parish priest in Cardston, but when Jacob died in 1944 several complications arose. Jacob willed the property to his niece, who lived in Germany, and with the Second World War underway, any proceeds from the sale had to be remitted to the Custodian for Enemy Property.

How it was sorted out is not known, but the following year physician Joseph J. Dobry, known in Cardston as "Doc" Dobry, purchased the residence. It became "social headquarters" for the bi-annual Glacier-Waterton Hamfest, a gathering of amateur radio enthusiasts. Dobry had become something of an amateur radio pioneer when he became the first radio inspector in Alberta in 1922.

The original residence was replaced in 1996 by Dr. Ed Dobry, son of Doc Dobry. Ed Dobry sold it about 2019.

---

612 Evergreen Ave.

First lessee: Robert W. Lynn

"Beth Lynn"

Builders: Doug G. Oland, Doug H. Oland

This residence, built at a cost of $4,000, has been continuously owned by members of Robert Lynn's extended family since 1931. Bob Lynn was a Cardston then Lethbridge physician who named both his boat and his residence for his wife, Beth Hunt Lynn. When he was killed in a car crash in 1936 on the way home from Waterton and Beth suffered serious and prolonged physical injuries, it became front page news. She later remarried but retained the residence throughout her life.

When a series of avalanches in the 1950s damaged residences near hers, she was willing to exchange lots, but there were only two said to be available and neither was suitable, so she remained in place.

The residence remains in the hands of relatives.

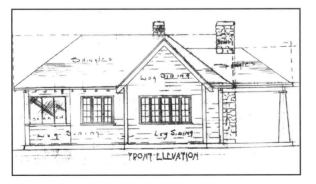

Residences on Fern Street

Fern is one of two short west-east streets in the town which are connectors between Evergreen Avenue and Fountain Avenue. The other short street is Fir Grove, *which has no residences facing onto it. Both streets were the result of a 1919 townsite survey. Fir Grove was initially called "B Street" and Fern was "C Street."*

101 Fern St.

First lessee: Lula Nielson

Lula Nielson of Cardston had a residence built on this lot in 1920 after she failed to come to a workable compromise with park officials for a lease elsewhere. Her sister and brother-in-law, Estella and Robert Oldroyd, had the lease next door on Evergreen Avenue. Nielson sold the residence in 1923 to Mark C. Rogers, the businessman who was attempting to renovate the Lakeshore Hotel. When Rogers died in 1924, the lease was transferred to his wife, Dorothy Rogers, who later married Slim MacLean of Waterton dance pavilion fame. They left the country and the residence remained in the Rogers' estate until 1958.

Finally, the deteriorating residence was sold to the government and this three-bedroom staff house,

Original residence replaced

whose front today is hidden by trees, was built in 1966 as residence for Waterton's first permanent naturalist, Kurt Seel, and his family.

It continues to serve as a park employee residence.

102 Fern St.

"Blue Moon"

First lessee: Archie MacLean

After two people withdrew their applications for this lot, Archie MacLean applied for it and had a residence completed by December 1929.

MacLean held the mortgage on the dance pavilion that burned down in 1938. When a new dance hall was built, Edward J. Schrempp of Twin Butte, Alberta, was financially involved for a short time.

The transfer of this lease to Schrempp may have had something to do with MacLean's departure from the dance hall partnership.

Schrempp owned the lot only a few weeks before it was transferred to James W. Fisher of Raymond, Alberta.

In 1949, it was transferred to Isabel Morrison of

New Dayton, Alberta. The family continues to own this residence.

104 Fern St.

First lessee: Logan McWhirter

Original residence replaced

The first residence was built on this lot in 1926. Logan McWhirter first applied for the lease in 1921 but required several extensions after he was struck by lightning and injured. The original residence was added to and became a mixture of log and frame construction.

McWhirter was a good friend of his neighbour to the immediate south, Bill Terrill of Twin Butte, Alberta, and sometimes worked with him in a backcountry guiding business.

McWhirter sold out to Jim J. Morrison, manager of the gas company in Lethbridge, in 1934.

Morrison and his wife Ethel were avid fishermen and aficionados of Waterton who used both boats and horses to get to good fishing spots. They sold the lease to Leo and Marion Schmidt of Pincher Creek in 1952. The Schmidts had Dorigatti Construction of Lethbridge build a new residence on the lot in the 1960s. Leo was the proprietor of the Tourist Café.

Norman Cristall purchased the house from Schmidt. Cristall worked as a bartender at the Bayshore, Prince of Wales Hotel and later as a clerk at the drugstore. His wife Margaret is buried in the park cemetery.

From 1994 to 2021 the house was sold to three successive owners.

Being on a corner lot, 104 presents two different faces when viewed from Fern Street, above, or from Fountain Avenue, below.

Residences on Fountain Avenue

This street is the only one named for a man-made feature. At one time there were two or three drinking fountains built by park staff in the townsite, giving thirsty pedestrians the opportunity to have a refreshing, cold drink on a hot summer day.

South along the avenue, at 202 Fountain, was another fountain that was part of the lessee's landscaping.

Postmaster Arthur "Pop" Harwood built his fountain from local stones, improving the curb appeal of his residence and providing wildlife with an opportunity to refresh themselves. A keen gardener, Harwood was known for growing a variety of plants and trees in his yard.

The only other private stone fountain in the townsite is non-operational and located between residences at 208 and 210 Evergreen Avenue.

103 Fountain Avenue

First lessee: Ernie Haug, Sr.   Original residence replaced

This is one of the few properties that was first occupied as a residence, followed by a business and then replaced by a new residence. Ernie Haug, Sr. erected the first building in 1927. Haug named it "Bide A Wee" and rented it to visitors, primarily for entire summers.

When Haug died in 1952, his widow sold the residence to Doug Allison, who in turn sold it to Jason Attwell, park painter and supervisor. Atwell and his wife, daughter and son lived there until 1978.

With their departure, the residence was turned into a place of business, starting with The Golden Crepe, which was followed by a pizza restaurant.

In 2009 the new owners, a couple from Lethbridge, tore down the original building and built this new residence, which was completed and landscaped in 2013.

104 Fountain Ave.

First lessee: Edna May Allison

Original residence replaced

The original residence on this lot was built in 1921 for Art and Edna May Allison. Art, a First World War veteran, was a temporary seasonal park warden until 1924.

When they left for Banff, the residence was rented in 1925 by Ralph M. "Chris" Christiansen and his wife Chrissie, but complications with the paperwork delayed transfer of the lease until 1947 because Mrs. Allison had moved away.

Christiansen, who served in the First World War, started working for the park as a labourer in 1923. He became a warden in 1936 and eventually became the town warden. Chris retired at the end of 1959. When he died in 1966, Chrissie moved to Cardston. They are both buried in the park cemetery along with Jacky, a grandson.

Lee Lerner, a park employee, and his wife Sandra bought the residence from Chrissie in November 1968, in turn selling it to Fort Macleod area turkey farmer Herman Lowen, who tore it down and rebuilt on the site. In 1993 Wendy and Rick Valley of Lethbridge bought the property, selling it in 2002. The lot, one of two in the townsite of extra-large size, was sold again in 2002 and redeveloped in 2010. The new residence is so stately, it was mistakenly thought to be a visitor centre following the demise of the one on the entrance road in September 2017. A discreet note and a locked door disabused visitors of their error.

105 Fountain Ave.

First lessee: Mabel Dilatush

Builder: Oland & Scott

Mabel Dilatush, co-owner of the Tourist Café and Stanley Hotel with her husband Nahor, applied for this lot in 1924, about the same time they bought the café. The house, which cost "well over $2,000," was finished by 1927. A distinctive architectural feature of a residence designed by W.D. Cromarty, well known Parks Branch architect and a one-time seasonal Waterton superintendent, is the "eyebrow" roof over the front door.

Since the lot is an irregular shape and the one next to it is substantially smaller than average, Mabel was allowed to lease the adjoining lot without building on it, which was an exception to park policy.

This was the first of several residences the Dilatushes owned in town. Most became rental properties. By the 1970s the house was sold to the government.

This is the only instance of an original residence, purchased by the government, still being used to house park staff.

106 Fountain Ave.

First lessee: Charles Carnell

Charles "Dippy" Carnell had his share of failures in Waterton, but it was not for lack of trying. His innovative boat dock at the marina was smashed to pieces in a winter storm in 1926, and his excursion and rental boat businesses failed to do well. He tried his hand at operating a store on Waterton Avenue but couldn't make a go of it.

In 1933, riddled with debts for the construction of this residence, which had been near completion in 1929, Carnell moved to British Columbia.

Ella Higgs, wife of Waterton pharmacist H.L. Higgs, acquired the residence through a court judgment in 1934. Their son and business successor, Ben Higgs, owned the residence in 1952. Barbara Tanner bought the lease in 1971.

It was sold in 2011 to a Lethbridge couple.

At this writing, it was intended that the residence would be replaced.

202 Fountain Ave.

First lessee: Arthur Harwood

"Kinnikinnik" "Hell Roaring Lodge"

Arthur "Pop" Harwood, the park's longest-serving postmaster, had this residence built in 1926 for about $1,500 and rented it to the RCMP until their own office was built on Waterton Avenue. Harwood and his second wife, Minnie, moved from a house/post office/telephone office across from Linnet Lake to this residence in 1927. This building served as both a residence and post office until 1949.

The corner property was neatly fenced and beautifully landscaped with trees and flowering plants, accented by the stone fountain Harwood built in 1930.

Harwood retired and sold the residence to Jessie Baalim, wife of Harry Baalim, whose parents owned a residence at 308 Fountain Ave. The residence has subsequently had two other owners.

The house has two names: one on each door.

Kinnikinnik, a plant native to the park, is an Algonquin word for "smoking mixture" as this plant was used by Indigenous people as tobacco. Hell Roaring Falls and Canyon are located on the east side of Upper Waterton Lake.

204 Fountain Ave.

First lessee: Nels E. Ekelund   Builder: Nels E. Ekelund

Swedish born Nels Ekelund, a Twin Butte, Alberta, builder and labourer, erected this $800 residence and a $15 outhouse in 1923. The site was said to be "one of the finest park locations, being at the crossroads of the main thoroughfare leading to the business section."

Ekelund was renowned as a skilled woodsman and man who could wield a broad axe. He built several residences in the park, as well as row boats which he sold to fishermen. He also did some prospecting in the park, finding traces of copper in the Blakiston Valley at Coppermine Creek. Nels and his wife Ingri homesteaded immediately north of the park's present-day border.

One of the couple's eight children, Aron, acquired the Waterton residence in 1934 and sold it in 1939 to Mary Sandin, whose husband was a chemistry professor at the University of Alberta in Edmonton.

It was transferred again in 1955 to Archie and Edna Willock of Milk River, Alberta, and changed hands again about 2012.

206 Fountain Ave.

First lessee: Katherine A. Fraser   Builders: Oland & Scott

Katherine Fraser, wife of William Fraser, a dry goods merchant in Pincher Creek, applied for the lease on this property in 1921. It was one of three Fraser properties in town.

The couple was forced to sell this property in 1943 when the aging and unwell William needed money to pay the taxes on his Pincher Creek holdings.

Elsie Baker, wife of William Baker, purchased this lease. When Mrs. Baker died, she left the residence to her daughter, Ella Baker Broomfield, sister to Waterton businessman George Baker.

Two years later, Reginald Cross, son of well-known Lethbridge photographer A.E. Cross, bought the residence and kept it until 1970.

Subsequent owners, Don and Sheila MacLennan substantially altered the residence prior to selling to new owners about 2012.

208 Fountain Ave.

First lessee: Percy Manning Wiltse

Original residence replaced

Percy Manning Wiltse of Foremost, Alberta, applied for a lease on this lot in 1921 and erected what was described by park officials as "not much more than a shack." In 1924, Wiltse applied for another lot (207 Waterton Ave.) but was not able to come up with the money to build and surrendered that application to concentrate on this lot. In 1933, he assigned this lease to Imperial Oil Ltd., which promptly transferred it to Laura Black of Medicine Hat. Black demolished the residence, but new construction was stopped when she died in 1939. Her son, Gordon Lewis Black, had the residence finished and in turn transferred it to George Wesley of New Dayton, Alberta, in 1943. Bill Snowden, a Calgary lawyer with family ties to the area, bought the lease in 1979. He sold it in 1996 to the current owners, who both worked in the park at the time.

210 Fountain Ave.

First lessee: B.B. Hoyt

"Magaguadavic"

Builder: George Robison

Creation of this residence was very much a family effort. Lessee Berton Beecher Hoyt, a Lethbridge hardware merchant and city pioneer, provided the funding. Construction was done by his father-in-law George Robison with the assistance of his brother-in-law George Watson and family friend Bob Hebert in the summer of 1923.

This log building employed the "pinned construction" method, using corner posts that made it quick and simple to erect. This residence has been owned by family members ever since. It was one of the last residences built before a moratorium was placed on leasing while the government struggled with the controversial issue of building a dam in Waterton.

The residence name, "Magaguadavic," reflects the heritage of Berton Hoyt and his second wife, Alma Jane, who were both born in New Brunswick.

The residence sign came from a railway station near the river of the same name.

212 Fountain Ave.

"Inn Haven"

First lessee: Katherine A. Fraser

This was the second residence on this street owned by Katherine Fraser. A former school teacher, Katherine was the wife of William Fraser, who was a Pincher Creek merchant. He later opened a store in Waterton's Stanley Hotel. Of three residences the couple owned (the others were at 206 Fountain and 416 Evergreen), this was the one they owned the longest.

It was built in 1926 and sold in 1945 to businessman Wilbur C. Mackenzie of Lethbridge. It was formerly called "Scots Haven." When the residence was owned by Jo and Dave Hodge of Lethbridge from 1963 to 1996, it was a tradition that the Canadian flag was flown when they were in the park and be taken down when they left. Dave spent the Second World War in the Canadian military overseas.

They sold the residence in 1996.

213 Fountain Ave.

"Teacherage"

First lessee: WSD No. 4233

Builder: Lethbridge Woodworking Co.

As the student body at the Waterton School grew, so did the need for staff. In 1952 a small coal and wood shed attached to the west side of the school was converted into an apartment for the teacher.

With year-round housing at a premium, the school board chose to build this two-bedroom house in

1954 which was suitable for a married teacher with a family.

In 1961, renovations to the basement created two more bedrooms.

When the school ceased to operate as an educational institution, ownership of the Teacherage was transferred to the Waterton Park Community Association and then the Waterton Community Joint Venture, which rents it as staff housing.

303 Fountain Ave.

First lessee: Nahor Dilatush

This building, originally a duplex, has been used as staff housing since it was built in 1960 and was situated on the east side of Waterton Avenue by Nahor Dilatush, immediately south of the old Fire Hall. The site of the duplex became green space after its first move in 1984.

At that time, it was purchased by Parks Canada and relocated to Clematis Avenue, immediately south of the Church of Jesus Christ of Latter-day Saints.

The second move of the duplex occurred in 2016 when park officials offered it to Improvement District No. 4 for $1 and moving costs, to make way for Phase 1 of staff housing on Clematis Cul-de-sac.

The move, rather than being such that the front of the building faced Fountain Avenue to conform to other buildings along that street, was simplified by shifting the structure to the west and resulted in the rear of the structure facing the street.

It was then renovated into three self-contained units for renting to employers. There are two upper units; the third unit is below the original two units and is about 30 per cent larger than the two upper units combined. It can be occupied by as many as 20 people. It has been used for staff housing since May 2017, with a hiatus for COVID-19 restrictions beginning in 2020.

304 Fountain Ave.

First lessee: William Terrill

William Terrill, a rancher from Twin Butte, Alberta, was a park foreman who in 1913 supervised the building of the Boundary Creek trail under the supervision of John George "Kootenai" Brown. In 1922 Terrill began constructing a 55.7-square-metre (600-square-foot) log residence which was completed the following year. At the time the residence was under construction, Terrill was the postmaster in Twin Butte. Good friends with Jack Hazzard and Logan McWhirter, Terrill was in partnership with them in a guiding business for a time.

The original residence was occupied, but not owned, by George David "Cap" Thomas, a long-time park employee best known for his work at the fish rearing ponds near Cameron Falls.

Ralph Thrall, later the owner of the McIntyre Ranch, bought the lease in 1945 and had Doug G. Oland replace the residence in 1953. Thrall was already familiar with Oland, who had done several projects at the ranch in the late 1930s.

Walter B. Foster, assisted by his son Rob Foster, was subcontracted for the cedar log and stone work on the residence. The residence is a larger version of the one at 303 Evergreen, but these logs came from British Columbia and are saddle-notched.

The residence remains in the family.

306 Fountain Ave.

First lessee: Carl Carlson

Local builder Carl Carlson completed this log building in 1925. Vincent W. Williams, secretary treasurer of Baalim Motor Co. in Lethbridge, bought the structure in the spring of 1929, just months before Williams was financially hurt by the stock market crash. Edgar B. Hill, a well-known Lethbridge merchant, bought the residence in 1931. The stone fireplace is reminiscent of the style used by Walter Foster, but it is not known who built it. The residence,

"Vimy View"

Builder: Carl Carlson

which faces Vimy Peak, was named for the vista.

The sign painter, however, apparently couldn't decide on the name's spelling or the owners did not want to confuse it with the rental residence named "Vimy Vue," then located in the lower compound across from Linnet Lake. One side of the original sign reads "Vimy View" and the other "Vimy Vu."

The residence is owned by a fourth-generation descendant.

308 Fountain Ave.

First lessee: Carl Carlson

Almost immediately upon completing the residence next door, Carl Carlson began construction of this one in 1926. He brought his wife from Blairmore, Alberta, to live in the new residence, but when the opportunity arose in 1929 to sell it, he did so. The residence was purchased by Gladys Baalim, wife of Lethbridge businessman Art Baalim. The couple

"Wigwam"

Builder: Carl Carlson

named the residence "Wigwam." In 1934 Gladys submitted plans for the first of a number of alterations to the residence which were made over the course of several years. Baalim was very active in the Lethbridge Chamber of Commerce, which often voiced its concern over the need for improvements in Waterton. He was instrumental in the formation of the Lethbridge Rotary Club and a charter member of the Waterton-Glacier International Peace Park committee. Many Rotarians enjoyed the hospitality of the Baalims over the years.

The residence's ownership was eventually shared among several family members from various parts of Canada in unequal percentages, a complicated arrangement, especially when it came time to share expenses.

In 2010 the residence was sold to new owners, who renovated it.

The work was nearly complete in 2021.

Residences on Harebell Road

This road was created by the 1924 townsite survey. Since then, it has been substantially changed by being twice shortened, first by development of the townsite campground and decades later by construction of the government-owned, Olympic-sized swimming pool. The residential nature of the road was changed by the *completion in 2022 of the Visitor Reception Centre, the park's largest building. The northern-most portion of Harebell, which resumes at Windflower Avenue, has no facing buildings. The road is named for a common and much-storied perennial which has sky blue bells on a thin stem about 10 cm (four inches) tall.*

104 Harebell Rd.

First lessee: Cyril and Marcel Hochstein

"Glendoe"

Builder: Carl Carlson

This residence, original to the lot, was completed for $3,000 in 1946, at a time when there was a postwar shortage of building materials. The Hochstein brothers, who had married sisters Edith "Toots" and Pearl, were Pincher Creek area ranchers. The parents of Toots and Pearl first brought their daughters to the park in 1918, when camping was the affordable type of family accommodation. This family retained ownership of the residence for 50 years and then sold it.

The name "Glendoe" reflects the Scottish heritage of the present owner.

106 Harebell Rd.

First lessee: William F. Gross

Original residence replaced

The Great Depression dashed many park cottagers' hopes. This lot was originally applied for in 1931 by Lillian Haug, wife of Ernie Haug, Sr., a long-time businessman in the park.

Unable to fulfill her building commitment, she had to accept a cancellation of her agreement to build. The lot remained vacant until 1952.

Postwar shortages of building materials delayed leasing of this lot, even though the one next door proceeded. William F. Gross was a Grassy Lake, Alberta, farmer who built a residence in 1952 and sold it in 1953 to Edith Emma Lillie, a widow from Warner, Alberta. When Lillie died in 1965, the property went to her daughter and was later sold.

Bryan and Pauline Currie had this modern house built in 1991 after they went into the grocery business at the last remaining grocery store, on Windflower Avenue.

The house was sold in 2004.

107 Harebell Rd.

First lessee: Art Batty and W.B. Hallifax

Builder: Batty & Hallifax

Arthur Batty and W.B. Hallifax were Lethbridge building contractors who put in a successful bid on the lot for $100. The lot had been thrown open to bids when park employee E.A. Gurney, supervisor of construction engineering, surrendered his application and was transferred to Cape Breton Highlands National Park in Nova Scotia. The residence was completed for $6,000 in September 1952. Batty & Hallifax built and sold the residence in short order, beginning a list of six subsequent owners.

Two owners of significant longevity were Derek Martin, who owned and operated a fast-food outlet called Virginia Dell (Cameron Falls Drive and Waterton Avenue), and George and Pat Meyer of High River, Alberta. George Meyer was a one-time mayor of Taber and a notable weekly newspaper publisher.

The Meyers sold the residence 25 years to the day they had purchased it from the Martins.

The lot immediately north of this one was designated a "government reserve" and was never leased. Today that lot is part of the Visitor Reception Centre development.

108 Harebell Rd.

First lessee: Bruce David Steed

It took three tries for the government to find a lessee who would live up to the obligation to build on this lot. Bruce Steed was a single school teacher who hoped to realize a profit by building and selling. He applied in 1950 and then required an extension. When his personal plans changed, he sold the unfinished residence in 1958 to his father, Orzie, for $900.

Orzie's wife Eula was able to recoup the price by renting the front room of "the big house" to tourists.

The residence has always been owned by family members.

109 Harebell Rd.

First lessee: Scott T. Low

Original residence destroyed by fire

Scott T. Low was a mechanic who worked in the park. It took him two years to have the residence built and the following year, 1935, he sold the residence to Dorothy M. Johnson.

Her husband, Ed, was a local carpenter who had built a residence on Cameron Falls Drive and built the original building that became an annex to the Kilmorey Lodge.

The Johnsons' residence burned to the ground early one morning in June 1937. They escaped with their baby and their lives and while they were unharmed, they lost everything. Dorothy's father was Bert Barnes, the Belly River warden.

Despite the tie to the park, the Johnsons soon moved away and, unable to pay their land rent arrears or build a new residence, lost their lease.

Another residence was erected sometime after 1947 by George Gruenwald of Lethbridge, who later sold it to long-time Waterton aficionados.

The existing house, the third on this site, is a man-ufactured building constructed by Mountain View Homes of Cardston that was carefully brought into the townsite in sections in July 2013 and required careful attention to overhead powerlines.

A crane was used to place each portion of the new residence.

---

110 Harebell Rd.

First lessee: Orzie D. Steed

Builder: Orzie D. Steed

Orzie and Eula Steed of Cardston, both school teachers, applied for this lot in 1948 while still trying to complete a residence at the corner of Vimy Avenue and Clematis Avenue. This was the second residence Orzie Steed undertook to build in the park, mixing the cement for the footings by hand. It took until 1954 to complete this residence. So difficult was it to get material in those postwar years that it was not unusual to buy bags of cement and other supplies individually in separate towns.

Added to the delay in completing this tiny residence was a proposal by Steed for two alterations to the plan, both of which were denied by park authorities. Over the course of several summers, Orzie worked at the Chief Mountain customs station, at Ben Higgs' pharmacy in the Stanley Hotel, and Eula rented the residence to tourists and ran Steeds Holiday Needs, a small store on Waterton Avenue.

111 Harebell Rd.

"Shield's Haven"

First lessee: Wilford F. Shields

Wilford Shields was a retired farmer who was living in Cardston when he applied for the lease on this property in 1946. By 1948 the frame-and-stucco residence was completed at a cost of $4,000 and named "Shield's Haven."

In 1959 Colin and Marguerite Hill Hedderick bought the residence, having sold a log residence at Cameron Falls Drive and Fountain Avenue.

The Heddericks, who lived in Pincher Creek, were long-time Waterton residence owners and were active in a variety of outdoor sports. Colin was a particularly keen golfer and fishermen.

The residence remained in the family until 2003.

It was sold and substantially renovated when new owners from the United States purchased the lease.

---

113 Harebell Rd.

"Research House"

First lessee: Government

Between 1946 and 1949 three applicants were interested in this lot, but none was able to build on the site, which needed filling and levelling. In 1950 the lot was withdrawn from public leasing until park officials could review their staff housing needs.

This three-bedroom house was built in 1957 for the Belly River warden and was located near Crooked Creek, off the Chief Mountain Highway. A mirror image of the house at 101 Windflower Avenue, it was built according to standard park service residence blueprints.

When the Belly River location was deemed redundant, the house was moved to this lot.

It continues to provide staff accommodation in the summer months.

It is known internally to park employees as the "Research House" because it is often used to accommodate visiting summer environmental scientists.

Residences on Lupine Lane

The fronts of these lots were originally supposed to face Cameron Creek, where Heather Road was to run along the creek from Cameron Falls southeastward to the lakeshore. Across the creek was to be Anemone Road, *which would have also ended at the lakeshore. Neither road was built. This dead-end lane runs northwest off Clematis Avenue.*

103 Lupine Lane   "Cedars"

First lessee: Alice Maria Stockdale

Alice Maria Stockdale, who came to Lethbridge in 1885, was 74 years old when she decided to get a lot in the park in 1946, making her the oldest person to apply for a first-time lease. She had the residence built by 1949. When she died in 1956, her three children inherited the residence after a lengthy hassle with officials that required the intervention of their member of Parliament.

When Johnny Black of Lethbridge purchased the lease from Stockdale's family, he was one of three men's clothiers in Lethbridge to have a park property.

The residence is currently owned by others.

105 Lupine Lane   "Welwyn"

First lessee: Charles Pace Hamill   Builder: Doug G. Oland

Charles Pace Hamill was a lawyer who lived in Belleville, Illinois, making him one of the most distant lease holders when he had the residence built in 1947. The Hamills, by then retired, spent the entire summer in Waterton and moored their boat at the marina. The boat was also named *Welwyn*.

The building was designed to provide winter storage for the boat, but little did the designer know that Heather Road, the only access to the other side of the building, would never be constructed.

Hamill's son, known as Charlie, was an aficionado of classic boats and utilized the park marina annually.

The lease has been in family ownership since it was acquired and the residence built.

107 Lupine Lane

First lessee: Gwendolyn Holland

Original residence replaced

Gwendolyn Holland was a businesswoman in Calgary who, like many eager to get a lot in Waterton, had applied in 1949 only to discover there was still a postwar shortage of building materials. She was able to solve the problem by having a foundation prepared and purchasing a small house from Harry Reeves (at 132 Waterton Ave.) which was moved to this lot in 1951.

She sold the property in 1954 to Cecil Edward Robinson of Lethbridge, who in turn sold it to Elinor C. Meisser, wife of Lowell. The Meissers farmed near Warner, Alberta.

When damage occurred from improper winterization of the residence, Lowell and his brother Rome did major repairs, replacing portions of the structure in 1963.

The lease was transferred to Elinor and Lowell's son Jerald. He died in 1990 and a family member took over the lease.

On Aug. 27, 2009, the tiny residence was moved north of the park to a rural location, where it was repurposed into a greenhouse and workshop.

A new residence, built by Castle Rock Homes of Coaldale, Alberta, was constructed over the winter of 2010.

109 Lupine Lane

First lessee: Donald L. Kirkham

Donald Kirkham was the son of a partner in the Waterton Lakes Hotel and Chalets. Like his father, he was in the hotel business in Lethbridge. He had this residence built in 1953 but sold it in 1954 to Bill and Betty Davidson of Lethbridge.

The Davidsons had originally planned to build another structure two doors away (113 Lupine Lane) in 1947 but failed to submit plans to the park and had to withdraw their application. They kept this residence until the 1980s, when it was transferred to son Roy Davidson, a fourth generation Lethbridge lawyer and veteran of the RCMP.

It has since changed hands outside the family and been renovated for year-round occupancy.

111 Lupine Lane

"Summer Place 1947"

First lessee: F. Charles Beny

F. Charles Beny was a Lethbridge car dealer when he applied for this lot in 1949. He had been a business associate of another Waterton home owner, Art Baalim of Lethbridge, since 1916 and now he was about to be a park neighbour. Beny had the $8,000, four-bedroom summer residence completed in 1952. It was no easy task.

Beny was advised by the park superintendent in 1950 that his plans were rejected because they were "not in keeping with what is desired for . . . a national park townsite." The plans were revised and approved. In 1957, an addition and boat house were joined to the residence. The 1964 flood broke through the banks of Cameron Creek cutting a new channel which inundated Lupine Lane, leaving rocks throughout the area along with mud and debris. This

residence required extensive cleanup. Damage resulting from the 1975 flood was mitigated thanks to the installation of gabions which prevented bank erosion.

One of the Beny sons, Roloff, became a world-renowned photographer whose collection is now owned by University of Lethbridge.

The residence remains in the Beny family.

113 Lupine Lane

First lessee: Henry Reuben Woitte

Henry Woitte was raised in Warner, Alberta, and after farming for several years, became a Lethbridge hardware store manager. This $6,000, two-bedroom residence was built in 1954.

Four years later when his wife Eleanor died, Woitte sold the lease to brothers Lowell and Rome Meisser, who were also farmers near Warner.

Rome Meisser made his first trip to Waterton with his brother in 1917, when it took an entire day to reach the park. Rome, Lowell and later Lowell's wife Elinor were all bitten by the "mountain bug" and when they retired, spent every summer here.

Rome lived here while Lowell and Elinor lived three doors up the lane. Rome was a golfer, fisherman and Waterton devotee in the extreme.

115 Lupine Lane   "Wildwood"

First lessee: Robert William Eagleson

Robert William Eagleson was, like others on this block, a Warner farmer. When this residence was built in 1947, it was described by the park superintendent as "one of the nicest to be built in the park for a number of years." Eagleson sold the lease in 1956 to Murton and Esther Harland, who raised cattle and horses north of the park. Despite the proximity to their other residence, the Harlands had a special attraction to Waterton. Both Harlands were First World War veterans. He was in the cavalry and she was with a nursing unit. When they married in 1920, they took over the Bar X Ranch.

A.Y. Jackson, a well-known Canadian artist and member of the Group of Seven, was among their friends and came to their ranch and their Waterton residence to paint. For many years his art hung in the home.

The couple is buried in the park cemetery.

The residence continues to be owned by Harland descendants.

The seldom seen front entrance of this residence faces a green space adjacent to Cameron Creek. The brackets below the windows were installed as supports for seasonal flower boxes.

Failure to build proposed roads along either side of Cameron Creek gave Lupine Lane residents a much better measure of peace and quiet, with less dust as well as more privacy. In the spring, the roar of the falls can be distinctly heard by residents.

Residences on Mount View Road

When the town was surveyed in 1910, a road later known as "The Boulevard" ran along the lakeshore from today's Kilmorey Lodge to the park administration office. This gave the lessees on this strip automobile traffic on two sides of their property. The Boulevard was finally closed to motor vehicles in 1926 and it became a pedestrian route, which has since been extended along the lakeshore to Cameron Creek.

Officials in Ottawa proposed in a 1967 master plan to purchase all of the lakeshore lots here and replace them with day-use facilities and a marina expansion. "In view of the increasing need for public waterfront facilities, private cottages occupying prime shoreline in this area can no longer be condoned," the report stated. Acquisition costs at the time were estimated at $126,000, more than Ottawa was willing to consider.

The proposal was abandoned, and the residences remain.

105 Mount View Rd.

First lessee: Carl Danielson

"Carl's Cottage"

Builder: Carl Danielson

Carl Danielson came to the park from Utah via Cardston, where he worked as a blacksmith. In 1911 he helped build the first flimsy bridge over Pass Creek. It was eventually swept away by the rapidly flowing creek. Danielson was, however, more successful in erecting buildings. In addition to constructing park buildings, he also built as many as five residences on his own, including this one in 1924. Officials had offered this lot for five years but could not find anyone who could build on it until Danielson applied.

He also built and operated a small boat into which he crammed visitors who wanted to tour the lake. The boat was the property of hotelier Jack Hazzard.

Months after Danielson died in October 1937, a fire of undetermined origin nearly consumed this building. It was one in a string of fires between 1936 and 1939 that had residents quite worried. In 1940, Ada Kemmis, who owned the Kilmorey Lodge next door and was the suspected arsonist, purchased the lease. It was sold again in 1965.

Despite its proximity, the residence was not damaged by the Kilmorey Lodge fire of 2009. However, it was put on the market in 2013.

106 Mount View Rd.

First lessee: J.E. Sherman

Original residence replaced

Waterton was a popular retreat for residents of Spring Coulee, Alberta, and the Shermans were among many from that town to visit the park. "Bert" Sherman, a farmer, built a home here in late 1922 because his wife May was prone to hay fever and the mountain air provided relief. They named their residence "Mountain Holm." After Bert's unexpected death in 1938, May moved to Waterton where she lived year-round and joined in the social activities of the day, grew flowers, occasionally shooed away bears, and shovelled snow. She sold the lease in 1957 to Florence and Peter Hominuke, who owned the lodge next door. Mrs. Sherman had seen Crandell Lodge rise from the ashes of Lee's Residences and grow into a popular accommodation, just as she had watched the growth and popularity of the Kilmorey Lodge across the street.

The residence remains in the extended Hominuke family.

The original residence was replaced in 2009 with a peeled log structure built by Twin Butte Log Homes.

107 Mount View Rd.

First lessee: Alice Hillier

Original residence replaced

Alice Hillier of Fort Macleod applied for this lot in September 1917 and committed to having a six- by 10-metre (20- by 34-foot) frame house built. While she did have a foundation constructed, she failed to build on it for a number of years. In 1932 she sold the property to brothers Benjamin and Gerald Harry Martin, both Lethbridge undertakers. Descendants of the brothers continue to operate the undertaking business, which began in 1907.

Benjamin was a First World War soldier who served in 61st Battery (Field Artillery), which was raised in Lethbridge.

Another Waterton and Lethbridge man who served in the same unit was Lieut. Gladstone Virtue, who later had a residence on Evergreen Avenue. It is not known if the two men were acquainted.

A modern residence replaced the original residence in 1991. It remains in the Martin family.

108 Mount View Rd.

First lessee: Carl Danielson

Mrs. Illa Laurie of Cardston tried for three years to come up with the means to erect a residence on this lot, but in the end was forced to surrender her application, which was picked up by Carl Danielson.

By 1929 he completed the structure, which was sold by his estate in 1946, nine years after his death, to Anna Bruns of Pincher Creek.

Bruns sold the lease to Meredith Going in 1952. Going and his family had lived in rental accommodations in the park since 1936. For the first few years, Going hauled mail from Twin Butte to Waterton and later went to work for George Baker at the Park Transport Garage. His wife, Linnea Hanson Going, was a cook at the Kilmorey Lodge. Linnea, who had been raised in Mountain View, Alberta, was the daughter of Waterton pioneers Henry and Julia Hanson. When Going died in 1963, Linnea left the park and sold the lease to Doris Williams of Cardston. It has since changed hands twice.

The most recent owner has substantially improved the appearance of the residence.

109 Mount View Rd.   "Emerald View"

First lessee: Mary Elizabeth Stacpoole

Although this was one of the first lots advertised for leasing, no one was able to meet the building obligation until the winter of 1918-19, when Mary Elizabeth Stacpoole of Cardston had a 6.6- by 7.2-metre (22- by 24-foot) summer home erected.

This was the first of two residences Dr. and Mrs. Stacpoole owned.

In one of the strangest unsolved park crimes, someone broke into the residence in the fall of 1937 and stole the bedding and housewares. Nothing was recovered.

After the Stacpooles died, the lease was sold to Robert John Fansett of Lethbridge. In 1948, it was sold to Edwin Ulysses Rylands, who renovated the residence, had a fireplace added by Walter B. Foster as well as a bedroom. Rylands named it "Noolook," giving it a Native flair, but then changed the name to "Emerald View." The original name had been "Seven Pines." Rylands was a prominent Lethbridge businessman who owned Rylands and Co., a womenswear and dry goods store, from 1911 to 1951.

The lease remains in family hands.

110 Mount View Rd.

First lessee: Herbert James McKenzie

Original residence replaced

Herbert J. McKenzie, a Waterton truck driver, built a residence on this lot in the winter of 1927 and added a garage in 1929. Known as "Foxy" McKenzie, he had been responsible for delivering the mail to Oil City in the Akamina Valley in the early 1900s. His wife Jennie was a rental agent for nearby properties. Their son Roy, of Coutts, Alberta, inherited the lease, which was family-owned for more than 30 years.

It was purchased by Peto Nicas of Lethbridge, who opened McGuire's Woolen Shop in Reeves Corner House in 1961. Nicas, who operated the store until 1987, was one of three Lethbridge men's clothiers to own a property lease in the park.

It changed hands in 2007 and was rebuilt the fol-lowing summer and winter by Jenex Contracting of Magrath, Alberta. It was ready for occupancy by the summer of 2009.

---

111 Mount View Rd.

First lessee: Thomas Herron Scott

"Carney"

Original residence replaced

Most of the lots on this side of the street were first used by campers in the early years, a practice forbid-den by authorities but ignored by visitors. Eventually the campers were directed elsewhere, "to keep the townsite clear of temporary squatters."

Lula Nielson of Cardston sought permission in 1915 to erect a residence and a suitable building for dancing on this lot. Officials could not agree among themselves whether her plans were appropriate for the location, so in disgust she dropped the request.

Tom Scott applied for the lot and built a residence in 1918. He was a pioneer Pincher Creek merchant and undertaker who had attended the 1916 burial of Kootenai Brown.

Scott sold the lease in 1934 to William Alexander Ross of Pincher Creek whose estate in turn sold it in 1954 to Ernest R. McFarland, a well-known Lethbridge merchant and community leader. He was inducted into the Kainai Chieftainship in 1950.

Doug H. Oland, son of the renowned Waterton builder, acquired the lease in 1958 and sold it in 1962.

The original residence was razed and this new structure completed in 1997.

112 Mount View Rd.

First lessee: Donald Thomson

Donald Thomson, a Pincher Creek lawyer, had this residence built in 1924 and a boat house was later moved onto the lot. Thomson's law partner, Harold Jackson, may well have encouraged him to obtain a lease in the park, since Harold's brother Cyril had built one a block away only three years before.

Thomson, who was among the invitees for the opening dinner at the Prince of Wales Hotel in July 1927, was active in petitioning Ottawa for park improvements. He was elected third vice-president of the Rocky Mountains Club in 1928, a local group headed by Walter B. Foster.

Thomson was a bachelor who died about 1931 without a will, despite his legal connections. His lease was purchased by Mary Jackson of Pincher Creek, who kept it until 1951, when Mabel Watson became the owner. Watson hired Walter Foster to build the stone fireplace in the residence.

The lease was later sold to Mrs. H. Mallison and it has changed hands twice since.

201 Mount View Rd.

First lessee: Elmer Ainsworth

Original residence replaced

As soon as lot applications were taken in October 1911, Timothie Lebel of Pincher Creek submitted his paperwork. Although Lebel was one of the most successful merchants in Pincher Creek, he was unable to build in the park and his application was cancelled. Between 1913 and 1915, Joseph William Bawden, a Lethbridge home furnishings merchant, went through a similar process.

Finally, in late 1915, Elmer Ainsworth of Lethbridge applied and by 1917 had built a 6.6- by 9.0-metre (22- by 30-foot) log home on the lot. A provincial public works inspector, Ainsworth went on to become responsible for construction of provincial highways. When he moved north in 1922, he sold the lease to William A. Buchanan, the senator from Lethbridge and publisher of *The Lethbridge Herald*. Buchanan became the park's strongest and most vocal advocate in Ottawa. When Buchanan died, Cameronian Mountain in the Akamina Valley was renamed Mount Buchanan. The lease was held by the Buchanan family until 1958, when it was transferred to a new owner.

In 1973 a new residence replaced the original log home. It was completed in 1974.

202 Mount View Rd.

First lessee: Mary Ann Wright

"Park Lodge"

The first applicant for this lot was Walter Samuel Deisman who, in 1927, was the secretary for the Alberta Motor Association. He wanted to build a tea room on this site, incorporating an AMA office from which he would broadcast road reports. Although he was given permission for the tea room-office, Deisman was unable to build and the lot went to Mary Ann Wright of Lethbridge, who had the residence completed in 1930. It was sold in 1944 for $1,000 to Jim J. Morrison of Lethbridge who transferred it to his son Jack A. Morrison of Burdett, Alberta, in 1945.

The residence had two units, one of which was sometimes rented. Jack sold the lease in 1953 for $3,250 to Lorne Burritt Collins, a Pincher Creek physician. Collins added a bathroom and the stone fireplace. The residence has changed hands several times since.

203 Mount View Rd.

First lessee: Truman Crofts

Original residence replaced

Truman Crofts, a Lethbridge dry land farmer, had his residence built in 1918, just two years before a proposed irrigation dam at the Narrows threatened to destroy the townsite. Despite his lease ownership, Crofts was a staunch supporter of irrigation and worked diligently for provincial funding of the Lethbridge Northern Irrigation District, of which he was the first chairman. When the Waterton dam was cancelled, Crofts had modest improvements made to the residence. In 1930 he transferred the lease to his wife, Julietta, and it was sold in 1935 to Dr. Douglas Bradshaw Fowler.

Fowler was a partner with Jesse Bigelow in founding Lethbridge's Bigelow-Fowler Clinic, which is still in business. Fowler had the Crofts residence demolished and rebuilt in 1936 by Art Auger, a local carpenter. It changed hands again in 1974 and was maintained without change until 2015, when a nephew of Dr. Fowler bought the residence.

It was demolished in 2018 and the third residence on the site was constructed.

204 Mount View Rd.

"Inglemere"

First lessee: John A. Mason

John Mason was a Lethbridge painter who had this residence built in 1930. Next door on the eastside, his wife Mary had a large cottage named "Inglenook." The two residences became home to the Lethbridge Kiwanis Mothers' Camp, but only this residence has survived.

"Inglenook" was rented through the Second World War and then purchased by Lillian Beswick of Spring Coulee, Alberta, in 1952. She sold the residence in 1958 and it was razed to allow for expansion of the El Cortez Motel (now Bear Mountain Motel).

John worked for the park until he died in 1937. Mary sold "Inglemere" in 1941 to Bernard Powlesland of Del Bonita, Alberta, and it subsequently changed hands three more times in the 20th century.

205 Mount View Rd.

First lessee: A.D. Cairncross

Andrew David Cairncross, a Cardston implement and auto dealer, leased this lot in September 1916. Cairncross ran into financial difficulties and he transferred the lease to his wife, Ida, in 1920. She sold the property to David Horton Elton in 1922. Elton was a long-time visitor to Waterton who had done some promotional writing for W.O. Lee and Sons, early park tent camp operators. Elton was a former newspaper publisher in Cardston, Magrath and Raymond who became a lawyer and was appointed a King's Counsel in 1921. A poet and public speaker, Elton sometimes served as an announcer at the Waterton Dance Pavilion.

Before he sold the residence to Mary Catherine Rice of Lethbridge in 1941, he was elected mayor of Lethbridge, an office he held for nine years.

The residence was demolished in the spring of 2021 to make way for a new one. Until that time, the 105-year-old building was the oldest original standalone residence in the townsite.

207 Mount View Rd.

First lessee: Byard Smith

This original residence is now the oldest in the park and until it was sold in the summer of 2021, had been continuously owned by descendants of the same family. It was completed in 1918 from a rough sketch.

Byard Smith was a Taber, Alberta, merchant who was in partnership for a time with his brother-in-law, Albert Lorenzo Wood (122 Evergreen).

Before the residence was built, the Smith family camped at the site. Smith and his wife Mae had three daughters, all of whom spent much time in the park. Best known was Mary, who met her husband Herb Healey at the Prince of Wales Hotel, where they both worked in the summer. Mary was a well-known sportswoman among park regulars and although she and Herb moved to St. Paul, Minnesota, she returned to the park every summer without fail for decades. She is buried in the park cemetery.

The lease changed hands in the summer of 2021 and was purchased by descendants of another longtime Waterton residence owner.

209 Mount View Rd.

First lessees: Doug Oland and Bert Kelley

Original residence replaced

The original 1919 structure on this site was a 61.3-square-metre (660-square-foot), three-room frame building valued at $1,200 and constructed by Doug G. Oland, Jim Scott and Shorty Glasgow. It was among the first residences built by Oland & Scott Construction in the park.

Bert Kelley lived in Spring Coulee, Alberta, where he and his wife ran the Spring Coulee Trading Co. After Kelley moved to Calgary, Mary Etta Faull of Twin

Butte, Alberta, bought the lease in 1929 and kept it for 20 years. For years it was known as "Miramichi" and its lakeshore frontage was filled with wild rhubarb.

Looking for a place to build a residence for her daughter, Violet Faye Broder of Broder Canning Co. in Lethbridge bought the lease in 1949. Broder also had a lease at 512 Evergreen. In 1951, she hired local contractor Carl Carlson to demolish the old residence, which the park superintendent had deemed dilapidated. When Broder's first plan for a new residence on this lot was rejected, she hired Fooks and Milne, a Lethbridge architectural firm, to design it. The $17,000 building was completed in 1959.

The property was sold in 1966 to Dr. Ralph Goates and his wife Katherine of Blackfoot, Idaho. Lethbridge born and raised Katherine was the daughter of Jobie Llewellyn, of Grassy Lake, Alberta, an avid Waterton fisherman.

The residence was built with an operating elevator to accommodate the aging Goates in getting to the upstairs bedroom. The lease continues to be held by the couple's daughter.

210 Mount View Rd.

First lessee: Carl Danielson

Original residence replaced

Carl Danielson, a Cardston carpenter, built the first residence on this property in 1928. Following his death in 1945, the lease was held by at least three other Cardston residents and in 1973 was purchased by Rae Baker, who demolished it in 2007.

The following year a detailed business survey was done in the townsite to determine accommodation requirements for businesses, both on a seasonal and year-round basis. Only about half of the housing needs were being met, with numerous employees living outside the park. By 2011, when additional surveying was done, there appeared to be a potential need for more staff accommodation in the community, a benefit to both staff and business owners.

Following release of the survey results, a new one-and-a-half-storey building for staff housing was

erected on this lot by the lessee in 2012-13. Siting the building on the lot with an east-facing front helps mitigate some winter weather problems arising from snowplowing and the north wind.

The winterized building can be occupied on a year-round basis.

211 Mount View Rd.

First lessee: Reed S. Eldridge

Original residence replaced

The first application for this lot was signed in 1911, but park officials were not successful getting someone to build. The lack of proper streets and the difficulty of getting material to the site discouraged all but the most determined.

Reed Eldridge, a Cardston farmer, applied for a lease on this lot in 1918, but was not able to put up a residence until the winter of 1922-23. Although brush was cleared and the foundation poured, work was suspended due to uncertainty about the proposed dam at the Narrows. Like several others on that street, the residence was built by Carl Danielson.

In the summer of 1923, Danielson acquired the lease from Eldridge. Danielson's estate sold the property to James A. Key, a Calgary doctor, in 1945.

It was purchased in 1956 by Cyril August Bonertz of Pincher Creek and has been in the family since.

The original residence was demolished in August 2009 and a new one built.

213 Mount View Rd.
"Glenshee"

First lessee: William Telford Laurie

William Laurie, a Cardston banker, had this tiny residence built in the summer of 1922. He transferred the lease in 1925 to his wife, Illa, who in turn sold it to Josephine Legh of Medicine Hat in February 1926. Legh proposed to operate a tea room here, but Herbert Knight, the acting park superintendent, did not like the idea because of concerns about parking and the need to widen the street for commercial purposes.

Despite the rejection, Legh opened the Tea Kettle Inn for one season, then disposed of the lease in 1928, selling it to George Millar of Taber, Alberta.

When park officials requested Millar grant them 4.5 metres (15 feet) of his lot to "round out the administration grounds" next door, he agreed, on the condition a hedge be planted to divide the two properties and his land rent be reduced by $3 per year.

Fearing the setting of a precedent, they declined.

He later transferred the property to J.G. and Angus Millar in 1941. Angus was a well-known, highly regarded Lethbridge optometrist, a member of a variety of service clubs and recipient of Rotary's Paul Harris Fellowship Award in recognition of outstanding service.

Family members continue to own the residence.

---

216 Mount View Rd.
"Rosedale"

First lessee: John Cox
Builder: Carl Carlson

This lot has a varied early history. John Cox, a park blacksmith from Pincher Creek, applied for the lease

on this lot in 1928 and two years later, still under Cox's ownership, it was announced that merchant W.A. Fraser would build a new store here.

Local builder Carl Carlson was contracted to do the job. By October 1930 the building was closed in, but Fraser was unable to finance its completion. By some accounts the building was merely a shell, but Cox intended to have it completed as a store and a tea room.

In 1931 the "Rose Tea Room" was rented to Erik and Olga Hagglund who, by 1932, bought the lease. The property was transferred to their daughter and son-in-law, Linnea and Frank Goble, in 1940. They enlarged it on the west side eight years later, renovating it into four apartments.

It became known as "Rosedale Apartments," but was eventually converted into a private residence and remains in family ownership.

217 Mount View Rd.

First lessee: Walter B. Foster   Builder: Walter B. Foster

Walter B. Foster began building this $4,000 structure in 1926 with the idea that it would be headquarters for the Rocky Mountains Club, an outdoor appreciation group he founded. Foster ran into financial difficulties because he had several other buildings under construction while building this one. He was forced to sell the building, which was purchased in 1929 by Frank Ellert of Milk River, Alberta. Ellert's daughter, Erma, became a teacher in the park from 1940-42.

Gilbert Moir of Barons, Alberta, won the residence in a Lions Club raffle in 1945 and rented it to Cliff Ott, who ran an excursion boat.

Andrew Hogg, a Lethbridge lawyer and son-in-law of David Elton (205 Mount View Rd.) bought the lease in 1947 and resold it to Howard Hays' Glacier Park Transport Co. Hays sold it to the Great Northern Railway, which then owned the Prince of Wales Hotel and *Motor Vessel International*. The residence became quarters for the boat's captain.

This building has had more names than any other: "Many Trails Lodge," "Deeidra Lodge," "Ellert House,"
"Captain's Residence" and "Cliff Hummel House." Cliff Hummel was manager of the Prince of Wales Hotel from 1976-78 and the brother of former owners of the cabin. The residence changed ownership in 2013 and was subsequently renovated.

218 Mount View Rd.

First lessee: John Lawrence Larson

John Lawrence Larson, a Cardston carpenter, built a residence at this location in 1926 and sold it in 1931 to Dell and Tay Ellison. The couple would eventually own many residential properties in Waterton which they skillfully turned into rentals, in addition to their commercial holdings: a store on Waterton Avenue (now the parking lot next to Trappers Mountain Grill & Smokehouse), a service station (now Pat's Waterton) and the Crystal Swimming Pool (now the site of Mountain Spirits and Welch's Chocolate Shop). The Ellisons had requested permission to add a large, four-unit apartment and garage to the residence, but

were turned down by park officials, so they sold to Mollie Cooper of Barons, Alberta, who in turn sold it to L.G. Turner of Barons in 1952.

The original residence was sold in 2009 and by
2015 it was replaced Laura and Rod Bullock of Zum's Eatery and Mercantile.

They sold the residence to new owners in the fall of 2020.

220 Mount View Rd.

First lessee: Dell H. Ellison

Dell Ellison signed the lease on this property in 1927. When the Ellisons decided to leave the park after more than 30 years, they sold this residence to brothers Don and Orzie Steed as part of a package which included a Waterton Avenue store which was renamed Steeds Holiday Needs.

The current owners have kept the classic "residence features" of this building, even as they updated and refurbished it in recent years.

Adjacent to this property on the east is a vacant lot, once the home to a two-storey rooming house built in 1927.

Over the years it changed hands several times and was known as Bungalow Apartments, Kootenai Motel, Coe's Motel and finally Alpine Motel.

After being bought by Parks Canada it was briefly used for staff housing, but was demolished in the early 1970s, becoming the last vacant commercial lot in the townsite.

In 2019 it was used as parking for Parks Canada vehicles, but was later restored to a vacant lot.

Residences on Vimy Avenue

In 1930, the government proposed that these lots had "secondary residential character" and officials were willing to allow the building of rooming houses and small rental chalets on them. Only one such chalet was begun on this street, but it was not completed.

There are two lots on this street which have always been vacant, although several applications for them were made in the 1940s and 1950s. Those lots are now designated as "green space" and will not be leased.

The avenue was named for its spectacular view of Vimy Peak (2,379 metres; 7,905 feet) which rises on the east side of Upper Waterton Lake and can best be seen at the eastern end of the avenue. Contrary to popular belief, Vimy Ridge, a namesake of the 1917 First World War battle in France, is a separate landform located east and south of Vimy Peak.

101 Vimy Ave.

First lessee: Orzie D. Steed

This was the first of several residences owned by Orzie Steed of Cardston. He and his sons used all their spare time to erect this residence, which was finished in 1947.

They built the stone fireplace themselves, without experience, from rocks collected in Taylorville, Alberta, 16 kilometres (10 miles) east of Cardston.

The residence was sold in 1948 to Daniel Boyle of Fort Macleod for $4,200. Boyle was a prominent businessman who owned Fort Macleod's Empress Theatre, served on many of that town's boards and was named Calf Chief as a member of the Blood Tribe's exclusive Kainai Chieftainship.

The residence was sold in 1962 to Dr. Syd Slen of Lethbridge, an animal geneticist who worked at the government research centre east of Lethbridge and later at the McIntyre Ranch.

The residence is owned by a family member and has been extensively renovated.

105 Vimy Ave.

First lessee: T. Van Wyk

"Varykino"

This residence was built in 1955 by T. Van Wyk, manager of the Burmis Lumber Co. Van Wyk had an agreement for another lot, 207 Clematis, but after the water and sewer work were done, the level of the road was about 90 centimetres (three feet) higher than the lot, so he requested and received a lot exchange.

The residence remained in the family until the 1980s and has since changed hands three times. The present owner named it after the cottage in the book and movie *Doctor Zhivago*.

107 Vimy Ave.

First lessee: John Robert Pisko

John Robert Pisko was a Lethbridge jeweller who had this Pan-Abode residence erected in 1958.

It is one of several in the park built within several years of each other when that construction company was getting started.

Pisko sold the residence in 1970 to Jack and Joyce Gorrie of Lethbridge who named it "Hobo Shack." Avid golfers, fishermen and general Waterton aficionados, the Gorries and sons Ken, John and Glen were summer regulars in the park. The family instigated the tongue-in-check "Deer Turd Invitational Golf Tournament" complete with a symbolic trophy.

They continued to own the residence until 2002, when it was sold to others.

301 Vimy Ave.

First lessee: William J. Morris

William J. Morris worked as a trail guide with his brothers, who ran a horse concession. Morris started building a "chalet" in 1931 which was to have five bedrooms, five sitting rooms and verandas suitable for renting. It was the kind of accommodation that was much sought after. Two years later, when the building was still unfinished, the Great Depression had deepened and the land rent was three years in arrears, Morris's lease application was cancelled.

W. Martin Madge, an implement dealer in Milk River, Alberta, proposed in 1939 to build a 111.4-square-metre (1,200-square-foot) residence on the lot with help from "some of his farmer neighbours" in 1939. His two-storey house, unfinished inside as many residences were, was erected the following year. Officials advised that the chimney had to be built from the floor up because a bracket chimney was a fire hazard. It is not known if Madge complied.

In June 1983 the residence, then owned by Madge's daughter Grace Snow, was destroyed by fire, the result of a faulty chimney. By the time the fire department arrived, the wind had pushed the fire out of control.

Some members of the family called the original residence "The Ponderosa."

A new residence was erected in 1986 and is owned by Martin Madge's descendants.

Residences on Waterton Avenue

Waterton Avenue was one of the first streets in the town to be properly cut to the standard width of 19.8 metres (66 feet), but only as far south as the last residence.

With some exceptions, the fronts of all the original residences on the east side of the street faced the lake because, like the strip along Mount View Road, a boulevard was planned between the property lines and the lake but never built.

By proposing construction of the boulevard along the lakeshore, park officials attempted to discourage leaseholders from claiming the waterfront as their own.

Today a footpath divides the public areas from private leases.

201 Waterton Ave.

First lessee: Carl Carlson

"Happy Landing"

Builder: Carl Carlson

In 1926 restaurant operator Win Chow proposed to build a $15,000, two-storey hotel on this and the lot adjoining to the south.

The lessees along this street, who openly objected to a Chinese neighbour, raised such a protest that park officials politely suggested Chow select another site. The Depression of the 1930s prevented Chow from proceeding with his idea.

Over the course of the next three years, two applicants expressed interest in the lot—James E. Fisher of Raymond, Alberta, and Elsie Baker of Waterton—but neither was able to build.

Carl Carlson, a Swedish-born carpenter, sawmill operator and ice cutter who had built and sold other park residences, wanted this site for his wife, son and daughter. He camped overnight outside the park office to be first in line in 1929 to file an application.

Framing began in 1931 with Erik Hagglund's help.

After an agonizing 12 years, the house was finished, although the family had moved in years before. Many years later, Carlson rented rooms to visitors, with space for 10 guests.

The residence remains in the hands of his descendants, with the interior completely renovated.

Carl, his wife Cecily and daughter Christina Mackay are buried in the park cemetery.

203 Waterton Ave.

"The Lewis's"

First lessee: Simpson J. Shepard

This lot was first opened to applicants in 1921.

William Laidlaw, a Pincher Station merchant, was first in line but failed to build, as did Mrs. Elizabeth Fisher of Raymond, Alberta, in 1927.

Simpson J. Shepard was a Lethbridge lawyer who applied for this lease in 1928 and completed the residence in 1930.

He transferred the lease to Mary McMahon of Lethbridge in 1940. In April 1947 the lease was transferred to Mary's daughter, Helen Lewis. It has been in her extended family since.

205 Waterton Ave.

First lessee: Perle A.E. Harris

Original residence replaced

The first residence on this lot was erected in 1928 for Mrs. Perle A.E. Harris, who transferred the lease to William H. Harris, an insurance and real estate agent. In November 1929, Margaret McNally of Lethbridge bought the lease. Scottish-born Margaret was a nurse's aide in the First World War in Europe where she met Capt. Dr. Alfred McNally, one of the first and most respected early doctors in Lethbridge.

The couple married in 1919 and had three sons. Dr. McNally died in 1935 and Margaret raised the boys by herself.

Despite her loss, she kept the residence, spending every summer in the park with her three sons, Jim, Bob and Ed, and her parrot Lolita, a gift from Ed.

All three boys had summer jobs in the park. Bob and Ed sold fishing worms and got into considerable trouble from Margaret when they placed a sign to advertise the worms on the new Kootenai Brown cairn before it was unveiled in 1936.

The original residence was believed to have been built by Carl Carlson. It was demolished in the fall of 2019 and replaced by a much larger one built by Neufeld Bros. Construction of Coaldale, Alberta.

The lease remains in the hands of family members.

206 Waterton Ave.

First lessee: Carl Carlson

"Metka"

Builder: Carl Carlson

This lot was not offered for leasing to the public until 1953 because, until then, officials thought it might be needed for government purposes.

Carl Carlson made the successful offer of $400 for the lease. It was not until the offer was formally accepted that park officials realized they had made an error under their new policy by granting the application to someone who already held a lease, but cancellation was not imposed.

Carlson built the residence for his son, Alton "Hoot" Carlson. It was a two-suite rental with basement bedrooms, which at the time were not allowed. Carlson deliberately flouted those rules, but since construction was completed according to the National Building Code, the lease was reluctantly issued in 1958.

Carlson originally named the residence "Kiruna"

for the northernmost town in his Swedish homeland.

It was sold in 1987 but it was not until 2019 that the residence was renamed for the family holding the lease.

207 Waterton Ave.

First lessee: Leslie T. Allen

Original residence replaced

Development of this lot had two false starts. In 1921, George Albert Bishop, a Calgary doctor, applied but failed to build, as did Percy Manning Wiltse of Foremost, Alberta, in 1924. Wiltse, however, already had a residence at 208 Fountain Ave.

Leslie T. Allen, a Lethbridge dentist, had the first residence on this site built in 1928. Rodney Whitson Ross, wife of prominent Aden, Alberta, rancher George Ross, bought the property in 1942 after many years of renting residences in the park.

George, who learned to fly during the First World War, never lost his enthusiasm for flying and was well-known as a charter member of the Flying Farmers of Alberta. His sons also took up flying. One son, Walter "Stubb" Ross, established Lethbridge-based Time Air in 1966, which operated until 1993.

Some descendants of George and Rodney continue

to ranch, and other descendants now own the Waterton lease.

The original 90-year-old structure was demolished in 2018 and replaced with a much larger log residence built by Pioneer Log Homes of British Columbia that showcases western red cedar.

208 Waterton Ave.
First lessee: Charles Benjamin Cheesman

"Dingley Dell"

Charlie Cheesman, a Cardston barber and an outstanding sports supporter, was one of the most well-respected men in his community. He applied for this lot in 1924 and by the following year Walter Foster had completed a stone foundation for the residence. The residence was built from plans supplied by Beaver (Alberta) Lumber Ltd. In 1936, the partnership of James Baird and Gerald Cahoon acquired the lease and sold it in 1941 to Alice May Creffield, the daughter of Elizabeth and Fred Meads. The Meads took over ownership in 1951. The residence became one of several that the Meads rented to visitors. It has been owned by the same individual since 1967.

"Dingley Dell," the name given to the residence by the Meads, comes from the Charles Dickens' novel *The Pickwick Papers*.

209 Waterton Ave.
First lessee: Charles S. Middleton

Original residence replaced

This lot was originally developed in 1947 by Charles Middleton, son of Rev. Samuel H. and Katherine Middleton. Because of a misunderstanding, Charles failed to pay land rent for many years, an error that was not quickly discovered because of the oversight by park officials who thought the Anglican Church held the lease. Once the matter was sorted, Charles was able to lease the property in his own name.

He began working with the Department of Indian Affairs in 1932 and for the next 18 years he was assistant vice-principal at St. Paul's Residential School near Cardston, where his father was principal.

Charles sold the lease in 1954 to Oswald E. Snyder and John Wobkenburg, both of the Coutts district. The pair converted Charles' residence into a small duplex which stood until August 2009, when it was demolished to make way for a new, larger residence that was built by Riviere Construction of Pincher Creek and Twin Butte Log Homes.

210 Waterton Ave.

First lessee: Nahor W. Dilatush

"Sun Dog"

Builder: Walter B. Foster

Claude Albert Ferguson, a partner in a garage and transportation business in the park, hired Walter B. Foster to design and build this residence in 1925, but Ferguson died suddenly in February 1926 without

clearing his debt to Foster. Foster was forced to put a lien on the building, and the lease was picked up by Nahor Dilatush, who owned the Tourist Café. The log residence was valued at $900. Ten years later, it was sold to William J. Baker, who rented this and other residences to visitors. Fred and Elizabeth Meads bought the property in 1949, also to rent to visitors. The Meads, who had several rental properties, gave it the name "Sun Dog."

George and Mary Bell of Lethbridge purchased the residence in 1966. Both Bells had long associations with the park. As a single woman, Mary had cooked for the Morris Brothers' horse concession crew and George, a blacksmith and welder, had been introduced to the park by his parents when he was a child. The residence was sold in 2020.

---

211 Waterton Ave.

First lessee: Anglican Diocese of Calgary

This lot and 213, the adjacent lot to the south, were leased to the Anglican Church in 1917. Rev. Samuel H. Middleton, principal of St. Paul's Residential School near Cardston, was given permission to build on this lot with relief from lease fees, paying a nominal $1 per annum.

Held in the name of the Anglican Diocese of Calgary, the lots became home to the "Kainai Kottage," a summer residence for Indigenous children from the Blood and Peigan reserves until the late 1940s. Middleton and assistants provided supervision.

While Kainai Kottage overlapped onto this lot only slightly, when the residence was demolished in 2019, this site was designated as a residential lot unto itself, despite being an irregular shape and slightly smaller than others along the

east side of the street. This was the first time in many years that an additional lot in the townsite was made available for building.

212 Waterton Ave.

First lessee: Elenora Hunter

When Claude A. Ferguson applied for this lot and the one next door in 1922, he had only enough money to erect a garage. When he died in 1926, he still had not built a residence, so the lot was open for applications. Cal and Elenora Hunter, local tent camp operators, had the residence completed in 1929.

The lease was transferred in 1941 to their daughter, Nellie Hunter Goble, wife of Ed Goble, son of Oliver and Arletta. The residence was later sold to Thelma Milne of Cardston, who was one of several Waterton lessees to be mayor of their hometowns.

The residence remains in the family.

Each exterior door on the premises, except the front door, has a name of its own: Blue Heaven (for the colour of residence), Robins Nest (for one of the lessees), and Goates Haunt (for the lessee's family).

---

213 Waterton Ave.

First lessee: Anglican Diocese of Calgary   Original residence replaced

This lot was granted in 1917 to the Anglican Church along with its neighbouring lot, 211, as a single lot and a residence, dubbed Kainai Kottage, was built, overlapping slightly onto 211.

See 211 Waterton for more about Kainai Kottage.

When the residence began to fall into disrepair, park officials suggested these lots be surrendered and a new residence be built next to All-Saints Anglican Church on Windflower Avenue.

Instead, the residence was demolished and in 1960 volunteers erected a three-bedroom, prefabricated Pan-Abode structure.

Following the removal of the All-Saints church in 2014, the leases on this lot and 211 were surrendered.

The Pan-Abode was demolished in 2019 and a new residence for another lessee was started the following year.

214 Waterton Ave.

First lessee: Edward H. Wagstaff

"Richardsons"
Original residence replaced

This was the site of the second residence built for Edward H. "Teddy" Wagstaff, the golf professional at the Waterton course. He sold his first one at 105 Cameron Falls Dr. and by January 1931 his new

residence was underway on this site. The following year, Wagstaff moved to Raymond, Alberta, to build a golf course there and work at the sugar factory. With money being tight and living away, Wagstaff saw little progress on the residence, and it wasn't finished until after 1933. Wagstaff sold the lease in 1938 to George Ballantyne, a Beaver Mines, Alberta, homesteader.

Five years later Ballantyne died at the residence, but his family kept it until 1956, when it was sold to Henry and Leone Hall of Cardston.

More than a decade later, it was sold to the Tanners of Calgary who had the residence demolished and replaced with this structure, which was sold to others in 2001.

---

215 Waterton Ave.

First lessee: Katherine Middleton

Original residence replaced

Kate Middleton was the wife of Rev. S.H. Middleton and matron and head nurse at St. Paul's Residential School on the Blood reserve, east of the park. She had a small residence built on this lot.

In 1943 Middleton sold the lease to Ada Kemmis, who held several other commercial and residential properties. Kemmis's daughter Sibyl and son-in-law Harry Reeves acquired the lease in 1951, sold the small residence, which was moved to 107 Lupine Lane, and hired J. Willie of Lethbridge Woodworking to build a new residence on this lot.

The Reeves had lived in the park since the 1930s, but this was the first house of their own.

The residence was sold in 1986 to Eddie McClain, who grew up in the region.

It has since changed hands.

216 Waterton Ave.

First lessee: Andrew Stratton

"Holiday House"

Original residence replaced

Andrew Stratton, a Cardston labourer, had the original wood frame, two-bedroom residence built in 1929. It was nearly identical to an existing one to the south. He owned the residence until 1948, when it was sold to Vella Carnell, who lived with her husband Pat at 307 Evergreen Ave.

Carnell sold this residence within six months to Francis Corbett Lynch-Staunton and his married sister, Victoria Georgina Cox, who in turn sold it to Marion Green of Pincher Creek in 1958. J.A. and Marion Green ran a summer grocery store and meat market on Windflower Avenue. The Greens sold the residence in 1978 and it was moved out of the park.

The lease was purchased by Ab and Lucille Cahoon, who had this new residence built but kept the original name, "Holiday House." The Cahoons were both school teachers. Lucille operated the Variety Market (114 Waterton Ave.) and Ab was a customs officer during the summers. He taught junior high school students for two years in Waterton.

The residence remains in the family.

217 Waterton Ave.

First lessee: S.H. Middleton

This lease was owned by Rev. S.H. Middleton, the husband of Kate Middleton, who had the lot immediately to the north.

The original residence was built in 1926 and was transferred to Kate Middleton two years later.

In 1943, Ada Kemmis bought this lease and held it until the fall of 1973, when it was purchased by the Almas family of Montana. They fell in love with Waterton and had been guests at the Kilmorey Lodge, which Ada Kemmis owned, for eight consecutive summers previous to the purchase.

Like many of the residences along this street, it suffered considerable damage during the 1964 flood, and was inundated to a lesser extent in the 1975 flood. The residence was sold in 2017 and has since undergone significant renovation by new owners.

218 Waterton Ave.

First lessee: Oliver Goble   Builder: Oliver Goble

Oliver Goble, a carpenter by trade, came to the park in 1926 with two of his sons, Ken and Ed, to work on the building of the Prince of Wales Hotel. Oliver and Arletta, who had six children, most of whom were then almost grown, applied for this lot in 1927. The residence was begun in 1929, but it took until 1932 to complete. Oliver went to work for the park and became construction foreman, supervising the building of kitchen shelters at Alderson, Crypt Lake and Bertha Lake, among others. Two sons had

long ties to the park. Frank Goble, who cooked for the crews building Chief Mountain Highway and other park projects in the 1930s, was later a restaurant and accommodation owner-operator. Ken was the assistant fish hatchery supervisor, later managed the fish ponds near Cameron Falls, and worked for the warden service in a variety of jobs.

The residence remains in the Goble family.

219 Waterton Ave.

First lessee: Enid Swanson   Builder: Walter B. Foster

The first applicant for this lot was H.C. Bellerby, a Fort Macleod farmer who expressed interest in 1922 but was unable to build.

Enid Swanson's husband, Cecil, was the rector of the St. Augustine's Anglican Church in Lethbridge when this residence was completed in 1927. Their three daughters, Vera, Bea and Cecilie (known as "Squish") came to know the park well. After the Second World War, while the couple was living out of the province, Enid transferred the lease to Bea.

Archdeacon Swanson and Squish were two of only three people associated with Waterton to attend the coronation of Queen Elizabeth II in 1953. Swanson's work on behalf of the Anglican Church was acknowledged when he was recognized by an award of the Order of Canada in 1979.

Enid, Cecil and Cecilie are buried in the Waterton

cemetery. The residence remained in the family until 2002 and was sold and resold several times.

The interior has been substantially renovated with a minimum of change to the exterior.

Residences on Windflower Avenue

Of all the streets in the townsite, Windflower is one of the longest and has seen more changes over the years than any other.

Once the site of the post office residence, a park house, two churches and several early cabins—now all long gone—it has been redeveloped and modernized. The west side of lower Windflower, now home to the Visitor Reception Centre, was once a thriving residential area with a kiddies' playground complete with the best slide anywhere. Adjacent to the playground, but first situated along Cameron Falls Drive, were four tennis courts owned and maintained by the government.

The playground and two of the tennis/pickleball courts are now located near the Community Centre.

Windflower Avenue is named for a flowering plant known as the Cut-leaved Anemone and is found in dry grasslands and open woods. Its small flowers can be white, bluish, pink to red or mottled. Seeds from this plant had medicinal value to the Blackfoot.

101 Windflower Ave.

"Red Rock House"

First lessee: Mabel Dilatush

As this street curves around toward the north to meet Fountain Avenue, the lots take on a peculiar shape, making them smaller than most others.

When Mabel Dilatush leased 105 Fountain Ave. in 1924, there was really very little that could be done with the tiny lot at 101 Windflower, and acting superintendent William Cromarty recommended she be allowed to lease both lots to avoid a crowded effect.

The lot remained vacant until 1966, when the government purchased the two lots.

The one at 105 with the residence on it was used for staff housing and 101 Windflower, vacant for years, became the site for a warden house, built in 1954, which was moved from Red Rock Canyon in February 1978.

This was done at a time when park managers were ending backcountry warden housing.

This residence is the mirror image of the government house at 113 Harebell Ave., also owned by the park and used for employee housing.

104 Windflower Ave.

First lessee: Government

Phase 2 Staff Housing

The southeast streetscape beginning at this location has been dramatically altered in recent years. The old structures, which included a post office and a residence near the corner of Windflower and Fountain Avenue, were demolished and replaced with new staff housing under one roof.

The free-standing park house to the east of the post office was sold to the highest bidder and moved out of the park. Built in 1959 as a single-family residence, for many years it was occupied year-round by Ernie and Maxine Haug and their family.

Ernie, with his usual dry wit, called the neighbourhood Information (post office), Damnation (his home) and Salvation (the Latter-day Saints church).

Active in the community, the Haugs left the park when Ernie retired in 1989 after working for Parks Canada for more than 32 years.

Parks Canada redeveloped the two adjoining lots in 2018. In their place, a 13-unit, 25-bed staff complex was erected. Nearby, around the corner on Clematis Cul-de-sac, is more new staff housing.

403 Windflower Ave.

First lessee: George Frederickson

Builder: Oland & Scott

Private residences on Windflower don't exist for some distance and run in a north-south direction south of Cameron Falls Drive to Vimy Avenue. Today they only occur on the east side of Windflower.

There have been a number of owners of this residence since George Frederickson had it completed in the fall of 1928. He didn't enjoy his new home for long. In 1934 Frederickson, who was in a business partnership with Ernie Haug, Sr., fell terminally ill and unable to support himself, subsequently became a ward of the government. He was forced to surrender his lease in exchange for medical care.

The government put the property up for tender and it was purchased by Advance Lumber.

Then businessman Nahor Dilatush purchased the residence in the 1940s and rented it to visitors for several seasons. After the Second World War, it was purchased by the Waterton Lakes Hotel and Chalets for staff housing. John Schlaht, a park employee who made the carved wooden signs with recessed yellow lettering used throughout Waterton, purchased the residence in 1957, living there with his wife and two children.

The next year park employee Charles S. Sanford, whose wife ran the Sanford Store at 113 Waterton Ave., became the owner of this property and kept it for several years.

It has since changed hands.

405 Windflower Ave.

"Berghem"

First lessee: Laura C. Black

George Frederickson applied for this lot in 1930 but when he fell ill, he had to surrender ownership to the government in 1934 while the residence was unfinished and the lease unsigned. His family, however, continued to live in the house until 1937, when they were finally evicted. The property was put out for public tender in 1938 for $400 and was purchased by Laura Cruickshank Black of Medicine Hat who held another lease on Fountain Avenue. But Black died in 1939 and her heirs sold the residence to Erik Hagglund in 1943. The Hagglunds named it "Berghem," Swedish for mountain home.

This residence was sold in 1956 to Alexander and Olive Long, who kept it for many years. It is now owned by others.

407 Windflower Ave.

"Strollin"

First lessee: Alice Rickmyer

When Win Chow's plans to build a hotel on Waterton Avenue collapsed (see 201 Waterton Ave.), he applied for this lot and had architectural plans drawn up, but he was unable to build, and his application was cancelled.

Alice Rickmyer of Woolford, Alberta, was a single woman who taught school when she applied for this lease in 1929 and had the residence built.

In 1932 she married LeRoy Cecil Hartman, a grain buyer from Raley, Alberta, and within a few years the residence was being rented to visitors, with William J. Baker serving as the agent.

The couple had four children who inherited the property in 1952 and it has long since been owned by others and renovated.

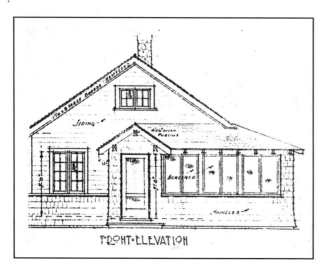

409 Windflower Ave.

First lessee: William Dayman

Original residence replaced

William Dayman was a railway agent in Carmangay, Alberta, who had a small frame house built on this lot in 1928. By 1933, however, the house had fallen into disrepair and park officials deemed it an eyesore.

Rather than improve the property, Dayman sold it to Charles R. Luchia, but it took until 1944 to complete the sale because of park requirements. Luchia made some repairs and sold the residence to A.M. Schow of Cardston.

Eventually, a new owner replaced the residence with this modern, one-and-a-half-storey structure.

411 Windflower Ave.

"Dahl House"

First lessee: Howard H. Oliver

This residence is named for 1952 owner Phoebe Evans Dahl of Raymond, Alberta. Dahl bought the lease from Howard H. Oliver, then a Cardston rancher and banker who had signed an agreement to build in 1945 and completed the residence to the satisfaction of officials by 1951.

Long before, others had tried to fulfill their obligations on this lot but were unable to do so.

The first was Amos T. Crawford, a butcher from Havre, Montana, who applied for the lot in 1927 but did not build. LeRoy R. Card, a truck driver-mechanic in Cardston, built a foundation and the first floor of the building, but was forced to quit the site.

And in 1936, Lee Land Card, a lumber merchant and truck driver from Cardston, failed to fulfill his agree-

ment when his health forced him to move to the coast.

After Howard Oliver sold the residence, he bought another, larger residence on Clematis Avenue to accommodate his family.

413 Windflower Ave.

First lessee: Cliff Ott

This is the original residence on this lot. Cliff Ott, an excursion boat operator who had lived in rental houses in the park for several summers, decided to apply for this then-vacant lot.

The first plan was for a Pan-Abode residence, but Ott later changed his mind and had this house built by 1958.

The lot was obtained through a tender in which Ott bid $135. From this location, Ott also sold ice to campers down the road.

The property had a fairly long history of unfulfilled applications between 1927 and 1958: Kenneth Alonzo Scott, a Cardston contractor; Kirkham L. Lee, a Cardston merchant; Kenneth C. Long, well-known Spring Coulee, Alberta, farmer; William A. Foote, a Pincher Creek merchant; and Alfred Scotter, a Cardston labourer had each applied.

414 Windflower Ave.

"Stagger Inn"

First lessee: Philyer Francis Lyman

This residence was built in 1931. First owner Philyer Lyman was a commercial traveller who lived in Lethbridge.

Lyman sold the property in 1935 to Rose Lynn, who in turn sold it to Ralph Waldo Greenway of Lethbridge.

Greenway was a prominent citizen who was the widely known manager of an International Harvester outlet, where he worked for 33 years.

He served four years on Lethbridge city council and was president of the Lethbridge Board of Trade. He was the sixth son of Thomas Greenway, eighth premier of Manitoba.

When R.W. Greenway died in 1948, the lease was transferred to his second wife, Annie Gordon, and continues to be owned by family members.

Residences on Entry Road

In its heyday, the north side of the entrance road across from Linnet Lake included privately leased lots with residences owned by park employees, and operations buildings including a horse barn and hay storage. The two dressing rooms at Linnet Lake were removed when the townsite swimming pool opened in 1960. The Kootenai Brown cabin was renovated into a seasonal staff house and eventually demolished. And the tents used to house summer employees were also removed.

No review of residential buildings in the park would be complete without mentioning those which stood along the entrance road below what is now the park compound, across from Linnet Lake and Middle Waterton Lake.

When lots were surveyed in December 1910, there were two sections to the plan. One was a 73-lot grouping laid out in the area now call the townsite. The other was a 214-lot subdivision that ran from Linnet Lake eastward following the shore of Middle Waterton Lake. The surveyor, W.F. O'Hara, was optimistic that this location would be appealing because it was near the water. Had he done his survey in the spring or early summer months, he would have seen just how unfavourable this area can be—prone to flooding and a strong prevailing wind from the south.

In 1918 park superintendent Robert Cooper told his Ottawa bosses these lots were too far from the town and businesses, and he felt "these lots will never be taken up within the next 50 years, no matter how prosperous the park may become." Eventually all of these lots were eliminated from the villa plan.

Only six of 10 lots in a single block were leased at various times over the 20th century. They were parallel to the entrance road and aligned in a row that ran from south to north facing the Middle Lake. About 1959, the government began to acquire these lots to centralize leases to just the townsite proper.

Lots 1, 2, 3 and 8 were officially never leased, but were used as sort of a no-man's land by the neighbours. Immediately to the west was an area used for government purposes and often referred to as "headquarters."

The family home of George Jr. and Bessie Annand was one of the last on the entrance road to be built, following the Second World War, and was used by the owners until the late 1960s. It was then sold to the park for staff housing and later removed.

This was where the government built its icehouse, stables, bunkhouse and dining room, and storage facilities. Additional buildings were added later.

George Baker built a log residence on Lot 4 in 1922 and started the Park Transport Co. from his private garage here, later moving to the townsite. Baker was the only lessee on this block who was not a government employee. Between 1933 and 1959, the lot was leased to park staff or members of their families: Mary McAllister, a warden's wife, in 1933; Simmons Moegenson, a park labourer, in 1952; and then Marion Woolf, a park mechanic, about 1959. Marion and his wife Helen sold the lot to the government and moved to Cameron Falls Drive.

In 1922, John T. Gladstone, the park's stable foreman, built a small frame house on Lot 5 and lived there until 1948, when he sold the lease to Joe English, a seasonal employee, who got special consideration under the Veterans Land Act, having served in both the First and Second World Wars. English sold the lease to the government in 1959.

The residence at left, "Lochvue," was built in 1921. It was purchased by Joe and Betsy Annand for use as their year-round residence. At right is "Vimyvue," built in 1945 as a seasonal rental duplex. Both of these residences on the entry road were eventually purchased by the government and removed.

270

Kootenai Brown and his wife Isabella lived in this building, which was originally a small hotel located across the road near Linnet Lake. After acquiring a lease, Brown purchased the building and had it moved across the road. He was the only park head to hold a lease.

Lots 6 and 7 were originally leased by Joe and Betsy Annand. Betsy operated a rental duplex on Lot 6 known as "Vimyvue." She and Joe, the park store-keeper, lived in the house on Lot 8. Next door on Lot 9 was the home of their son, George Annand, Jr., who got the lease from his mother in 1947 and built a house on it in 1952. The lot had originally been the site of a post office and telephone exchange operated by post-master "Pop" Harwood. When Harwood moved into a new home on Fountain Avenue, he sold his residence to two of the Morris brothers, Scott and William. The seven-room log structure had just been renovated when it caught fire in October 1930 and burned to the ground.

Lot 10 had been leased by Kootenai Brown before he retired. He and his wife Isabella lived in the reno-vated Jensen hotel building, which had been moved to this lot in 1913. Brown died in 1916 and his wife sur-rendered the lease in 1922. The building was later used as a park carpentry shop.

The last of the stand-alone staff residences was removed from this area in winter of 2002-03 and the sites restored with vegetation. The only residential occupancy in this area was a two-storey, quadrangle modular bunkhouse installed in 1977 for 64 seasonal employees in the compound. It was demolished in 2018, when new staff accommodations were built in the townsite on Clematis Cul-de-sac and on Wind-flower Avenue.

204 Cameron Falls Dr.   Pumphouse

This building, erected in 1987, houses the chlorination and pumping equipment for the town's water supply, as well as a standby generator in the event of a power failure. It is part of a water supply system that took two years to complete at a cost of just under $1 million. Included in the cost was a 2.2-million litre (500,000-gallon) reservoir located above the townsite just off the Akamina Parkway, along with the drilling of four water wells in the location of the pumphouse. The use of well water was a preventive measure against the risk of Giardia, bacteria often found in surface water which can cause prolonged digestive upset in both humans and pets.

The pumphouse also provides easier access to the electronic equipment which tests water around the clock for turbidity and chlorine levels, and ensures satisfactory reservoir volume for domestic use and fire suppression.

Before this system was installed, the water intake was located above Cameron Falls. The first water system, built in 1924, was operational only during the summer months. In the winter, when the system was shut down, residents drew their water by hand from the lake or the creek. Some residences had indoor cisterns for winter use.

In 1953 the government installed a year-round water and sewer system, which raised hopes that Waterton would become a 12-month resort, something that was not previously possible.

Prior to the pumphouse being built, this site was vacant, but not for want of interested residential applicants. In 1928, Ivan Y. Reddin, secretary with Alberta Gas and Fuel Co. in Twin Butte, Alberta,

made an application for the lot but moved away and surrendered his interest. The following year, Cardston farmer E. Rasmussen proposed to build a log residence on the lot and had his building plans approved, but his application was cancelled in July 1931 for failure to build. George L. Flawn, a Calgary restaurateur, applied for the lot in 1931 but he, too, was unable to build. Lula Nielson applied in 1946. She received some added time to build because of a postwar shortage of materials, but by 1947, when she still had not built, her application was cancelled.

Ray William Johansen, a farmer from Woolford, Alberta, subsequently applied and failed to build by a 1948 deadline. Joseph Robert Dickson, a physician and surgeon from Chinook, Montana, made application in September 1949 but it was cancelled when he did not respond to correspondence from the park superintendent. Finally, by 1950, after 21 years of trying to lease this lot and six cancelled applications, park officials gave up. They said they would not tender the lot unless there was a special demand for it.

404 Cameron Falls Dr.

Visitor Reception Centre

Builder: Graham Construction

The location of the new Visitor Reception Centre, which takes up 10 building lots between Cameron Falls Drive and Vimy Avenue, has been one of controversy. Despite public meetings and protests asserting the site to be inappropriate, park management refused to consider any other location in the townsite or outside of it.

The site of this huge development, budgeted at $17.3 million, had long been eyed by park authorities, starting more than 40 years ago. (See Residences on Windflower Avenue)

Six lots adjacent to Cameron Falls Drive had never been privately leased, having been devoted to public tennis courts starting in 1918 and children's playground in 1920. Both facilities were relocated west along Cameron Falls Drive, near Fountain Avenue. The balance of five residences on that block, one on Windflower Avenue and four on Harebell Road, were left intact—four privately leased and one owned by the government.

With the site confirmed in November 2017, construction of a year-round visitor centre at this site began in 2019. When the Kenow forest fire of 2017 destroyed the long-time visitor centre on the entrance road at the Bear's Hump trail head, a temporary visitor site was created in the former Lions Community Hall on Fountain Avenue.

Graham Construction, based in Calgary, was awarded the contract for the new visitor centre.

This project is one of the most significant investments in visitor facilities in Waterton in 50 years. It includes a theatre for presentations, an area for displays, space for administrative offices in an adjacent building, a service counter, and a sales counter for permits, maps, books, etc. along with Parks Canada branded merchandise.

Interpretive elements are also incorporated into the visitor centre's outdoor plaza, which will serve as a meeting place in the community. In addition, a new, nature-based playground will provide a place for play and learning for families with children.

At the end of October 2021, information services were available at the new facility, but Alberta's CO-VID-19 restrictions were still in force. It was not until February 2022 that it was announced construction of the facility and all of the interpretive exhibits were completed. The cost was estimated to be $25 million.

The park's first information bureau was located for decades in the administration office on Mount View Road and was moved to a dedicated building on the entrance road in July 1958 at the Bear's Hump trailhead. It served the public for 59 years.

102 Clematis Cul-de-sac

Builder: Remington Construction

Church of Jesus Christ of Latter-day Saints Chapel

This chapel is the most recent of the four churches built in Waterton. It was constructed in 1963 on land that was until then vacant. Mormons had been holding services in the park since 1941, utilizing the theatre, the school and Lions Hall. For many years they were under the direction of Ora L. Nielson of Cardston, presiding elder.

With the demise of the Crystal Swimming Pool (now 504 Cameron Falls Dr.) in 1948, members of the Church of Jesus Christ of Latter-day Saints hoped to acquire that site for a chapel. Owner Dell H. Ellison was willing and so were park officials. There were two major problems, however. One was the costly removal of the concrete pool at the site and the other was a need for plans to be approved not only by park officials, but also church officials in Utah. Both problems proved insurmountable, and the Mormons put the project on hold. A final slap in the face was that instead of a new church going up at that site, the Alberta government bought the lease and built a liquor store.

When another location for a chapel was found close to the three other churches, plans were approved and funds set aside. In July 1963 construction of the chapel began on two lots at the corner of Windflower and Clematis avenues. Designed by N.H. Fooks and Associates of Lethbridge, the $80,000 building was contracted to Remington Construction of Cardston. Services were held the following summer, but dedication was delayed until July 17, 1966, when Nathan Eldon Tanner, a one-time Alberta politician and former residence owner in Waterton, was able to attend. He was then living in Salt Lake City, Utah, where he was second councillor to church president David O. McKay.

Although there was seating for 300 people, an estimated 560 attended the dedication. Conducting the meeting was Alberta stake president Dr. Roy R. Spackman of Cardston, a park residence owner who spoke along with presidents of other southern Alberta stakes that provided financial support for the construction. Other presidents attending were Dr. Elmo E. Fletcher of Lethbridge, J. Richard Evanson of Taber and Fay H. Walker of the Taylor stake, Raymond.

Local resident and park employee Marion Woolf served for 23 years as the president of the Waterton branch, under the Mountain View Ward.

108 Clematis Cul-de-sac   United Church of Canada

Builder: Holte & Nordlund Construction

The United Church is a Protestant denomination formed by the merger of Methodist and Congregationalist churches, with the majority Presbyterians. Interest in the denomination was growing in the mid-1950s, so a church for the park was proposed to accommodate both year-round residents and summer visitors. Services had been held for several years in the Lions Hall.

James D. Paterson of Lethbridge, the finance chairman of the building committee, dedicated the vacant lot on June 18, 1956. The design of the church was avant-garde and created quite a buzz in the community. Architect George Watson of Meech, Mitchell, Robins and Associates of Lethbridge came up with the concept, which included native stone and clear glass windows offering a mountain view.

Park superintendent James H. Atkinson didn't like the "odd design," as he called it. As a practical matter, he advised against the roofline for such a windy location and on a personal level he said that such an extremely modern design was inappropriate "where we have enough natural beauty to absorb people without trying to impress them with a building, especially a church."

The Waterton congregation was formalized in June 1959. About 135 people attended a service conducted by Rev. F.G. Holbertson, chairman of the South Alberta Presbytery. Five local residents were given charter memberships on profession of their faith: Ella Baker, Ethel Carnell, Mr. and Mrs. William Akitt and Betty Baker.

In September 1960, the public was invited to a social evening at the Lions Hall to see the plans for the new church. Tenders were called the following spring. Alf Baker, William Henderson and Allen Berry were in charge of local arrangements for construction, and Andy Russell was appointed chairman of the board of stewards.

Mrs. Hannah Carnell Presley, the oldest member of Waterton's congregation and a long-time park resident, was given the honour of turning the sod on April 8, 1961. Construction began two days later. Holte and Nordlund Construction of Lethbridge finished the church later that summer at a cost of $32,000.

The first wedding in the Waterton United Church was held Nov. 4, 1961. The groom was Lawrence Yucytus, and the bride was Marla McIntosh, both of Lethbridge. Rev. Willington Dormer of Pincher Creek presided.

Fountain Ave.   Community Centre

Builders: Harry Cummings; Oland & Scott

This building served for over 70 years as the town's school. Classes began in 1925, but the first one-room school wasn't built until 1927. Harry Cummings, a local carpenter who lived across the street, erected the building under contract to George Baker. Almost too small when it opened, the school was enlarged by Oland & Scott Construction, which added another room and merged the old structure into the new in 1929. It became the largest public building in the townsite.

The school never had a street address and today the front doors face a green space on the east. It was purposely positioned on the site to capture the early morning light at a time when there was no electrical service in the winter.

It was not until the swimming pool was built in 1960 that Clematis Avenue was extended from south to north, cutting across Cameron Falls Drive and in front of the school to connect with Windflower Avenue. When a playing field was built in 1991, the portion of Clematis Avenue on the east side of the school was removed and replaced with fenced-in sod and a baseball backstop.

The school district, which comprised this one building, was under the direction of an elected school board which was responsible for hiring teachers, collecting and spending school taxes, and making decisions about education.

A teacherage was initially built onto the Fountain Avenue side of the school to provide living quarters for one teacher, and in 1954 a separate two-bedroom house was built immediately north of the school to accommodate a married teacher with family.

In July 1961 a gymnasium was added to the west side of the school. Bird Construction was contracted to build the $41,800 addition. Although preliminary plans were drawn in 1964 for a new school and supported by the province, which claimed the life of a school house was 25 years, no new facility was built.

The school's last year of operation was 1995. The school leases and improvements were transferred that year to the Waterton Park Community Association. The deteriorating building got a new life in 2011 when financial support was provided by the Improvement District with a $1.1-million grant, a $375,000 government grant and local donations. Preservation and restoration went forward right down to the blackboards. A northwest addition was built to provide an office and kitchen with commercial equipment.

All lessees within Improvement District No. 4 are assessed school taxes while governments make payments in lieu of taxes. This money goes directly to Edmonton and the Alberta School Foundation Fund.

207 Fountain Ave.

Fire Hall

Builder: Kenwood Engineering

It was the construction of this new fire hall in the winter of 1978-79 that led to a requirement for street addresses on residences. Until then, designation of residences was formally by lot and block numbers and informally by the name of either the owner or the building itself.

Fire protection in the townsite has, until recently, been provided by a volunteer brigade of park employees and other year-round residents. As fewer and fewer people decided to live in the park year-round, formation of a brigade became problematic. Parks Canada, which provides the equipment, was forced to hire the services of out-of-park firefighters during the summer.

The Waterton townsite has been no stranger to structural fires over the years. Fanned by strong winds, fires have claimed two lodgings, a dance hall and numerous residences. Originally, fire equipment was stored at the park compound, but the distance from the residential area made response times longer than necessary. Construction of the RCMP detachment building on Waterton Avenue provided a more central location for the equipment, but its use in winter was limited since there was no water supply. A permanent, all-season water system built in 1952-53 provided for fire hydrants and the town's first fire hall was completed in 1952 on Waterton Avenue, now the Paahtómahksikimi Cultural Centre. The installation of a fire alarm system in 1964, since updated, completed the fire suppression requirements.

As important was the trained volunteer brigade, which conducted weekly drills in the summer of 1952 in conjunction those held at the Prince of Wales Hotel. Initial members were chief park warden Bob Hand, park warden Bert Pittaway, W.W. MacLeod, and G.M. Walker of the RCMP, C. Underwood, Leonard Zorn, Pat Carnell, Jr., Carl Carlson, Alf Baker and Ernie Haug, Jr.

This $235,000 Fountain Avenue fire hall provides space for the town's ambulance, fire truck and year-round public washrooms, as well as office space now used by park wardens. Fire protection is now provided from Cardston.

209 Fountain Ave.

First lessee: Lions Club

Community Hall

Originally known as the Lions Hall, this building came about through the efforts of Waterton's only service club, Lions International. It took five years, hundreds of hours of volunteer time and donations of cash to bring the hall to fruition.

The hall was the local Lions Club's first project. It was launched with a fundraising drive in March 1948. The original idea had been to build the hall from scratch, but the lowest preliminary estimate was $18,000, far beyond anything the small community could raise. With the moral support of Senator William A. Buchanan of Lethbridge (also a Waterton residence owner), members of the Lions Club visited the site of the Fort Macleod flight training school in the hope of acquiring a surplus building from the then-closed facility. The Lions had to buy the 20.4-metre (68-foot) long building, move it, build a basement, and bring it up to the national building code.

Each Lions member donated money, and more was canvassed from business people, residents and tourists. Together with what had already been collected, the Lions had just enough: $1,800. Eager to get the project going, volunteers came out in force to prepare the site, just north of the school, in October 1948. Erik Hagglund supervised preparations, even getting some assistance from General Contracting of Lethbridge, which was in the park working on Akamina Highway.

The move, however, didn't go as planned. Halfway to Waterton the building collapsed on the road, smashing the walls. The Lions had to renew their search and their fund drive. Carnivals were held each summer at the dance pavilion to raise money for a hall. "Pop" Harwood came up with a plan to sell "name bricks," which were drawn on a Masonite board. For $1, a purchaser could buy a "brick" and write his or her name on it for permanent display. Women in the park helped by hosting card parties to raise money and by selling needlework and baked goods.

In 1949 the Lions were able to find another building, this one an officers mess hall at the Pearce Flight Training School, east of Fort Macleod. The building, however, was slightly longer than anticipated and when set on the site, encroached 2.4 metres (eight feet) on to the neighbouring lot, which was leased by the Catholic Church. Unable to contact park officials, the Lions simply asked church officials for their permission, and they agreed. When officials in Ottawa learned of the Lions' solution, superintendent Herbert A. DeVeber was severely admonished for his "gross negligence" in supervising the move.

The hall was dedicated on May 9, 1952, by Rev. S.H. Middleton "to the glory of God and the service of the community." It cost a total of $10,000 to complete.

The most northerly part of the hall was converted into a tiny post office in March 2017 and following the 2017 Kenow forest fire, an adjacent visitor information outlet and office space was temporarily provided in the same building until the opening of the new Visitor Reception Centre on Cameron Falls Drive in 2022.

211 Fountain Ave.

Our Lady of Mount Carmel Catholic Church

There have been two Roman Catholic churches in Waterton. The first, built by William and Eugene Morris, was begun in early 1929. The Morris brothers, who operated a horse rental concession and were Catholic, were chosen as much for their willingness to build it as for their membership in the church. Located near the corner of Windflower Avenue and Harebell Road (now part of the Aspen Village Inn site), the 7.8- by 15-metre (26- by 50-foot) shell cost $1,800.

It was built from green logs, a choice that would prove fateful. The interior work was contracted to Alexander Turcotte of Lethbridge. Bishop J.T. Kidd of Calgary, assisted by Father Doriste Moreaux of Cardston and Father Reoux of the Blood Tribe reserve, dedicated the church on May 25, 1930, before a crowded congregation. It was called Precious Blood, a name not widely understood even then, except by the most devout.

The south side of the log church took the full brunt of the winter winds and after five years, the green logs had dried substantially, adversely affecting the building's integrity. Repairs were made and services were held though 1947, but the building was condemned and finally demolished in 1950 by George Baker, who was contracted to do the job.

The leases were sold in 1951 for enough money to pay off the debt owed by the diocese. A new lot on Fountain Avenue was selected and plans were drawn up for another church. Meanwhile, services were held in the Lions Hall next door and in the school, and donations were collected for the required $7,000 building fund.

Ole Olson of Pincher Creek and a crew of carpenters began work on the new church on May 21, 1951. George Hole of Twin Butte, Alberta, hauled the lumber from British Columbia sawmills, H. Scott of Cardston dug the basement and G. Smith of Pincher Creek hauled the gravel for the foundation. Numerous Waterton residence owners, including the Bonertz family

and others from Pincher Creek, donated labour. The first mass was held July 1, 1951, and the church was named Our Lady of Mount Carmel. It was dedicated on July 16 by Rev. A.J. Hetherington, vicar general of the Calgary diocese. Mass was said by the Waterton priest, Rev. J. McElgunn.

The first wedding performed in the church was for Ronald Keith LaFournie and Maria Louise Gladstone, July 19, 1969. Wedding records for the first Catholic Church have been lost.

215 Mount View Rd.

Administration Office
Demolished 2021

The north and east sides of the park administration office as it looked in 1932. Over the years the building underwent several changes, including exclusive access from Mount View Road and removal of two fireplaces.

The administration office was one of the most renovated buildings in the park. First constructed in 1919 as a single office space for the park superintendent, it was enlarged in 1925. The stonework over the lakeshore entrance was reminiscent of similar work done next door, at 217 Mount View Rd. Both were done by Walter B. Foster.

In 1928 a visitor information bureau was included in the building. In the summer of 1935, an addition to the south of the existing office was proposed. The new portion was to be office space and the old portion was to house a museum. While the museum idea was nixed, later that year Doug G. Oland was hired to enlarge the office and add a basement to the new addition. The front of the building was then changed to Mount View Road. The addition of the basement provided additional storage.

When the new visitor information centre on the entrance road opened in 1958, additional office space was created in this building. However, during the 1964 and 1975 floods, water seeped into the basement, destroying or damaging a number of park documents.

The most recent alteration took place in the fall of 2002, when the north section of the building was de-

What was left of the administration building once the wreckers were done with it in November 2021.

molished, and a demonstration garden planted there.

With transfer of the park staff to the new Visitor Reception Centre at 404 Cameron Falls Dr., this building was demolished Nov. 2, 2021, to make way for construction of better marina access for buses and to improve traffic flow near the marina.

117 Waterton Ave.

Paahtómahksikimi Cultural Centre

This building, the park's first fire hall, was built in 1952. The lot was originally suggested as a location for a post office, but the practicalities of traffic in summer and drifting snow in winter finally dissuaded officials from locating the post office here. In fact, they were reluctant to build the fire hall at this location for the same reasons but changed their minds when they were able to purchase a rotary snowplow which could be housed in the fire hall.

Ron Simmons, a First World War veteran, was hired as the first fire hall attendant. The $10,000, two-bay building accommodated his sleeping quarters as well as the Bickle-Seagrave firefighting unit and snow plow.

In the winter of 1978-79 when a new fire hall was erected on Fountain Avenue, this building was scheduled for demolition. But it found new life in 1986 when it was set aside to house a small museum and bookstore for the then three-year-old Waterton Natural History Association, a non-profit group. The building, owned by the government, was leased to the association for a nominal fee and gave it a retail presence to raise funds in support of its educational activities in the park.

With the demise of the association in 2018, the building was leased to the Blood Tribe and renamed Paahtómahksikimi Cultural Centre. Pronounced "BUCK-toe-MOCK-sick-ih-mee," the word means the inner sacred lake within the mountains and recognizes the area as a sacred place in Blackfoot history.

The Waterton Natural History Association also had a business office at 306 Waterton Ave., on the eastern edge of the townsite campground which, in recent years, has been the site of various Parks Canada uses. Initially the building was the park interpreters' office. It was built in 1926, added to in 1929 and renovated in 1961. Designated as a federal heritage building, it originally had a two-room area for a live-in interpreter. It has since been renovated to make better use of the building, but its future is unknown.

202 Waterton Ave.

RCMP Office and Garage

Builder: Oland & Scott

Credit for the decision to build an elaborate office and residence for the Royal Canadian Mounted Police goes, in part, to completion of the Prince of Wales Hotel in 1927. The hotel set a new tone for park buildings in general and this one in particular.

The $18,000 building was constructed in the winter of 1927-28 by Oland & Scott Construction, which had built the hotel. Situated on two lots, the office is angled to give it a striking presence. The building is similar, but a mirror image, to another in Jasper National Park designed by William D. Cromarty, acting superintendent of Waterton and head of the Parks Branch's architectural division.

The structure was designed to be multi-purpose. It provided office space for police work and holding cells, storage space and a coal bin in the full basement, complete residential quarters with two bedrooms and a recreation room, and two stone fireplaces. The adjacent building, first a stable and then a garage, provided space for hay storage in the early days.

The first of the two buildings to be erected was the stable-garage. The prisoner cells and cage barrier, built to standard, were sent from Kingston Penitentiary in Ontario by train and trucked to the site. By the end of October 1927, both buildings were ready to be stuccoed. Oland & Scott got a rare opportunity to complete the exterior in January 1928 when a chinook raised the winter temperature. They used tarps and a salamander during the stucco application.

In the summer of 1928, Oland & Scott was also hired to have the landscaping completed to a maximum of $1,000, which included filling, grading, construction of flagstone walks, stone walls, and the planting of flowers. The deer repellant peonies, which still grace the stone fence, are documented to have been in place in 1937.

While the buildings have been renovated several times to accommodate changing requirements, the exteriors remains nearly the same as built and they have been designated Federal Heritage Buildings. This is the oldest RCMP building in use in a national park in Canada.

Near Cameron Lake

Alpine Club of Canada

Winter rental

The Alpine Club of Canada (ACC) came up with a creative idea in 2015. It proposed to renovate the oldest remaining seasonal warden residence in the park, near Cameron Lake, and rent it as overnight accommodation for cross-country skiers and snowshoers.

After consulting with the public, Parks Canada granted the club

a licence of occupation and the club completed the improvements. Up to eight people can be accommodated in the rustic, spruce log structure built in 1929-30.

Located in a clearing about 35 metres (38 yards) east of the Akamina Parkway near the end of the road, the log building was originally intended to house a seasonal warden and his family.

The warden enforced park rules in the Cameron Lake area and also served as a public relations contact for summer tourists.

Commercial Buildings

504 Cameron Falls Dr.

First lessee: Isaac L. Allred

This building was designed by the provincial government as a seasonal liquor store and opened its doors in July 1961. It became the second provincial liquor outlet in town, replacing the one at 305 Windflower Ave.

From 1924 to 1948, this lot and the one immediately to the west were the home of the Crystal Swimming Pool, which had its beginnings as an open-air pool and was eventually covered. There were many problems associated with its operation. The pool building was condemned as unsightly and in need of either major repair or removal, but even as late as 1956 nothing was done to improve it. There was considerable acrimony between the lessee and park officials over the two lots, yet no one was willing to take responsibility for either the taxes or the condition of the property.

Mountain Spirits

The expense of removing the building and the concrete pool discouraged others from buying the lease until the Alberta Liquor Control Board and the Alberta Motor Association next door, now Welch's Chocolate Shop, stepped up.

The liquor store was sold to Dave Rylands in 1994, when the provincial government privatized its retail liquor business. Rylands sold the business in 2014.

101 Clematis Cul-de-sac

The Lodge at Waterton Lakes was the original name of this 80-room accommodation, opened in 1998 after several years of public controversy and planning. The facility replaced the government-owned swimming pool and parking lot that had opened in 1960. Prior to construction of the swimming pool, the site was a sports field. The removal of the pool and redevelopment of this site in this configuration angered members of the public, who expressed their views vehemently at numerous meetings.

The last prime 1.6 hectares (four acres) of townsite, this location is now home to 11 individually named buildings containing guest rooms, a 20-bed hostel, a recreation facility with small swimming pool, restaurant, lounge, retail outlets and a meeting space. It was built at a cost of just over $8 million as an environmentally friendly complex under the management

Waterton Lakes Lodge Resort

of Ed Romanowski of Edmonton. It was later sold to Waymarker Hospitality, which owns several other accommodations in the park.

At the corner of Cameron Falls Drive and Windflower Avenue in the "Founder's House" is the Taco Bar, an independent business in the renamed Waterton Lakes Lodge Resort. This one-of-a-kind Mexican eatery opened in late 2012.

117 Evergreen Ave.

Kilmorey Lodge
Builder: Oland & Scott

This lodge is often erroneously referred to as the oldest accommodation in the park. That honour goes to the Prince of Wales Hotel. Part of the Kilmorey Lodge dated from 1935, while the Prince of Wales is eight years older.

The Kilmorey has had several incarnations. Ada Kemmis of Pincher Creek applied for just one lot in 1911 and by August 1914 a three-room residence was built on it. According to some sources, the lumber for the original residence came from the buildings erected near Cameron Falls by an oil company that had drilled there, found no oil and then abandoned them.

In 1926, Ada Kemmis had the residence razed and a 12-bedroom rooming house, over four times larger than the first residence on the property, constructed, naming it Kilmorey Lodge to reflect her estranged husband's Irish heritage. The lodge, built by Oland & Scott Construction, opened the same year as the Waterton Dance Pavilion on Waterton Avenue which attracted many new visitors to the park.

In 1929 Kemmis bought the 11-year-old residence next door from Clarence Watson Pickup, a Cardston doctor, and razed it. In 1931, taking inspiration from a magazine ad for Flint Paint and Varnish, a new, two-storey house was built there by local contractor and residence owner Edward Johnson. Kemmis's future son-in-law, Harry Reeves, was hired to do the interior. It was intended to provide a dining room for her guests at the lodge next door but was primarily her private residence. It was here that Kemmis and her daughter Sibyl were living when the Kilmorey Lodge next door caught fire and burned to the ground in February 1933. It took until 1935 for Kemmis to come up with the money for the second Kilmorey Lodge, which was built by Doug Oland.

Kemmis wanted very much to join her private residence to the Kilmorey, but permission was denied until 1940. That year, Oland joined the two buildings, giving them an almost seamless appearance from the lakeshore side. Other exterior additions were made by other owners over the years, including a patio on Mount View Road, a gazebo on the lake front, and a deck on Evergreen Avenue.

Purchased by Waymarker Hospitality in 2007, the Kilmorey burned to the ground Jan. 20, 2009, the result of spontaneous combustion of laundry, according the Cardston fire chief. Construction of a replacement building began in late fall of 2018 and as of this writing (2022) remained unfinished.

This view of the Kilmorey Lodge is how it looked after Doug G. Oland had joined the 1936 building, on the right, to owner Ada Kemmis's house next door, presenting a nearly seamless facade. The building was destroyed by fire in 2009.

118 Evergreen Ave.

Telus

Park officials had second thoughts about leasing this lot after two applicants failed to meet their obligations. Leaving this lot vacant later allowed for expansion of the 1919 superintendent's residence, which was situated on this lot and the one to the north. Most of the lot sat vacant until 1960, when Alberta Government Telephones (AGT) leased it to house its new telephone exchange, which later became automated. The new building was stucco finished and designed specifically to match the nearby residences.

The new equipment meant park customers had continuous telephone service for the first time since service was established in 1920. Telephone rates, however, were raised accordingly. A residential line went from $2.25 a month to $2.75, which included rental of the phone set. There was no charge for extensions, bells or switches. Prior to the installation of automated equipment, a phone exchange had been located in the post office on the entrance road and then at George Baker's Park Transport Garage, where since 1938 women were hired as operators. It was not until June 1964 that direct-dial local and long-distance calling went into operation. Telus became the successor company to AGT in 1990.

408 Evergreen Ave.

Northland Lodge
Builder: Oland & Scott

The Northland Lodge, tucked in the middle of a row of residences on Evergreen Avenue, blends in so well it is sometimes overlooked as a historic public accommodation. Originally named Carthew Lodge, for a mountain well to the west, it was erected in 1928 as a personal residence for Louis W. Hill, head of the Great Northern Railway, whose company had opened the Prince of Wales Hotel the summer before.

It cost $9,600 to build the lodge, but there is no indication Hill ever used it. In Hill's absence, Fred and Grace Udell became caretakers for the property. Fred Udell held successive positions at the Prince of Wales Hotel, first as the house detective, then as doorman and winter caretaker. Through the Depression, the Udell family continued to live in the lodge and the couple's three sons and two daughters attended school in Waterton.

Hugh Black of St. Mary, Montana, purchased the lodge in 1949 for $6,000 cash. But in those days Americans wanting to do business in Canada had to meet certain requirements. The easiest way around the formalities was to take on a Canadian partner, which Black did in the person of Earl Hacking of Cardston. Hacking and his wife Bessie refitted the building for guests and renamed it Northland Lodge.

Bessie Hacking's participation in the lodge's operation was a reflection of her father's entry into the same business in 1911 at a hotel near Linnet Lake. She was the second generation of her family to provide hospitality in Waterton. The Hackings bought out Black in the 1960s and Northland Lodge has remained under family ownership since.

102 Mount View Rd.

Crandell Mountain Lodge
Builder: Erik & Hilding Hagglund

When the Emily Lee's two rental residences on this site burned down, the leases were sold in 1939 to Hilding Hagglund, son of Erik and Olga.

Hilding initially proposed to build auto bungalows similar to those operated by his father to the south, along Cameron Creek, but the government did not accept the idea.

Hagglund got permission to build one large apartment building over the two lots, something that until then was against policy. The government's architectural division drew up the plans.

The Crandell went up in 1940 and was completed just before wartime restrictions cut off building supplies.

The lodge has been renovated and redecorated several times over the years, but the original lines of the exterior are obvious.

Above is the manager's residence, located at the back of the lodge.

A deck has been added to the front and a private, stand-alone residence constructed at the rear.

The lodge is owned and operated by Waymarker Hospitality.

208 Mount View Rd.

Bear Mountain Motel

Builder: Forry Construction

This motel was built incrementally, with the first 14 units ready for the public in 1956. Originally called the El Cortez, the name reflected a mid-1950s trend for all things Spanish, the result of completion of the Pan-American Highway from Canada to Mexico.

The motel is built on two lots. One was owned by Lula Nielson, who had a residence built there in 1917. She sold it to Maxwell Bradshaw, an award-winning draft horse breeder who owned Bird's Eye Ranch east of the park. His heirs sold the crumbling residence in 1953 and it was torn down.

The other lot was leased by Mary Mason, who ran the Mothers' Camp for the Lethbridge Kiwanis Club. Mason sold the property to Lillian May Beswick in 1932 and she in turn sold it to Wilfred and Peggy Forry for expansion of the motel in 1958.

The motel was owned and operated by the Forrys until 1971, when it was purchased by Joe and LaRue Roberts of Lethbridge. They sold it 1973 to Alf and Rae Baker, whose father George owned the nearby Park Transport Garage. Over the years, the Bakers contracted the operation of the motel to a number of resident managers.

When new owners Beth Russell-Towe and Andy Towe took over in 2004, they changed the name to Bear Mountain Motel, an early name given to Mount Crandell, which rises above it to the northwest.

The Towes sold the motel in 2015 to the Uibel family.

214 Mount View Rd.

"Tamarack"
Builder: Carl Carlson & Erik Hagglund

This building, now a mountain equipment outlet, was erected by Carl Carlson and Erik Hagglund for George Baker in 1932 as the Park Transport Garage. The building was designed to include an automobile showroom, a garage and an office. Originally a residence had been constructed on the lot in July 1924 for Elsie Baker, sister to George, but it was demolished to make way for this large commercial building.

The garage became the headquarters for all of George Baker's many enterprises, as well as a gathering-information place for locals and regular summer visitors. While the lines of the building are essentially unchanged, the interior has been substantially altered and in 1978 "Tamarack Mall" was developed with space for 14 shops. It was altered again for the mountain equipment outlet.

For many years, this was the oldest retail outlet for Imperial Oil fuel in Canada. The gas pumps were removed in 2005, leaving Pat's on the same street to the east as the only gasoline retailer in the park.

The business is known as Tamarack Outdoor Outfitters and is owned by the Baker family.

219 Mount View Rd.

Park Transport
Builder: Oland Construction

This storage building was completed in the fall of 1954 and its design was purposely similar to the original Park Transport Garage (now the Tamarack), both of which were owned by George Baker. The original 1922 residence which stood on the site was demolished to make way for the garage.

This building was erected as a place to keep new and used cars and trucks which were sold by Baker. The red tour buses owned and operated by Howard Hays' Glacier Park Transport Co. were stored overnight here during the summer season. The buses operated daily between Waterton and Glacier parks.

This building freed space in the Baker garage, down the street to the west, where new equipment was installed, including a steam heating plant for the garage and a larger office. It also gave the garage mechanics additional working room.

Four years after it was completed, parks officials expressed regret in giving approval for this building in such a conspicuous location but acknowledged there was nothing they could do about it. Its unsightly condition was frequently brought to park managers' attention by visitors, but they did nothing to demand improvements.

Today it provides storage space for the owner.

224 Mount View Rd.

First lessee: Dell Ellison

Built in 1927 as a service station for Dell Ellison, an early Waterton entrepreneur, this structure was close to competing garages. Also nearby were Dell and Tay Ellison's rooming houses and store.

The business opened as Waterton Motors and was operated by a series of individuals, including Charles Nixon (son of restaurant owner Florence "Ma" Nixon), and W. Bogart, who lived at the garage in a small apartment.

This became the go-to place for hardware, fishing licences, fishing tackle, souvenirs, snacks, dairy products, shirts, information and sometimes local gossip.

By the time it was sold to Pat Carnell Jr. in May 1953, the name had been changed to Waterton Service Station and featured Texaco products. Carnell, a residence owner in the townsite, had worked for the park for many years and was well-known for his stonework here and elsewhere in the park.

Pat's Waterton

He sold the station to Wallace "Butch" Sloan of Cardston in 1968. In addition to Texaco products and a towing service, Sloan offered bicycle and pedal surrey rentals, and sporting goods.

Sloan sold the business to Pat Seerey in 1986 and the name was changed. Seerey sold the business in 2013. Pat's Waterton is now the sole retailer of gasoline and provider of limited mechanical services in the townsite.

106 Waterton Ave.

First lessee: Florence Nixon

This property had its beginning as Nixon's Café, later renamed the Waterton Lakes Café, which was owned by Florence "Ma" Nixon of Twin Butte, Alberta. She and her husband William built the town's second stand-alone café following her employment across the street at the Hazzard Hotel.

In 1928, the café was enlarged on both the north

Trapper's Mountain Grill and Smokehouse

and south sides and became a convenient and popular eating establishment. Florence worked diligently to ensure her premises were well decorated and attractive, and that the meals were moderately priced.

Frank and Linnea Goble bought the restaurant in the spring of 1941 and renamed it Frank's. In 1951 they began building a new, modern structure to house not only a 150-seat restaurant, but also a photo shop and souvenir outlet on the south side. Two years later, they added living quarters at the rear, along with a laundry room for the Frank-Lin Motel and Rosedale Apartments, which the Gobles also owned and operated.

Frank's became "New Frank Restaurant" in 1970, owned and operated by Lucy Lee and Co., and specializing in Chinese food.

In 1992 David C.M. Yee proposed redevelopment and while conditional development was granted, little changed. In 2008 the restaurant was closed. The West family, long-time Waterton businesspeople, purchased the property in 2009, renovated, redecorated and renamed it.

Waterton Avenue

Bayshore Inn Resort & Spa

First lessee: Jack Hazzard

There are eight commercial lots on the lake side of Waterton Avenue that make up the current property. But it started as four lots and was the site of the first visitor accommodations in the townsite, beginning even before the lots were surveyed and leased starting in 1911. It was a natural spot for development: the lakeshore appealed to visitors who came from the dry prairies and wanted to be close to both the mountains and water.

No property in the town has seen more redevelopment and upgrading.

Jack Hazzard claimed the first four lots when he erected several small buildings amid the existing brush, and

later built a two-storey hotel, the first in the townsite. In 1920 Isaac L. Allred bought the Hazzard Hotel and leases, adding the north half of a fifth lot. Then things got complicated, with half the lots belonging to various people, including Ernie Haug, Sr., Eudor Brosseau and Allred, and the buildings belonging at various times to Allred, Eddie Poulin and Mark C. Rogers. In 1924 leases and improvements all came under the same name, Associated Breweries of Canada, simplifying ownership.

By the 1970s, a total of eight adjoining lots were taken up by the hotel and related facilities. They included the Ballinacor Hotel, which was completed in 1938 for Ada Kemmis and amalgamated into the current Bayshore as Kootenai Lodge in 1956.

Two lots south of this complex were the site of the

original Waterton Dance Pavilion built by Oland & Scott in 1926. The unheated, unoccupied pavilion burned to the ground in January 1938 and while arson was determined as the cause, no charges were laid for lack of proof.

A new but smaller building was erected on the same site as the destroyed Waterton Dance Pavilion and continued as a place for dancing under the ownership of Pat MacLean. It was sold in 1976 and became part of the Bayshore Inn operation, taking on new life as an arcade and roller-skating rink. It was saved from the wrecking ball in 1984, when it was renovated into a convention centre as part of an upgrading of the hotel complex.

The entire complex was sold by the Kratz family to the Suleman family in 1991.

108 Waterton Ave.

First lessee: Dewitt Talmadge Johnson

Dewitt Talmadge Johnson of Fort Macleod was an enterprising young man who saw the potential of Waterton as a post-First World War tourist destination. This is the oldest commercial building in the townsite. It was built in 1919 as a full-service garage for Johnson's transport line, which ran between Fort Macleod and Waterton, and it was also the first gas station in the park.

Johnson had thought to convert the garage into a swimming pool but held back until the matter of a proposed dam at the Narrows was settled. Then he took on a partner, Julius L. Lockead of Fort Macleod, and they renovated the garage into The Palace Dance Hall. In 1925 Johnson sold his half of the lease to Lockead and when the big, modern dance pavilion was built across the street in 1926, the building was converted again. This time it became the Beach Café.

Lockead sublet the café to a series of Chinese operators. Among them were Win Chow, Ming Yee and then Charlie Yip, all of whom had big city restaurant experience. Ada Kemmis of Kilmorey Lodge fame

Akamina Gifts & Book Nook

purchased the building in 1945.

The building was renovated yet again and became the Good Hunting China Shop and was transferred in 1958 to Helen Aileen Rhodes, Kemmis's daughter. When she retired in the mid-1970s, the lease changed hands. Subsequent owners were Eric Hedlich of Pincher Creek, Waterton residence owners Roy and Donna Spackman of Cardston and, in 1994, Cathy Wood of Cardston, who sold clothing, souvenirs and books.

Dave Cruickshank purchased the shop in 2013.

---

110 Waterton Ave.

First lessee: Dewitt Talmadge Johnson

This is the oldest original restaurant building in the townsite. Erected for Dewitt Talmadge Johnson of Fort Macleod by Oland & Scott Construction, it was opened in 1922 as the Tourist Café.

Johnson sold it in 1924 to Mabel Dilatush, who operated it with her husband Nahor.

The Tourist Café was a hot spot in town. During the 1930s it stayed open until 3 a.m. to accommodate the crowd from the dance pavilion across the street. The goings-on sometimes prompted complaints about late-night noise. By 1958 the café was open around the clock during July and August.

Leo Schmidt, brother of Florence Dilatush, Nahor's second wife, bought the restaurant in 1957 after working there for nearly 25 years. Schmidt added staff quarters at the rear of the property and later built a new home on Fern Avenue for his family. Leo died in 1988.

Waterton Park Café

Builder: Oland & Scott

The Tourist Café was sold and renamed Waterton Park Café in 1990, outdoor seating was added, then the name was changed sequentially to Little Italian Café, Tuscana Ristorante, Bel Lago Ristorante, Grizz Café & Steakhouse and Larkspur Coffee House, becoming Waterton Park Café in 2020.

112 Waterton Ave.

Stanley Hotel
Builder: Oland & Scott

The Stanley Hotel was the second accommodation built on this street, but it was small compared to the Lakeshore Hotel. The Stanley, built in 1927 and named for Nahor and Mabel Dilatush's son, had only 11 rooms and one shared bathroom.

Its focus was as a commercial block, with two retail shops on the main floor that were initially sublet to a Cardston druggist H.L. Higgs and a Pincher Creek merchant, William A. Fraser.

Arguably no sublet was longer lived than the drugstore. From 1929 to 1968 it was operated by Higgs and then his son. McCready-Baines Pharmacy took over until 1977, when the business, but not the lease, was sold to pharmacist Dave Cruickshank.

In 1936, merchant William Fraser moved back to Pincher Creek. The Dilatushes decided to operate the general store themselves, eventually specializing in woollens and linens, boasting it was the largest retailer of Hudson Bay blankets in Western Canada.

Dave Cruickshank bought the building in 1994. Dill's General Store was given over to Evergreen Gifts under the management of Joanne Meisser. Wendy West, who was a co-owner of Zum's Restaurant and R & W Woolens to the south, took over Evergreen Gifts and then the shop was converted again, in 2006, to a high-end ladies clothing store operated by Carol Cruickshank, Dave's wife. Hotel rooms were no longer rented after 2003, and the upstairs became staff quarters. Gust Gallery, a fine art gallery operated by Edith Becker, took over the space where the drug store had been, and the hotel lobby became Lost Art Jewelry, operated by artist Daniel Sommerfeld.

114 Waterton Ave.

Caribou Clothes; Big Scoop Ice Cream; My Sister's Room

Two unattached buildings have been erected on this lot. The first, now home to My Sister's Room giftshop, right, was completed for Mabel and Nahor Dilatush in 1930 as a butcher shop. It has been occupied by more businesses than any other building in town. They include Tinney's Butcher Shop, Cahoon's Variety Market, Stan's Store, MacLennan's Store, Sanford's Store, Mas' Grocery, Ruffles Clothing, Trail of the Great Bear, Worth the Splurge, and since 2014, My Sister's Room.

The separate building immediately to the south was erected in 1982 as home to Caribou Clothes and Big Scoop Ice Cream.

116 Waterton Ave.

Zum's Eatery & Mercantile; BeaverTails

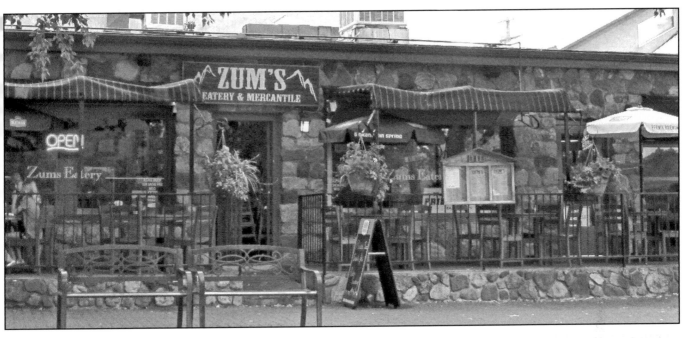

This corner lot was the last vacant land in the business section in 1961 when Harry and Sibyl Reeves purchased the lease and built Reeves Corner House. The fact that it had remained vacant since the 1920s, when an existing livery stable was removed, was an oversight by usually ever-vigilant park officials.

The lease was transferred from Isaac L. Allred to Carl Danielson in 1926, and then to Ernie Haug, Sr. in 1930. With the help of investors, Haug wanted to build the Kootenai Hotel on this and lots to the west, a proposal that did not come about, nor did a later proposal for another building.

William Sykes Wallace, a Lethbridge financial broker, bought the lease from Haug's estate in 1958 with the intention of building a three-section store on the lot, but sold it to the Reeves instead. Their building provided space for their own retail operation, plus that of McGuire's Woolens.

The lease was sold after 1971 to Doris and Bill Huculak and was renamed "Red Rock Imports," which sold Irish linen, imported china and souvenirs. Along the Cameron Falls Drive section of the building was a small, popular fast-food outlet known as Virginia Dell.

In the 1980s the building was purchased by Rod and Wendy West, who redeveloped the larger portion of the building into Zum's Burger Haus restaurant. It

was sold to Dave Cruickshank in 2005.

In September 1995 an extension was built onto this building along Cameron Falls Drive right up to the alley. It had both basement space and residential space, but once Cruickshank took over, the above-ground section was made into The Bear Shop, a retail operation associated with the restaurant.

On the Cameron Falls Drive side of the building, BeaverTails, a chain pastry business, was added in May 2018.

This was the third chain-food operation in the park to open, with Kentucky Fried Chicken being the first but now defunct, and Subway on Windflower Avenue being the second.

209 Windflower Ave.

Aspen Village Inn

This facility is the amalgamation of what were once two separate accommodations: the Frank-Lin Motel on the east and Windflower Motel on the west.

The Frank-Lin Motel was built by Frank and Linnea Goble in 1956-58, owners of Frank's Café on Waterton Avenue. The $63,000 deluxe motel had 16 units in seven separate, flat-roofed buildings to accommodate 56 guests. It was ideally located in a relatively quiet area, across from the Olympic-size swimming pool but close to the marina, restaurants and shops. Originally, these lots were home to the Precious Blood Catholic Church.

The Gobles sold the property in 1968 and it was renamed Ponderosa Motel by owners Wayne and Arminta Anderson of Lethbridge.

Immediately to the west was the Central Auto Court, operated by Enid Briosi of Lethbridge who had bought the leases in 1962. This was originally two residences altered for rental purposes into eight units to accommodate 38 people. They had been built separately, one in 1928 for Thomas Spackman and

the other for William Baker in 1929. They were both purchased in 1949 by Fred and Elizabeth Meads, who continued to rent rooms in them.

When fire destroyed the buildings in 1966, the leases for the two lots were sold to Arlen and Flora Leavitt of Calgary, who built the 23-unit Windflower Motel in 1970. The Leavitts later purchased the Ponderosa, which they operated for eight years.

Under the ownership of Leslie and Gerry Muza, the two motels became the Aspen Village Inn. Renovations to the exteriors were made in the mid-1990s to visually unify and update the two facilities. The complex was sold in 2007 to Waymarker Hospitality Inc.

107 Windflower Ave.
Builder: Gero Construction

Waterton-Glacier Suites
Red Rock Trattoria

These two lots had been occupied by two private residences, which were eventually used for staff housing. Since they were once owned by Jack and Kay Kerr, who operated the Kentucky Fried Chicken outlet in town, and were used for staff housing, they were sometimes referred to as the "chicken coops." The house next to the Windflower Motel, which had been scheduled for demolition, burned to the ground in an early morning fire in 1997. It had been built in 1934 by Walter and Rachel Rickmyer, farmers from Woolford, Alberta. Its distinctive mansard roof made it decidedly different from other residences. Next door, on the west, was a smaller residence completed in 1935 and owned by Glen William Peacock, a theatre manager from Carmangay, Alberta, and later Calgary.

The lots were cleared in 1997 to make way for the 26-unit Waterton-Glacier Suites, owned by the Suleman family, which also owns the Bayshore Inn.

The $2-million complex was built by Gero Construction of Pincher Creek and opened in May 1998.

A small fountain was created within the complex, out of street view. The latest addition was an on-site restaurant, Red Rock Trattoria. Both the accommodation and restaurant are open year-round.

301 Windflower Ave.

Builder: Schaffer Construction Ltd.

Alvin Caldwell of Hillspring, Alberta, opened the park's first butcher shop on this site in 1924. He sold out to the Strate brothers of Hillspring who continued the butcher business. They sold out in 1946 to George A. Delany, who added living quarters. Nahor Dilatush purchased the building in 1952 from Sara Delany and rented it as a two-family dwelling.

In 1962 under the ownership of Doug Allison, a concrete block coin laundry was built. Allison named the business Itussiststukiopi Coin Op Launderette. In the Blackfoot language, "Itussiststukiopi" means "wash tub." This was the first use of a Blackfoot word for any establishment in the townsite. Later, Paul Shaw of Cardston ran the laundry for a few years, adding Greyhound bus service. He was followed by NeWana Holt of Cardston, who added a one-hour photo service. This laundromat served until 2001.

In 2002 new owners Lorin Low and Dal Zemp hired Schaffer Construction Ltd. of Cardston to redevelop the site to include a new coin laundry, plus

Wieners of Waterton; Cogs; Waffleton

three other retail spaces and four staff suites. Wieners of Waterton is the cornerstone at the north end of the building. Next door is Cogs, an art and gift shop, then Waffleton, a breakfast and brunch takeout café. There is another space that was empty at this writing.

303 Windflower Ave.

First lessee: Joseph Atkinson

This lot has had a long history of being associated with garages. The first lessee, Joseph Atkinson, a Hillcrest Mines carpenter, proposed in 1931 to build a full-service garage but before it was completed, part of it was altered into a milk bottling and retail dairy outlet. Atkinson sold the property in 1937 to Imperial Oil Ltd., which in turn sold it in 1938 to Ernie Haug, Sr., who had been operating it on a rental basis.

After Haug's death in 1954, Ernie Haug, Jr., took possession and it continued to be operated as an Imperial Oil outlet. It was sold in 1959 to Doug Allison, a long-time Waterton businessman, who operated it under the Shell Oil banner. The old garage was torn down in 1964 and replaced with a concrete block building constructed by Eric French and Sons that was a full-service station. Art Widmer of Cardston operated the station, which included a coffee shop.

In 1967 the coffee shop became home to a Kentucky Fried Chicken outlet, the first fast-food fran-

chise in the park. It was operated by the Jack and Kay Kerr family of the Crowsnest Pass. The site was sold and became Kootenai Fried Chicken, operated by Pat Seerey, but gasoline sales were discontinued. The building has since been used by a series of short-lived, food-related businesses. Most recently, in 2015, the structure became 49th Degree North Pizza, which was closed in 2020, presumably temporarily because of the COVID-19 pandemic.

305 Windflower Ave.
Builder: Oland Construction

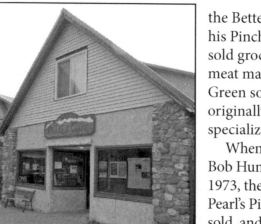

There are two buildings and food businesses at this site. The smaller, older building on the south was built by Oland Construction in 1936. In 1943 Oland sold the property to Bert Wood and Glen Fisher, who had been renting it for a few years under the name Glendell Market, which sold groceries. Wood was Fisher's father-in-law and a long-time Waterton residence owner. In 1944, ownership was transferred to Vic and Anne Harrison, former employees at the Prince of Wales Hotel. The Harrisons added the large dormer at the front. The building became the park's first Alberta Liquor Control Board outlet in 1950. It continued to be used for this purpose until 1961.

J.A. Green purchased the building and operated

"Pearl's Café"
"Pizza of Waterton"

the Betterway Store, a branch of his Pincher Creek operation, which sold groceries and had a custom meat market. In the early 1970, Green sold the lease to Pearl Irvine, originally of Magrath, Alberta, who specialized in pizza.

When Dave Cruickshank and Bob Hunt bought the building in 1973, they continued the business as Pearl's Pizza. In 1984 the lease was sold, and it became home to Pearl's Pantry until the winter of 1986-87, when Terry and Franci Hammell built a restaurant and accommodation on the north side of the lot. Since that time, the smaller building on the south has served as a souvenir shop, Levi's Pub and Willock and Sax Art Gallery until 2007, when the two buildings were sold to new owners.

307 Windflower Ave.
Builders: Carl Carlson & Erik Hagglund

During the Depression this was one of three adjoining lots that were offered to the public for leasing as the last on this street. Money was so tight in 1932, however, that no one came forward to put in a bid. They were tendered again in 1934. George A. Delany was interested in building a grocery store on this lot, only if he were granted the right to occupy it on a year-round basis. Even though this was an exception to existing policy, park officials accepted his condition. Delany's combination grocery-meat store and residence was built by Carl Carlson and Erik Hagglund, local contractors, in the winter of 1935-36.

Delany was a Lethbridge grocer who had started in the meat business in the 1920s. The Waterton store soon became a year-round hub for shopping and conversation. Delany was known as an amiable person who was missed when he died in June 1949.

His son George, Jr., the eldest of seven children, took over the business and ran it until he and his wife Mary Edith retired in 1967 and moved to Cardston.

Rocky Mountain
Food Mart

The store was sold to Rod and Wendy West, who operated it as a summer business until May 1990, when it became Rocky Mountain Food Mart under the ownership of Cheri Currie and Paulette and Gene Low. New owners, Layne and Stacey Cook of Cardston, who had opened a Subway sandwich franchise in the north end of the store, purchased the building, which is now the town's only grocery store.

309 Windflower Ave.

Builder: Carl Carlson & Erik Hagglund

Waterton Lakes
Opera House

There were several attempts to lease this lot before it became a theatre. William A. Nixon, whose wife operated Nixon's Café, applied but was not able to build.

In 1928 the Kootenay Co-operative Fruit and Produce Association of Creston, British Columbia, surrendered its application when it couldn't build.

Claresholm, Alberta, mechanics Brett and Hugh Grainger hoped to erect a garage in 1926 and Eugene Morris hoped in 1924 to put up a "business house."

Gordon Brewerton of Raymond and Cardston, however, proved to be the man to make things happen. He applied for the lot, came up with the plans and the $6,500 to build the movie theatre here, opening it in 1936. Brewerton was a pioneer in the theatre business, opening his first in 1916.

The name of the building was changed over the years from Brewerton's to Mayfair Theatre to The Centre, but Brewerton continued to own the lease. After his death in 1959, his wife ran the business, which stayed in the family until 1976, when it was named Alpine Theatre and was sold to Larry and Edith Becker of Pincher Creek.

Changing technology that went from celluloid film to digital projection, requiring specialized equipment, saw Becker move away from showing movies at end of the 2011 season.

Becker sublet the facility on a rent-to-own basis to Phil and Jenny Akitt, proprietors of a Twin Butte Store who turned it into a Mexican restaurant, bar and entertainment stage. In 2014 an outdoor patio was built on the south side of the building.

Two years later the Beckers resumed showing movies. Despite the building's name, Waterton Lakes Opera House, no operas have yet to be performed there.

In 2019 the theatre was sold and the new owner, Maribeth Pollock Douglas, began showing movies again.

On the north end is an outlet for Blakiston & Co. Adventure Rentals and on the south is Windflower Corner Coffee.

401 Windflower Ave.   Welch's Chocolate Shop

First lessee: Isaac Allred

The site of Welch's Chocolate Shop was once partially that of the Crystal Pool, below. When the pool was removed, the lot lines were redrawn to create two adjacent business sites.

This lot and the one immediately to the east (Mountain Spirits) were originally developed by Isaac L. Allred, who built a swimming pool here in 1924. It was permanently closed in 1948, but it was not until the early 1960s that new owners came forward and this lot was leased to the Alberta Motor Association (AMA). A sod-turning ceremony was held for the new building in April 1960. It was attended by Jack Giesen, southern Alberta manager of AMA; Ludvik Pahulje of Pahulje Construction of Lethbridge; AMA building committee chairman Tom Snowden of Milk River; and park superintendent T.W. Pierce.

By July the $20,000 building was opened for business. Carole Bates was the first AMA employee in Waterton. The new facility was seen as a turning point, acknowledging Waterton's part in Alberta-wide tourism.

In the 1980s the AMA closed its office and sold the lease to Jim and Chris Thompson, who operated a bakery there for two years. They were followed by Lance and Loural Meeks.

When it became Welch's Chocolate Shop in 1992, the building was renovated and enlarged, with its main entrance on Cameron Falls Drive but officially the business address is Windflower Avenue, the intersecting street.

Prince of Wales Hotel
Builder: Oland & Scott

The only hotel outside the boundaries of the townsite is the Prince of Wales Hotel. Built in 1926-27 by Oland & Scott Construction of Cardston, the 82-room hotel was once the pride of the park for its railway ownership, imposing size, location, and class of service. Eventually the hotel became the identifying symbol of Waterton. Operation of the hotel has always been seasonal, now from late May to mid-September. Staff is generally comprised of university students, under the guidance of professional hotel and kitchen managers. Three dormitories, located below the hotel to the west, provide staff accommodation.

The Prince of Wales Hotel was named a National Historic Site in 1995 before a standing-room only crowd that watched as a large bronze plaque was unveiled in the lobby. It is the only building in the park with such a designation. Changes to the building are restricted and reviewed because of this designation. In recent years the building has undergone a few structural renovations, some required by the ravages of weather and some by age. Most recently, the pillars supporting the balcony above the entrance have been replaced and restored to their original appearance.

The Kenow forest fire of 2017 endangered the hotel, but it received special protection with the arrival of aerial ladder fire trucks seconded from the Calgary Fire Department, supplemented by firefighters and equipment from other southern Alberta fire departments. Apart from one storage building which was destroyed and minor roof damage, the hotel was relatively unscathed by the fire.

The hotel has had only had three owners, all of which have been U.S.-based: the Great Northern Railway (1927-1960), Don Hummel's Glacier Park, Inc. (1960-1980) and Viad Corp.'s Glacier Park, Inc. (1980-2016), which was rebranded in 2017 under the same ownership as the Glacier Park Collection by Pursuit.

Photo Credits

Page

Chapter 1

6 Waterton Valley: Galt Museum & Archives

7 Kootenai Brown: Galt Museum & Archives

8 Isabella Brown: Galt Museum & Archives; Joe Cosley: Glacier National Park archive

9 Boundary marker: U.S. Geological Survey

11 Grave marker: Chris Morrison

12 Frederick Godsal: Galt Museum & Archives

13 Drilling rig: Library & Archives Canada; oil pool: Chris Morrison

15 Waterton road: Dave Allison; creek crossing: Chris Morrison

16 Early townsite & riders: both Galt Museum & Archives

17 Three visitors: Quenton Wagstaff; early campers, Waterton Lakes National Park (WLNP) Archives

18 Both photos: Ray Djuff

19 First school: Goble Family Collection; park registration office: Waterton Natural History Association (WNHA) Collection

20 Akamina Highway: Galt Museum & Archives; buffalo entry badge, Chris Morrison

21 Boat: WNHA Collection; fire: Goble Family Collection

22 Chief Mountain Highway: Galt Museum & Archives; car on road: WLNP Archives; registration office: Galt Museum & Archives

23 Road arch: Chris Morrison

24 Rev. S.H. Middleton: Ray Djuff

25 Andy Ford: Quenton Wagstaff; Chuck Underwood: Goble Family Collection; Hockey players: WNHA Collection

26 War Hut: Sommerfeldt Collection

27 Ice cutting: Goble Family Collection

28 George Annand with boys: Bessie Vroom Annand Ellis

29 Pittaway men and Art Holroyd: WNHA Collection

30 Lions club: Goble Family Collection

31 Farmers Bay: Robins Family Collection

32 TV antenna: Galt Museum & Archives; Playground: WNHA Collection

33 Firearm seals: WLNP Archives

34 Cross country skiers; dog in snow: Goble Family Collection; ski badge: Mackay Collection

35 Couple in boat: Mackay Collection; Jim Morrison and fish: Chris Morrison

36 Swimmers: Library & Archives Canada; Linnet Lake, WLNP Archives

37 Fish hatchery and fish ponds: Goble Family Collection

38 Campground: Robins Family Collection

39 Four-wheel trek, Galt Museum & Archives

40 Main street in flood: Goble Family Collection; two cabins in flood, Galt Museum & Archives

41 Ranson Photography Edmonton

42 Horses: WLNP Archives

43 James Marshall and cemetery wall: Chris Morrison

44 Kenow fire: Michelle Stuart

45 Waterton at night: Robins Family Collection

Chapter 2

46 Hazzard Hotel: Ray Djuff

47 William O. Lee: Lee Family Collection

48 Postcard: Lee Family Collection

49 Hazzard's first accommodation: Galt Museum & Archives; Christian Jensen: Stacy Tangren

50 Jack Hazzard: Chris Morrison; Hazzard Hotel: Quenton Wagstaff

51 Steamboat *Gertrude*, Ray Djuff

52 Lee's Cabins: Chris Morrison

54 Waterton Lakes Hotel and Chalets: Ray Djuff

55 Cal Hunter: Goble Family Collection; Ladies Lodge, Robert Miles

56 Kilmorey Lodge: Galt Museum & Archives

57 Prince of Wales crew: Quenton Wagstaff; kitchen annex: Ray Djuff

58 Hotel ad: Ray Djuff

59 Stanley Hotel: Ray Djuff

60 Cameron Lake boats, Ray Djuff

61 The Tavern: Galt Museum & Archives; Bellevue Lodge, Goble Family Collection

62 Kilmorey Lodge: Glenbow Museum

63 Both photos: Goble Family Collection

64 Ballinacor: Chris Morrison

65 Cameron Lake store and café: WNHA

66 International gas station: Ray Djuff

67 Crandell Lodge: Robins Family Collection

68 *Lady Cameron*: Bessie Vroom Annand Ellis Collection

69 James S. Kirkham: Galt Museum & Archives; International Service Station: WLNP Archives

70 Cabins: Esplanade Arts & Heritage Centre

70 Northland Lodge: Stacy Tangren

71 Postcard: Chris Morrison

72 Frank-Lin Motel: Ray Djuff

73 Marina: Robins Family Collection; Emerald Bay Motel: WLNP Archives

74 Hugh & Ann Craig: Linda Mackenzie

75 Kootenai Lodge: WNHA Collection;

76 Lakeshore Hotel flooding top: WNHA Collection; bottom: Ray Djuff

77 Cameron Lake bungalow, WLNP Archives

78 Fred Weatherup: Ray Djuff

79 Bayshore Inn: Chris Morrison

80 Kretz Family: Galt Museum & Archives

81 Waterton Lakes Lodge: Chris Morrison

82 Waterton Glacier Suites: Chris Morrison

83 Kilmorey construction: Chris Morrison

Chapter 3

84 Waterton Avenue: Earle Coverts Collection

85 Baker at boat house: Ray Djuff

86 Central Garage: WLNP Archives; men at garage: Bessie Vroom Annand Ellis Collection

87 Gas attendant: Mackay Collection

88 Park Transport Garage: Ray Djuff

89 Dairy wagon: Ray Djuff

90 Ernie Haug, Sr.: Galt Museum & Archives; first dance hall, Quenton Wagstaff Collection

92 Women at dance hall: Stacy Tangren; dance ticket: MacLean Family Collection

93 Dance pavilion, Waterton Natural History Association Collection; interior of pavilion, Chris Morrison

94 Waterton Avenue: Ray Djuff; tin fish: Chris Morrison

96 Mart Kenney & his Western Gentlemen: Galt Museum & Archives

97 Goathaunt Chalet: Chris Morrison; MacLean Brothers: MacLean Family Collection

98 Hupp Huston Orchestra and rebuilt dance hall: WLNP Archives

99 Anderson Sisters: Galt Museum & Archives

100 Bonnie & Archie MacLean: MacLean Family Collection; Carl Carlson, Galt Museum & Archives

101 Tourist Café and staff: WNHA Collection

102 Stanley Hotel and Leo Schmidt: Ray Duff

103 Nixon's Café: WNHA Collection

104 Inside Delany's: Galt Museum & Archives; Linnea and Frank Goble: Goble Family Collection

105 Both photos: Goble Family Collection

106 Ellison family: Goble Family Collection

107 Good Hunting China Shop: Chris Morrison

108 Alpine Theatre: Goble Family Collection

109 Hanson and Foster at Goat Haunt: WLNP Archives

110 Goathaunt Chalet: WLNP Archives

111 *Alleas* at dock: WNHA Collection; Les Morrow: Chris Morrison

112 Carnell's boat house: Ray Djuff

113 *M.V. International*: Ray Djuff

114 Ott's *Deeidra*: Ott Family Collection

115 *Miss Waterton*: top, Isabell Morrow Holladay; middle: Robins Family Collection; bottom: Chris Morrison
116 Kretz couple: Kretz family
117 Riders: WLNP Archives; Russell: Galt Museum & Archives
118 Horses in water: WLNP Archives; Dee Barrus: Chris Morrison
119 Horses: Library & Archives Canada

Chapter 4

120 Golfers: Library & Archives Canada
121 William E. Thomson: Whyte Museum of the Canadian Rockies
122 Both photos: Quenton Wagstaff
123 Both photos: Quenton Wagstaff
124 WLNP Archives
125 Both photos: Quenton Wagstaff
126 Starter's shack: Quenton Wagstaff; gathering a first hole: WLNP Archives
127 Tee off: Glacier National Park Archives
128 Top photo: Quenton Wagstaff; bottom: Dave Allison
129 Ladies: Quenton Wagstaff
130 Putting: Dave Allison; Rackettes: Chris Morrison
131 Lonesome Lake: Galt Museum & Archives
132 Stanley Thompson: Ray Djuff
133 Aerial view: Chris Morrison
134 Club house: Glacier National Park Archives
135 Wagstaff: Quenton Wagstaff

Chapter 5

136 Camp councillors: Galt Museum & Archives
137 Boy Scouts: Galt Museum & Archives
138 Fathers and sons: Raymond and District Historical Society
139 Kainai Kottage: WLNP Archives
140 Both photos: WLNP Archives
141 Buchanan and Long: Galt Museum & Archives
142 Boys at cabin: Robins Family Collection
143 Jim Sampson: Galt Museum & Archives; camp activities: Robins Family Collection
144 Group of boys: Galt Museum & Archives; Fred Botsford: WLNP Archives

145 Hospital hut: Galt Museum and Archives
146 Camp bell: Galt Museum & Archives
147 Fire rubble: WNHA Collection; Russell Bennett: Chris Morrison
148 Fred Botsford: Robins Family Collection
149 Both photos: Robins Family Collection
150 Inglenook: WLNP Archives
151 Boys and deer: Robert Miles; Anna Tilley: Galt Museum & Archives
152 Needs credit
153 Both photos: Galt Museum & Archives
154 Maintenance: Kathy Yamashita
155 Vespers area: Chris Morrison; lodge and infirmary hut: Galt Museum & Archives
156 Galt Museum & Archives
157 Galt Museum & Archives
158 Camp committee members: Raymond and District Historical Society; fire rubble: WLNP Archives
159 Bell: Chris Morrison
160 Camp Columbus: Chris Morrison
161 Ball game: WLNP Archives

Chapter 6

162 Trailers: Galt Museum & Archives
163 Speedwagon: Chris Morrison; Kathryn Leighton: Ray Djuff
164 RV with helicopter: Chris Morrison
165 Radio equipment: Glacier-Waterton Hamfest Association
166 Alberta hams: Glacier-Waterton Hamfest Association
167 Tennis winners: Library and Archives Canada
168 William Rodney: Ray Djuff; Kootenai Brown: WLNP Archives; cairn dedication: Glenbow Museum
169 Crane and cairn: Galt Museum & Archives
170 Both photos: Chris Morrison
171 Both photos: Galt Museum & Archives
172 Both photos: Chris Morrison
173 Hatchery: Peel's Prairie Provinces; Gerald Bailey: Gwyneth Bailey
174 Fish ponds: Goble Family Collection; William Cable: Kathleen Cable; Art Colbeck: Dave Colbeck; Ken Goble: WLNP Archives

175 Church: WNHA Collection
176 Church interior: WLNP Archives
177 Scrolls: Chris Morrison
178 Demolition: Chris Morrison
179 Middleton and Nielson: WNHA Collection

Chapter 7

Unless noted below, all photos in this chapter: Chris Morrison

195 Superintendent's house: Waterton Natural History Association Collection
269 Compound: Travel Alberta
270 Two residences: Galt Museum & Archives
271 Browns at home: WLNP archives
279 First Catholic church: WNHA Collection
280 Administration office: WLNP Archives; demolition: Jo Slen
281 Fire hall: Galt Museum & Archives
298 Crystal Pool: WNHA Collection
299 Prince of Wales Hotel: Ray Djuff

Index

Achtem, John 214
Administration Office (former site) 26, 240, 273, 280
Ainsworth, Elmer 244
Aitken, Alexander 176
Akamina Gifts & Book Nook 86, 91, 101, 103, 106 291
Akamina Highway 20, 41, 60, 65, 77, 212, 278
Akamina Ski Championships 34
Akamina-Kishinena Highway proposal 34, 38
Akitt, Phil & Jenny 297
Alaska Highway 28
Alberta Government Telephones (Telus) 89, 285
Alberta Liquor Control Board store 283, 296
Alberta Motor Association 245, 283, 298
Alberta Railway & Irrigation train 47
Aldridge Bay (Middle Waterton Lake) 11, 48
Aldridge, William, & family 11, 48, 49
Alleas 87, 111
Allen, Les T. 151-152
Allen's Lakeshore Motel 76, 78
Allison, Art & Edna May 225
Allison, Dick 30
Allison, Doug 38, 202, 295
Allred, George & Esther 68, 73, 74, 204
Allred, Isaac 50, 52-53, 58, 86, 104, 105, 283, 290, 293, 298
All-Saints Anglican Church 175-178
Alpine Cinema 297
Alpine Club of Canada 119, 282
Alpine Stables 44, 117, 119,161
Altyn 87
Anderson, Robert & family 197

Anderson Sisters 99-100
Anderson, Wayne & Arminta 294
Annand Dairy 88
Annand, "Joe" George family 29, 270 271
Annand, George Jr.& Bessie 270
Aspen Village Inn 279, 294
Associated Breweries 58, 290
Atkinson, James H. 32, 132, 195, 275
Atwell, Jason 224
Auger, Art 183, 210, 245
Auger, John C. 201
August singularity 83
Avalanches 34, 80, 217, 221
Ayris, Robert 28
Baalim, Art Jr. 31
Baalim, Arthur & Gladys 35, 231,238
Baalim, Harry 226
Bailey, George E. 172, 173, 178, 179
Bailey, Reg 179
Baird, James 258
Baker, Alf 28, 31, 275, 275 287
Baker, Rae 28, 78, 89, 248, 287
Baker, Brian
Baker, George 19, 28, 34, 36, 37, 64-66, 68, 77, 85-89, 112, 113, 198, 200, 202, 276, 279, 255, 288
Baker, Elsie 55, 86, 88-89, 227, 288
Ballantyne, George 261
Ballinacor Hotel 64, 69, 74-75, 94, 98, 106, 186, 290
Barnes, Bert 211, 234
Barrus, Dee & Family 118-119
Bates, Carole 298
Batty, Art 233
Bayshore Inn 11, 69, 75, 79, 81, 83, 170, 198, 204-205, 290
Beach Café 92, 106, 291
Bear attack at Camp Inuspi 149
Bear Mountain Motel 71, 83, 89,

246, 287
Beargrass Days 42
BeaverTails 101, 293
Becker, Edith 109, 292, 297
Becker, Fred 151
Becker, Larry & Edith 297
Beckett, J.T. 53
Beer parlour 59, 71, 75-76, 81, 100
Bell, Art 38
Bell, Eddie 28, 213
Bell, George & Mary 259
Bell, Kirk & Jean 70, 72
Bellevue Lodge 61, 63
Belly River Campground 41, 167
Bennett, Russell 141, 142, 145, 146, 147, 168
Beny, F. Charles 238
Beny, Roloff 238
Beswick, Lillian 246, 287
Betterway Store 296
Betts, William 219
Bevan, George Ace 14, 24, 52, 195
Big Scoop Ice Cream Parlour & Big Chunk Fudge Shop 83, 292
Bigelow, Dr. Jesse 151, 216, 245
Bigham, Orson 211
Bissett, Geddes 221
Black, Dr. Brian O. 215
Black, Gordon Lewis 228
Black, Hugh 70, 285
Black, Johnny 236
Black, Laura C. 228, 266
Blakiston & Co. Adventure Rentals 297
Blakiston, Thomas Wright 8-9
Blood Tribe 21, 23, 138, 139, 144, 146, 176, 252, 279, 281
Blunt, Rev. Neville 175
Bogart, W. 289
Bond, Frank 218
Bonertz, Cyril August 248, 279
Boswell, Harley H. 64
Boswell, William 10

Botsford, Fred Albert ("Gramps") 143, 144, 146, 148
Boulton, C.W. 206
Boundary survey 9-10
Bowie, Clarence 72
Boy Scouts 23, 30, 137, 138, 152, 169, 174
Boyce, Bill 114
Boyle, Daniel 252
Brandvold, Lars 171
Brewerton, Gordon 98, 108, 297
Bridgeview Cabins 37, 69,78
Briosi, Andy 73-74
Briosi, Enid 294
Broder, Violet Faye 218, 247
Broomfield, Ella Baker 89, 227
Brosseau, Eudor 89, 290
Brown, Dr. Duncan & Patricia 201
Brown, Isabella 8
Brown, John George "Kootenai" 7-8, 10, 12-14, 23-24, 32, 45, 48-50, 168-170
Brown, Olivia 8
Brown, Urvilla Isabel 170, 198
Bruns, Anna 242
Buchanan, Senator William A. 7, 23, 24, 53, 92, 131, 141, 145, 168, 244, 278
Bullock, Rod & Laura 250
Bundy, Clarence & Freda 207
Burch, Art 208, 115
Burns, Dianne 154
Doris Burton 48
Burton, Edward D. 118
Bus service 19, 295
Byard, Smith 196, 247
Cable, William 173
Cahoon, Ab & Lucille 262
Cahoon, Gerald 258
Cahoon, Kent 30
Cahoon, Lynn 30
Cahoon, Merlin 94
Cairncross, Andrew David 246
Caldwell, Alvin 102, 295
Calgary Power Ltd. 33, 68, 158
Calvert, G. R. Rev. 32
Cameron Lake Auto Bungalows 37, 68, 88, 204

Cameron Lake campground 37
Camp Columbus 137, 159-161
Camp Inuspi 37, 136-37, 141-150
Camp Tee-La-Daw 157-159
Campbell, Roy 184
Campbell, Ruby Elaine 176
Canadian flag 72, 229
Canadian Legion War Services 28, 68
Canadian Pacific Railway 12, 89, 121, 146
Canadian Radio Broadcasting Commission 96
Canadian Rockies Hotel Co. 78
Canyon Church Camp 137, 148, 150, 152-157
Card, LeRoy R. 267
Caribou Clothes 292
Carlson, Alton "Hoot" 257
Carlson, Carl 17, 27, 35, 52, 87, 100, 104, 108, 154, 187, 216, 231, 232, 247, 249, 255, 256, 257, 277, 288, 296, 297
Carlson, Cecile Ada 32, 35
Carnell, Charles "Dippy" 87, 111, 112, 226
Carnell, Jean & Ethel 28
Carnell, Michael 30
Carnell, Pat Jr. 105, 211, 277, 289
Carnell, Patrick Sr. 204
Carnell, Vella 211, 262
Carnell, William Joseph 201
Carpenter, Silas 109
Carson, Joseph E. 215
Carthew Lodge 285
Casey, Gordon & Lil 82
Cemetery 24, 32-33, 43, 184, 197, 202, 203, 209, 216, 219, 223, 225, 239, 247, 255, 263
Central Auto Court 78, 294
Central Garage 86, 87, 89
Cahoon's Variety Market 292
Cheesman, Charles Benjamin 258
Chief Mountain International Highway 19, 20- 22, 66, 263
Chow, Wing 255, 266, 291
Christiansen, Ralph D. & Chrissie 225
Christou, Van 189

Church of Jesus Christ of Latter-day Saints 137, 138, 157-58, 219, 265, 274
Civilian Conservation Corps 21
Clark, Garnet 187
Coates, Fred J. & Faye 207
Cody, Gene 159
Cogs 295
Cohen, Donna 38
Cohen, Emanuel & Sam 39, 78, 81
Colbeck, Art & family 174
Collett, W.J., Rev. 154
Collins, Lorne Burritt 245
Combs, Bill 152
Community Centre 44, 264, 276
Community Hall 29, 172, 278
Coombs, Leo 178
Cooper, Mary 205
Cooper, Robert 14, 90, 269
Cooper, W.C.L. 217
Cordiero, Arthur Joseph 161
Cosley, Joe 8
Costello, Lenore 60, 213
Coulee Cruisers Club 38
Cox, John 249
Craig, Hugh, Ann & family 74-75, 77-79, 83
Crandell Mountain Campground 41
Crandell Mountain Lodge 51, 52, 286
Creffield, Alice May 258
Cristall, Norman & Margaret 223
Crofts, Truman W. 15, 245
Cromarty, William 91, 94, 264, 282
Cronkhite, Goldie & Otto 206
Cross, Reginald 227
Cruickshank, Dave 80, 291, 292, 293, 296,
Cruickshank, Dave & Carol 101, 187, 292,
Crystal Swimming Pool 105, 127, 143, 250, 274, 283, 298
Culler, Marvin Carl & Alice 190
Cummings, Harry 19, 64, 184, 186, 276
Cummings, Sara 186
Currie, Bryan & Pauline 232
Currie, Cheri 296

Dance pavilion 17, 18, 24, 56, 90-93, 97-98, 100-101, 112, 184

Danielson, Carl 17, 49, 109, 240, 242, 248, 293

Davidson, Agnes 144

Davidson, Bill, Betty & Roy 237

Dayman, Art 27, 28, 204

Dayman, Sadie 203

Dayman, William 267

Deak, John, 185

Deak, John & Elayne 209

Deeidra 30, 112-116,

Delany, George family 29, 36, 104, 295, 296

DeLong, Eleanor 17, 184

DeVeber, Herbert A. 28, 69, 131, 132, 153, 166, 278

Dickson, Silas 28, 199

Dilatush, Florence 103, 291

Dilatush, Mabel 28, 58, 101, 102, 225, 264, 291, 292

Dilatush, Nahor 17, 28, 29, 59, 95, 101, 102, 103, 113, 178, 217, 230, 259, 265, 292

Dilatush, Stanley 28

Dixon, Luella & Lawrence 183

Dobry, Dr. Joseph J. & Dr. Ed 166, 221

Dominion Day 50, 142, 159

Dorigatti Construction 185, 223

Douglas, Maribeth Pollock 297

Dowsing, Julie 30

Dray, Albert 76

Eagleson, Robert William 239

Eddy, Wesley 220

Ekelund, Nels 227

El Cortez Motel (Bear Mountain Motel) 33, 71, 83, 151, 246, 287

Eldridge, Reed S. 248

Ellert, Frank 250

Ellison, Dell & Tay 23, 27, 55, 68, 87, 97, 104, 105, 107, 108, 250, 251, 274, 289

Elton, David Horton 48, 104, 246, 250

Emerald Bay Motel 38, 72, 73, 81, 89

Enerson, Peter O. family 198

Engler, Bruno 34

English, Joe 270

Ensign, Jack 69

Evacuation orders 22, 44

Fairweather, Charles A. 89

Fairy, 111

Falls theatre 37, 42

Fansett, Robert John 242

Fatal bear attack 41

Ferguson, Claude A. 86, 259, 260

Field, Bruce 159

Fire halls 277, 281

Fires, forest 21, 43, 44, 119, 133, 157, 161, 178, 273, 278, 299

Golf tournaments 122, 131, 253

First hole-in-one 123-125

First motorized RV 163

Fish hatchery 172-174

Fish ponds near Cameron Falls 37, 42, 174, 175, 263

Fisher, James W. 63, 68, 99

Floods 39-41, 47, 76, 78, 83, 169, 185, 189, 190, 195, 238, 262, 269, 280

Ford, Agnes 203

Ford, RCMP Cpl. Andy 23, 25, 203

Forry Construction 71, 287

Fortis Alberta (formerly Calgary Power) 33, 68, 158

Foster, Walter B. "Waddy" 91, 109, 110, 134, 149, 217, 230, 244, 258

Fowler, Dr. Douglas 216, 245

Frache, Alwin & Winnie family 176, 209

Frank-Lin Motel 33, 72, 78, 104, 289, 294

Fraser, William & Katherine 102, 216, 227, 229, 249, 292

Frederickson, George 87, 95, 265, 266

French, Eric 295

Frey, Frank 189

Gairns, Peter & Florence 189, 209

Galbraith, Hugh & Jean 125, 178, 186, 198

Ganske, Fred 72

General Construction, Lethbridge 148

Gero Construction 183, 206, 294

Gertrude 51, 211

Giddie, Ellen & Jack 188

Gilborn, Danny 159

Giles, Dr. George 206

Girl Guides 23

Glacier National Park (MT) 16, 22, 34, 48, 53, 58, 70, 110, 128, 165

Glacier Park Hotel golf course 126

Glacier Park, Inc. 33, 78, 116, 299

Glacier-Waterton Hamfest 165-167, 221

Gladstone, John T. 270

Glendell Market 296

Goat Haunt, MT and Midnight Frolics 21, 96, 97

Goates, Dr. Ralph & Katherine 247, 260

Goathaunt Chalet 90-91, 95, 109, 111

Goble, Calvin 28

Goble, Ed & Nellie 206, 260

Goble, Frank 23, 33, 34, 36, 40-41, 60, 105, 249, 289, 294

Goble, Ken 174

Goble, Linnea 23, 33, 104, 249, 289, 294

Goble, Oliver & Arletta 263

Godsal, Frederick 10-12, 15,

Going-to-the-Sun Highway 22, 34

Going, Linnea Hanson 242

Golf course clubhouse 126, 133-135

Golf course evaluation 129

Good Hunting China Shop 291

Gorrie, Jack, Joyce & family 253

Graham, Ray & Olive 72

Granger, H.H. 54

Great Depression 20, 22, 59, 60, 66, 68, 94, 102, 108, 127, 128, 141, 150, 179, 200, 201, 210, 212, 232, 254, 255, 285, 296

Great Northern Railway 53, 56, 58, 78, 87, 126, 163, 202, 250, 285

Green Timber Apartments 61

Green, J.A. 61, 262

Green, Marion 262

Greenway, Thomas & Ralph Waldo & Annie Gordon 268

Gregory, Percy & Helen 64, 178, 212

Grinnell, George Bird 17
Gruenwald, George 234
Gust Gallery 292
Gyro Club of Lethbridge 145
Hacking, Bessie 33, 70, 285
Hacking, Earl 70, 285
Hagglund, Erik & Olga 61, 63, 66-68, 87, 104, 108, 187, 216, 249, 255, 266, 278, 286, 288, 296, 297
Hagglund, Florence (née Moss) 67
Haibeck, Todd 218
Hall, Henry & Leone 261
Hallifax, W.B. 233
Hamfest, Amateur Radio Assoc. 165-167
Hamill, Charles Pace 236
Hammell, Terry & Franci 296
Hand, Bob 186
Hanson, Henry & Julia 47, 51, 91, 109-111, 170, 242
Harkin, James B. 15, 17, 53, 109, 139, 141, 179
Harland, Murton & Esther 239
Harris, Mrs. Al 144
Harris, William & Perle 256
Hartman-Rickmyer, Alice 266
Harwood, Arthur "Pop" & family 23, 29, 88, 168, 169, 170-171, 178, 197, 224, 226, 271, 278
Haslam, Dean 187
Haslam, John 133
Haug, Ernie Jr. & Maxine 34, 91, 265, 277, 295
Haug, Ernie Sr. 29, 32, 66, 69, 87, 89, 90-91, 94, 95, 168, 190, 224, 265, 290, 293, 295
Hays, Howard 250, 288
Hazzard, Jack F. 13, 46, 48, 49-50, 52, 75, 79, 85, 89, 103, 109-110, 199, 209, 230, 290
Healey, Herb & Mary 247
Hedderick, Colin & Marguerite Hill 185, 235
Helicopter on trailer 164
Helicopter ski service 80
Hembroff, Verna 191
Herron, John 12
Heuer, Emmanuel 152-153
Hewlett, Frances &

Hilda 103, 214, 215
Higgs, Ben 26, 102, 106, 226, 234, 292
Highway, Lethbridge-Waterton 30, 66
Hill, Edgar B. & Lawrence 127
Hill, Louis W. 56, 87, 163, 175, 179, 285
Hillier, Alice 241
Hilton, Bill 134
Hochstein, Alan & Doris 82
Hochstein, Cyril, Marcel, Edith "Toots" & Pearl 232
Hodge, Dave & Jo 229
Hodges, Jim & Meredith 202
Holladay, Isabell Morrow 112
Holland, Gwendolyn 237
Holm, Mary Yvonne 219
Holt, NeWana 210, 295
Holt, Stephen 218
Holte, Gunnar 74, 275
Hominuke, Peter & Florence 67-68, 241
Honour Roll, Second World War 176, 177
Horse pasture for public 37
Houston, Fred K. 187
Hovan, Joe 159
Hoyt, Berton & Alma Jane 228
Hummel, Don 33, 78, 250, 299
Hunt, Bob 296
Hunt, Dr. John & Leone 194
Hunter, Cal, Elenora & Nellie 26, 51, 54, 58-60, 66, 206, 260
Hurlburt Auction 78
Hurlburt, Ken & Renee 214
Huston, Merv "Hupp" 98-99
Hutchinson, Harold 187
Hutchinson, Leonard & Victoria 69, 78
Hutchison, J.A. 32
Hy's Steak House 79
Ice (for refrigeration) 27, 31
Imperial Bank of Commerce 75
Imperial Oil 66, 88, 95, 288, 295
Improvement District No. 4 230, 276
Inglemere 150, 152, 246
Inglenook 150, 151, 152, 246

International Coffee Shop, Service Station & Auto Bungalows 66, 69, 95
Irma Peach 58
Irrigation dam proposal 15, 17, 245
Jackson, A.Y. 207, 239
Jackson, Cyril Frederick 196
Jackson, Frances 196
Jackson, Walter 124
Japanese Canadians 154
Jensen, Christian F. 13, 49, 50
Jitney dances 91, 92, 97, 99, 100
Johansen, Frank 213
Johnson, Dewitt T. 85, 86, 90, 101, 103, 183, 291
Johnson, Ed 61, 185, 234, 284
Johnson, Ed & Dorothy Barnes 234
Johnson, Julia 183
Jones, Samuel 206
Kainai Kottage 138-140
Kanouse, H.A. "Fred" 7, 8
Karim, Karim 83
Kelley, Bert 47
Kemmis, A.C. 55, 60-64, 66, 68, 69, 106, 186, 200, 240, 261-262, 284, 290-291
Kemmis, Helen Aileen 107, 291
Kenley, Kay 40-41
Kenney, Mart & his Western Gentlemen 95, 96, 99
Kenow Fire 43, 44, 45, 119, 133, 135, 157, 161, 273, 278, 299
Kentucky Fried Chicken 293, 294, 295
Kerr, Jack & Kay family 294, 295
Kesler, Shirley & Bart 189
Key, Dr. James A. 248
Kilmorey Lodge 24, 55, 60, 61, 62, 66, 67, 68, 70, 72, 82, 83, 89, 186, 208, 234, 240, 262, 284
Kirkham, Donald L. 237
Kirkham, James Stanley 58, 68
Kiwanis Club of Lethbridge 144, 150-152, 216, 287
Knapik, Leonard 159
Knight, Herbert 24, 53, 62, 87, 128-130, 132, 142, 169, 249
Knights of Columbus 159

Kootenai Brown cairn 168-170, 256
Kootenai Lodge Hotel Co. 94
Kratz, Mary & Rick 80, 81, 83, 101, 205
Kratz, Miriam & Luke 80
Kretz, Stan & Vivian 30, 114, 116, 185
Kuschel, Leigh & Flora 69, 74, 94, 193, 194
Kuschel, Paul 58, 68
Ladies Lodge 55
Lady Cameron 34, 68
Lakeland Golf Management (Alberta) Inc. 135
Lakeshore Hotel 50-53, 54, 101, 103
Lakeshore Village 74-75
Lakeview Apartments 68
Larkspur Café 291
Larson, John Lawrence 250
Latter-day Saints father-sons camp 137-138
Laurie, Illa 242
Laurie, William Telford 249
Lawson, Bristol 172
Lear Construction 81
Leather, Augustus 185
Leavitt, Arlen & Flora 78, 294
Leavitt, Hugh 29
Lebel, Timothie 244
LeCapelain, C.K. "Cap" 21, 28, 65, 99
Lee, Armenia 47, 49
Lee, Harry Calder & Emily 51-52
Lee, Lucy 104, 289
Lee, William O. 47-49, 51, 83
Lee's Cabins 52, 55, 66-67, 286
Leighton, Kathryn & Edward 163
Lerner, Lee & Sandra 225
Lethbridge Nursing Mission 151
Lethbridge Woodworking Co. 194, 215, 229, 261
Levi's Pub 296
Lewis, Helen 256
Lieff, Bernie 135
Lillie, Beattie C. 187
Lillie, Edith Emma 232

Lineham, John 11, 170
Lineham, Mabel 216
Linnea 21, 109-112, 140
Linnet Lake swimming 35, 36
Lions Club 29, 30, 100, 250, 278
Lockead, Julius 90, 291
Lodge at Waterton Lakes 82, 189, 283
Lomas family 194
Long Lance, Sylvester C. 140
Long, Alexander & Olive 266
Lost Art Jewelry 293
Low, Gene & Paulette 296
Low, Scott T. 234
Lowen, Herman 225
Lower horse corral at Crypt landing 37
Luchia, Anne C. 202
Luchia, Charles R. 267
Lundgard, Oscar 72
Lundstad, Reidar 72
Lyman, Philyer, Francis 268
Lynn, Dr. Bob 150
Lynn, Dr. Bob & Beth Hunt 221
Mas Grocery 292
MacIntyre, Col. D.E. 28
MacKay, Christina 255
Mackenzie, Wilbur C. 229
MacKenzie, Linda Craig 74-77
MacLean, Archie 91, 97, 99, 100, 205, 222
MacLean, Dave 91, 92, 95
MacLean, Dorothy Rogers 222
MacLean, Elizabeth "Bonnie" 97, 100
MacLean, Laurie 99, 101
MacLean, Neil "Pat" 95, 97, 98, 100, 205, 222
MacLennan, Don & Sheila 227
MacLennan's Store 292
Madge, Nola 39-41
Madge, W. Martin 254
Mallison, Mrs. H. 244
Mani Krupa Investments Inc. 83
Margach, W.T. 12
Markus, Larry & Vilma 202
Marshall, Jim 43
Marshall, Locke 114, 170

Martin, Ben & Harry 241
Martin, Derek 233
Mason John & Mary 151, 152, 246
Matkin, Mr. & Mrs. Bert 68
Matkin, Henry & Joe 40
Matkin, Mrs. W.H. 134
Mayfair Theatre 297
McClain, Eddie 261
McClain, Maxine 192
McClung, Owen Spencer 192
McCready-Baines Pharmacy 292
McCulloch, Babb Irene Baalim 191
McDonald, Harriet 156
McFarland, Ernest R. 243
McGuire's Woolen Shop 107, 293
McKenzie, Herbert James "Foxy" 243
McKenzie, Rex 152
McMahon, Mary 256
McNally, Dr. Alfred, Margaret & sons 256
McNeill, Leishman 26
McNellis, Elmer D. 217
McWhirter, Logan "Loggie" 223, 230
Meads, Fred & Elizabeth 217, 258, 259, 294
Meeks, Lance & Loural, 298
Meisser, Jerald 237
Meisser, Joanne 292
Meisser, Lowell & Elinor C. 237
Meisser, Rome 238
Metal collection for war fund 28
Metcalfe, Ben 54
Metka family 257
Meyer, George & Pat 233
Middleton, Charles 258
Middleton, Lilly 177, 219
Middleton, Rev. Samuel H. & Katherine 23, 24, 29, 32, 130, 138-141 145, 168-169, 176-179, 197, 202, 219, 259, 261, 262, 278
Miles, June Rackette 23, 29
Miles, Robert 27
Millar, George & Angus 249
Milne, Thelma 260
Miniature golf 127

Miss Waterton 115, 116
Moir, Gilbert 250
Montalta 87
Moroz, Mariette 159-161
Morris Brothers 116, 200, 254, 259, 271, 279, 297
Morrison, Gordon & Grace 87, 208
Morrison, Isabel 222
Morrison, Jack A. & Dorothy 245
Morrison, James J. & Ethyl 35, 223
Morrison, Peter 69
Morrison, Phil, Glenda & Cathy 183
Morrow, Les 21, 87, 91, 111, 112, 208
Morrow, Thomas D. & Kate 208
Mothers' Camp 150-152, 216
Motor Vessel International 18, 21, 87, 91, 110, 113, 116, 152, 166, 250
Mount Atkinson sand bunker 132
Mountain Spirits liquor store 127, 250, 283, 298
Mountain Square Dance Jamboree 100
Movie theatre/opera house 108, 109, 297
Mount Cleveland ascent 178
Muser, Allison 41
Muza, Gerry 80
Muza, Gerry & Leslie 82, 294
My Sister's Room 292
Nathani, Andy 83
Neils, E. Al 59
Neilson, Wes 170
Neville, Nina 171
New Dayton Trail Rangers 152
Nicas, Peto 243
Nielson, Lula 12, 89, 107, 178, 206, 213, 222, 243, 272, 287
Niven, Mary & Bob 197
Nixon's Waterton Lakes Café 103, 104
Noffsinger, George W. 53
Nordlund, Hans 74, 275
Norris, Bill 152
Northland Lodge 33, 61, 70, 285

O'Bray, Violet 203
O'Brien, Mary Oland 71, 214
O'Hara, W.F. 12, 49, 269
Oil City 11, 85, 243
Oland & Scott Construction 18, 19, 56, 92, 94, 98, 125, 126, 140, 172, 184, 201, 206, 207, 213, 214, 217, 276, 282, 284, 291
Oland Construction 89, 148, 149, 171, 199, 288, 296
Oland, Doug H. 221, 243
Oldroyd, Robert & Estella 60, 205, 206, 213, 222
Oliver, Howard H. 191, 267
Olsen, Dee 118
Ott, Cliff 89, 112, 113, 114, 116, 250, 268
Our Lady of Mount Carmel Catholic Church 279
Paahtómahksikimi Cultural Centre 281
Packrats 74
Palace dance hall 90, 91, 92, 291
Palliser Expedition 8
Palmer, Delbert 188
Park Meat Market 97, 102
Park Saddle Horse Co. 53, 111, 112
Park sizes & designations 14
Park Transport Co. 87, 89, 210, 270, 288
Park Transport warehouse 288
Parke, Cecilie "Squish" Swanson 211
Parry, Kate 155, 156
Pat's Waterton 104, 289, 295
Patching, Charles & Gladys 202
Patterson, T.E.H. 102
Peace Park dedication in Waterton 168
Peace Park Plaza 49, 78, 169
Peacock, William 107, 108, 294
Pearce Flight Training School 27, 179, 278
Pearl's Café, Pearl's Pizza 296
Penhove, Ivy & Bay 78
Pepper, Enid (nee Dowdle) 167-168
Perrett, June 113

Peszat, Stan 192
Pickup, Dr. Clarence Watson 60, 61, 284
Pierson, Byron 170
Pilling, Frank & Peter 97
Pincher Creek Oil & Refining Company 11
Pisko, John Robert 253
Pitcher, Clara 213
Pittman, U.J. 159
Pittman, Victor 159
Pizza, 49th Degree North 295
Pizza of Waterton 296
Platt, Etta 198
Pohl, John 185
Ponderosa Motel 294
Porter, Gordon 151
Poulin, Louis "Eddie" 54, 56, 58, 59, 92, 178, 290
Precious Blood Catholic Church 279
Pressley, Hannah Carnell 28, 201, 204, 205, 275
Primrose, Capt. Peter & Winnona 21
Prince of Wales Hotel 18-23, 27, 33, 41, 44, 56-62, 64, 68, 71, 78, 80, 87-88, 92, 94, 97, 108, 111, 126, 129, 133, 168, 175, 176, 206, 208, 247, 250, 263, 277, 282, 285, 296, 299
Pruegger family 217
Pumphouse 272
Putney House 186
Queen Elizabeth Fund 26
Queen's Canadian Fund for Air Raid Victims 131
R & W Woolens 292
Rackette, Jim & Adelle 26, 28, 29, 130
Rankin, Jean 98, 116, 117, 184
Ranson, Carl & Elsie 142, 145, 193
Ranson, Denny 144, 149
Record fish 55
Red Cross 26, 29, 166
Red Rock Gifts 107
Red Rock Trattoria 83, 294
Redfern, Cy & Gladys 190

Reeves Lakeshore Bungalows/ Motel 71, 72, 76
Reeves, Brian "Barney" 30, 106, 107
Reeves, Harry Northover & Sibyl 70-72, 76, 106, 107, 237, 261, 293
Reilly, Charles F. 60, 213
Remington, D.C. & D.H. 220
Rent review of 1960 35
Rexford, Leonard J. 86-87
Rhodes, Aileen & Dusty 106, 107, 291
Rhynas, Mel 125
Rice, Mary Catherine 246
Riddle, Jim & Ashley 83
Riggall, Bert 48, 117
Riviere, George 116
Riviere, Henri "Frenchy" 16
Roberts, Joe & LaRue 78, 287
Robins, George 148
Robinson family 116
Rocky Mountain Development Co. 11
Rocky Mountain Food Mart 104, 296
Rocky Mountains Club 178-179
Rocque, Steve 156
Rodney, William 167-168
Rogers, Mark C. 53, 59, 222
Roller skating 101, 108, 109, 290
Rollins, Leroy 157
Romanowski, Ed 83, 283
Roper, Albert 29, 68
Rosedale Apartments 69, 104, 249, 289
Ross, George & Rodney Whitson & Stubb 257
Ross, William Alexander 243
Rotary Club 22, 34, 145, 231, 249
Royal Canadian Mounted Police 282
Ruffles Clothing 292
Ruperell, Dee 81
Russell, Andy 117, 275
Rylands, Dave 283
Rylands, Dr. D.A. 217
Rylands, Edwin Ulysses 242
Saddle horse businesses 86, 98,

111, 112-113, 116-119
Sampson, Jim 143, 144
Sampson, Marie Lovering 144
Sandin, Mary 227
Sanford, Charles S. 265
Sanford, Eunice 292
Sanford's Store 292
Saran, E.R. 72
Saruwatari, Mary 145
Sartoris, Charles 216
Schaffer, Jennifer 171
Schlaht, John 265
Schmidt, Florence 102
Schmidt, Leo & Marion 102, 103, 223, 291
School taxes 20, 43, 276
Schrempp, Edward J. 27, 98, 99, 116, 222
Scott, James C. "Jim" 17, 18, 55, 92, 124
Scott, Thomas Herron 243
Seel, Kurt 222
Shaw, Joseph C. 67, 201
Shaw, Paul 205, 295
Shaw, Robert & Beryl 220
Shell Oil 295
Shepard, Simpson J. 256
Sherman, Bishop R.L 168, 175
Sherman, J.E. & May 241
Shields, Wilford F. 235
Shimamura, John "Shig" & Hamagi 209
Simpson, Dave 117-119
Sisters of St. Martha 219
Skiing, Bertha Peak 34
Skyline Pack Train & Saddlehorse Co. 117
Slen, Syd 252
Sloan, Wallace "Butch" 38, 105, 289
Smith, Byard 196, 247
Sneyd, Sam 143
Snow, Grace 254
Snowden, Bill 228
Snowshoe Cabin Road 37
Snyder, Oswald E. 258
Sommerfeld, Daniel 292
Spackman, Roy & Donna 274, 291
Spackman, Sara 193

Spackman, Thomas Alfred & Amy 207, 294
Spence, Ken 150
St. Paul's Residential School 138, 139, 219 259, 261
Stacpoole, Dr. Harry 202
Stacpoole, Mary Elizabeth 242
Stadnicki, Mary 159
Staff housing on Clematis 189
Staff housing on Windflower 265
Stan's Store 292
Standige, William 216
Stanley Hotel 292
Steadman, Bobbie 147
Steed, Bruce David 233
Steed, Don & Orzie 106, 234, 251, 252
Steed, Eula 106, 234
Steeds Holiday Needs 106, 234, 251
Stewart, Arta 134, 210
Stewart, Charles 53
Stewart, George 29, 130, 132, 210
Stewart, MP John 130
Stewart, William & Alice 208
Stockdale, Alice Maria 236
Strate Brothers butcher shop 102, 295
Strate, Delance & Theresa 24, 28, 51, 205, 211
Strate, Orene 184
Stratton, Andrew 262
Stratton, Jean 200
Stretton, Bert 147
Stubbs, Thomas 53, 59
Subway (food outlet) 296
Suicide Ski Run 29, 34
Suleman family 83, 290, 294
Swanson, Cecil, Enid & family 123, 175, 263
Swedish, George 28, 143, 145
Swimming pool 34, 35, 53, 83, 161, 189, 234, 265, 269, 276, 283, 294
Swinarton, Ab 74, 75, 77, 78
Syroteuk, Merv 135
Taco Bar 283
Tamarack Outdoor Outfitters 288
Tanner, Barbara 226
Tanner, Earl & Vinessa 191

Tanner, N. Eldon 193, 196, 219
Taylor Stake 157-159
Telegraph 89, 96
Television 31, 32
Telus 89, 285
Tented Villages 47, 48
Terrill, William 223, 230
Texaco Service Station 289
The Tavern boarding house 60, 61, 213
Thomas, George David "Cap" 87, 230
Thompson, Clara 15, 218
Thompson, Jim & Chris 298
Thompson, Ralph & Harlan 218
Thompson, Stanley 132, 134
Thomson, Donald 244
Thomson, William E. 121, 129
Tidball, Ollie & Nellie 171, 199, 265
Tilley, Anna 151
Timberline Saddle Horses 118, 119
Tinney's Butcher Shop 292
Tourist Café 58, 59, 95, 101, 102, 103, 183, 223, 225, 291
Tourond, David V. 200
Towe, Beth & Andy 83, 287
Townsite land survey 12, 14, 47, 49, 181, 183, 193, 232, 240, 269
Trail of the Great Bear 292
Transient camp 38
Trapper's Mountain Grill & Smokehouse 289
Turner, Herbert M. 219
Udal, Slim & June 203
Udell, Fred & Grace 61, 64, 70, 285
Uibel, Ross & Lorna 83, 287
Ully, Leonard 76
United Church of Canada 43, 74, 152-157, 275
Valley, Rick & Wendy 225
Van Wyk, T. 253
Viad Corp. 81, 299
Virginia Dell 233, 293
Virtue, Gladstone & Marion 215
Virtue, Marion 37
Viscount Alexander of Tunis 117
Visitor Reception Centre 61, 233, 264, 273, 278, 280

Vroom, Bessie & Don 117
Wacher, S.J. 117
Waffleton 295
Wagstaff, Edward H. "Teddy" 121-127, 129-130, 132, 135, 185, 261
Walchli, Blanche 130
Wallace, William Sykes 293
Wally Byam Airstream Caravan 162, 164
Walsh, Lt.-Gov. W.L. 23, 168
Wanda Mae & Roddy Paul 115
War hut 26
Water-skiing 30
Waterton Auto Bungalows 63-66, 68, 73, 78, 204
Waterton Chamber of Commerce 38, 42, 70, 231
Waterton, Charles 9
Waterton Community Joint Venture 229
Waterton Glacier Suites 82, 83, 294
Waterton Inter-Nation Shoreline Cruise Co. 115, 116, 186
Waterton Lakes Lodge Resort 81, 82, 83
Waterton Lakes Hotel & Chalets 58, 59, 68, 69, 92, 265
Waterton Lakes Opera House 109, 297
Waterton Natural History Association 42, 43, 169, 170, 281
Waterton Park Café 291
Waterton Park Community Association 30, 42, 43, 135, 229, 276
Waterton Pavilion Dance Hall 17, 18, 24, 56, 71, 91, 92, 93, 97, 98, 100, 101, 112, 184, 222, 246, 278, 284, 290, 291
Waterton Pharmacy 58, 102, 106, 234, 292
Waterton School 19, 20, 43, 199, 204, 219, 229, 274, 276, 285
Waterton Ski Club 34
Waterton-Glacier International Peace Park 22, 23, 178, 231
Waterton-Glacier Suites 82, 83, 294
Watmough, Cyril James 48

Watson, George 228
Watt, Carol 43
Waymarker Hospitality 82, 83, 283, 284, 294
Weatherup, Fred 78-80, 82, 100, 198
Webb, Harold 134
Welch's Chocolate Shop 298
Wesley, Anna 188
Wesley, Charles Leonard 184
Wesley, George 228
West family 289, 293, 296
West, Mary 75
Westbrook, James & Harold 208
Western Oil & Coal Co. 11, 295
Widmer, Art 295
Wieners of Waterton 295
Wild weekends 37
Williams, Doris 242
Willie, John Henry 194, 215, 217, 261
Willock & Sax Art Gallery 296
Willock, Archie & Edna 227
Wiltse, Percy Manning 228
Wind storm of 1926 111, 112
Windflower Corner Coffee 297
Windflower Motel 78, 82, 294
Wismer, Harry 167, 168
Wobkenburg, John 258
Woitte, Henry Reuben 238
Woolf, Marion & Helen 184
Wood, Albert Lorenzo 196
Wood, Cathy 291
World War, First 14, 16, 23
World War, Second 26, 28, 66, 99, 112, 130, 173, 176, 177
Worthington, Bob 149
Wright, Ernest & Mary Ann 199, 211, 245
Wright, Harry & Bill 135
Yee, David C.M. 229
Yee, Ming 291
Yip, Charlie 291
Zorn, Leonard 210, 277
Zum's Burger Haus 293
Zum's Eatery & Mercantile 293

About the author

Chris Morrison is a journalist and former public relations specialist who has been writing about Waterton since 1986, when she was hired by the *Lethbridge Herald* "to cover the park like a blanket."

She did so for 13 summers. During that time, she developed an enduring interest in the past of both Waterton and Glacier national parks, and began digging into the wealth of information about the human history of the parks.

This is her 10th book, either as an author or contributor.

She and her husband Jim spend summers in Waterton, the third generation of Morrisons who have delighted in Waterton's mountains, lakes and other wonders.

Manufactured by Amazon.ca
Bolton, ON

25733050R00171